The Early Creeds

The Mercersburg Theology Study Series
Volume 8

The Mercersburg Theology Study Series presents attractive, readable, scholarly modern editions of the key writings of the nineteenth-century theological movement led by Philip Schaff and John Nevin. It aims to introduce the academic community and the broader public more fully to Mercersburg's unique blend of American and European, and Reformed and Catholic theology.

Founding Editor
W. Bradford Littlejohn

Series Editors
Lee C. Barrett
David W. Layman

Published Volumes

1. *The Mystical Presence and the Doctrine of the Reformed Church on the Lord's Supper*
Edited by Linden J. DeBie

2. *Coena Mystica: Debating Reformed Eucharistic Theology*
Edited by Linden J. DeBie

3. *The Development of the Church*
Edited by David R. Bains and Theodore Louis Trost

4. *The Incarnate Word: Selected Writings on Christology*
Edited by William B. Evans

5. *One, Holy, Catholic, and Apostolic: John Nevin's Writings on Ecclesiology (1844–1849): Tome One*
Edited by Sam Hamstra Jr.

6. *Born of Water and the Spirit: Essays on the Sacraments and Christian Formation*
Edited by David W. Layman

7. *One, Holy, Catholic, and Apostolic: John Nevin's Writings on Ecclesiology (1851–1858): Tome Two*
Edited by Sam Hamstra Jr.

"In these writings, John Williamson Nevin and Philip Schaff develop their conviction that the foundation of the catholic and ecumenical Christian tradition is to be found in the Apostles' Creed, which expresses the transforming presence of the triune God in the continuing incarnation of the Son of God in the church. The editors do an exemplary job of placing these texts in their theological and cultural contexts. These writings are essential for an understanding of Mercersburg theology."

—**RANDALL C. ZACHMAN**
Professor Emeritus of Reformation Studies, University of Notre Dame

"Nevin's and Schaff's articles championing the early creeds provide a fascinating window into the entire range of their 'catholic and Reformed' theology. Best of all, their spirited debates with then-dominant American 'Puritan' 'anti-creed' Protestant views anticipate, as the editors rightly note, continuing issues in contemporary American constructive theology. Brilliantly edited, with immensely helpful historical footnotes, this volume is a gift for anyone concerned with recovering the centrality of the early creeds for Christian confession."

—**DAVID J. GOUWENS**
Professor Emeritus of Theology, Brite Divinity School

"In this important volume, Professors Yrigoyen and Barrett carefully introduce and annotate key writings by Nevin and Schaff. The Apostles' Creed emerges here as the hermeneutical lens through which the Mercersburg theologians read Scripture—anchored in an understanding of incarnation as the crucial work of Christ (in contrast to prevailing theories of atonement) and shaped by social practices and communal language (instead of immediate experience). Contemporary religious debates will be enhanced through engagement with these writings."

—**THEODORE LOUIS TROST**
Professor of Religious Studies, University of Alabama

"Church debates are worth revisiting only if something crucial is at stake. Nevin and Schaff used a debate regarding the creeds to affirm that Christianity is about the incarnation and new life in Christ and the Spirit, in contrast to thinking that we believe as solitary individuals cut off from the community of Christ, sacraments, and tradition. That makes the book worth reading. The introductions are an added bonus."

—**PETER SCHMIECHEN**
Professor of Theology and President Emeritus, Lancaster Seminary

"This most welcome addition to The Mercersburg Theology Study Series brings together for a twenty-first-century audience seminal and incisive documents from the Mercersburg efforts to appropriate the great creedal heritage of the church for their own nineteenth-century context. Lucidly and carefully edited by Charles Yrigoyen and Lee Barrett, the volume also serves as a fitting capstone to Yrigoyen's many significant contributions to Mercersburg studies. It will be of interest to those concerned with the perennial questions of religious authority, theological hermeneutics, and the relationship of the individual and the corporate in Christianity."

—**WILLIAM B. EVANS**
Younts Professor of Bible and Religion, Erskine College,
and author of *A Companion to the Mercersburg Theology*

The Early Creeds

The Mercersburg Theologians Appropriate the Creedal Heritage

By
JOHN WILLIAMSON NEVIN
PHILIP SCHAFF
and JOHN WILLIAMS PROUDFIT

Edited by
Charles Yrigoyen Jr.

Introduction and Footnotes by
Charles Yrigoyen Jr.
and Lee C. Barrett

General Editors
Lee C. Barrett
and David W. Layman

Foreword by
Anne T. Thayer

WIPF & STOCK · Eugene, Oregon

THE EARLY CREEDS
The Mercersburg Theologians Appropriate the Creedal Heritage

Mercersburg Theology Study Series 8

Copyright © 2020 Wipf and Stock. All rights reserved. Except for brief quotations in critical publications or reviews, no part of this book may be reproduced in any manner without prior written permission from the publisher. Write: Permissions, Wipf and Stock Publishers, 199 W. 8th Ave., Suite 3, Eugene, OR 97401.

Wipf & Stock
An Imprint of Wipf and Stock Publishers
199 W. 8th Ave., Suite 3
Eugene, OR 97401

www.wipfandstock.com

PAPERBACK ISBN: 978-1-5326-9791-3
HARDCOVER ISBN: 978-1-5326-9792-0
EBOOK ISBN: 978-1-5326-9793-7

Manufactured in the U.S.A.   07/23/20

Contents

Contributors | vii
Foreword by Anne T. Thayer | ix
Editorial Approach and Acknowledgments | xi

General Introduction | 1

Chapter 1: "The Apostles' Creed" | 21

    Editors' Introduction | 23
    The Apostles' Creed | 35

Chapter 2: "Puritanism and the Creed" | 99

    Editors' Introduction | 101
    Puritanism and the Creed | 103

Chapter 3: Nevin and Proudfit: Opposed Views of the Early Creeds | 123

    Editors' Introduction to John Williams Proudfit's "The Apostles' Creed" and to John Williamson Nevin's "The Anti-Creed Heresy" | 125
    The Apostles' Creed | 128
    The Anti-Creed Heresy [John Williamson Nevin's Response to Proudfit] | 196

Chapter 4: "The Athanasian Creed" | 211

    Editors' Introduction | 213
    The Athanasian Creed | 217

Chapter 5: "Origin and Structure of the Creed"
          and "The Unity of the Apostles' Creed" | 251

  Editors' Introduction | 253
  Origin and Structure of the Apostles' Creed | 255
  The Unity of the Apostles' Creed | 262

Bibliography | 267

Index | 275

Contributors

Lee C. Barrett earned his PhD degree in Religious Studies from Yale University in 1984. He has taught at Presbyterian theological institutions and at Lancaster Theological Seminary. Much of his research and writing focuses on the thought of Søren Kierkegaard. He is the author of *Foundations of Theology: Kierkegaard*, and *Eros and Self-Giving: Intersections of Augustine and Kierkegaard*. He is the editor of *The T. & T. Clark Reader in Kierkegaard as Theologian*, and *Kierkegaard in Context*.

David. W. Layman earned his PhD degree in Religion from Temple University in 1994. Since then, he has been a lecturer in religious studies and philosophy at schools in south-central Pennsylvania. He is editor of volume 6 of the Mercersburg Theological Study Series, *Born of Water and the Spirit: Essays on the Sacraments and Christian Formation*.

Charles Yrigoyen Jr. earned his PhD degree from Temple University. He is a prominent pastor, teacher, and scholar. He has written numerous books and articles on the history of Methodism and on the Mercersburg Theology. He has co-edited two volumes of the highlights of the Mercersburg Theology, *Catholic and Reformed: Selected Theological Writings of John Williamson Nevin*, and *Reformed and Catholic: Selected Theological Writings of Philip Schaff*.

Foreword

The Apostles' Creed has had remarkable staying power in the life of Christian churches, especially in the West. Shorter and more accessible than its widely ecumenical sibling, the Nicene Creed, or its more pedantic relative, the Athanasian Creed, this is the creed that many western Christians know, if they know a creed at all. This would not surprise John Williamson Nevin who wrote in 1867:

> The Apostles' Creed . . . is the deepest, and for that reason, most comprehensive of all Christian symbols. It lies at the foundation of all evangelical unity; it is the last basis and bond of comprehension in the conception of the Church. No sect refusing to stand on this basis can have any right to claim footing in the Gospel, or fellowship with the Apostles. All right theological thinking then, as well as all true evangelical believing, must start where this fundamental form of faith starts, and keep step with it at every point as far as it goes.[1]

According to the Mercersburg theologians, the Apostles' Creed had risen organically out of the early church's experience of Christ, and thus became an important through-line, indeed a vital plumb-line, for Christian theology in all subsequent centuries. In it, they found affirmed the doctrines of the trinity and the incarnation, the central theological pillars grounding the unity of the church, itself an article of faith but visibly fractured in their day and in ours.

Indeed, the 19th-century church was fractured over whether it was appropriate to use creeds in worship or even in catechesis. This is evident in the amount of time and ink spent in theological argumentation over it. Was the Bible the sole religious authority for Protestants, albeit read under the influence of the Holy Spirit? Did creeds fall under the tradition so vigorously decried by their Reformation champions? Did the use of creeds constrain the work of the Spirit? Were ancient creeds hopelessly out of date?

And what was the overarching goal of Christian faith itself? While many in 19th-century America stressed the need for a cathartic conversion experience, the Mercersburg theologians, drawing on the understandings expressed in early Christian creeds, especially the incarnation, upheld Christianity as a life, a life that ultimately would

---

1. Nevin, "Theology of the New Liturgy," in *MR* 14 (Jan., 1867) 34.

reconcile all things to God, not simply a system of doctrine that would save sinful individuals, important as that was. As Nevin taught, "The whole world, in the deepest sense, is longing and striving after union with God. Nothing less than a union with its divine creator can satisfy the soul."[2]

This new volume in the growing Mercersburg Theology Study Series draws us in to the scholarly, theological, and ultimately pastoral and liturgical debates over the use of early creeds and the significance of their teachings in the United States in the mid-19th-century. Dr. Lee Barrett has done a masterful job continuing the substantial work begun by the Rev. Dr. Charles Yrigoyen. The General Introduction offers a fine overview of important Mercersburg principles and the historical contextual factors that made the issue of the use and interpretation of creeds so contentious in 19th-century America. Through the seven essays offered here, with their illuminating introductions and explanatory annotations, readers are introduced to the influential pro-creed arguments of the Mercersburg theologians, John Williamson Nevin and Philip Schaff, as well as the opposing ones of the classicist, theologian and historian, John Williams Proudfit. Overall one gains appreciation for robust 19th-century debates about what constitutes the vital center of Christian faith.

Mercersburg Theology has been described as part of a "Copernican revolution in theology." Perhaps we are on the verge of a Copernican revolution in ecclesiology. As I write this foreword, I am working from home during Holy Week in the context of the COVID-19 pandemic. Congregations, institutions, and individual Christians are busily learning how to maintain their communities and nurture their common life, without physically gathering together. Certain perennial questions are being asked with new urgency. What is authoritative for Christian faith? How should we worship? What should guide our reading of scripture? How are we connected to Christians in other times and places? What hope does our faith offer? And such questions are taking on new features. What will provide or ensure the continuity of virtual communities with physically gathered ones? How will we recognize one another as kindred in Christ through our screens? Will our shared vulnerabilities propel a new ecumenism? And we might add, What role will traditional affirmations of faith, like the Apostles' Creed, with its trinitarian and incarnational teachings, play in our theological reflections?

As a historian and teacher, I welcome the arrival of new and readily accessible editions of primary sources. Because substantial debates help illuminate deep questions, volumes such as this will serve us well by facilitating our engagement with historical answers to questions with ongoing ramifications.

Anne T. Thayer
Paul and Minnie Diefenderfer Professor of Mercersburg
and Ecumenical Theology and Church History
Lancaster Theological Seminary

2. See Erb, *Nevin's Theology, Based on Manuscript Class-Room Lectures*, 131.

Editorial Approach and Acknowledgments

The purpose of this series is to reprint the essential writings of the Mercersburg theologians in a way that is both fully faithful to the original and yet accessible to non-specialist contemporary readers. These twin goals, often in tension, have determined our editorial approach throughout. We have sought to do justice to both by being very hesitant to make any alternations to the original texts, while at the same time being very generous with supplemental information in the form of annotations and explanatory footnotes.

We have decided to leave spelling, capitalization, and emphasis exactly as in the original documents, except in cases of obvious typographical errors, which have been corrected. We have, however, taken some liberties with altering punctuation, which is sometimes quite awkward and idiosyncratic in the original texts, and which can be confusing to modern readers. In several articles the volume editor has added quotation marks to the original author's citations as required by modern conventions. The entirety of the texts have been re-typeset and re-formatted to make it as clear and accessible as possible; consequently, the pagination of the original editions has been changed.

The author's original footnotes have been retained, although for ease of typesetting they have been subsumed within the series of numbered footnotes that also include the supplemental informational footnotes added by the editors. Our own supplemental footnotes are wholly enclosed in brackets, while the footnotes of the original author are not. Often material in brackets (such as birth and death dates, biblical citations, or translations of foreign language words) appear within the original author's footnote, because that information has been added by the editors. Sometimes entire sentences in brackets will appear at the end of the original author's footnote; these have been supplied by the editors to provide contextual information.

Source citations in the original text have been retained in their original form, but where necessary we have provided expanded citation information in brackets or numerated footnotes, and often have sought to direct the reader to more modern editions of these works, where they exist. Where citations are lacking in the original, we have tried as much as possible to provide them in our footnotes. Before the nineteenth century it was not a universal practice for books to include the name of their publishers; often only the place of publication was supplied.

In the annotations that we have added (either in the footnotes or in the form of brackets in the main body of the text) we have attempted to be comprehensive without being overly cumbersome. In addition to offering citations for works referenced in the original text, these additions fall in six major categories:

1. Translation
2. Explanations of unfamiliar terms
3. The identification and brief descriptions of individuals mentioned by the author
4. Additional source material
5. Clarifying commentary
6. Contextual information

We have attempted to be comprehensive in providing translations of any untranslated foreign-language quotations in these texts, and have wherever possible made use of existing translations in standard modern editions, to which the reader is referred. At times the translations have been done expressly for this volume.

Additional annotations serve to elucidate any terms, concepts, or historical figures with which the non-specialist reader may not be familiar. We have also sought to provide references to sources where the reader may find further information. For these additional sources, only abbreviated citations are provided in the footnotes; for the full bibliographical information, see the bibliography.

Throughout the volume we have sought to shed light on the issues being wrestled with by these authors. Much of the commentary and contextual information appears in the General Introduction and in the Editors' Introductions to each document. Further brief commentary on specific points has been provided in the footnotes in order to facilitate understanding of the significance of the arguments and counter-arguments of the various authors.

Many of the themes articulated in these texts may sound arcane and strange to modern ears. This is to be expected, because the culture of these authors was in many respects markedly different from our own. Nevertheless, the ultimate issues that gripped their hearts and minds are of perennial significance. We hope that our practice throughout will bring these remarkable texts to life for contemporary readers, while also allowing the authors to be heard in their own authentic voices and with the accents of their own era.

Acknowledgments

The libraries that have made the research for this project possible must be recognized. Without the resources of the Library of Lancaster Theological Seminary and the

Archives of the Evangelical and Reformed Historical Society this volume could not have been completed. Myka Kennedy Stephens, the Seminary Librarian, has provided invaluable assistance with questions ranging from the most mundane to the most esoteric. Alison Mallin, the Archives Assistant in the ERHS, has helped us locate elusive documentary material in the proverbial cardboard boxes.

Others who helped enormously are: Frederick E. Maser (now deceased), Robert Golon and Kenneth Henke (Princeton Theological Seminary librarians of Special Collections), seminary librarians Richard Berg (Lancaster Theological Seminary) and Terry Heisey (Evangelical Seminary, Myerstown, PA), and Scott Vine (Franklin and Marshall College Information Services librarian). Those who assisted with translating include Robert G. Hunsicker (German), Anna van den Broek (Greek), and Robert P. Yrigoyen (French). Michael J. Stell aided with content and stylistic matters. Tony Poulos, Michael J. Floriani, and Jean Yrigoyen assisted with thorny computer issues on formatting, charts, etc.

The founding editor of the Mercersburg Theology Study Series, Bradford Littlejohn, deserves continuing gratitude for his publishing initiative and his herculean efforts to actualize this project. His enthusiasm for the irenic vision of the Mercersburg theologians is exemplary and contagious.

I am grateful for the labors of my fellow general editor, David W. Layman, whose keen eye for detail removed many infelicities from these pages. His knack for spotting minute formatting irregularities is a sheer wonder to a detail-oblivious personality like myself. Anne Thayer, Lancaster Theological Seminary's professor of church history, helped with the Latin translations, and Rev. Warren C. Riedel, who recently passed away, aided with the Greek. Tekoa Robinson's assistance with the laborious task of preparing the index is much appreciated.

Expansive gratitude must be extended to the members of the Mercersburg Society. Their financial support and their passion for this under-appreciated theological movement have made this series possible. The leadership of Thomas Lush, Carol Lytch, and Deborah Rahn Clemens has been the sustaining pillar of this enterprise.

Most of all heartfelt thanks must be extended to the volume editor, Charles Yrigoyen. For Charles this has been a labor of love. While much of his scholarly work has been devoted to the history of Methodism, the Mercersburg Theology has been woven throughout his long career. His dissertation focused on the work of Emanuel Gerhart, the systematic theologian of the movement, whose long career of teaching at Lancaster Theological Seminary lasted into the 1890's. Later Charles collaborated with George Bricker in editing two volumes of the highlights of Mercersburg Theology, *Catholic and Reformed: Selected Theological Writings of John Williamson Nevin*, and *Reformed and Catholic: Selected Theological Writings of Philip Schaff*. Charles' meticulous research into Nevin and Schaff's sources and his comprehensive knowledge of the nineteenth century theological environment in the United States have been invaluable.

General Introduction

Charles Yrigoyen Jr. and Lee C. Barrett

I. The Mercersburg Theology and Nevin and Schaff's Interest in the Early Creeds

Over the centuries Christians have confessed their faith personally and corporately in numerous ways. They have chanted passages of Scripture, intoned litanies, sung familiar hymns, and have even repeated the words of ancient creeds. This last activity is the focus of this volume. In some Christian traditions creeds have performed a central role in worship and have been recited regularly and fervently. Certain communions have even insisted that they are absolutely essential for preserving the well-being, the "*bene esse,*" of the church. It is claimed in these ecclesial circles that creeds encapsulate the saving truths of the Christian message in succinct and compelling ways. But in other traditions creeds have been rarely used, and in some, creeds have never been employed at all. In those heritages where they have been totally omitted, the reasons often given for their neglect are that they have lost their meaning through mindless repetition, or that they have become irrelevant due to their antiquarian language and arcane conceptuality. Sometimes it is proposed that creeds were mere human inventions that were always unnecessary, given the clarity and sole authority of Scripture. These two divergent assessments of creeds, one approbative and one critical, clashed in American Protestantism in the nineteenth century, and the spiritual value of creeds became an often bitterly contentious matter.

The progenitors and most influential exponents of the Mercersburg Theology, John Williamson Nevin (1803–1886) and Philip Schaff (1819–1893), believed that creeds, especially the early creeds, must always have a prominent place in the lives of individual Christians and the church as a corporate body. They urged careful and devout recitation of the early creeds as an essential way of professing one's personal belief, the convictions of one's congregation, and the faith of the church through the ages. They also valued the regular use of the creeds as a primary and even indispensable vehicle for nurturing faith and for expressing and undergirding the unity of the church across time and space. Even more boldly, for Nevin and Schaff the recitation of the creeds was a crucial life-giving channel through which the spiritual vitality of Christ was communicated to the ecclesial community.

Nevin and Schaff's high estimation of the early creeds was an intrinsic feature of the theological movement that they had spawned. Their valorization of the early creeds cannot be understood without situating it in the broader context of their theological schema as a whole. The Mercersburg Theology, as it came to be known, was accused almost immediately of being heterodox by many influential Reformed leaders, and was even condemned for promoting an insidious crypto-Catholicism. Shrill and vicious as these criticisms often were, they were manifestations of the fact that Nevin, Schaff, and their theological compatriots were articulating a vision of Christianity that diverged significantly from the spiritual universe of most of their Reformed cousins in North America.

This controversial theological movement from an obscure village in Pennsylvania was characterized by a distinctive set of interlocking convictions that required a reinvigorated appreciation of the early creeds. Most essentially, it encouraged a new emphasis on the incarnation as the perfecting of human nature through its union with the Second Person of the Trinity. It proclaimed the joyful spiritual union of the faithful with Christ and their consequent participation in Christ's life. That participation would fuel the individual's, the church's, and humanity's growth in godlikeness, a process stretching from creation to the eschaton. The sacraments were given new prominence by the Mercersburg theologians, for they were primary vehicles for the communication of Christ's glorified and transforming life. The church was reconceived as the Body of Christ that enables participation in the new creation. Even more shockingly to some detractors, Nevin and Schaff celebrated the organic development of the church through the centuries, its movement toward its eschatological consummation, in a way that embraced its patristic and medieval (and therefore Roman Catholic) heritage.[1]

This was a dramatic departure from the prevailing sensibilities of American Protestantism. For one thing, the Mercersburg theologians based the perception of the truth of Christianity on the immediate experience of Christ's self-communication in the life of the church rather than on a logically prior belief in the Bible's inspiration and veracity. In effect, they treated the authority of the Bible as being derivative from the authority of Christ. For them, the Bible should not be accepted as authoritative because its reliability can be demonstrated by arguments concerning the fulfillment of prophecy or the historicity of the miracles, as was common in much of American Protestantism. Instead, according to Nevin and Schaff, the Bible's authority resides in its ability to witness to Christ and thereby to communicate Christ's presence to the

---

1. See Nevin, "Its Material Structure or Organization" in this volume, .

believing community.² The faithful do not believe in Christ because they have been convinced of the truthfulness of the Bible; rather, they trust the testimony of the Bible because they have experienced new life in Christ. This Christocentric focus rather than a bibliocentric focus would enhance the Mercersburg theologians' sensitivity to the variety of ways in which the vitality of Christ is communicated to believers, including the pedagogical and liturgical use of the Christ-centered early creeds.

Even more momentously, the Mercersburg movement shifted the center of theological gravity away from the atonement and the drama of sin and salvation toward the incarnation and the saga of the perfecting of creation. In contrast to this, the more traditional and wide-spread Reformed view, typified by Charles Hodge of Princeton Theological Seminary, construed the plot-line of the Christian story as a movement from paradise lost to paradise regained.³ In this schema, the goal of human life was perfect obedience to the will of the righteous God and the adoration of God's glorious ordering power. In this view, prelapsarian Adam and Eve had originally possessed the capacity to obey God and enact perfect righteounsess, but they had lost that ability through their primal rebellion. To make matters worse, by violating God's order humanity as a whole has rendered itself worthy of condemnation and punishment. Consequently, the saga of Christianity is the tale of the restoration of a right forensic relation with God and the recovery of the power to obey God that Adam had forfeited.

Nevin and Schaff discerned a different metanarrative in the Bible as they interpreted it through the lens of the church's liturgical and confessional traditions. For them the fulcrum of the Christian saga was the fact that through Christ's incarnation and ascension the supernatural had entered the natural realm as an historical reality and had transformed it. Fall and restoration were no longer the centerpieces of the Christian story; rather, the new creation's completion of the old creation, with time being transmuted into eternity and the earth sublated into heaven, took center stage. For the Mercersburg theologians, the basic problem propelling the whole cosmic drama was not sin (although sin was a major complicating factor for them and they certainly attended vigorously to the issues of sin and redemption) but the more basic ontological incompleteness of Adam and Eve's original human nature. The perfecting of human nature, and of the cosmos as a whole, would only be achieved through the union of finite creatures with the infinite God. In lectures delivered about the same time that the essays in this volume were written, Nevin declared, "The whole world,

---

2. See DiPuccio, *The Interior Sense of Scripture*.

3. See A. A. Hodge, *Life*, 181. Charles Hodge (1797–1879) was a celebrated Presbyterian theologian at Princeton Theological Seminary, who in the 1820's had taught Nevin and allowed him to be his instructional replacement while he engaged in an academic tour of Europe. Hodge developed a scholastically orthodox version of Calvinism known for its logical rigor and its effort to generate doctrines from biblical "facts" in the way that physical scientists derive conclusions from the data of the natural world. Hodge thought that he was following the principles of the Baconian induction, with the qualification that for Christian theology the data to be collected, analyzed, and schematized were bits of supernaturally revealed information.

in the deepest sense, is longing and striving after union with God. Nothing less than a union with its divine creator can satisfy the soul."[4]

This recasting of the basic Christian narrative, so different from the theological vision of the majority of American Protestants, inspired a reconceptualization of almost all critical topics in Christian theology. Even the foundational discourse about God was modified. The traditional Reformed theologians like Charles Hodge had preferred to describe God in terms of sovereign power, awesome majesty, ordering will, and the standard metaphysical perfections associated with absolute transcendence, staunchly adhering to the traditional Reformed dictum that the finite cannot contain the infinite.[5] While not rejecting these motifs, Nevin and Schaff tended to define God in terms of love, relationality, and the power of unity-in-difference, and spoke glowingly of the reconciliation or even the union of the infinite and the finite.[6] Whereas their Reformed cousins articulated the relationship of God and humanity with judicial and constitutional vocabulary, favoring concepts like law, disobedience, guilt, punishment, and reprieve, the Mercersburg theologians (while not entirely abandoning that forensic conceptuality) shifted the core of their discourse to the interpersonal language of alienation, reconciliation, and union.[7] Nevin and Schaff severely qualified the sharp metaphysical dualisms of the natural and the supernatural, of time and eternity, of flesh and spirit, and of earth and heaven that had become common currency in the doctrinal economy of theologians like Charles Hodge.[8] In his chapel sermons Nevin in particular was more likely to identify the core human problem with the limitations of finitude than he was to construe it in terms of sin and guilt.[9]

The Mercersburg theologians were not alone in making the reconciliation of the infinite and the finite the leitmotif of the Christian metanarrative. By so doing they were manifesting their participation in a broader transatlantic theological shift in theological sensibilities.[10] In Germany, England, Switzerland, and Denmark theologians influenced by either Romanticism or Idealism (and usually by both), including

---

4. See Erb, *Nevin's Theology, Based on Manuscript Class-Room Lectures*, 131.
5. See Hodge, *Systematic Theology*, I, 366–441.
6. See Nevin, "Christianity and Humanity," and Schaff, *Christ and Christianity*.
7. See Erb, *Nevin's Theology*, 125–32.
8. See De Bie, *Speculative Theology and Common Sense Religion*, 93–99.
9. Nevin, *College Chapel Sermons*, 52–78, 140–61, 167–74, 194–231.
10. See Aubert, *The German Roots of Nineteenth-Century American Theology*.

Philipp Marheineke,[11] J. A. W. Neander,[12] F. A. G. Tholuck,[13] Carl Ullmann,[14] Hans Lassen Martensen,[15] and Isaak Dorner[16] had already been describing the goal of the Christian life (and world history) as the mediation of the immanent and the transcendent, of the natural and the supernatural, of time and eternity, and of the world and God. Philip Schaff had been educated and nurtured by these theologians during his academic maturation in Germany,[17] and he conducted a voluminous correspondence with many of them during his American career, particularly with Isaak Dorner.[18] Nevin, although he had been raised in what he identified as "Old School" Presbyterianism, began absorbing the works of some of these mediators while he was teaching at Western Seminary in the 1830's, and became even more familiar with them through his association with his colleagues Friedrich Rauch[19] and Philip Schaff. While it may be

11. Philipp Marheineke (1780–1846) was a prominent "right-wing" Hegelian who sought to make G. W. F.Hegel's speculative Idealism compatible with an orthodox understanding of divine transcendence.

12. Johann August Wilhelm Neander (1789–1850) was a professor of church history at the newly founded University of Berlin. Neander popularized the understanding of the history of the church as a chronologically extended developmental and organic process, rather than as a repository of changeless doctrinal propositions or as a tale of Christianity's fall from apostolic purity to Protestant restoration. Nevin began to read Neander's works during his early years of teaching at Western Seminary.

13. Friedrich August Gottreau Tholuck (1799–1877) was a neo-Pietist theologian and biblical scholar, teaching at Halle, who had been influenced by Schleiermacher. He was widely regarded as one of the primary leaders of the more orthodox and pietistic branch of the "mediating" school. When Schaff had been studying at Halle he lived in Tholuck's home and had regular conversataions with him.

14. Karl Ullmann (1796–1865) was a German theologian and church historian who also became an influential exponent of the "mediating" tendency in German theology. Nevin translated portions of his works for the *Mercersberg Review*. Schaff patterned his later book, *The Person of Christ* (1882) on Ullmann's *Über die Sündlosigkeit Jesu* (1833).

15. Hans Lassen Martensen (1808–1884) was a Danish theologian who eventually became primate of Denmark. He, like Marheineke, was a right-wing Hegelian who had been partially influenced by Schleiermacher. He is best remembered for being the nemesis of Søren Kierkegaard. Schaff persuaded Henry Harbaugh to translate Martensen's treatise on baptism (the German edition) for *The Mercersburg Review*.

16. Isaak August Dorner (1809–1884) was a leading theologian of the "mediating" school that attempted to synthesize elements of Hegel, Schelling, and Schleiermacher in ways that were compatible with orthodox doctrine, at least in a reconceptualized form. Dorner made the divine-human personhood of Christ the centerpiece of his understanding of the Christian faith and wrote extensively about the historical development of Christology. Schaff had studied under Dorner at Tübingen and maintained a life-long friendship with him. Dorner was one of the primary voices that had urged Schaff to accept the call to Mercersburg.

17. See Penzel, *The German Education of Christian Scholar Philip Schaff.*

18. See The Philip Schaff Papers, Evangelical and Reformed Historical Society, Lancaster, PA.

19. Friedrich Augustus Rauch (1806–41) was Nevin's German émigré colleague at Mercersburg for about one year, right before Rauch's premature death. Rauch had been influenced by the German philosopher Karl Daub (1765–1836), who himself had been influenced by both Hegel and Schelling. Daub reinforced for Nevin the themes of the social nature of experience, the dialectical progress of history, and the need to mediate the infinite and the finite. Nevin wrote the introduction to the second edition of Rauch's very Hegelian magnum opus, *Psychology*, and used Rauch's lecture notes to teach Rauch's courses after he had died.

fruitless to speculate about the question of whether these German thinkers were the primary catalysts of the deviation of Nevin's understanding of Christianity from the scholastic American Reformed norm, or whether they simply provided a conceptuality that enabled him to express ideas that were gestating in him anyway, the striking thing is that the Mercersburg theologians were part of broader Copernican revolution in theology. The structures of classical Calvinism that focused on sin and salvation and the absolute transcendence of God could not do total justice to their vision. Nevin was much more than a "high church Calvinist" who adjusted his thinking to an ethnically German constituency.[20] As W. Bradford Littlejohn has argued, Nevin's sense that the *telos* of Christianity is communion with, or even participation in, the life of God may have more in common with the "*theosis*" theme in many forms of Eastern Orthodoxy than it does with the metaphysical dualisms of scholastic Calvinism.[21]

The Mercersburg theologians' shift of focus did not leave Christology and soteriology unaffected. Whereas theologians like Hodge construed God's atoning act in Christ as a legal transaction accomplished *extra nos* and imputed to sinful human beings, Nevin and Schaff regarded the entirety of Christ's life, death, and resurrection as the glorification of human nature in which believers participate.[22] Although Nevin did affirm Jesus' satisfaction of God's justice, he preferred to speak of Jesus's earthly career as the infusion of his theanthropic life into humanity,[23] which brought with it victory over sin, death, and all the ills that afflict humanity. The incarnation for the Mercersburg theologians was not just a necessary precondition for the work of Christ in the atonement for sin, as it was for many American Reformed theologians. Rather, for Nevin and Schaff the very constitution of Christ's divine/human personhood has saving power, for in Christ's person the universal form of human nature was glorified and suffused with divine life. From the perspective of Mercersburg, Christ is the Second Adam in whom the divinely intended actualization of human nature, a process derailed by Adam and Eve, has been finally achieved.

This new emphasis of the soteriological efficacy of Christ's personhood had profound implications for the way that Christ's atonement for sin was understood. The righteousness of Christ is imputed to us because that righteousness has been imparted to us through our union with Christ.[24] Nevin insisted that there is no basis for the imputation of Christ's righteousness and his satisfaction of divine justice to us sinners apart from the believer's living union with Christ.[25] God declares us to be righteous and justified because the life of Christ the righteous one has entered us, and therefore

---

20. See Hart, *John Williamson Nevin*, 32–34.
21. See Littlejohn, *The Mercersburg Theology*, 124–46.
22. See Evans, *Imputation and Impartation*.
23. Referring to Christ as "theanthropos" was a linguistic habit of the German mediating theologians that they borrowed from the Greek Fathers.
24. Again, see Evans, *Imputation and Impartation*.
25. See Erb, *Nevin's Theology*, 226, 296.

what belongs to Christ has become ours. For Nevin, this mutual indwelling of Christ in the believer and the believer in Christ is not only the basis of justification, but also of sanctification. Sanctification is the organic unfolding and blossoming of the new life of Christ that has become resident in us. Living in our hearts, Christ's spiritual core gradually permeates and transforms our spiritual core as we absorb Christ's affections, motivations, and dispositions. Faith's identification with Christ fuels a life-long process of growth in Christ-likeness. Given this understanding of the soteriological importance of participation in Christ, it was natural that the Mercersburg theologians would gravitate toward the early creeds with their focus on the incarnation.

For Nevin and Schaff this perfecting of the original creation made possible by the incarnation was effected through the ongoing potency of Christ's life in the church. The glorified Christ has not deserted the finite realm; quite the contrary, he continues to be active in it through the medium of his body, the ecclesial community, particularly through its sacraments. According to Nevin and Schaff, the church is much more than an aggregate of converted individuals, as their more evangelistic brothers and sisters would have it. The Holy Spirit, working through the church, brings about the union of the believer with the ascended Christ in heaven, enabling Christ's divine-human personhood to become soteriologically effective. Because of this understanding of the church as the Body of Christ, Nevin and Schaff naturally stressed the efficacy of the church's communal nurture through its historic liturgies, creeds, confessions, and catechisms.[26] Consequently, they applauded the fact that the church was an article of faith in the Apostles' Creed. This valorization of the transformative power of the communal, historical traditions of the church would be the point at which the divergence of Mercersburg Theology from the theory and practice of the majority of Protestants in the United States would become most glaringly evident.

Given these theological emphases and their concern for the creedal heritage of the church, it was no accident that the principal periodical of the Mercersburg Theology, *The Mercersburg Review*, which began publication in January 1849, carried two articles by Nevin on the Apostles' Creed in its opening issue. A third article on the Creed in the fourth issue (July 1849) concluded his published three-article treatment of the Creed. Nevin contributed four more articles on the Creed in later issues: November 1849, November 1852, January 1869, and April 1869. Each of these provides evidence of his profound regard for this early creed and his continuing defense of it as a confession of faith and a premier normative document of the early church.

On the faculty at Mercersburg Nevin was not alone in his enthusiasm for the spiritual power of the early creeds. His German-born colleague Philip Schaff's equally high regard for the creeds is evident in his article on the Athanasian Creed which was published in *The Mercersburg Review* in its April 1859 issue. The full texts of the articles penned by Nevin and Schaff are included in this volume as well as an article by

---

26. See Barrett, "The Distinctive World of Mercersburg Theology: Yearning for God or Relief from Sin?" See also Evans, *A Companion to the Mercersburg Theology*.

the classicist, theologian, and church historian John Williams Proudfit (1803–1870) of New York University and New Brunswick Seminary which appeared in *The Biblical Repertory and Princeton Review,* October 1852. Proudfit's passionate and often caustic essay advocated for a rather one-dimensional view of the venerable Protestant doctrine of *"sola Scriptura"* and challenged Nevin's opinions regarding the significance of the Apostles' Creed.

Schaff's views on the nature and importance of creeds continued after his 1863 move from Mercersburg when he took up residence in New York City. In 1870 he joined the faculty of Union Theological Seminary, New York, where he published his *History of the Christian Church*, edited his monumental *Nicene and post-Nicene Fathers*, and compiled his three-volume *The Creeds of Christendom*, the groundwork for which was undoubtedly laid throughout his academic career including his tenure at Mercersburg. Reference is made to his work on the creeds in many places in this volume, especially to various sections of his collection of primary source documents on creeds, confessions, catechisms, and other important documents in *The Creeds of Christendom*.

II. The Nature and Significance of Creeds

Because the significance of the early creeds was a contested matter in the American Protestantism of the nineteenth century, Nevin and Schaff had to explain to their readers what exactly a creed is and why the early church (and most subsequent Christians) had ascribed such importance to them. When studying the church's early creeds, Nevin and Schaff occasionally encountered the term "rule of faith" (*regula fidei*). This concept would become crucial for their efforts to defend the nature, origin, and vitality of the creeds. The rule of faith was a brief statement of faith intended to define fundamental components of Christian belief, sometimes functioning to distinguish orthodoxy from erroneous (heretical) views. These rules of faith, sometimes also called "rules of truth," often varied in wording from Christian community to community, but reflected what was regarded as genuine apostolic teaching.[27] Among the earliest Christian thinkers who referred to rules of faith were Irenaeus[28] and Tertullian.[29] According to the historians upon whom Nevin and Schaff relied, the early creeds evolved from these rules of faith.

---

27. Much of Nevin's familiarity with this nomenclature was gleaned from Joseph Bingham, *The Antiquities of the Christian Church*, III, 497–98.

28. Irenaeus of Lyon (c. 130–c.202) was a bishop of Lyon in southern Gaul. Born in Smyrna in Asia Minor, he became one of the most influential shapers of the theological trajectory that became accepted as orthodoxy. He carefully distinguished what he considered to be the apostolic tradition from various gnostic heresies. His understanding of Jesus as the Second Adam in whom the history of the race was recapitulated and human nature was perfected would be critically important to the Mercersburg theologians.

29. Tertullian (c. 155–c. 240) was a North African Christian polemicist and apologist whose impact on theology was enormous. Writing in Latin, his vocabulary of "one substance" and "three persons" shaped the subsequent development of Trinitarian theology in the West. He also stimulated the

GENERAL INTRODUCTION

What is a creed? Definitions were provided in numerous theological works, dictionaries and encyclopedias that Nevin and Schaff consulted. Synthesizing all this material Schaff himself offered a succinct definition in the first volume of *The Creeds of Christendom*. He wrote, "A Creed, or Rule of Faith, or Symbol,[30] is a confession of faith for public use, or a form of words setting forth with authority certain articles of belief, which are regarded by the framers as necessary for salvation, or at least for the well-being of the Christian Church."[31]

In his masterwork on Christian creeds Schaff observed that creeds (as well as confessions, catechisms, and other official doctrinal declarations of a church with creedal standing) may emanate from at least five sources.[32] (1) A creed may have originated in a particular era of the church's life without specific authorship attributed to any individual, event, or action. Such is the Apostles' Creed, for many centuries thought to have been a collection of phrases contributed by Jesus' twelve apostles, but since the Renaissance era considerable and justifiable doubt had been cast on this explanation. The Athanasian Creed (after 428) in earlier centuries had been commonly thought to have been composed by Athanasius of Alexandria (c.296–373), but by Schaff's generation the attribution of its authorship to Athanasius had been generally rejected and the identity of no particular author had been agreed upon. (2) Some creeds had their origin in one of the ecumenical councils of the church. This would include, for example, the Nicene-Constantinopolitan Creed which had its birth in the Councils of Nicea (325) and Constantinople (381), and the Chalcedonian Creed which was produced by the Council of Chalcedon (451). (3) Other confessional documents had their origin in an official assembly of a particular church such as the Roman Catholic Council of Trent which promulgated the Profession of the Tridentine Faith (1564), or the Orthodox Confession of the Eastern Church (1643), or the Canons of Dort of the Dutch Reformed Church (1618–19). (4) A group of theologians may have been commissioned by an ecclesiastical body to draft a creedal statement as in the case of the Church of England's Thirty-Nine Articles (1563), which though not technically a creed, briefly set forth the official doctrine of the church. (5) Sometimes the statements of one individual became the basis of the particular church's faith and practice. Included in this category were documents such as Martin Luther's Small Catechism and Lutheranism's Augsburg Confession (1530), the last of which was largely the work of Philip Melanchthon.[33]

---

type of reflection on original sin that became prevalent in the Latin church. See Kelly, *Early Christian Creeds*, 76–88.

30. Symbol (*symbolum* in Latin, συμβολον in Greek) was a name given to creeds in both Western and Eastern churches. See Kelly, 52–61.

31. Schaff, *The Creeds of Christendom*, I:3–4.

32. Schaff, *The Creeds of Christendom*, I:6–7.

33. Philip Melanchthon (1497–1560) was a close theological collaborator of Martin Luther at Wittenberg. He was the chief author of the Augsburg Confession and is often regarded as Lutheranism's first systematic theologian.

Since our interest in this volume is Nevin's and Schaff's concern for the church's early creeds, namely the Apostles' and Athanasian creeds, we confine our attention to these two. It was evident to the two Mercersburg leaders that both of these creeds have been given special attention by the church ever since its earliest centuries, especially in liturgical use and catechetical instruction. Both the western and eastern ecclesiastical communities were familiar with them, but the two creeds gained much more attention and wider use in the former.

Roman Catholicism, of course, has utilized the Apostles' Creed for centuries. Illustrations of its importance include the *Roman Catechism*, also known as the *Catechism of the Council of Trent* (1566), which described the Creed as a major component of the church's official handbook of instruction. The more recent *Catechism of the Catholic Church* (1992) cites the Creed as one of its four major sections. The *Catechism* asserts, "*The Apostles' Creed* is so called because it is rightly considered to be a faithful summary of the apostles' faith. It is the ancient symbol of the Church of Rome. Its great authority arises from this fact: it is 'the Creed of the Roman Church, the See of Peter, the first of the apostles, to which he brought the common faith.'" The Athanasian Creed is also mentioned as an important articulation of Christian faith, but is not granted the high regard given the Apostles' and Nicene creeds.[34]

The Apostles' Creed was never as popular in Eastern Christianity as it was in the West. Rather, the Nicene Creed emanating from the Councils of Nicea (325) and Constantinople (381) was considered Eastern Christianity's primary statement of faith. According to Schaff, Eastern Christianity was unfamiliar with the Athanasian Creed until the eleventh century and thereafter rejected or modified it because of its pronouncement concerning the procession of the Holy Spirit from the Father *and* the Son. Schaff also observed that, "The Greek texts [of the Athanasian Creed] moreover differ widely, and betray, by strange words and constructions, the hands of unskilled translators."[35]

The confessional traditions within Protestantism generally recognized the authority and value of the Apostles' and Athanasian creeds, a fact that Nevin and Schaff emphasized. Many Protestant churches employed the Apostles' Creed for both liturgical and instructional purposes. The Athanasian Creed, however, was mainly utilized for educational purposes.

Martin Luther (1483–1546) regarded the Apostles' Creed as the most important statement of the faith since the era of the apostles themselves. He made it a centerpiece of his 1529 *Small Catechism* and urged that "it should be clearly and simply explained to every household by the head of the family."[36] He valued the Athanasian Creed because,

---

34. http://www.usccb.org/beliefs-and-teachings/what-we-believe/catechism/catechism-of-the-catholic-church/epub/index.cfm (accessed August 12, 2014).

35. Schaff, *Creeds*, I:35–36.

36. Schaff, *Creeds*, III:77–79.

he asserted, it "is a symbol in defense of the first symbol," the Apostles' Creed.[37] One of the most important statements of Lutheran theology, *The Formula of Concord*, drafted in 1577, perpetuated Luther's high estimation of the two creeds (as well as the Nicene), all of which are to be embraced as confessions of the "orthodox and true Church."[38]

John Calvin (1509–1564), one of the principal founders of Protestantism's Reformed tradition, like Luther highly valued both the Apostles' and Athanasian creeds, especially the former. In his *Catechism of the Church of Geneva* (1545), in which he said that the Apostles' Creed "was always received among all the pious, and because it came from the lips of the apostles [although he doubted this] or was faithfully collected from their writings," Calvin claimed that it is worthy of study and should be spoken aloud. He then included the entire text of the Creed in the catechism.[39] Calvin also used the Apostles' Creed as a pattern for the exposition of parts of his *Institutes of the Christian Religion* (1559).[40]

Creeds and confessions continued to play an important role in the liturgical and instructional life of many Christian traditions. For example, in Protestantism's Gallican Confession (*Confessio Fidei Gallicana*), 1529, originally prepared by John Calvin and later revised by Antoine de la Roche Chandieu, asserts that in addition to the Bible, ". . . we confess the three creeds, to wit: The Apostles', the Nicene, and the Athanasian, because they are in accordance with the Word of God."[41] Likewise, the Church of England in early versions of its Thirty-Nine Articles of Religion (1563, 1571) stated: "The three Creeds, Nicene Creed, Athanasian Creed, and that which is commonly called the Apostles' Creed, ought thoroughly to be received and believed: for they may be proved by most certain warrants of holy scripture."[42]

III. The Animus against Creeds in the Early Nineteenth Century

However, in spite of the enthusiastic valuation of the early creeds by the magisterial Reformers and their theological heirs, by the early nineteenth century the appreciation of the creeds had waned in many Protestant circles. A conjunction of shifts in cultural and ecclesial sensibilities fueled this eclipse of interest in the early creeds even in the Protestant traditions that had formerly treasured them. These shifts account for the virulent hostility that the Mercersburg theologians' foregrounding of the creeds provoked.

Some of these shifts had remote roots in tensions in European ecclesial politics that were transplanted across the Atlantic due to the impact of German theology on

---

37. Luther, "The Three Symbols or Creeds of the Christian Faith," *Luther's Works,* 34:202.
38. Schaff, *Creeds,* III:98.
39. Calvin, "Catechism of the Church of Geneva," *Calvin: Theological Treatises,* 22:92.
40. Calvin, *Institutes of the Christian Religion,* 20:507–28, 21:101–2.
41. Schaff, *Creeds,* III:362.
42. Schaff, *Creeds,* III:492.

the Mercersburg movement and other German-derived denominations.[43] Many of these tensions were functions of the complex relations of the church and the state in the German principalities, and were often motivated by a desire to foster a comprehensive national church untroubled by confessional differences.[44] For example, during the early nineteenth century the United Church of Prussia, the state sponsored union of Reformed and Lutheran traditions, effected in 1817 by a series of decrees from King Frederick Wilhelm III, was reconsidering its liturgical, political, and doctrinal foundations. Those who sought to emphasize the commonalities of the Reformed and Lutheran traditions, as well as their shared divergence from Catholicism, tended to favor the creation of a new pan-Protestant statement of faith that would replace the confessions and catechisms of the Reformation era in the worship life of the union church. The early creeds, however, would continue to be honored, for they were the common heritage of the Lutheran and Reformed groups, but the possibility of a new confession that could unify the Prussian state (and the other German principalities that had formed union churches) attracted the most attention, excitement, and controversy.

However, the desire for national theological unity could cut in the opposite direction if its vision of a comprehensive state church was even broader than an integration of the Lutheran and Reformed traditions. The party of Ludwig von Gerlach, who enjoyed the support of the very conservative Prussian king, hoped to include Roman Catholics in its more ecumenical vision of the established church. The return to the early creeds, particularly those jointly recognized by magisterial Protestantism, Roman Catholicism, and Eastern Orthodoxy would have the additional advantage of helping to unite the conservative monarchies of Europe, including Prussia, Austria, and Russia, against the destabilizing forces of liberalism and revolution. Therefore Gerlach's faction opposed the use of any modern formulae for baptism, confirmation, or ordination, and sought to restrict ecclesial authority to the pre-Reformation ecumenical creeds. Both of these movements, of course, triggered a reaction from stalwart Lutheran parties in the various states who insisted upon preserving their own unique doctrinal heritage and theological ethos, and who therefore looked to the confessional documents of Lutheranism, particularly the Augsburg Confession, Luther's Catechism, and the Formula of Concord to ground their specific identity rather than the creeds shared more generically by most Christians, including non-Lutherans. Many of these disgruntled confessional Lutherans would emmigrate to the New World.

In muted and transfigured forms, this dispute would be transplanted in the United States, in spite of its lack of a European-style established church. In the New World those Protestants who yearned for a trans-denominational evangelical alliance sought

---

43. Annette Aubert has drawn attention to the importance of the German philosophical, theological, and literary heritage for the development of the Mercersberg theology. See Aubert, *The German Roots of Nineteenth Century American Theology*.

44. See Conser, *Church and Confession*, 13–96.

to downplay confessional differences, including those associated with the early creeds, which were not valued by all American Protestants. But the champions of the early creeds also had their counterparts in America, particularly among the Mercersburg theologians. According to Nevin and Schaff the early creeds could serve as the foundation for an even wider ecumenical vision than that imagined by the evangelicals, a vision that could include Catholics and Orthodox Christians. Through the influence of Philip Schaff, who in his youth had been befriended by von Gerlach in Berlin, the *"evangelische Katholizität"* (evangelical catholicism) of conservative Prussia would help fuel Nevin's enthusiasm for the Apostles' Creed as the basis for a capacious ecumenical hope.[45]

Other powerful forces in addition to this drive for an a-creedal evangelical ecumenism began to erode the importance of the early creeds in the lives of many American congregations. Many of these forces were a function of cultural and political dynamics more characteristic of the New World than of Europe. Perhaps most importantly, a plethora of restorationist movements had begun to popularize the motto "No creed but Christ" and relegated the creedal traditions of the early church to the category of unnecessary and deleterious human innovations. The Campbellites,[46] who helped create the Disciples of Christ, and the followers of John Winebrenner,[47] who founded the Church of God, were expressions of this pervasive suspicion of the corrupting and divisive impact of humanly authored creeds upon an otherwise unified and pristine church. For these groups, the meaning of the Bible was clear, needing no authoritative ecclesial interpretation, summary, or supplement. In a way, this was an intensification of the Protestant commitment to the principle of the priesthood of all believers, including the imperative that all Christians should read Scripture for themselves, in conjunction with an augmented trust in the perspicuity of Scripture.

This heightened sense of the clarity of Scripture was reinforced by a deep cultural trend in the United States. In the relatively new American Republic confidence grew in the abilities of ordinary people to think for themselves and to make their own political decisions. This valorization of the cognitive and volitional powers of

---

45. Nichols, 72–74.

46. Thomas Campbell (1763–1854) was a former Presbyterian minister who was influenced by both John Locke and the Second Great Awakening. After having had his ministerial credentials revoked by the Presbyterians, he eventually formed an independent congregation that helped inspire the "restorationist" movement. This movement hoped to reduce the tenets of Christianity to the essentials that reasonable individuals could agree upon and which could be clearly demonstrated to be rooted in Scripture. Campbell sought to return Christianity to what he imagined was the theological simplicity of the apostolic church and therefore rejected the contentious creeds that had allegedly disrupted the unity of the primitive Christian community.

47. John Winebrenner (1797–1860) was a German Reformed pastor who was disaffiliated from that tradition because of his enthusiasm for the "new measures" of radical revivalism and for his insistence upon a personal conversion experience as a hallmark of genuine Christian faith. His commitment to the doctrine of the clarity of Scripture eventually led him to reject the use of all creeds and catechisms. His views were adopted by the Church of God, General Conference, which he helped found with five other pastors in 1830.

ordinary, unlearned people would spill over into a conviction that laypeople can and should discern the meaning of Scripture for themselves. As Nathan Hatch has persuasively argued, the early nineteenth century witnessed an upsurge in egalitarianism, epitomized by the Jacksonian lionization of the "common man" and its consequent distrust of hierarchies and elites, including spiritual ones that based their authority on tradition.[48] In the new nation, the older European habit of deference to authority and authoritative institutions waned as individual initiative and self-reliance were celebrated and the spectrum of life-choices was extended. The right of private judgment in religious matters seemed to be the natural analogue of the right of private judgment in political matters.

This twin belief in the sole authority of the Bible and in the capacity of all believers to discern its clear message had a profound impact not only on the overtly schismatic groups, but also on the more established Protestant traditions from which they emerged. For example, even the theologically orthodox factions among the Congregationalists, in boasting of their Puritan ancestry, observed that "The experience of two centuries has shown that the [Apostles'] Creed and Puritanism have not a kindred spirit," and denounced the creedal heritage as an idol venerated by Papists and the other enemies of the Puritan spirit.[49] This anti-creedal animus did have roots in the Puritan heritage, for New England congregations had sometimes used their own individual covenants for catechetical instruction (some of which were based on the Westminster documents of the seventeenth century), but not the testimonies of the early church. By the early nineteenth century, even some Lutheran and Dutch Reformed ministers had joined in the disparagement of the normativity of the early creeds even though they usually conceded their limited pedagogical utility.

Moreover, even in many Calvinist circles the conviction had spread that a benevolent deity would necessarily have provided humanity with a clear, unambiguous revelation. The "New Divinity" of Joseph Bellamy[50] and Samuel Hopkins[51] defended the principle that God cannot hold people responsible and culpable for failing to do something that they are actually incapable of doing. God, Hopkins argued, would never condemn individuals for what they could not do.[52] Therefore, if God morally evaluates people according to whether they respond to God's revelation in Scripture or not, people, including the unlearned, must be capable of understanding that revelation. The cognitive capacities of sinners must remain functional, rather than being

---

48. See Nathan Hatch, *The Democratization of American Christianity*.

49 Cited in Nevin, "Puritanism and the Creed," in this volume, . Also cited in Nichols, 175.

50. Joseph Bellamy (1719–1790) was a Congregational pastor in western Connecticut who had studied under Jonathan Edwards and was sympathetic to the Great Awakening. He trained several ministers and was a pioneer of the Sunday School movement.

51. Samuel Hopkins (1721–1803) was another student of Jonathan Edwards who served pastorates in Connecticut and Newport, Rhode Island. He emphasized God's "disinterested benevolence" toward creation as a whole.

52. Hopkins, *System of Doctrines*, I:84.

totally corrupted and debilitated by original sin. Hopkins announced that "depravity or sin lies wholly in the heart, and not in the intellect or faculty of understanding."[53] Moreover, God must ensure that the salvific essentials of God's revelation in Scripture, in principle at least, are comprehensible to all people, without undue external help. If divine revelation involves the communication of saving information, then that information cannot be so cryptic as to baffle an ordinary individual's interpretive capacities. Nathaniel Taylor, a leader of what became known as the "New Haven Theology," intensified this theme, arguing that a benevolent deity's chief concern was to promote the well-being of his creatures.[54] Such a God would not deliver a revelation that, for the purpose of salvation, necessarily required decoding by a clerical elite well-versed in ecclesial lore. Nor would God reveal saving truths that would not be intelligible without the supplement of an interpretive key (a creed). Although the proponents of the New Divinity and the New Haven Theology did value the early creeds as helpful pedagogical aids, they could not regard them as being necessary for the interpretation of Scripture.

The evolution of American political sensibilities and legal principles also contributed to the erosion of trust in historical traditions. The absence of an established religion at the federal level and the disappearance of established denominations at the state level (Congregationalism was not entirely disestablished in Massachusetts until 1833) provided fertile soil for the flourishing of private interpretations of Scripture independent of any hermeneutic tradition. As denominations and sectarian groups multiplied, the range of available religious options expanded. Given that dizzying plurality, with the religious landscape fissured by conflicting denominational truth-claims, no single religious tradition could claim immediately obvious validity or plausibility. The principle of religious voluntarism coupled with religious pluralism undermined any automatic ascription of authority to any particular historic religious institution and its normative documents.

The sense of the significance of the early creeds was also damaged by the acute focus on dramatic personal conversion experiences that was the legacy of the American religious awakenings. The Second Great Awakening, beginning at the very end of the eighteenth century and waxing ever more intense during the early nineteenth, spawned a wave of revivalism that shifted the focus of the Christian life away from the pedagogical efficacy of confessional and creedal traditions to the dramatic transformation of the individual's heart. The revivals had a profound impact on virtually every denomination, often dividing them into rival parties. The surge of evangelical piety affected the German Reformed Church in Pennsylvania, particularly from 1828 to 1844, when many local

---

53. Hopkins, *Two Discourses*, 37.

54. See Nathaniel Taylor, *Lectures on the Moral Government of God*. Taylor (1786–1858) was pastor of First Congregational Church in New Haven, and then a professor of theology at Yale. He stressed God's benevolence and justice even more than the "New Divinity" theologians had done. In order to safeguard moral culpability he insisted that even sinners know what sin is and possess the freedom to refrain from it (even though they fail to use that freedom appropriately).

pastors began to employ in their congregations the highly emotive strategies used in the camp meetings.[55] The denomination suffered two major defections, an early one led by William Otterbein[56] who helped found the United Brethren, and a later one led by John Winebrenner who, as we have seen, founded the Church of God. Similarly, the Presbyterian Church (of which Nevin was a member until his call to Mercersburg) was by no means immune to the allure of revivalism. In 1834 in Pittsburg, a city thick with Scots-Irish Presbyterians, the revivalist James Gallaher employed Charles Finney's[57] controversial "new measures" in a high-pressure evangelistic campaign. In all these instances sudden episodes of being moved by grace to make a personal decision to embrace Christ began to upstage the slow nurture provided by historic communal traditions. The church became less a mediator of grace through its worship, liturgies, catechisms, and confessions, and more the site where individuals gathered for the recharging of their spiritual batteries. The sense of being united by the common experience of Christ's saving grace diminished the importance of doctrinal differences and fostered a pan-Protestant revivalistic, a-creedal ecumenism.

In a very different way Rationalism had also undermined confidence in the authority of the early creeds. Skepticism about religious traditions had been encouraged by many strands of the eighteenth century Enlightenment, including the *philosophes* in France and the "neologians" in Germany. Many English Deists had famously denounced "priest-craft," railed against the guiles of the clergy who sought to manipulate the credulous masses, and cautioned rational individuals to be wary of the superstitions embedded in the historic traditions of the church. The spirit of critical rationality reached its premier expressions in Immanuel Kant's[58] exhortation "Dare to think!" and, in a more Romantic idiom, in Ralph Waldo Emerson's[59] claim that the only truths that an individual should hold are the ones that he discovers for himself. Truth cannot be acquired at second-hand through the testimony of third-parties, not even through the witness of the venerable saints of the church and their ancient

---

55. Good, *History of the Reformed Church in the Nineteenth Century*, 130–34.

56. William Otterbein (1726–1813) was a university-trained German immigrant and a pastor in the German Reformed tradition. Although he never formally left that denomination, along with the Mennonite Martin Boehm he organized and inspired the more revivalistic and more Wesleyan religious communities that evolved into the United Brethren.

57. Charles Finney (1792–1875) was a maverick Presbyterian preacher and ardent revivalist who became a professor and president of Oberlin College. He vociferously advocated Christian perfectionism, social reform, abolition, and developed a confrontational "decisionist" style of mass evangelism.

58. Immanuel Kant (1724–1804) was an exceedingly influential Prussian philosopher who proposed that the structures of the mind shape experience, and that much of traditional metaphysics transgressed the boundaries of what the mind could legitimately comprehend. Religious convictions, he argued, must be kept within the limits of reason alone, particularly our capacities for moral reasoning.

59. Ralph Waldo Emerson (1803–1882) was a celebrated American essayist, poet, philosopher, and lecturer. A member of the Transcendentalist movement, his essay "Self-Reliance" made him a premier champion of individualism in all spiritual and intellectual matters.

councils. Moreover, confessional disagreements were particularly odious to Enlightenment enthusiasts because they were thought to provoke needless dissensions within and between nations. Political tranquility would become more attainable if Christians would simply restrict their convictions to a minimalist "reasonable" core and would practice toleration free of confessional dogmatism.

The general spirit of Enlightenment skepticism did not exempt the early creeds from suspicion and critique. In the late seventeenth and early eighteenth centuries a spate of critical histories of the Creed had appeared, building on the doubts of Renaissance humanists. Most of these works had compared the citations of creedal formulae in such ancient Christian authors as Rufinus, Clement, Irenaeus, Origen, Tertullian, Ambrose, and Jerome in order to expose discrepancies and later additions. The critical scholars concluded that the Creed did not issue from the apostles themselves, and did not receive its final form until the fourth or fifth century. In the eyes of many, the undermining of literal apostolic authorship diminished the authority of the Creed in general. Even the very conservative Presbyterian theologian Charles Hodge of Princeton Seminary proposed that the undeniable plurality of theological traditions in the early church argued against the ascription of divine authority to any rule of faith other than the canonical scriptures themselves.[60]

IV. Nevin's and Schaff's Responses to the Neglect of the Creeds

In Nevin's articles on the Apostles' Creed which follow we will see that he was especially disturbed by those churches that did not recognize the critical importance of the Creed, did not understand its content, and failed to employ it for the instruction and liturgical occasions for which it was intended. He was notably annoyed by the Puritans (Congregationalists) of New England who set aside the Creed in favor of having congregations compose their own creeds or "covenants." We will see that he denounced this practice in strong terms as the "anti-creed heresy."

The concern of both Nevin and Schaff for the early creeds of the church, in this case the Apostles' and Athanasian creeds, fit well with two of their major concerns: their high regard for the importance of the historical nature of the church including the development of its creeds, and their commitment to the theological content of the creeds which reflected the views of the early Christian community. In his critical review of John Winebrenner's *History of all the Religious Denominations of the United States* published in 1849[61] Nevin regretfully noted the proliferation of "sects" in American Protestantism. In that review Nevin exhibited his commitment to the high authority of history as a crucial factor to be considered in any attempt to understand the origin and development of Christian faith and the church. The "sects" denied such

60. Charles Hodge, *Systematic Theology*, I, 104–16.
61. Nevin, "The Sect System," in *One, Holy, Catholic, and Apostolic, Tome 1*, MTSS 5, ed. Hamstra, 238–71.

authority to their detriment. In the first of his two articles on the sects Nevin wrote that Winebrenner's book illustrated the "unhistorical" nature of the "sect system." He exclaimed, "The independence which [the sect] affects in pretending to reduce all Christianity to private judgment and the Bible, involves, of necessity, a protest against the authority of all previous history, except so far as it may seem to agree with what is found to be true [by the sect]; in which case, of course, the only real measure of truth is taken to be, not this authority of history at all, but the mind, simply, of the particular sect itself."[62] This appears to be Nevin's main concern with the "unhistorical" substance of the "sect system" and the groundwork of his concern to emphasize the Apostles' Creed and other historically accepted creedal statements in worship and the believer's faithful life. He was committed to recognizing and employing the "authority of history," for God has been active in the life of the church, energizing and guiding its organic development. Little needs to be added regarding Philip Schaff's position on the importance of history and the creeds which is clearly and persuasively stated in his three-volume work *The Creeds of Christendom* as well as in his essay on the Athanasian Creed in this volume.

Recognizing the importance of the worship of the church, the weekly gathering of the faithful to offer praise, to sing and pray together, to hear God's word proclaimed, and to participate in the Lord's Supper comforted and empowered by receiving the elements of bread and wine through the presence of their Lord, Nevin and Schaff argued vigorously that the creeds were indispensable. Both Nevin and Schaff played important roles in designing a liturgy for the German Reformed Church which made its first appearance as a "Provisional Liturgy" in 1857. After a decade of experimentation, this liturgy was replaced by a permanent revised "Order of Worship." In worship on a regular Lord's Day, the Apostles' Creed was a significant component of the liturgy. On days when the Lord's Supper was celebrated the Nicene Creed was employed. A future volume in this series will more adequately examine the liturgical developments related to the Mercersburg theology. Our intention here is simply to point out the important place of early creeds in the Mercersburg theologians' efforts to revitalize the liturgical life of the German Reformed Church.

As one reads through the essays on the creeds in this volume, many of the major themes of the Mercersburg theology that we have outlined will appear. The movement's criticism of American Protestantism's "sect system" and its condemnation of the unhistorical, unchristological, unchurchly, and unsacramental nature of much of American Protestant church life are pervasive. The essays manifest the intrinsic connections between Nevin's and Schaff's enthusiasm for the early creeds and the foundational christological, soteriological, and ecclesiological themes of the Mercersburg theology. And, of course, the Mercersburg corrections of the perceived shortcomings of "sectarian" American Protestantism are forcefully and repeatedly advanced.[63]

---

62. Nevin, "The Sect System," 251.

63. For the recurrence of these themes in the works of the Mercersburg theologians, see Philip

As will become clear, it was not just an appreciation of the power of historical doctrinal and liturgical traditions that drew Nevin and Schaff to the early creeds. Even more importantly, their significance resided in their theological content. The ancient creeds placed the foundational doctrines of trinity and incarnation in the foreground where they belonged. The narrative of the saving work of Christ was implicitly presented as a function of his divine-human personhood. This focus differed from the sin-fall-redemption pattern that structured large portions of the confessions of faith that emanated from the Reformation and post-Reformation eras (even including Nevin's beloved Heidelberg Catechism). The early creeds were theocentric and Christocentric, not anthropocentric. Attention to salvation was derivative from the concentration on the triune nature of God and the constitution of Christ's person (which was inseparable from his soteriological work). The spiritual world of the creeds was radically different from American revivalism's obsession with the morphology and dynamics of individual salvation. The early creeds revolved around the enacted being of the divine persons, not around the *ordo salutis.*

This rather obscure theological dispute about the significance of the early creeds was not a mere tempest in a teapot with no relevance to future generations. In unintentional ways it prefigured many of the most urgent questions that would vex subsequent theological reflection in the twentieth and twenty-first centuries. It foregrounded the tension between claims about the accessability of the "objective" meaning of texts and the growing sensitivity to the role of interpretive communities and their hermeneutic traditions in producing textual meaning. In later years this tension would erupt in arguments about the value of exclusively historical-critical methods of biblical interpretation as over against the more theological and ecclesial readings championed by the "post-liberal" and "radical orthodoxy" movements. Even more broadly, in literary critical circles this divergence would manifest itself in arguments between textual formalists and reader-response critics. Moreover, by grounding the power of Scripture in its testimony to the incarnation, the Mercersburg theologians also presaged debates about the relation of biblical authority to the actual theological content of Scripture. The controversy problematized the issue of which is logically prior: the doctrine of revelation or the doctrine of the incarnation? One trajectory (the Hodge/Proudfit strand) would lead to J. Gresham Machen and the other (the Mercersburg strand) would point to Karl Barth. Finally, the nineteenth-century argument raised questions about the relation of the individual and the community, and the community's history, in Christianity and religion more generally. Is religious experience primarily a matter of individual inwardness,[64] originating in the private depths of

---

Schaff, *The Principle of Protestantism*, in *The Development of the Church: "The Principle of Protestantism" and Other Historical Writings of Philip Schaff*, MTSS 3, ed. Bains and Trost, 27–205. See also John Nevin, "Antichrist; or the Spirit of Sect and Schism," and "The Sect System," in *One, Holy, Catholic, and Apostolic: John Nevin's Writings on Ecclesiology (1844–1849)*, Tome One, MTSS 5, ed. Hamstra, 163–232.

64. In extreme form, this view would be expressed in Alfred North Whitehead's dictum that

the soul, or is it fundamentally birthed and shaped by social practices and communal language?[65] Does the spiritual life basically flow from the inside out, or from the outside in? If Christian faith is the fruit of the interaction of both currents, what is the relation of the two? By raising the question of the relation of the work of the Spirit in transforming the interiority of individuals to the work of the Spirit operating through the practices of the church, the Mercersburg theologians opened a Pandora's Box. The issues that Schaff and Nevin foregrounded would become the ultimate questions with which succeeding generations of Christian theologians would wrestle.

"religion is what the individual does with his own solitariness." See Whitehead (1861–1947), *Religion in the Making*. New York: Macmillan, 1926, 16.

65. For a statement of this perspective, see Berger and Luckman, *The Social Construction of Reality*. Garden City: Anchor Books, 1966.

Chapter 1

"The Apostles' Creed"

(By John W. Nevin)

Editors' Introduction

By 1849 the professors of the German Reformed Theological Seminary at Mercersburg, John Williamson Nevin and Philip Schaff, were generating interest in their work and fomenting controversy in their own denomination and beyond. Nevin's *The Anxious Bench* (1843) and *The Mystical Presence* (1846), and Schaff's *The Principle of Protestantism* (1845) had especially stirred minds in the German Reformed Church by developing theological themes that were becoming known as the Mercersburg Theology.

In addition to their published books and pamphlets both men were contributors to regularly circulated periodicals. Nevin was a frequent author of articles in the *Weekly Messenger of the German Reformed Church*. Schaff was founder and editor of *Der Deutsche Kirkenfreund*, a journal which sought to provide American denominations of German-language background, such as the Lutheran and German Reformed communions, with information on "theological and practical religious" topics.[1] As the Mercersburg movement took shape, however, some of its proponents thought it necessary to reach a wider audience for the thought of Nevin and Schaff by publishing a periodical devoted especially to the main themes of their theological perspective.

In 1848 the Alumni Association of Marshall College, the sister institution to the Theological Seminary at Mercersburg, moved to establish a periodical primarily intended for clergy and other readers with theological, philosophical, and literary interests. It would become a special voice for the views of Nevin and Schaff as well as their theological kinsmen. Although Nevin refused the invitation to be the editor of the proposed journal, he offered to support its publication and promised to be a principal contributor. It was named *The Mercersburg Review* and its first issue appeared in January 1849. True to his promise Nevin wrote an introductory item ("Preliminary Statement") and the journal's first main article, "The Year 1848," and was a regular writer for many years thereafter. The journal continued to be published under various names until 1926.

Given the theological and historical interests of the Mercersburg movement, it is not surprising that Nevin contributed three articles on the Apostles' Creed to the first

---

1. Richards, *History of the Theological Seminary*, 303.

volume of the *Review*.² They are published together here in the order of their appearance since in the opening article Nevin announced that he intended them to be three parts of a whole. In fact, almost immediately the three articles were subsequently republished together in booklet form without significant modification.³ They are treated here as Part 1, Part 2, and Part 3.

Nevin's decision to begin the fledgling journal with an extended discussion of the Apostles' Creed was not adventitious. During the early and middle nineteenth century in some ecclesial circles the role of the Apostles' Creed in the life of the church had become a contested matter. In many sectors of the Protestant churches in North America the Creed was suffering from a kind of benign neglect or even overt hostility. This waning of enthusiasm for the Creed was even true of many congregations of the German Reformed, Dutch Reformed, and Presbyterian traditions, all of which had highly valued it during the period of their European birth and growth.

Nevin himself later lamented that in his early days he had failed to appreciate the power and significance of the Creed. As a student at Princeton Seminary he had learned church history from the text books of the mildly rationalistic J. L. Mosheim,⁴ whose tomes had narrated a tale of the church's fall from apostolic integrity to a period of superstition and papal despotism. Nevin's professors at Princeton did not emphasize the Creed, nor did his colleagues at Western Seminary where he taught from 1830 to 1840.⁵ Even worse, Nevin admitted that he had not encountered the use of the Creed in worship in any substantive way in the Presbyterian congregations of his youth and young adulthood. Nevin's student and biographer Theodore Appel recollected, "The probability is that neither Dr. Nevin at Pittsburgh, nor many other Presbyterian divines, if they had been called upon to repeat it from the pulpit, would have been able to have gone through with it without stumbling, or travestying it from beginning to end."⁶

Nevin credited his discovery of the work of the ecclesial historian Johann August Wilhem Neander⁷ as a primary catalyst for his appreciation of the significance of

---

2. Nevin, "The Apostles' Creed." *The Mercersburg Review* 1 (1849). The three parts of the series were: "Outward History of the Creed," (March 1849) 105–27; II. "Its Inward Constitution and Form," (May 1849) 201–21; III. "Its Material Structure or Organization," (July,1849) 314–47.

3. Nevin, *The Apostles' Creed: Its Origin, Constitution, and Plan*.

4. Mosheim, *An Ecclesiastical History: Ancient and Modern, from the Birth of Christ to the Beginnings of the Present Century*. Johann Lorenz von Mosheim (1694–1755) was a German historian of Christianity. He claimed to pursue the ideal of objectivity and therefore has often been regarded as the founder of modern church history. Nevin and Schaff, however, feared that he lacked any real sense of the organic development of Christianity and tended to think in terms of a mere institutional chronology spiced with some anti-Catholic polemics.

5. Appel, *The Life and Works of John Williamson Nevin*, 86.

6. Appel, 86–87.

7. Johann August Wilhelm Neander (1789–1850) was a professor of church history at the newly founded University of Berlin. Neander popularized the understanding of the history of the church as a chronologically extended developmental and organic process, rather than as a repository of changeless

the evolution of the church, and therefore of the power of the Creed in Christianity's maturation. Later Nevin would rely extensively upon the work of Rev. Joseph Bingham, an early eighteenth century Anglican historian of ancient Christianity, to deepen his knowledge of the history of the Creed and its antecedents and increase his enthusiasm for them.[8]

Part 1: "Outward History of the Creed"

Nevin's series of articles on the Apostles' Creed were intended to resist the anti-creedal tendencies that dominated American ecclesial culture. The origin of the Creed had been questioned ever since the Renaissance when the celebrated humanist Lorenzo Valla[9] raised serious doubts about its apostolic provenance (and thereby incurred the wrath of the Roman heirarchy). Even John Calvin did not hesitate to conceal his skepticism about the Creed's apostolic authorship, even though he valued it highly and affirmed that it did communicate the apostolic consensus.[10] The issue of apostolicity again became a matter of heated controversy in the seventeenth century, with critiques of theories of its origins being leveled by many English and Dutch classical scholars. But the notion of apostolic authorship continued to have its defenders throughout the eighteenth and early nineteenth centuries. During Nevin's youth the Danish theologian N. F. Gruntvig had even argued that the words of the Creed had been dictated by Jesus himself, and therefore the Creed possessed even greater authority than the gospels.[11]

Because these issues of origin and authorship were in the air, Nevin grappled first with the history of the Creed, especially the source of its name. He rejected the opinion, once popular among some scholars and church leaders, that Jesus' twelve apostles actually wrote sections of the Creed. Here he followed Bingham's critique of the view of Baronius,[12] who, having accepted the testimony of a sermon erroneously ascribed to

---

doctrinal propositions or as a tale of Christianity's fall from apostolic purity to Protestant restoration.

8. See Bingham, III:495–550. Joseph Bingham (1688–1723) was an Anglican antiquarian and historian of the early church. During Nevin's life-time, Bingham's *Orignes Ecclesiasticae, or the Antiquities of the Christian Church* was quite popular with English-speaking theologians, serving as a definitive and synoptic catalogue of the rituals, polity, liturgical calendars, and disciplines of early Christianity.

9. Lorenzo Valla (1407–57) was an Italian philosopher, grammarian, humanist, and literary critic. He notoriously defended the philosophy of the ancient Epicureans. He also discredited the spurious document known as "The Donation of Constantine" which allegedly gave virtually imperial authority over Christendom to the papacy.

10. Calvin, *Institutes of the Christian Religion*, I:527.

11. Nikolai S. F. Grundtvig (1783–1872) was a Danish Lutheran pastor, theologian, poet, educational reformer, and an enthusiast for Norse mythology. He insisted that the Bible should be interpreted through the lens of the church's creeds and liturgies, for the church was older than the Bible and logically more foundational.

12. Caesar Baronius (1538–1607) was an Italian cardinal and controversialist who polemicized against Protestantism. His considerable historical scholarship was intended to defend the legitimacy

Augustine, had maintained that the Creed was called a "symbol" (used as a synonym for "collation") because each of the apostles had contributed a separate written article to it.[13] Nevin also rejected the conclusion of Thomas Comber that the twelve apostles had jointly fashioned the exact wording of the Creed in a special editorial meeting.[14] According to Nevin, the Creed was the product of no one individual author or identifiable group of authors. The early surviving versions of the creed, he observed, exhibit variations, with some articles, such as "the descent into hell" and "the communion of saints," missing entirely. In fact, Nevin's source for much of this material, Joseph Bingham, had concluded that an historian should refer to "apostolical creeds" in the first four centuries, rather than one "Creed," for none of them enjoyed "perpetual and universal use for the whole church."[15] Following Bingham, Nevin pointed out that before the composition of the Nicene Creed, local variants of creedal formulae were common. Irenaeus,[16] for example, cited a much longer and more elaborate "rule of truth" that he claimed was used by the church dispersed throughout the world, while Origen[17] quoted a formulaic summation of the apostolic teaching that was different, but equally lengthy.[18] Tertullian[19] cited the words of the apostolic creed three times, but the citations do not match, even though he claimed universality and authenticity for each version. Nevin noted that even later authors, referring to the period before the Council of Nicea, displayed a lack of uniformity, for different wordings were used by the churches of Jerusalem, Caesarea in Palestine, Alexandria, Antioch, Aquileia, and Rome.[20] According to most of the Protestant scholars whom Nevin read, it was the Roman Creed that was the ancestor of the formula that was eventually named the "Apostles' Creed."

---

of the Roman Catholic Church.

13. Bingham, III:495.

14 Comber, *Companion to the Temple*, 132. Thomas Comber (1645–99) was an Anglican priest and apologist whose writings sought to convince Dissenters to return to the Church of England.

15. Bingham, III:504.

16. Irenaeus of Lyon (c. 130–c. 202) was bishop of Lyon in southern Gaul. Born in Smyrna in Asia Minor, he became one of the most influential initiators of the theological trajectory that would be regarded as Christian orthodoxy, which he carefully distinguished from gnostic heresies. His interpretation of Jesus as the Second Adam in whom the history of humanity was recapitulated and perfected would have a profound impact on both Nevin and Schaff, partly mediated to them by Friedrich Schleiermacher.

17. Origen (c. 182–c. 251) was an important theologian and teacher of the early church, who was influential in the Greek-speaking East, particularly in Alexandria. Borrowing from Platonic thought, he engaged in allegorical exegesis, speculative theology, and reflection on spiritual practices.

18. Bingham, III:512–14.

19. Tertullian (160–240) was an innovative and widely read theologian from Carthage in North Africa. His influence was so strong that he is often regarded as the parent of Latin theology. Tertullian is credited with developing the terminology translated as "nature" and "person" used in Trinitarian doctrine and with stimulating speculation about the nature and transmission of original sin.

20. Bingham, III:526–35.

However, Nevin vigorously affirmed that the Creed's name indicates that it does indeed reflect the faith of the original apostles even if they did not compose it. He was comfortable with the theory that the wording of the Creed had slowly evolved, and that its authority did not rest upon its authorship by specific apostles. Rather, its spiritual power and normativity resided in its expression of the Christ-infused communal spirit and life of the developing apostolic church. Its content, he believed, is from the "old church tradition" from earliest times. Following Bingham, Nevin concluded that some formulae, very much like the spirit of the received Creed, had been used in admitting catachumens to baptism.[21] According to Nevin, the Creed was preceded by a number of "rules of faith" or "rules of truth" which varied in wording, but essentially embraced the same basic core message affirmed by the primitive Christian communities. He cited outstanding early church theologians—Irenaeus, Tertullian, Origen, and Cyprian[22]—to provide evidence for the claim that there was one "apostolical tradition" which formed the basis for the Apostles' Creed. For Nevin, its primitive basis was rooted in Peter's confession recorded in Matt 16:15–16. In answer to Jesus' question, "Who do you say that I am?" Peter declared, "You are the Christ [Messiah], the Son of the living God." According to Nevin, this is Christianity's central theological affirmation, confessed at the time of one's baptism into the life of Christ and his church. Again following Bingham, Nevin maintained that this core confession was elaborated and became more robust than the bare affirmation of beleif in God the Father, the Son, and the Holy Ghost, as Episcopius had argued. It must have included material that predated the Council of Nicea, for that Council presupposed a normative, common phraseology.[23] He also rejected Basange's theory that the core of the Creed was a late product of the second century, developed in response to various Gnostic heresies that drove a wedge between creation and redemption.[24] For Bingham, who relied upon the work of Grabe, most of the central tennets that eventually appeared in the Creed were in circulation during the late first century.[25] The essentials of the Creed were not written on paper, but "in the fleshly tables of the heart."[26]

21. Bingham, III:504.

22. Cyprian (c. 200–258), bishop of Carthage, is regarded as one of the most significant early leaders of the Latin-speaking church. After many Christians had offered sacrifices to the Roman emperor during a period of persecution, Cyprian attempted to forge a middle course between the lax policy of easy readmission to the church and the rigorist position of no readmission. He himself died as a martyr during a subsequent persecution.

23. Bingham, III:505. Simon Episcopius (1583–1643) was a Dutch theologian who vigorously defended the Arminian position against the predestinarian doctrinal conclusions of the Synod of Dort.

24. Bingham, III:506. Jacques Basnage (1653–1723) was a French Reformed pastor. He was the author of several theological works, some of which dealt with the sections of the Creed that seemed to be condemnations of various heresies.

25. Bingham, III:509. Johannes Ernst Grabe (1666–1711) was a German-born Anglican priest who questioned the apostolic validity of Lutheran clerical orders. He authored many tomes concerning patristic theology, usually trying to determine which parts of the heritage were truly ancient.

26. Bingham, III:510.

Chapter 1: "The Apostles' Creed"

In addition to citing early Christian theologians in support of the historic importance of the Apostles' Creed, Nevin believed that both the Protestant and Roman Catholic traditions had continued to hold the Creed in highest regard. Among the Protestants Nevin referenced the Lutheran, Reformed, and Anglican customs of paying tribute to the Apostles' Creed by mandating its use as an indispensable statement of faith. By doing so, Protestants and Catholics revealed that they were rooted in a common foundational heritage. That conjunction of positive valuations of the Creed shared by the two major branches of western Christianity, branches that were opposed to each other on so many other matters, had to be taken with utmost seriousness.

Near the closing of this section of his treatment of the Creed Nevin chose to criticize "rationalism" and "sects," both of which he alleged denigrated the value and use of the Creed. Rationalism held that the affirmations of the Creed had been superseded by the insights of human reason. The unhindered operations of natural intellectual powers found the assertions of the Creed to be mostly unfounded or meaningless. Philip Schaff commenting on the Apostles' Creed echoed his colleague's negative assessment of this rationalist critique. Schaff wrote:

> . . . if we look at the several articles of the [Apostles' Creed] they are all of Nicene or ante-Nicene origin, while its kernel goes back to the apostolic age. All the facts and doctrines which it contains are in entire agreement with the New Testament . . . The rationalistic opposition to the Apostles' Creed and its use in the churches is therefore an indirect attack upon the New Testament itself. But it will no doubt outlive these assaults, and share in the victory of the Bible over all forms of unbelief.[27]

According to Nevin, the "sect system," which he vigorously condemned in other places in his writings, viewed the Creed "as a venerable relic of early Christianity" which had no place in worship; it should either be abandoned entirely, or replaced by more modern statements of belief.[28] In this section he hesitated to include Puritanism [mainly American Congregationalism and Presbyterianism] in the "sect system," although he was clearly annoyed by Puritanism's view that the Creed was "antiquated" and required more contemporary and congregationally-created statements of faith. He would be forced to confront Puritanism's "heresy" concerning this matter and explicitly voice his displeasure with it in a later essay included in this volume. Nevin obviously believed that the Apostles' Creed could not be improved upon as a creedal affirmation of the core beliefs of Christian faith.

---

27. Philip Schaff, *The Creeds of Christendom*, I:20.

28. See Nevin, "Antichrist," in *One, Holy, Catholic, and Apostolic*, Tome One, MTSS 5, ed. Hamstra, 165–76; Nevin, "The Sect System," *One, Holy, Catholic, and Apostolic*, Tome One, MTSS 5, ed. Hamstra, 238–71.

EDITORS' INTRODUCTION

Part 2: "Its Inward Constitution and Form"

In Nevin's second article on the Apostles' Creed in *The Mercersburg Review*, included here as Part 2, he continued to advance his view that the Creed represents the true core of apostolic Christian faith and should necessarily be employed in the worship and teaching of the church. According to Nevin, it is "the direct utterance of the Christian faith itself." Since he spoke about the Creed as a statement of faith, Nevin felt it necessary to discuss next the nature of faith, a task that he accomplished in several pages of the article. He began with the familiar quotation of Heb 11:1 and the definition of faith in the Heidelberg Catechism.[29] Nevin obviously thought of this as a significant and substantive section of his essay. He wrote, "Faith turned towards Christ, as he stands revealed in his own life, finds itself filled with the sense of a new spiritual world, the proper consciousness of the Christian Church; and all this comes to its right expression, under such form, in the solemn language of the Creed."[30]

Nevin's understanding of faith was indebted to Johann August Wilhelm Neander,[31] and ultimately to Neander's theological inspiration, Friedrich Schleiermacher.[32] This trajectory was mediated to him initially not only by Neander, but also by Wilhelm Martin Leberecht de Wette,[33] a biblical scholar influenced by Schleiermacher, who stimulated Nevin's growing conviction that the meaning of the Bible must be apprehended by the "heart" rather than by the inductive reasoning that was constitutive of the historical and grammatical methods of biblical interpretation.[34] The truth of Chistianity must be felt experientially in the interior life of the spirit, and not known through the analysis of evidences and rational arguments.[35] Genuine faith is not a matter of intellectual conviction, not even if the content of the belief system is perfectly orthodox or supported by ecclesial authority. By 1838 Nevin was using Schleiermacher's vocabulary, describing religion as a life rather than as a matter

---

29. See *The Heidelberg Catechism*, Question 21.

30. Nevin, "The Apostles' Creed," 65 (in this volume).

31. Johann August Wilhelm Neander (1789–1850) was professor of church history at the newly founded University of Berlin. Neander popularized the view of the history of the church as a chronologically extended developmental and organic process, rather than as a static repository of doctrinal propositions or as a narrative of Christianity's fall from apostolic purity to Protestant restoration.

32. See Schleiermacher, *The Christian Faith*. Friedrich Schleiermacher (1768–1834), a professor at Halle and then at the University of Berlin, was one of the most important theologians of the modern era. He pioneered what has been dubbed "the subjective turn" in theology by describing the contents of the experiential dimension of faith. He was also a scholar of Plato, a biblical critic, and a theoretician of hermeneutics, as well as being instrumental in the founding of the University of Berlin and the creation of the Prussian Union Church.

33. Wilhelm Martin Leberecht de Wette (1780–849) was a German theologian and biblical scholar who employed the techniques of historical criticism but ultimately associated the meaning of a text with the impact it had on the subjectivity of the reader.

34. Nichols, 38.

35. Nichols, 38.

of cognition.³⁶ This vitalistic language was reinforced by his early engagement with the works of Samuel Taylor Coleridge, excerpts of whose work he often included in a journal that he published in his early years.³⁷ An American edition of Coleridge's *Aids to Reflection* had appeared in 1829, and an American edition of his essays had been published two years before Nevin began using Coleridge-like vocabulary in his journal *The Friend*. In the mid-1840's Nevin was so taken by the description of Christianity as a "life" (rather than a system of doctrines) in the work of Carl Ullmann that he attached an abridged translation of one of Ullmann's texts to his own *The Mystical Presence*.³⁸ Nevin later recalled that diverse appropriations of Schleiermacher by German scholars, mostly of a more "orthodox" variety, such as Neander, Dorner,³⁹ and Ullmann,⁴⁰ had nourished his theological development.⁴¹ This understanding of the foundation of faith in the immediate experience of the heart was a sharp divergence from the "evidentialism" that dominated most of American Reformed theology.⁴²

The influence of Schleiermacher was so striking that in 1848 Charles Hodge of Princeton Seminary accused Nevin of being a Schleiermacher epigone. In self-defense, Nevin replied, "I have read Schleiermacher some, and consider him certainly a

36. Nichols, 40.

37. Samuel Taylor Coleridge (1772–1834) was an English Romantic poet and literary theorist. His most influential work on religious language and biblical interpretation was *Aids to Reflection* (1825). There is some controversy about the extent and depth of Coleridge's influence upon Nevin. David Layman has argued that Nevin may not have been responsible for all the editorial decisions to include Coleridge's pieces in his journal, and that he seldom mentions Coleridge in his later work. See David Layman, "Was Nevin Influenced by S. T. Coleridge?" William DiPuccio, however, has pointed to the prevalence of Coleridge's terminology in Nevin's writings from this period. See DiPuccio, "Nevin and Coleridge."

38. See Ullmann, "Preliminary Essay," in Nevin, *The Mystical Presence*. This can be found in Nevin, *The Mystical Presence and the Doctrine of the Reformed Church on the Lord's Supper*, edited by Linden J. DeBie, 15–39. The Mercersburg Theology Study Series, Vol. 2. Eugene, OR: Wipf & Stock, 2012. Ullmann's German original was Über *den unterscheiden charakter oder das Wesen Christenthums* (Trans. *The Distinctive Character or Essence of Christianity*).

39. Isaak August Dorner (1809–1884) was a leading theologian of the "mediating" school that attempted to synthesize elements of Hegel, Schelling, and Schleiermacher in ways that were compatible with orthodox doctrine, at least in a reconceptualized form. Dorner made the divine-human personhood of Christ the centerpiece of his understanding of the Christian faith and wrote extensively about the historical development of Christology.

40. Karl Ullmann (1796–1865) was a German theologian and church historian who also became an influential exponent of the "mediating" tendency in German theology.

41. See Nevin, "Antichrist," in *One, Holy, Catholic, and Apostolic*, Tome One, MTSS 5, ed. Hamstra, 166.

42. See Holifield, *Theology in America*, 467–81. However, it must be remembered that the focus on faith as a supra-cognitive inward phenomena, not based on a logically prior conviction about the reliability of the Bible, had roots in certain varieties of the English-speaking Reformed tradition with which Nevin was familiar from his early years. He appreciated the introspective Christocentric piety of such seventeenth-century Puritans as John Owen (1616–1683) and Richard Baxter (1615–1691), as well as the moderate revivalism of Jonathan Edwards. He also had been moved by the spirituality of some of the Cambridge Platonists, many of whom had Reformed roots. See Hart, 72–74. See also Payne, 4–35.

genius of the very highest order in the modern theological world. But I am not aware at all of having taken him, in any sense slavishly, for my master and guide."[43] Nevin did, however proceed to admit that he did owe much to Schleiermacher. He credited Schleiermacher with helping him to appreciate the centrality of the incarnation and the person of Christ and the fact that Christianity is a "life in which God and humanity are united in an organic way."[44]

In spite of his indebtedness to Schleiermacher and those influenced by him, throughout his life Nevin did express a reservation that they did not attend sufficiently to the dimensions of faith that transcend human subjectivity, including the creeds and liturgies of the church. His worries about Schleiermacher were functions of his fear that Schleiermacher may have over-identified Christianity with the affective life of believers and not attended enough to the "objectivities" of the faith, such as the ontological composition of Jesus, the efficacy of the sacraments, and the importance of the foundational doctrines of church, such as the Trinity, that were enshrined in its creeds and confessions. Nevin wanted to make clear that the ultimate agent in the production of a person's faith is Christ himself, and not the potency of the individual's volitional and affective powers (actually, Schleiermacher would have agreed with Nevin). A divine power, objectively existing outside and beyond the individual's consciousness, is responsible for the inception of faith. Because of this, Nevin concluded, the objective media graciously chosen by this very objective God to awaken and nurture the experience of faith must be honored, preserved, and used.

In spite of these reservations, Nevin appreciated and appropriated much of Schleiermacher's Copernican revolution in the understanding of faith. Schleiermacher had initiated a new approach to Christian theology by suggesting that faith was not a matter of cognitive assent to doctrinal or philosophical propositions, as such unlikely allies as Protestant scholastic orthodoxy and Enlightenement-style rationalism had both assumed. Faith is not grounded in the alleged proofs of the truth of Christianity from miracles or the fulfillment of prophesy. Nor was faith to be identified with moral rectitude or the virtuous discharge of ethical obligations. For Schleiermacher, faith was a phenomenon in the deep foundations of a person's inner experience; it was a transformation of self-consciousness that pervaded every aspect of a person's life. Christian faith was the immediate feeling of being absolutely dependent upon God, including the feeling of being dependent upon grace to overcome the sense of being separated from God.[45] Theology, from this perspective, was the systematic exposition of this Christian self-consciousness in a way that would be intelligible and attractive to a particular cultural context. Theology, Schleiermacher proposed, articulated the faithful person's sense of being given new life through the communication of Jesus'

---

43. Nevin, "Antichrist," 165.
44. Nevin, "Antichrist," 168.
45. Schleiermacher, *The Christian Faith*, 5–31.

perfect God-consciousness through the church community.[46] As the Second Adam, Christ made a new kind of God-reliant existence available to humanity through the church, and thereby recreated it at the very center of its life.[47] By expounding these themes, Schleiermacher synthesized the affective orientation of the Pietism in which he had been raised with the focus on subjectivity that was typical of the Romantics. This synthesis would have a profound impact on Nevin's understanding of faith as a phenomenon that was far deeper than cognitive assent to doctrinal propositions.

From his readings in Johann Gottfried von Herder[48] Nevin had learned the necessity of looking beyond the surface historical meaning of biblical texts in order to discern their deeper spiritually edifying sense.[49] This discovery was reinforced by Neander's insistence that Christianity was not based upon "speculative cognitions of God and of divine things," but upon the communication of a new "religious consciousness,"[50] a "new life" that changes human nature "from its inmost center."[51] It is a "common consciousness" that unites the church in the "fellowship of the divine life."[52] In a similarly way Nevin claimed that the authority of the Creed is rooted in the fact that it expresses faith's immediate apprehension of God's self-revelation in Jesus Christ, and has the power to awaken such a recognition in subsequent believers.[53] Accordingly, Nevin insisted that the Creed is the "direct immediate utterance of the Christian faith itself."[54] It is not a condensed systematic theology addressed to the mental faculties, but is rather "the free spontaneous externalization of the Christian consciousness" that can nurture new life in Christ.[55]

According to Nevin, the Creed issued from the church's early life in a "collective" manner. It is not possible to assign a specific time or location when the Creed appeared in its present form. It evolved. "The Creed was not *made*, not manufactured like a watch; it *grew*, self-produced, . . . out of the great fact of Christianity itself. The early Church was not the artificer that hammered it into shape, part by part, and one article after another; but the organ, through whose life as an actual fact it brought itself to pass." Here Nevin was following the trajectory of Neander, who had rejected the theory that the apostles themselves had deliberately composed a written formula

---

46. Schleiermacher, *The Christian Faith*, 52–60.

47. Schleiermacher, *The Christian Faith*, 367–69.

48. Johann Gottfried von Herder (1744–1803) was a German philosopher, literary critic, philologist with ties to both the Enlightenment and Romanticism. He proposed a developmental view of history and emphasized the shaping power of language upon the general ethos of a culture.

49. See Hart, *John Williamson Nevin*, 74–75.

50. Neander, vol. 1, 557.

51. Neander, 1:1.

52. Neander, 1:2.

53. Nichols, 182.

54. Nevin, "The Apostles' Creed," 58 (in this volume)..

55. Nevin, "The Apostles' Creed," 69 (in this volume)..

and who regarded the Creed as emerging much more spontaneously and organically from the Christian spirit.[56]

Drawing Part 2 to a close, Nevin again made clear his assessment of the Creed's value and importance. However it may have reached its precise present form, he concluded that "the Creed is still, at all events, that old living tradition, nothing more or less, expressing itself in the one sense of the Universal Church. To reject it, is to reject the ancient faith; to make light of it, is to make light account of the very substance of Christianity as it stood in the beginning."

Part 3: Its Material Structure or Organism.

Nevin's third and final article on the Apostle's Creed series begins with references to the trinitarian shape of the Heidelberg Catechism, a fundamental theological text of the German Reformed Church, and the trinitarian form of the Creed. Nevin approvingly stated that both confessional documents affirm the Holy Trinity and the central importance of the incarnate life of Jesus Christ. He asserted again his belief that Peter's confession that Jesus is indeed the Christ and the Son of God [Matt 16:16] is the core of the Christian faith. Then Nevin launched into a description of a main theme of the Mercersburg theology, namely, the centrality of the incarnation. He asserted, "The incarnation is the deepest and most comprehensive fact, in the economy of the world." The incarnate Christ "constitutes the sum and substance of Christianity, as it lives in the consciousness of the Church and finds its expression in the Creed."[57] While Nevin devoted several pages to a treatment of the Creed's affirmation of the three Persons of the Trinity, the second Person received a more extended consideration than the Father and the Holy Spirit, a focus that reflected Nevin's sense of the centrality of the incarnation.

It is not surprising that Nevin also emphasized the Creed's mention of the Holy Catholic Church and the communion of saints. According to Nevin, the Creed understood the church to be "an object of faith; a new divine economy . . . the mystical mother of saints" whose "sacraments convey grace, where the way is open for its reception; the remission of sins, in order to a Christian life, comes under God from her hand."[58] The essential role of the church and its sacraments as conduits of the continuing presence of Christ was another essential and foundational theme of the Mercersburg theologians.

Having discussed the structure of the Creed, Nevin closed Part 3 with six "Practical Reflections." He presented these "Reflections" as follows: (1) the relationship of the Creed to the Bible; (2) the nature of the church and the role of the Bible in it; (3) Christianity and theology as an historical phenomenon; (4) the fact that authentic theology

56. Neander, 1:306.
57. Nevin, "Its Material Structure or Organism,".
58. Nevin, "Its Material Structure or Organism,".

Chapter 1: "The Apostles' Creed"

evolves from the Creed; (5) the claim that sound church life and thought (as opposed to the errors of "sect and schism") must hold a high regard for the Creed; and (6) adherence to the Creed as the ground for settling theological and ecclesiastical disagreements.

Nevin's articles on the Apostles' Creed did not go unnoticed by those sympathetic to his insights and also by those who raised serious objections to his understanding of the significance of the Creed. The latter category included John Williams Proudfit,[59] a pastor and professor of ancient languages, whose lengthy article that was published in *The Princeton Review* challenging Nevin is included in this volume. Proudfit argued two points that were deeply embedded in American Protestant sensibilities. The first was that the great Reformers had affirmed the principle of *sola Scriptura*, and thereby had rejected the Creed as a rule of faith. The second was that the Creed dated from the post-Nicene era, and therefore represented the sentiments of post-Constantinian Roman Catholicism.[60]

Nevin published other articles on the Creed, some answering Proudfit and other critics, and still other articles reciting his basic views on the Creed in later issues of *The Mercersburg Review* which are also included in this volume. The longevity and virulence of this controversy about the Creed reveals the extent to which Nevin had exposed a fissure in American Protestantism.

---

59. John Proudfit (1803– c. 1870) was a pastor and a professor of ancient languages at New York University and Rutgers University. He had been theologically educated at Princeton Seminary. Although Nevin and Proudfit had been classmates at Union College, Proudfit became one of Nevin's most caustic theological critics.

60. Nichols, 176–77.

The Apostles' Creed[1]

[by John Williamson Nevin]

To understand properly the religious significance and value of this most ancient symbol, we must take into consideration, first, its *outward history;* secondly, its *constitution,* or *inward form*; and thirdly, its *material structure,* or *organism.* All this may be regarded as forming a proper introduction to the study of its actual contents, the glorious world of truth which it throws open to our contemplation

I. Outward History of the Creed.

The title of the symbol[2] seems, at first sight, to refer its authorship at once to the Apostles; and it has been in fact a very widely prevalent opinion in the Church, resting in long tradition, that it came originally complete in every part, as we now have it, from their hands. In the Romanist communion, it has been looked upon almost universally indeed, as profane to call this in question;[3] and many in the Protestant world, have made it a part of their religion to believe the same thing. The first distinct statement of the opinion, we find in Rufinus,[4] a church father of the fourth century; who speaks of it, however, as a common belief, handed down from an earlier time.

---

1. [J. W. Nevin, "The Apostles' Creed: I. Outward History of the Creed," *The Mercersburg Review* 1 (March 1849) 105–27; "... II. Its Inward Constitution and Form," (May 1849) 201–21; "... III. Its Material Structure Or Organism," (July 1849) 313–47.]

2. [The term "symbol" derives from the Latin term *symbolum* and the Greek term σύμβολον and came to be a common term meaning "creed." For more information on the term's provenance, see Kelly, *Early Christian Creeds,* 52–61.]

3. [The Catechism of the Council of Trent (1566) assumed that the twelve Apostles had composed the Creed under the guidance of the Holy Spirit, although this conviction did not acquire dogmatic status in the Roman Catholic Church.]

4. [Tyrannius Rufinus (c.345–411), an early Christian monk and historian, was born near Aquileia, a Roman village on the edge of the Adriatic. He was the author of *Commentarius in symbolum apostolorum* (c. 404), a treatment of the Old Roman Creed that was considered to be a forerunner of the Apostles' Creed.]

According to this tradition, he says, the Apostles, before separating to their different fields of service, that they might not fall into any confusion subsequently, met together, and under the guidance of the Holy Ghost, by joint contribution of views, framed and adopted this compend, as a rule of faith,[5] to be everywhere received by the infant churches. Some allusion to such joint composition, was found in the Greek name *symbol* itself, which signifies, primitively, a collation or throwing together of different things; and it is in conformity with the same thought, that we find the tradition elsewhere so far improved, as to refer to each Apostle, separately, a distinct article or clause of the Creed, as his particular quota contributed towards its formation.[6]

This whole opinion, however, is one which cannot be maintained with any tolerable show of success. Not only is it destitute of all positive historical foundation, but insuperable difficulties stand in the way of it on every side. No such apostolic creed or rule is mentioned in the New Testament. Some, indeed, have pretended to find it in St. Paul's "analogy or proportion of faith," Rom. xii. 6, the "good deposit" committed to Timothy, 2 Tim. i. 14, the "first principles of the oracles of God," mentioned in Heb. vi. 12, the "doctrine" on which so much stress is laid by St. John, 2nd Epis. v. 10, and "the faith once delivered unto the saints," as noticed by St. Jude, Ep. v. 3. But there is nothing in these passages to require any such interpretation. Still more significant is the silence of the early church writers. None of the fathers before Rufinus, Greek or Latin, makes any mention of the tradition to which he refers; and in all their controversies and discussions, we meet with no appeal whatever, to any such single and fixed form of words, as of established authority from the time of the Apostles. On the contrary, the way in which they touch the subject, shows clearly that no fixed form of this sort was in existence. They refer frequently to a Christian rule or canon of faith, and occasionally give us the sum of its contents; but this always with such free variation, as plainly implies that it was regarded as standing in the substance of what it taught, rather than in any particular forms of expression. Nay, the testimony of Rufinus himself,[7] is conclusive as regards this point. He affirms expressly, that the form was not the same precisely in all the churches; but that additions were made to it, in some cases, in opposition to particular local heresies. He himself chose to follow, as he tells us, the form to which he stood pledged by his own baptism in the church at Aquileia. This, of course, he accepted, as of apostolical authority; and yet he admits, that it contained one article which was not found in the Latin or Greek symbols generally; as in use elsewhere at that time. This was the article on Christ's descent into Hades. It has been made clear besides, that the article on the communion of saints, was wanting

---

5. [Predecessor to formal creeds, the rule of faith, or rule of truth, was a brief statement of orthodox Christian belief intended to distinguish what were taken to be genuine Christian teachings from rival heretical views, and to provide a very brief synopsis of essential convictions. Although there were various rules of faith, they were considered to contain essentially the same apostolic truth.]

6. [This view was reported by Rufinus. See Bingham, III:501–2].

7. [See Rufinus, *A Commentary on the Apostles' Creed*.]

altogether, and the article on the life everlasting, to a very considerable extent, in the symbols of the first four centuries; the truth asserted in each case, being held only, as something involved in the article going immediately before. Such variations in the form of the Creed, forbid the supposition of any fixed system of words, recognized and received as the composition of the Apostles. For no one, surely, would have felt at liberty to alter any such normal scheme of faith; and the use of other different forms altogether in Gaul, Spain, Alexandria, Antioch, Jerusalem, &c., must be counted in this case a problem admitting no rational solution.

Against such weight of evidence, the mere *inscription* of the symbol cannot be taken as of any particular force. It is called, indeed, the *Apostles'* Creed. But this title might have come into use gradually, under a mistaken idea of its being derived from the Apostles, when it had no such origin in fact; or the title may be taken as referring, in its original application, only to the substantial contents of the Creed, and not to its particular phraseology and form. The last supposition, we have every reason to assume as true and correct. The testimony of Rufinus himself, while it shows that there was a current general tradition in the Church at that time, referring the authorship of the Creed to the Apostles, indicates clearly enough at the same time, that this was to be understood only of its soul and substance, and not of the very terms in which it might happen to be uttered in any given case. For he does not pretend to confine the character of apostolic dignity to any single form of it, as then in use, to the exclusion of all the rest; but takes it for granted, rather, that all the churches enjoyed in this respect, the same advantage. He seems to allow, indeed, a certain central normality to the Creed as used at Rome; but chooses, nevertheless, as we have just seen, to abide by the form it earned in his own church at Aquileia, as strictly answerable to his idea of apostolical authority, although including a clause, which by his own confession, had no place in it as it had been in use to that time in other places. This shows plainly, in what sense he took it to be from the Apostles; and it was no doubt only in the same view, that the title which it now bears, came in the first place into general use.

The title indeed, was by no means confined originally to this particular symbol, as distinguished from others; but was applied frequently also to other symbols, that of Nice [Nicea] for instance, that of Constantinople, &c.; since with all their difference, they were regarded as alike embodying and representing in a true form, the one catholic faith of the Church as it had been handed down from the Apostles.

In this way, we are prepared at once to meet the vanity of those who affect to run away with the point now granted and proved, as though nothing more were needed to overthrow the apostolical credit of the Creed entirely, and turn it into the character of any mere ordinary human composition.[8] Of the two extremes, it is hard to say which in this case most deserves our commiseration: the superstition, which in the face of all historical evidence to the contrary, still clings to the dream of an outward construction of the symbol as we now have it, on the part of the Apostles; or the shallow frivolity,

---

8. See the essay by Proudfit in this volume.

that in detecting the untenable character of this prejudice, is ready at once to chuckle over its great discovery as the revelation of a "pious fraud," which it feels itself at liberty ever afterwards to scout from its presence as deserving of no regard whatever. With such mechanical *illumination,* that is so soon and so easily conducted to the end of its subject, it becomes us of course to have no patience or correspondence.[9] Its superior wisdom is, after all, in the case before us, of a most sophomorical complexion. "What men call the Apostles' Creed," this spirit exclaims, "though very ancient, was no more an apostolical invention than was Christmas-pie."[10] Admitted, so far as any particular outward structure is concerned. But is *this* a discovery to be paraded in such style, over against the ancient fathers and the belief of the early Church? The puerility here falls not on the fathers, but on the modern rationalism, that thinks to dispose of the whole question in such poor outward style. Even Rufinus himself, refers the Creed to the Apostles, only in such a way, as to leave room for much liberty and variation in its external form. But all this was not felt, either by him or by the Church in general, to conflict at all with the reigning tradition, which carried back its origin to the time of the Apostles. The true power and value of the symbol were felt to stand, not in a given fixed version established for its universal use, but in the divine substance of its contents, which was capable of retaining its identity under very considerable changes of expression. So far as this was concerned, the Christian catholic world considered itself in possession always of one and the same faith, however much freedom it might see fit to exercise with the utterance of it in different places. It was known well enough, that the general symbol admitted an utterance more or less full, as circumstances might require; that particular additions had been made to it with the progress of time, which did not belong to it in the beginning; and that it was not the same thing precisely, as to all its details, in any two leading provinces of the Church. And yet, notwithstanding all this, it was felt that the Church had but one Creed, and that this was of truly

---

9. [The reference to "mechanical illumination" may be a critique of Charles Hodge and the scholastic Calvinists. For an example, see Hodge's review essay (written after this exchange) "The Inspiration of Holy Scripture," *The Biblical Repertory and Princeton Review* 29 (Oct. 1857) 660–698.]

10. See the notice of Dr. Bushnell's address at Andover in the October number of the Boston "Observatory," for 1848, p. 479: "We are at a loss to understand what is meant by the boasted progress of theological science. So far as we can see, the foot-prints of this progress are all *back-tracks*. The Puseyites are advancing stern-foremost towards the Dark Ages, and Dr. Bushnell is backing up to what he calls the 'Apostles' Creed,' which, though very ancient, was no more an apostolical invention than was Christmas-pie. Such hind-part-before 'progress,' like the 'man with his head turned,' with his reversed stridings and grotesque backslidings, does not promise that the 'new era of Christianity,' which is said to be at hand, will be any improvement on the past." This may be allowed to be sufficiently smart, but is it not also sufficiently profane? *Christian Observatory*, II, no. 10 (October 1848), p. 479. [Horace Bushnell (1802–76), American Congregationalist pastor and theologian, has often been credited with helping to lay the foundations for American Protestant liberal theology by reconceptualizing the doctrines of atonement, sin, and the Trinity. The reference to Puseyites in this note refers to those sympathetic to the views of the Oxford Movement leader Edward Bouverie Pusey (1800–82) who sought to recover much of the liturgical and theological heritage of the pre-Reformation church. Nevin feared that Pusey paid too little attention to the positive insights of the Protestant Reformation and that his movement could degenerate into a kind of nostalgic ecclesial antiquarianism.]

apostolical dignity and authority. It expressed not only the same faith that was held by the Apostles, but it was their faith itself handed forward thus, under a living character, in the good confession of the Church from age to age. It was no product of private thinking here and there, as though the churches being left all to frame their several creeds in a separate way, had simply happened to come so near together, without yet reaching a full harmony; but it was something that came to them from a common source and under a common character, and which in this view was of broader and deeper force than any merely private confession as such. The unity of the Creed was determined by the realness of its contents, and the relation under which these were apprehended by all parts of the Church alike. It stood bound thus to the new order of life, which was revealed by Christ, through the Apostles, in the Church. Its stability was not in the outward letter, so much as in the inward spirit. It was written and preserved, as one of the fathers expresses it, not on plates of metal or stone, but on "fleshly tables of the heart," by the Spirit of the living God.[11]

In this way then, the old church tradition, as it is has passed down to us from the earliest times, is still entitled to our earnest respect; and we may easily see in fact, how with all its changes and variations, the symbol before us may be said to have taken its rise in the very age of the Apostles, and in a certain sense, under their very hands, and to have represented from the beginning, the one unvarying faith of the universal world. It needs no very close inspection to perceive that the manifold ways in which it was uttered come all to the same thing at last, and fall back always to a single fundamental formula as their general and common ground. They are at most, different translations, more or less full, of one and the same Creed, comprising in itself the sense of the new creation in Christ Jesus.[12]

It lies in the nature of the case, that the profession must have involved some common rule of faith from the beginning. "The word is nigh thee," Paul says, "even in thy mouth and in thy heart, that is the word of faith which we preach; that if thou shalt confess with thy mouth the Lord Jesus, and shalt believe in thy heart that God hath raised him from the dead, thou shalt be saved. For with the heart man believeth unto righteousness, and with the mouth confession is made unto salvation" (Rom. x. 8, 9). Faith comes to its proper completion only in the way of utterance; the inward word to be truly real must pass over into the form of an outward word; which becomes thus, at the same time, the bond of union and fellowship with others who have been made to partake of the same grace. Such an utterance of faith, in what may be considered

---

11. Jerome, Epistle lxi. as quoted by Bingham: Ab apostolis traditum, non scribitur in charta et atramento, sed tabulis cordis carnalibus. [Trans. "Handed down from the apostles, not written with paper and ink, but on fleshly tables of the heart." See Bingham, III:510. Bingham's attribution of Jerome's letter 61 to Pammachius is incorrect. Letter 61 is addressed to Vigilantius. The correct letter is to Pammachius "Against John of Jerusalem," Section 28.]

12. [It is significant that Nevin identifies "the new creation in Jesus Christ" as the essence of the Creed, rather than "salvation" or "redemption," which would have been the opinions of most other American Reformed theologians.]

Chapter 1: "The Apostles' Creed"

its primary central form, is presented to us in the memorable confession of Peter: "Thou art the Christ, the Son of the living God;" or, as we have it in another place: "To whom shall we go but unto Thee? Thou hast the words of eternal life; and we believe and are sure that thou art that Christ, the Son of the living God" (Matt. xvi. 16; John, vi. 68, 69). The whole Creed, as we shall see hereafter, is in truth wrapped up in this foundation article, and grows forth from it with inward necessity. Afterwards we have it, more full and clear, in the form of baptism, as presented by our Saviour himself: "Go teach all nations, baptizing them in the name of the Father, and of the Son, and of the Holy Ghost." [Matt 28:19] Christ is the revelation of God, under the three-fold character here brought into view; and this revelation may be said to constitute the sum and substance of Christianity, as the object of the faith we profess in coming into his Church. To be baptized into Christ [Rom 6:3], is to be baptized into the whole mystery of the Trinity, as inseparably joined with his person; and the formal acknowledgement of this mystery accordingly, in the way of solemn response or confession, was associated with the ordinance, no doubt, from the beginning.[13] It is allowed almost universally, that reference to such a confession is made by St. Peter, where he speaks of the answer of a "good conscience" (1 Pet. iii. 21), as necessary to be added to the outward washing of water, to complete the idea of baptism. The good profession of Timothy "before many witnesses" (1 Tim. vi. 12), is taken by many to refer also to the same thing. It is not necessary to suppose, that the profession thus required of all who came into the Church, was even in the age of the Apostles, under the same invariable form. It was sometimes more and sometimes less full, but it always carried in it, explicitly or by implication, a full assent to the contents of the baptismal formula. How far it may have become usual, before the death of the Apostles, to connect with this foundation the secondary clauses of the Creed as it now stands, cannot be clearly determined. But no one familiar with the early history of Christianity, can well fail to see that this must have been the case, at least to some extent; and the probability is certainly strong, that early in the second century, if not before, nearly all the particulars now embraced in it were found more or less in current use.

Still, as before said, the current use itself remained irregular and free. Each church considered itself at liberty to employ its own particular style of expressing its faith; just as each exercised the same sort of liberty in its general liturgy; while at the same time the faith itself was considered to be of a common character, belonging alike to all the churches and handed down from the Apostles. The variety and freedom thus allowed, were not suffered to trench upon the unity of the general tradition or rule. In the midst of it all, this was still felt to be one and the same, and is frequently appealed to accordingly, by the early writers as of acknowledged and easily intelligible authority.

Irenaeus speaks of such an "immoveable rule of truth," belonging to every Christian by his baptism; and describes it as proclaiming:

---

13. [See Bingham, III:462–72; 562–64.]

THE APOSTLES' CREED

> One God, the Father Almighty, maker of heaven, earth, the sea, and all that they contain; one Jesus Christ, the Son of God, incarnate for our salvation; and one Holy Spirit, who by the prophets preached the dispensations and the advents; the generation from the Virgin, the passion, the resurrection from the dead, and the ascension with the flesh into heaven of our Lord Jesus Christ, the Beloved, and his coming from heaven in the glory of the Father, to gather all things together into one and to raise all human flesh, that to Jesus Christ our Lord, and God and Saviour and king, according to the good pleasure of the invisible Father, every knee may bow of things in heaven, and things on earth, and things under the earth, and every tongue confess, and that he may execute just judgment upon all; remanding wicked spirits, and sinning apostate angels, and the impious, unrighteous, disobedient and blasphemous among men, into eternal fire; but on the righteous, and holy, and such as have kept his commandments and continued in his love, some from the beginning and others from their repentance, bestowing life, the gift of immortality and everlasting glory.[14]

Irenaeus does not mean, of course, to quote literally in this case, any certain formula, as of established and fixed use in the churches.[15] His whole manner implies the contrary, and may be taken as evidence that no fixed formula of this sort, as afterwards settled in our present Apostles' Creed, was then in ecclesiastical use. But he appeals nevertheless to what he regards as a well defined and clearly intelligible rule of faith, as forming the substance of the Christian profession; and it is easy enough to see, that this agrees entirely with the contents of the Creed now mentioned, showing it to reach back in the use of the Church, so far as these are concerned, to the age in which he lived. We have his testimony moreover, that it was in this view of apostolical and universal authority. The Church, he tells us, disseminated throughout the whole world, held it from the Apostles and their disciples, keeping it carefully, as though she occupied but a single house, accepting its contents everywhere as with one heart and soul, and preaching them as from one and the same mouth. Irenaeus writes:

> The dialects in which it is uttered are different; but the tradition is in force the same. The churches founded in Germany, have no other faith and doctrine; nor those in Spain; nor those among the Celts; nor those in the East; nor those in Egypt; nor those in Libya; nor those of more central situation; but as the sun, God's workmanship, is over the whole globe one and the same, so also the evangelical truth shines everywhere and illuminates all who are willing to come to its light.[16]

---

14. Irenaeus, *Adversus Haereses* [*Against Heresies*], Book l, Chapter x. Quoted in full by Joseph Bingham, *Orig. Eccles.* Book 10, Chapter iv. [See Bingham, III:512–13.]
15. [See Bingham, III:511–14.]
16. [Richardson, ed., *Early Christian Fathers*, 360–61.]

Chapter 1: "The Apostles' Creed"

The testimony of Irenaeus is very important, as illustrating both sides of the true doctrine concerning the origin of the Creed. It started with no such fixed form of words, in the beginning, as it carries in its repetition now. Irenaeus, and the Church in his time, knew of no apostolical tradition in this outward form, and none should be pretended by any part of the modern Church.

But Irenaeus, and the Church in his time, were perfectly familiar notwithstanding, with the idea of a *regula fidei* or creed, of universal force, and in actual use among all the churches. Still more, this rule was regarded as strictly and truly the *Apostles' Creed*. It was no product of private opinion, and it stood not at all in articles of convention and agreement adopted by the general Christian body. It was accepted everywhere as a system handed down from the Apostles; not merely as supposed to be in the spirit of their teaching, but as carrying forward in the faith of the Church, the very substance and contents of the divine revelation itself, which they were sent to proclaim. Finally, we gather from Irenaeus, that this Rule of Faith, in living use with the universal Church of his time, embraced in itself, under a free character, all the leading features of the Apostles' Creed, as afterwards settled in its present form; in which view it may well continue to challenge the reverential homage of all Christendom still, and onward to the end of the world, as a true apostolical symbol. This testimony of Irenaeus, it is well always to bear in mind, carries us back to the second century, and into close proximity thus with the immediate disciples of the Apostles themselves.

Tertullian appeals frequently, in the same free way, to the Christian Rule of Faith, and recapitulates several times its general contents, always in harmony with the sum of it as given by Irenaeus, for the purpose of confuting and confounding the heretics of his own time. His recapitulations are indeed always different, sometimes more and sometimes less full, showing that the Creed was more life than mere word; but they assume throughout, notwithstanding the clear identity belonging to it, as a single apostolical tradition.[17] The amount of it is always: One God, the almighty maker of the world; his Son, Jesus Christ, born of the Virgin Mary, constituted Messiah, crucified under Pontius Pilate, raised the third day, exalted to heaven and set at the right hand of God, from whence he shall come to judge the quick and the dead; the Holy Ghost sent forth vicariously, according to his promise, to sanctify those that believe in his name; the resurrection of the flesh, the damnation of the wicked, and the reception of the righteous into eternal life and the blessedness of heaven.[18] This rule, he says, instituted by Christ, allows no questions, other than such as spring from heresy and go

---

17. "Regula fidei una omnino est, sola immobilis et irreformabilis." [Trans. "The rule of faith is entirely one, uniquely fixed and unalterable." Bingham, III:515–18.]

18. [Tertullian] De veland. virginibus [Trans. "Of the Virgin's Veil"]. Chapter 1. De praescript. adv. haereticos [Prescriptions Against the Heretics]. Chapter 13. Adversus Praxean [*Against Praxeas*]. Chapter 2. [Tertullian considered Praxeas (c.200) to be guilty of heretical views concerning the Trinity by asserting that God the Father in Christ suffered on the cross. The passage from *Against Praxeas* is quoted in full by Bingham, III:517.]

to make heretics; it is older than all heresies; their novelty, as exposed by it, serves to establish its antiquity; to know nothing beyond it, "is to know all that is necessary."[19]

Origen, in like manner, gives a summary statement of the heads of Christian doctrine, "as plainly received by apostolical tradition," which corresponds in substance with the same rule.[20]

From Cyprian, we have an insight into the general Creed of the Church in Africa, as it stood in his time. The Novatians,[21] he admits, proposed the same questions at baptism that were used in the Church catholic, calling for faith in God the Father, his Son Jesus Christ, and the Holy Ghost. But still, he contends, that as schismatics, their rule and interrogation could not be regarded as the same; "for when they say: Dost thou believe the remission of sins and eternal life through the holy Church? They interrogate falsely, since they have no Church." This shows that the whole Creed, nearly as we have it now, was in common use in Africa, at this time, as an apostolical rule of faith, in connection with the baptismal service.[22]

These private testimonies show the presence everywhere in the early Church of an evangelical tradition, agreeing in its general contents with the Creed as it now stands, and accepted as of strictly apostolical origin and weight. They show also, that this tradition was regarded, not as a slavish form of words, but a free doctrine rather, that might be uttered in various ways. Still it would be a great mistake, to conceive of it as wholly loose and floating, in the style of these notices. In the nature of the case, the different churches must have held it from the beginning, under some regular and standing form. This may have varied some with the progress of time, as circumstances seemed to call for new points and specifications; and in this way, there would be room of course, for considerable peculiarity in the several churches, compared one with another; but the reigning type of the Creed in each case must have continued always the same. So much may be said to lie in the primitive design of the thing itself. It was the profession of faith that accompanied the sacrament of baptism, and that grew originally out of the baptismal formula as spoken by our Lord in its institution. Its use in the first centuries, was especially for those who were about to be introduced into the Church by this holy sacrament, after having gone through all proper previous steps, in the way of preparation for the solemnity. It was first delivered to the catechumen

---

19. "Nihil ultra scire, omnia scire est." [Trans. "To know nothing more is to know everything." Bingham, III:517.]

20. [See Bingham, III:514–15.]

21. [Novatian (c. 200–258) was a Roman priest who opposed the readmission to the church of those who had "lapsed" during the latest Roman persecution by offering sacrifices to the Emperor. He was elected bishop of Rome by a handful of dissident bishops who shared his extreme rigorist views. These views, and his claim to be the legitimate bishop of Rome, were eventually rejected by the majority of the church's hierarchy.]

22. Epistle lxxvi. [Cyprian, Epistle 76, 313–18, addressed to bishops, clergy, and others. This was cited in Bingham, III:518.]

by the bishop *(traditio symboli)*,[23] orally as it would seem, though possibly at times, also in writing; and then afterwards, in the course of a few days, publicly spoken back again and returned, *(redditio symboli)* ["the public proclamation of the creed"] as being effectually laid up in the meantime in the candidate's memory.[24] This was followed by an open solemn profession on the part of the candidate, at the time of his baptism itself, in the way of response to distinct interrogatories embracing the symbol in its several parts. Such an "answer of good conscience," is referred to by the earliest ecclesiastical writers wherever the subject comes in their way, and is to be regarded as starting undoubtedly in the practice of the Apostles themselves. All this implies, however, a short standing form, of established use in each particular church. Cyprian gives us a glimpse into the general African formula, as it was everywhere of force in the first part of the third century.[25] Other sections of the Church had similar standing forms; some more full perhaps than others; those of the East different from those of the West; but all handed down from the earliest time, and palpably expressing one and the same faith, as they belonged to one and the same baptism. In the fourth century, these public formularies begin to come more distinctly into view; always, however, in such a way as to show them in full, actual, and undisputed possession of the authority they claim, as of the most ancient right and force.[26] Take for instance, the symbol then in use at Rome. It is not specially presented to us, before this time. But what could well be more monstrous, than to fancy that it was for this reason of any comparatively recent date? It meets us in no such form; it tolerates from us no such doubt. We might just as well question the antiquity of the church itself in Rome, as question the antiquity of its creed. We meet it not in the fourth century, as a new thing, the creation, possibly, only of that age, or the one going before; it is the old baptismal symbol, as all the world then might know it to have been in use there from time immemorial; it is the Christian rule of faith, the Creed of the Apostles, in the particular form in which it had come to be woven into the very life of this ancient church from the beginning. So with the church at Aquileia; and so with the churches generally. Their particular creeds are regarded always as dating, in their main character, from the most remote Christian antiquity.

The very early origin of nearly all the elements presented in these church symbols of the fourth century, is shown not merely by the outward tradition going along with them in each case, and their general agreement with one another, but very strikingly

23. [Trans. "the handing on of the creed."]

24. The brief form of this confession, says Johann August Wilhelm Neander, as a matter of course, did not need a written communication; it was to pass over into the soul of the catechumen, out of *the living word into the life*; it must be the utterance of his own conviction. Christianity stands primarily, not in letter, but life. So Augustine, Hujus rei significandae causa, audiendo symbolum discitur, nec in tabulis, vel in aliqua materia, sed in corde scribitur. [Trans. "In order to show this, the creed is learned by hearing; it is not written on tablets, nor any material, but on the heart." Augustine, Sermon 20. See Neander, 308.]

25. [See Bingham, III:518–19.]

26. [See Bingham, III:526–42.]

also by the historical relations that are found imbedded as it were in their own form. The Creed is, of course, primarily positive, and not simply negative, in its contents. It affirms a substantial reality, which is not produced in any way by the mere denial of the various errors and false doctrines to which it stands opposed. At the same time, to be thus positive and affirmative, it must include in itself, from the start, a steady protest against such false doctrines as they came in its way. The Christian consciousness can evolve itself only by a process of continual critical separation, by which all that is foreign to its true life is sundered from this, and made to stand over against it as its antichristian opposite and contradiction. It lies moreover in the nature of this process, that the errors which are thus cast out will not come into view confusedly and by chance, but must be conditioned and determined always by the posture which has been reached by the Christian consciousness itself at the time of their appearance. In the history of the Church, accordingly, each age has its own forms of heresy, as well defined, we may say, as the successive geological formations that show themselves in the structure of the earth. The "fossil remains" of each period, are found wrought into the solid rock by which it is represented for all subsequent time.

In this way, the Apostles' Creed, aside from all outward historical evidence in the case, falls back plainly, in its main composition, to the earliest period of the Church. Its various propositions carry in them, beyond all doubt, a reference to certain false tendencies, which at the time of their original utterance, were actively at hand, and working towards the overthrow of the Christian faith. This has been very generally seen and felt; and great pains have been taken by such writers as Vossius,[27] Pearson,[28] Basnage,[29] King,[30] &c.,[31] to identify the relation of the several clauses of the Creed, in this way, to specific forms of heresy mentioned in early church history. Thus one clause is explained as springing out of opposition to Ebion, Cerinthus, and others; a second, as in contradiction to Menander, Cerdo and Saturninus; and so most of the

---

27. [Gerardus Vossius (also Gerhard Jan Voss, 1577–1649) was Dutch humanist scholar, active in Leiden and Amsterdam, who sought to formulate a mediating position between the Arminians and the Calvinists. Much of his irenic work was based on his reconstruction of the history and texts of the early church.]

28. [John Pearson (1613–86) was Lady Margaret's Professor of Divinity at Cambridge and later Bishop of Chester. He was celebrated for his exposition of the Creed and for his moderate Reformed theology.]

29. [Jacques Basnage (1653–1723) was an expatriate French theologian and ecclesial historian who was active in the Netherlands. Much of his historical work served to advance his anti-Catholic polemics.]

30. [Peter King (1669–1734) was an English jurist, politician, and baron. In his youth he penned a history of the worship of the church during the first three centuries.]

31. [Nevin cites these four Protestant writers to provide examples of Christian scholars who dealt with the question of the dating of the allegedly anti-heretical sections of the Creed.]

rest, as directed against Gnostic, Montanistic, Novatian, or other errors.[32] Walch[33] in his *Introd. in Lib. Symb.* p. 101,[34] justifies this view in a general way, while he considers, at the same time, that it has been carried by some quite too far. Bull[35] and Grabe[36] are disposed to dispute its correctness a good deal farther; the latter especially, holding that all the clauses of the Creed, with the exception of those on the *descent into Hades* and the *communion of saints* (possibly also that on *the church*), came into use in the age of the Apostles themselves, by their authority, or at all events, with their knowledge and approbation, and are to be explained out of relations existing at that time. The question cannot be brought probably to any such absolute determination as this; but in any case, a proper familiarity with the early history of the Church, must lead us to feel that we have no right to come lower than the first part of the second century, in order to fix, to the extent just mentioned, the rise of the several parts of the Creed. The errors excluded by them, are such as lie close around the inmost life of Christianity. They belong to the very first stage of the process by which this life was

32. [Nevin mentions five heretical individuals and three heretical movements against whom the four writers previously mentioned had marshaled credal evidence to undermine the heretics' unorthodox views. Among the heretical leaders were: Ebion, thought to be the founder of the Ebionites, a heretical Jewish Christian sect described by several early church fathers; Cerinthus (second century), a Jewish Christian Gnostic teacher, branded a heretic by Irenaeus and Epiphanius for his dualism and his Docetic Christology which asserted that Jesus only appeared to be genuinely human, but actually was not; Menander (second century), a Samaritan Gnostic, who denied the world's creation by the Jewish God Yahweh and was considered to be heretical by Irenaeus; Cerdo (second century), a Syrian Gnostic teacher, who denied that the Jewish God was the Father of Jesus Christ; and Saturninus (late first century), a prominent Gnostic trained by Menander who held heretical views on creation and viewed Jesus as the redeemer who would destroy the Jewish God. The heretical movements cited by Nevin were: gnostics, some of whom are named as individuals above; Montanists who were founded by Montanus (second century), an apocalyptic prophet who claimed that he was a representative of the Holy Spirit initiating the final era of divine revelation; and Novatians (mid-third century) a sect founded by Novatian who questioned the legitimacy of lapsed church leaders who had compromised their faith by submitting to pagan authorities during the reign of the Roman emperor Decius. See Everett Ferguson, ed., *Encyclopedia of Early Christianity* and F. L. Cross and E. A. Livingstone, eds., *The Oxford Dictionary of the Christian Church*.]

33. [Johann Georg Walch (1693–1775) was a German theologian and historian of Lutheranism. He edited Luther's works and Reformation confessional documents, and composed histories of the Reformation, focusing on Lutheran doctrinal controversies.]

34. [Johann Georg Walch, *Introductio in libros Symbolicos ecclesiae Lutheranae*, 20.]

35. [George Bull (1634–1710) was an Anglican theologian who became Bishop of St. David's. From that position he tried to combat what he took to be the doctrinal laxity of the Latitudinarians. He authored treatises defending the doctrine of the Trinity and a polemical work refuting the theory that the concept of the divinity of Christ had been invented by early heretical groups who then influenced the broader church.]

36. [John Ernest Grabe (1666–1711) was an Anglican theologian who had left the Lutheran church in Prussia because he feared that it failed to meet the critera for apostolic succession. He critically edited the manuscripts of some of the works of Justin Martyr and Irenaeus. Both Bull and Grabe are cited because they convincingly argued that evidences for the early age of the Creed precludes the possibility that some of the articles were post-apostolic attacks on heretical movements that developed later in the church's experience.]

required to unfold itself in the form of history. They come in the way of that process, by a sort of inward necessity, from the very start. We meet them, accordingly, under full revelation, in the second century. There is no occasion then to descend lower than this, for the rise of the Creed. It was *needed* for the second century; it forms the proper utterance of the Christian life as it then stood, in the face of all sorts of Gnostic and Ebionitic[37] unbelief. Still more, we have good evidence that those spurious forms of thinking were actively at work in the century before. Gnosticism, as it meets us in the second century, sprang not abruptly and with a single stroke, like a full armed Minerva, on the arena of church history. We have traces enough in the New Testament, of the chaotic workings at least of the same antichristian spirit in the very age of the Apostles. Indeed, to assert itself at all, the Christian life must be supposed to have been brought into conflict with the substance of these primitive forms of heresy from the beginning. It was then practically an utterance of faith from the first, answerable to these circumstances, and no good reason can be shown why the utterance should not have passed over, in the apostolic period itself, to a free form of words also in substantial agreement with the ancient symbol as it now stands. Let anyone but have in his mind a lively sense of the terrible aberrations from the truth, that are revealed to us darkly from the first days of the infant Church, in the writings of Paul and John and Peter and Jude, and he will not be likely to feel that there is any necessity whatever for coming down to the heresies of a later time, as broached by Cerdo, Marcion, Saturninus, Valentinus, Basilides, &c., much less to the age of the Novatians, or that of the Donatists,[38] in order to explain the sense and force of the testimony here handed down in the Apostles' name. Was not the same testimony, at almost every point, called for by the relations of the Church in the first century? And if so, what right have we to overlook these altogether, and refer its origin mainly to another time? No one, at all events, can study attentively the structure of the Creed, without finding in its whole formation clear monumental evidence of the very highest Christian antiquity.

With the advance of time, as the aspects of heresy changed, the old elementary style of the Creed was made to undergo naturally, in different quarters, partial and circumstantial modifications, in the way of direct testimony over against such new errors. Thus, for instance, in the church at Aquileia, the first article read in the time of Rufinus: I believe in God the Father Almighty, *invisible and impassible;* with clear

---

37. [Ebionism was a form of ascetic Jewish Christianity that probably arose after the destruction of the Temple and lasted until the fifth century. The Ebionites regarded Jesus as the Messiah, but rejected the ascription of divinity to him.]

38. [Nevin asserts that the writings of the New Testament authors Paul, John, Peter, and Jude reveal such serious criticism of the presence of heterodox ideas in the churches of their own era that the erroneous ideas of the later heretical groups need not be posited as a major polemical concern of the authors of the Apostles' Creed. This was a part of Nevin's argument that the spirit of the Creed, if not the exact letter, dates from the era of the apostles.]

reference to the Sabellian[39] and Patripassian[40] heresies, which affirmed that it was the Father himself who had become incarnate and suffered under Pontius Pilate.[41] This symbol also included the article on the *descent to hades,* as we have before seen, when it had no place, as Rufinus supposed, in the other creeds generally existing in his time. In the Oriental [Eastern] Church, the tendency of the Creed to adjust itself, by expansion and modification, to new necessities, prevailed more actively than it did among the Latins; by reason of the manifold phases and forms, in which false doctrine was always starting into fresh life, on that field, during the first ages. Thus we find in Cyril,[42] the creed of the church at Jerusalem, as it had stood before the Council of Nice [Nicea], bearing upon it such significant amplification at various points.[43] Still, different from this again, was the old creed used at Caesarea, in Palestine, recited by Eusebius,[44] in the Nicene Council, as the formula of faith which he had received there at his baptism. It approached closely to the symbol adopted by this Council. It is a probable supposition, that the Nicene Creed was made to embrace the reigning type of the older Oriental symbols, with such additions only as were needed to meet effectually the false doctrine of Arius.[45] As issued at Nice [Nicea], however, (a.d. 325) it was made to close abruptly with the article of the Holy Ghost, leaving out all that should follow concerning the Church and the course of the new creation in Christ Jesus; by which some have been led to question the presence of these concluding topics

---

39. [Sabellianism was a doctrinal position that flourished in the eastern church in the third century. It was a form of modalism, which was a cluster of related views that the Father, Son, and Holy Spirit were different activities of the one God. It was later condemned as a heresy.]

40. [Patripassianism was a modalistic belief in the early western church that the Father, who was absolutely identical with the Son and the Spirit, suffered in Jesus Christ.]

41. [Nevin relies on Bingham, III:535.]

42. [Cyril (c. 376–444) was a politically and theologically influential Patriarch of Alexandria. He was a pivotal participant in the Council of Ephesus (431) and was a fierce opponent of the position of the Nestorians. Against the Nestorians, who tended to dichotomize the divine and human natures of Christ, Cyril argued for a more intimate union, maintaining that Mary could be addressed as "the Mother of God," and that the Incarnate Son of God truly suffered in the flesh. Here Nevin relied on Bingham, III:528–29.]

43. "I believe in one God, the Father Almighty, Maker of heaven and earth, maker of all things visible and invisible: And in one Lord Jesus Christ, the only begotten Son of God, begotten of the Father before all days, the God by whom all things were created, who was incarnate and made man; was crucified and buried, the third day rose from the dead, and ascended into the heavens, and sat down at the right hand of the Father; who shall come to judge the quick and the dead, and of whose kingdom there shall be no end. And in one Holy Ghost, the Paraclete who spake by the prophets; in one baptism of repentance for the remission of sins; in one holy catholic church; and in the resurrection of the flesh and in life everlasting." [Philip Schaff, *The Creeds of Christendom*, II:31–32. The wording in Schaff is slightly different than that given by Nevin.]

44. [Eusebius (c. 260–c.340) was a Roman ecclesial historian and bishop. His *The Ecclesiastic History* is one of the earliest histories of the Christian church, and partly functioned as an apology for Constantine's revolution in the relation of the church and the empire.]

45. Walch, [*Introductio*], 20. [Arius (c.250–336) was a priest in Alexandria who proclaimed that the Son was subordinate to the Father. His teachings were rejected by the First Coincil of Nicea in 325 which declared that the Son and the Father are one in essence ("consubstantial").]

in the earlier creeds altogether. But we have ample evidence to show the contrary, and the omission here is accounted for very easily, by the consideration that the object of the Nicene Creed was simply to repel the errors of Arius and his party in regard to the Trinity.[46] The topics following had not been called in controversy, and were left to stand untouched accordingly, as already found in the creeds generally. Subsequently, by the second general Council, (held at Constantinople, a.d. 381)[47] this omission was formally supplied, and the Creed re-adopted, with some other improvements, in the form in which it is now known and used; with the exception only of the clause that makes the procession of the Holy Ghost to be *from the Son,* as well as from the Father, which was added at a later period by the Latin Church. The older Oriental creeds naturally gave way to this oecumenical Nicene, or rather Niceno-Constantinopolitan, symbol. It passed very soon into general use, as it would seem in the administration of baptism; and was adopted subsequently into the stated liturgical church service. It is agreed on all hands, however, that the practice of reciting it in this way, was not introduced before the middle of the fifth century.[48]

Among the earlier symbols of the Western Church, which differed somewhat among themselves, as we have already seen, though their reigning type was always the same, a sort of central dignity and pre-eminence was gradually claimed and allowed in favor of the formula used at Rome.[49] When speaking of the occasional slight variations of the Creed, in different churches, Rufinus tells us, that nothing of this sort was to be found in the Roman church, a fact which he accounts for in this way, that no heresy had started there, and that those who were to receive baptism were required always to repeat the creed before the whole congregation, which stood ready at once to object to the slightest innovation in its terms. Still Rufinus chose to abide by his own symbol, as he held it from the church at Aquileia; and whatever the stability of the Roman formula might have been previously, we find it at a later period consenting to complete itself by the admission of a little material at least, which did not belong to it from the beginning. As it stood in the time of Rufinus, it lacked the articles on the *descent to hades,* and the *life everlasting,* as well as the title *catholic,* in connection with the Church. In reality, however, of course, the descent to hades was involved in the clause on *Christ's death and burial,* and the life everlasting in the idea of the *resurrection;* while the Church, as an object of faith, includes the conception of catholicity as

46. [Nevin gets this material from Bingham, III:536–37.]

47. [The First Council of Constantinople, accepted by many Christian traditions as the second ecumenical council, was called by the Emperor Theodosius in 381 as an effort to theologically unify the empire. The Council opposed the residual Arianism that was still common and reaffirmed the Nicene Creed. It expanded the Creed by adding an article on the divinity of the Holy Spirit.]

48. See Bingham, III:535–38, 541–45.]

49. Credatur symbolo apostolorum, quod ecclesia Romana intemeratum semper custodit et seriat. Ambrose, Epistle 81. [Trans. "The Apostles' Creed, which the Roman church guards and keeps pure, is to be believed." In Epistle 81 addressed to "Certain of the Clergy," the reference to the Creed does not appear.]

an attribute inseparable from its constitution. When precisely the Roman creed was brought to include, in common use, the separate distinct utterance of the points now noticed, is not known. They were, however, in due time fairly installed in their place; and in this form, having come in the fifth and sixth centuries into general use, it has come down to us, with the veneration of the whole Christian world, as the standard edition of the ancient rule of faith, the best and truest representation of the fundamental realities of the Christian religion, the proper Apostles' Creed.

In this character, it forms the basis of all sound Christian profession, in the Protestant Church no less than in the Roman Catholic. In the great religious revolution of the sixteenth century, its credit and authority remained inviolate and unimpaired. The object of the Reformation was to sweep aside the rubbish which threatened to smother the life of the ancient faith, not by any means to bring this faith itself out of the way. Both divisions of the Protestant Church accordingly, the Lutheran and the Reformed, united in acknowledging the binding authority of the ancient oecumenical symbols, and especially the root of all symbols as found in the Apostles' Creed. They did not pretend to abjure all connection with the past, but professed to build on a foundation already laid, and to carry forward a work already long since begun. In the Lutheran Church, the three primary creeds, (Apostolical, Nicene and Athanasian) are made to precede the Augsburg Confession, in the Form of Concord; to show, says Walch, "that Lutherans embrace not a new doctrine, but such as is old and apostolical, and profess thus the truly catholic faith."[50] How fully it lay at the foundation of all Christianity with Luther himself, we all know. It was part of his piety, a necessary means of grace with him, he tells us himself, to repeat the Creed with the Lord's Prayer, throughout his life, in the spirit of a little child. His sense of the authority that belongs to the ancient catholic faith altogether, was very earnest and deep. "It is dangerous and terrible," he writes in his memorable letter to Albert of Prussia, "to hear or believe anything, against the united testimony, faith and doctrine of the universal holy Christian Church, as held now and from the beginning, for 1500 years, throughout the world."[51] The Creed, of course, occupies a conspicuous place in his catechism.[52] In this, however, we see only an image of the universal Protestant feeling in that age. Every such formulary of religious instruction was expected, as a matter of course, to take in the Creed, along with the Lord's Prayer and the Ten Commandments.

The Reformed Church here was of one mind with the Lutheran. Thus in Calvin's Catechism, the first section treats of *Faith;* which is said to have the sum of its contents in the "formula of confession held in common by all Christians; commonly

---

50. [See Walch, *Historische und theologische Einleitung in die Religionsstreitigkeiten der evangelishe-lutherischen Kirche* (Jena: Meyer, 1736).]

51. [Martin Luther to Albrecht of Brandenburg, December, 1523, *Luther's Works, Letters II*:59–68. Duke Albert of Prussia (1490–568) was a convert to Lutheranism and one of its primary poltical and military defenders. His territory was the first state to adopt Lutheranism as its official established religion.]

52. [Schaff, *The Creeds of Christendom*, III:77–80.]

THE APOSTLES' CREED

called the *Apostles' Creed*, and always received from the beginning among the pious; as being either derived from the mouth of the Apostles, or faithfully collected from their writings."[53] After this it is recited and expounded in full. So in the admirable symbol of the Palatinate, the Heidelberg Catechism, "it is the articles of our catholic undoubted Christian faith,"[54] as comprehended in the same Creed, which are made to underlie the doctrine of salvation from beginning to end. It formed part of the regular church service in the Reformed liturgies, accompanied their baptisms, and entered into their celebration of the holy eucharist. The Gallican Confession, art. 5. approves the three Creeds, Apostolic, Nicene and Athanasian, as agreeing with the written word of God.[55] "We do willingly receive the three creeds," it is said in the Belgic Confession, art. 9, "namely, that of the Apostles, of Nice, and of Athanasius; likewise that which conformable thereunto, is agreed upon by the ancient fathers."[56] In the Helvetic Confession, art. 11, the symbols of the first four general councils, together with that of Athanasius, are cordially approved and professed.[57] The three Creeds are endorsed in the Articles of the Church of England, as worthy of all reception.[58] In the Declaration of Thorn, we are said to be all baptized into the Apostles' Creed, as a compendium of the Christian faith; and the Nicene and Constantinopolitan Creeds are taken still farther as a sure interpretation of the same heavenly doctrine, forming thus the common ground on which all who profess Christ, must of necessity come together, and the one firm foundation against which the gates of hell shall never prevail.[59] It is part of the true Protestant faith, undoubtedly, as held by the Reformed Church, no less than the Lutheran, to abide by the ancient Christian Creed. Whatever else it may include, it starts from this and rests in it throughout, as its sure and necessary foundation.

---

53. [John Calvin, "Catechism of the Church of Geneva," *Calvin: Theological Treatises*, 22:92.]

54. [Schaff, *The Creeds of Christendom*, III:314.]

55. [Schaff, *The Creeds of Christendom*, III:362. The Gallican Confession of 1559 was a statement of Reformed faith adopted by the first national synod of the Reformed Church of France. It was largely based on a draft prepared by John Calvin.]

56. [Schaff, *The Creeds of Christendom*, III:393. The Belgic Confession was a summary of the Reformed faith adopted in the Netherlands in 1561. It stressed the continuity of Reformed theology with the creeds of the early church.]

57. [Schaff, *The Creeds of Christendom*, III:277. The Helvetic Confessions were two confessional documents adopted by the Swiss Reformed churches, the first in 1536, and the second in 1566. The first one was largely composed by Heinrich Bullinger and Martin Bucer and had a somewhat irenic tone, trying to avoid giving offense to Lutherans. The second document, composed by Bullinger, was much longer and more specifically Reformed. Although its immediate provenance was Switzerland, its enormous influence reached from Poland to the Netherlands and Britain.]

58. [Schaff, *The Creeds of Christendom*, III:492.]

59. [The Declaration of Thorn was the documentary fruit of the Colloquy of Thorn held at Torún, Poland in 1645. Representatives of the Lutheran, Roman Catholic, and Reformed communions were present. The goal of the conference was the religious reconciliation of the three traditions. Although that goal was not achieved, the Declaration is considered an important statement of Reformed theology. See Schaff, *The Creeds of Christendom*, I: 560–63.]

Chapter 1: "The Apostles' Creed"

It must be acknowledged, however, that the honor thus put upon the Creed in the original Protestant Confessions, has undergone, practically at least, no slight eclipse, in a wide portion of the modern Protestant world. So far as Rationalism has had power in Europe, the authority of the ancient church faith, of course, fell into discredit; and it is felt now by those who seek the revival of pure Christianity, that all turns on the power of the Church to intone with full emphasis again, in her public formularies and services, every single article of the *symbolum apostolicum,* most especially those of the incarnation, the descent into hades, and the resurrection of the body. But the low esteem for the Creed, of which we now speak, has not been confined to Rationalism, technically so styled. We see it widely displayed in other sections also of the Protestant world, which we are accustomed to distinguish as orthodox and evangelical. The other great disease of the Protestant system, the spirit of *Sect*,[60] shows a striking affinity here, no less than at other points, with the Rationalistic tendency of which it is the natural counterpart. Sects, in proportion as they *are* sects, that is in the same measure that they lack all sympathy with the idea of the Church, and substitute sectarianism for catholicity, will be found all the world over to have no taste for the Creed. They may possibly extend to it some cold token of respect, as a venerable relic of early Christianity; but it has not their heart, falls not in with their habit of Christianity, and is admitted to no place of course in their worship, public or private.

More than this, *Puritanism,* which we do not wish to confound certainly with Rationalism and the Sect System, although it carries in itself undoubtedly a more direct tendency towards both than can be said to lie in original Protestantism, being in truth, an advance on this, whether for weal or for woe, and such an advance as places it in closer natural proximity to the evils now mentioned; Puritanism,[61] we say, taking the term in the broad sense, to designate a special form of the religious life, which is just as well defined in history as early Protestantism itself, may be said to carry with it this universal character, that it makes no account practically of the Apostles' Creed. The remark is not made here of course in the way of censure or reproach, and ought not to be taken as disrespectful in any way to the system in question. We are dealing simply with the history of the subject; and the fact now stated, is one which no well informed person will pretend to call in question. It matters not that the authority of the Creed may be recognized, in some general way, in this or that old confession still retained in

---

60. [Nevin, "Antichrist" and "The Sect System," in *One, Holy, Catholic, and Apostolic, Tome One,* MTSS 5, ed. Hamstra, 165–232, 238–71.]

61. [By "Puritanism" Nevin generally meant the type of Reformed faith that arose in many sectors of Congregationalism in New England and in Presbyterianism in the Middle Atlantic colonies, as well as their antecedents in Great Britain and the European continent. In his view, Puritanism construed the visible church as a voluntary society of individuals who had made similar personal commitments. Nevin also feared that it regarded the Lord's Supper as a memorial meal or as a personal pledge to follow Christ. In his eyes Puritanism lacked a sense of the church as the Body of Christ that communicated Christ's vivifying presence through its sacaments, liturgies, and nurture. See his "Evangelical Radicalism," in *Mercersburg Review,* 4:508–12. There he referred to the "modern Puritanic system" thought to be the "very perfection…of evangelical religion (510)."]

the Church; so far as the Puritan spirit in its modern form is found to prevail in any ecclesiastical body, all actual use of the Creed, and all hearty interest in it, are to the same extent wanting. It is not used, for example, in the religious education of families. Children, generally, are not made to lay it up in their minds, as the sum and substance of the Christian faith. It comes not into view in catechetical instruction; if indeed this itself be still upheld, under any form, in regular use. It is not repeated of course in public worship; the minister who should take upon him any such innovation as that, would be suspected of some secret hankering after Rome. It is not made in any way a rule of Christian profession or public teaching. It is quite common, for instance, in Congregationalist churches, to make use of "covenants," or forms of profession and engagement, when members are received into full communion, each congregation varying the form to suit its own taste;[62] but it would be hard to find one among all, that would be content to make use of the Apostles' Creed in this way, or even to be guided by it at all in the construction of its own formulary.[63] The feeling is, plainly enough, that this old symbol has had its day, and is now antiquated if not absolutely obsolete; that it bears upon it the marks of a rude and imperfect Christianity, not without some touch of tendency towards superstition; that the evangelical faith of the present day may be more clearly and satisfactorily expressed, in other schemes and summaries altogether, any one of which, as taken from the Bible and common Christian experience, is to be held just as much entitled to honor as that which is thus

---

62. [The concept of "covenant" was common in Reformed theology, with roots in the writings of John Calvin and Heinrich Bullinger. The term possessed a variety of nuances, ranging from God's unconditional promises to God's conditional injunctions. As elaborated by the Puritan William Ames and his Dutch student Johannes Cocceius, "covenant" suggested reciprocal obligations and commitments, and began to be used as the lens through which social relations and ecclesial polity were viewed.]

63. A striking exemplification of this independence is furnished in the manufacture of a new confession of faith, a few years since, for the use of the *Protestant Armenian Church*, lately started, under the auspices of our New England missionaries, in the city of Constantinople. In other ages, the casting of a creed for a whole church has been counted an enterprise of not common size and weight, but here it was the work of one or two hands only, brought happily to a full conclusion in the course of a few hours! To expedite the business and guard against all bias, the precaution was adopted, we are told, of shutting out all consultation whatever had been adopted by an part of the Church as of symbolical authority previously, the primitive foundation Creed of the Oriental [Eastern] Church, of course, along with the rest, so as to draw the whole by purely original deduction direct from the Bible, *as traditionally understood in New England*. Not a syllable accordingly does this new confession contain, in recognition of the ancient symbol of universal Christendom. The greatest marvel of all, perhaps, is that this bold way of going to work in so momentous a case, should be quietly accepted so generally, by the whole American Board for instance, as nothing out of the way, a mere matter of course. So, it will be remembered, the late World Convention of London, in undertaking to construct an oecumenical platform for the union of *evangelical* sects, found it necessary to ignore the Apostles' Creed in full, and brought in a new set of articles altogether of its own invention, as better suited for the purpose. [The Armenian Protestant Church was founded in 1846 through the labors of the American Board of Commissioners for Foreign Missions, reputed to be the first American foreign mission society. The London conference to which Nevin makes reference is the 1846 London meeting of the Evangelical Alliance.]

falsely ascribed to the Apostles. It is felt to be on the whole a loose and careless production; without much plan or method, and governed by no principle in the choice of its articles; introducing some points of no necessary importance, and leaving out several others that should be counted indispensable. One thing is beyond all controversy certain, that if Puritanism were called upon to form a fundamental, universal creed, it would fall on something very different from this ancient symbol, both in conception and style. All this, as before said, is noticed here neither in the way of blame nor of praise, but simply as a matter of history which is open to common observation. In this view, however, it is entitled to earnest attention. The fact, in its own nature, is curious. Nor can it easily be allowed to be of only small significance. Such variation from the mind and posture of the ancient Church, in regard to the Creed, implies necessarily a serious variation from the life of primitive Christianity in general. The difference between Puritanism and original Protestantism here, argues necessarily a very considerable remove in the whole inward habit and being of the first from the proper spiritual constitution of the second. Such a fact has a right to challenge notice. Whether it be looked upon as right or wrong, an occasion for congratulation or a reason for censure and complaint, it is entitled at all events to earnest consideration, and should if possible be fairly understood and explained.

The force of what is now said will become still more evident when we take into view the interior constitution of the Creed, its rise and structure in the living sphere of faith, to which it primarily and natively belongs.

II. Its Inward Constitution and Form.[64]

To estimate properly the merits and claims of the *apostolical symbol,* it is not enough to be acquainted with the facts of its history outwardly considered. We need still more to understand its interior history; its rise and progress under an inward view; the idea which is developed in its constitution, and the manner in which the development is to be regarded as taking place.

In the first place, the Creed is no work of mere outward *authority,* imposed on the Church by Christ or his Apostles. It would help its credit greatly in the eyes of some, no doubt, if it could be made to appear under this view. Their idea of Christianity is such as involves prevailingly, the notion of a given or fixed scheme of things to be believed and done, propounded for the use of men, on the authority of heaven, in a purely mechanical and outward way. If there were evidence that some several of the Apostles together, or even the Apostle Paul, or the Apostle John alone, had formed the Creed as it now stands, and handed it over in this shape as something finished and complete, to the keeping of the Church, it would be looked upon, of course, as at once a divine tradition, the sacredness of which it would be no better than infidelity

64. [(May 1849) 201–21.]

to doubt or call in question.[65] It is plain, however, from the history already presented, that no such origin as this can be asserted in its favor. It is not in this sense it has claimed to be apostolical from the beginning. Its relation to the faith of the Church, is not that of an outward dead *traditum* or deposit, in any way. On the contrary, the idea of such a relation in the case, contradicts its whole nature. In no such form could it be the glorious Christian *creed*, which we now find it to be in fact.

In the next place, it is no product of *reflection*, exercised on the contents of Christianity, as an object of thought and study. This it might be conceived to have been, in two ways. We can suppose some gifted individual, well versed in the great truths of the gospel, to have addressed himself to the work of reducing them to the form of such a brief system or compend, in a merely private character; or we may imagine a body of competent persons met together for this purpose, as a council or synod, and furnishing the formulary as the result of their joint deliberation and discussion. This last view, especially, would suit the taste of many; more particularly if it could be made to appear that the Bible had been taken as the source and rule of all evidence in the case, and that the formulary was exhibited throughout as an extract simply, and summary, of what is to be found in its inspired pages. It would assist the respect of such persons greatly for the Apostles' Creed, if in the acknowledged default of a strictly apostolical *imprimatur*, it were possible still to refer to some ecclesiastical convention of this sort, in which with all due formality and deliberation it was brought out for the use of the Church, at the very beginning of its history; if that famous synod at Jerusalem [Acts 11:1–18], for instance, or some other solemnly convened for the purpose after the destruction of Jerusalem, were known to have taken the matter in hand (after the fashion of the great *world convention* in London[66]) and to have produced finally, what they conceived to be, in this shape, a truly *scriptural* platform of Christian doctrine. But it must be admitted that the ancient Creed comes down to us in no such form as this. We ask in vain for the private study or private theological brain to which it owes its birth; and we are equally disappointed when we think of tracing its origin to any more public theological or ecclesiastical source. In this respect, its rise is more obscure seemingly, than that of all modern confessions. It comes with far less "observation," than the Heidelberg Catechism, or that of Westminster.[67] No trumpet tongue proclaims its "articles of agreement," for the whole world to hear, as

---

65. [Nevin probably feared that such an attitude characterized such scholastically inclined Reformed theologians as Charles Hodge, who had been one of Nevin's mentors at Princeton Theological Seminary. As a theology textbook, Hodge used the *Institutes* of the seventeenth century theologian Francis Turretin (1623–1687), who had treated theology as a set of propositions referring to supernatural realities that must be arranged in a logically organized system of axioms and corrolaries, and whose plausibility (including the plausibility of an infallible divine revelation) must be demonstrated. See Hodge, "The Idea of the Church."]

66. [Nevin is referring to the 1846 Evangelical Alliance convention in London which received strong but varying support from world Protestant denominations.]

67. [The texts of the Heidelberg Catechism and Westminster Confession are located in Schaff, *The Creeds of Christendom*, III: 307–55 and 600–673.]

in the case of the *late* "Evangelical Alliance." There is no evidence whatever, of plan, or calculation, or forethought, of any sort, in its production; not even to the extent of what is implied in the fabrication of a modern church "covenant," for the use of a single congregation. There is nothing in the case to match even the independent private manufacture of that new creed lately originated for the use of the Protestant Armenian Church, in Constantinople. We can see and understand easily how *that* was made; the missionary goes into his upper room, takes the Bible into his hands, forgets as far as possible all creeds besides, and so through the medium of his own head, with such theological shape as it has already at hand, contrives and puts together a scheme or plan of necessary Christian truths; which in such form is presented, at the end of a few hours, all done and complete, and at once ready for use. All this however, we miss in the Creed which bears the name of the Apostles. No one can tell exactly whence or how it comes. Its beginning is vague and uncertain. It seems to spring up at different points, and its appearance is not at once well settled and defined. Plainly there has been no method or plan, no process of intellectual reckoning, no comparison of views and observations, no outlay of theological thought and reflection, in the production of the Apostles' Creed. The authorship of it, be it such as it may, does not hold at all in the form of any such relation to its contents as would be implied in this supposition. It is not the work of any mind, or set of minds, placing themselves over against the contents of Christianity in the way of consideration, holding them off as it were objectively for the notice of thought, and so reducing them to logical statement for the understanding. We hear of no such process; and we read no trace of it in the formulary itself. That is not in any view its constitution and form. The Creed, it deserves to be well understood and well borne in mind, is not a confession in the common modern sense. It is not like a catechism. It is no summary of Christian doctrine, no theory of divinity in miniature form. To be appreciated properly, it must be apprehended under a wholly different character.

We would not be understood, in what is here said, as undervaluing or disparaging at all, schemes of Christian doctrine; as though the vital power of religion must be supposed to suffer, from any attempt to make it the subject of intellectual contemplation. There is a certain way, indeed, of using the understanding here, which is not to be approved; when its notions and abstractions, namely, are made to pass for the matter or substance of religion itself, as though this stood primarily in such mere acts of thought. To make reflection or intelligence, in this way, the principle of Christianity, is to fall at once fully over into the arms of rationalism.[68] But allowing the Christian substance or reality to be already at hand, under a different form, there is no reason why it should not be made the object of thought, like any other material with which the mind is called to work. On the contrary, it lies in the very conception

---

68. [Nevin is arguing against some of the Reformed scholastic theologians who proposed that faith begins with the cognitive conviction that certain theological propositions are true. See Hodge, "Inspiration," 660–98.]

of Christianity, that it should thus take possession of the thinking of men, as well as of their outward activity. It seeks continually to become objective, in the way of reflection and knowledge. Where there is no religious thought, no doctrinal scheme for the understanding, no theological science, it is in vain to expect that the life of religion can be truly prosperous in any other view. We undervalue not systematic divinity. We speak not a word against modern catechisms and confessions. They are all good and highly necessary in their place. Only we must not think of the Apostles' Creed, as belonging to the same order of ecclesiastical productions. It is no work of religious reflection, no product of the understanding, no digest in the form of thought. It holds altogether in a different element, and carries in itself quite another constitution.

What then is the true distinctive character of the Creed? How has it come to pass, and in what form does it now challenge our homage and respect?

We have the answer in its name. It is the *Creed;* that is, the substance of Christianity in the form of faith. Here we reach at once its last ground and inmost constitution. It holds immediately and entirely in the element of *faith,* and it can be rightly appreciated only as it is apprehended under this view.

Are not, however, our ordinary confessions and catechisms, in this respect, of the same nature? Is it not precisely as compends or summaries of the Christian faith, the things which Christianity requires us to believe, that they are prized and counted sacred?

They are indeed, we reply, summaries of what is regarded as the Christian faith, and it is only as the contents of this faith are truly represented by them, that they can deserve respect; but still they do not hold immediately and directly in the life of faith itself, as the very element and inward form of their representation. They give us the contents of faith, as projected in the first place from the mind which has them, and made the object of thought or reflection. This reflection is not itself faith, but something different from it altogether; which only in this case employs its force on what faith has caused to be at hand for its use. So apprehended, truth is before the mind not immediately, but mediately. The mind separates itself, as it were, from its own contents under the first form, and then turns round to gaze upon them, for the purpose of coming if possible to some clear knowledge of their sense. The process is indirect, circuitous, reflex; whereas in the first case, the apprehension is immediate, and without any intervening mental operation. The difference between such mediate and immediate apprehension, is very great, and is not confined of course to the sphere of religion.[69] All knowledge starts in the second form, and from this passes forward into the first. So we have said already, the substance of Christianity carries in itself the same necessary tendency. It requires to be translated into both thought and action. In this mediated form, however, it is no longer the same thing precisely which it was before. Thus it is, that our summaries of faith, in the form which they carry as the product of theological reflection, are always materially different from the Apostles'

---

69. [In this distinction of mediated reflection and immediate faith the influence of the tradition of Schleiermacher is evident. See Schleiermacher, *The Christian Faith,* 76–93.]

Creed. They represent Christianity under a reflex view; whereas in the Creed we have it in its primitive form, as the direct immediate utterance of the Christian faith itself.

The full import of this distinction requires, however, that we should now direct our attention more closely to the nature of faith. If our conception of this be defective and false, it must involve the whole subject for us necessarily in more or less confusion.

Faith, it is said, Heb. xi. 1, is the substance of things hoped for, the evidence of things not seen. With this agrees well the definition given of it in the Heidelberg Catechism: "True faith is not only a certain knowledge, whereby I hold for truth all that God has revealed to us in his word, but also an assured confidence, which the Holy Ghost works by the gospel in my heart, that not only to others, but to me also, remission of sin, everlasting righteousness and salvation, are freely given by God, merely of grace, only for the sake of Christ's merits."[70] It is fully distinguished here from all mere fancy or opinion. It can hold only in regard to what is true; it can never be sundered from the actual substance of that which it is called to embrace. The idea of faith in a falsehood, and the idea of faith in no actual union with its object, are alike contradictions, which come in the end to the same thing. Faith carries in its very nature its own warrant and guaranty.[71] It is the "substance and evidence" of the realities it brings into view. Thus related to its object, it is no blind assent of course to mere outward authority. Just as little, however, can it be regarded, as the product of ratiocination. Certain knowledge, as the Catechism has it, even if such a thing could have place on other grounds, engaging us to give full credit to the declarations of the Bible, as we believe the Copernican system, or the facts of common history, would not come up at all to the conception. Our knowledge or conviction, in such view, springing from no apprehension of the things themselves, but based on something out of them and beyond them altogether, would be in fact no knowledge whatever, but a system only of unsubstantial notions and abstractions pretending to the name. It is just as impossible for ratiocination to do what is wanted here, as it is for mere outward authority and blind tradition. It is not by thinking of invisible realities, that they are made to be really present for the soul. This real presence is accomplished by faith, and by faith alone; whose very nature it is to bridge over the chasm which divides the two worlds, and to bring them into actual substantial union, as the "hypostasis of things hoped for and the demonstration of things not seen"; and which for this very reason must ever go before, and not follow after, all true intelligence in the sphere of religion, according to the deep sense of our motto borrowed from St. Anselm,[72] and through

---

70. [Heidelberg Catechism, Question 12. See, Schaff, *The Creeds of Christendom*, III:313.]

71. [Again the influence of the tradition of Schleiermacher is evident. See Schleiermacher, *The Christian Faith*, 591–94.]

72. [Anselm of Canterbury (1033–1109), was a proto-scholastic theologian, prior of the abbey in Bec, Normandy, and later archbishop of Canterbury. He is known for his metaphysical speculations, including his "ontological" proof for the existence of God, and his effort to demonstrate the reasonableness of the incarnation and the satisfaction view of the atonement.]

him we may say from St. Augustine: "*Neque enim quaero intelligere ut credam, sed credo ut intelligam.*"[73]

Faith stands thus in the same relation to its objects, that holds in the case of sense. It brings the mind into direct communication with them, as actually present and at hand. Such is the apprehension we have of things immediately around us, in the world of nature, by means of our senses. As thus apprehended, they may be made the object of reflection and thought; but such reflection and thought are not themselves this primary apprehension. It goes before all thought, and lies at the ground of it, as that without which it could be of no force or worth whatever. In itself, it turns on no ratiocination, no intermediate bridge of any sort, between itself and the things to which it refers. It is in its own nature, the evidence of these things, the very form we may say, in which their existence is actualized and brought to demonstration. The relation of vision to light, for instance, is such as allows no room to intervene between them, no connecting link to bring them together. It is not in any sense external, but altogether inward. They are different sides only of the same fact, each being what it is wholly by the correspondence in which it stands with the other. Light asserts its character and power by means of vision; that is the form in which it comes to its revelation in the natural world. And so on the other hand, vision takes effect only through the presence of light; this constitutes the very matter or substance, by which it becomes real in the process of actual life. The light is in the eye, and not simply beyond it; the eye, or its capacity of seeing, is itself the power of what is seen, as made in this way to fill with its own immediate presence the mind that sees. It is the organ for light, which can never be exercised without it, and whose exercise then, of course, carries in itself the guaranty that its object is really at hand. In this natural vision differs from all impressions of mere fancy, however vivid. It can have no place, without real natural light for its contents. The form here can never be sundered from the substance it is required to embrace. To talk or think of sight, that sees nothing, is an absurdity.

And now parallel with all this, we say, is the connection that holds between faith and the world of invisible realities, the true home of the spirit, revealed and thrown open by its means. It is the organ by which we perceive and apprehend the spiritual and eternal; the telescope, through which our vision is carried far over the confines of time and sense, into the regions of glory that lie illimitable beyond; the very eye itself rather, that enables us to "look at things unseen," and causes their presence to surround us as a part of our own life.[74] Our nature is formed for such direct commu-

---

73. [Trans. "I do not seek to understand in order that I may believe, but rather, I believe in order that I may understand." Augustine, "Tractate 29:6 (John 7:14–18)," *Opera omnia*.]

74. [Here Nevin's vocabulary and rhetoric reveals the influence of various forms of Romanticism. In the early 1830's, while still at Western Seminary, Nevin absorbed the writings of the English Romantic poet and literary theorist Samuel Taylor Coleridge (1772–1834), particularly his reflections on hermeneutics. In those works Nevin discovered the concept of an organ of interpretation in the human heart, an intuitive spiritual capacity that was utterly distinct from the powers of empirical induction and logical deduction. Coleridge most fully articulated this theme of the immediate sensing

nication with the world of spirit; carries in itself an original capacity for transcending the world of sense, in the immediate apprehension of a higher order of existence; and can never be complete without its active development. Sin indeed overwhelms this capacity and prevents its proper use; natural men are said to do violence to the truth by their unrighteousness (Rom. i. 18–20), closing their inward sense as it were, to the revelation of it that surrounds them, and allowing it no room in their minds; but the corruption of our nature in this respect, is not its destruction. The great object of religion, accordingly, is, to restore it to its proper freedom and power, by infusing life into the spiritual sense of which we now speak. Thus called into exercise by the power of the Holy Ghost, faith makes way for the apprehension of divine things at once in their own light. The barrier which had place previously between them and the mind, is made of itself to fall away. They touch it, and make themselves felt by it, on the side of its original capability for such sense of the unseen; just as the things of the natural world touch it also, and are felt, on the side of its corresponding sense for what is outward and seen. As in the case of vision and light, so here also the relation between perception and object, is of the most inward and necessary character. It is the relation which holds between contents and form. Faith is the form in which divine truth comes to its proper revelation among men. As a word in the Bible, merely, or upon the tongue, or in the brain even, it is not made to be truly and fully in the world; only where it is "mixed with faith in them that hear it" [Heb 4:2], only where it finds access to the living soul under this form, can it be said to be revealed actually in its proper constitution. For truth is life; and it can hold as such only in an element answerable to its own nature. The words that I speak unto you, said our Saviour (John vi. 63), they are *spirit* and they are *life;* not letter for the eye only, nor sound for the ear, nor notion for the understanding, but truth whose very form is active power, and the apprehension of which accordingly is not to be imagined under any *other* form.[75] The word lives, and is the word truly, only by faith. And so faith necessarily includes it also as its own proper substance and contents. Faith does not create truth; as little as our natural vision creates light; but without truth for its contents, it can no more be in exercise or existence, than the same natural vision can be where all light is wanting. As sense is developed by the world of sense, and subsists permanently only by union with it as its own substance; so faith is called into exercise only by the presence also of its

---

of supernatural realities in *Aids to Reflection* (1825). This concept of a more spiritual mode of perception was reinforced by Nevin's engagement with Herder's *The Spirit of Hebrew Poetry* and Wilhelm Martin Leberecht de Wette's (1780–1849) *Psalms*, both of which articulated Romantic apologia for the power of intuition to apprehend the invisible realm of the spirit. Readings in the seventeenth century Cambridge Platonists further reinforced his growing sense that the world of mundane phenomena is but a veil and a symbol of a more real and more ultimate transcendent dimension. See Nichols, 37–39. This positing of an intuitive spiritual sense was a dramatic divergence from the religious epistemology of the culturally dominant Scottish Common Sense philosophy. See DeBie, *Speculative Philosophy and Common-Sense Religion.*]

75. [The concept of language as an active power that communicates life may have been derived from Coleridge and/or from Herder. See Herder, *Treatise on the Origin of Language* (1772).]

proper objects, and can have no subsistence apart from them. Faith filled with fiction, is as great a contradiction as sight that sees nothing. It stands just in the apprehension of invisible things, in their own true and proper reality. The direct and immediate communication of our nature with this higher world, in virtue of its original capacity for such purpose, the state or activity in which this communication holds, is itself precisely what we are to understand by faith. It is the form or inward habit of a soul, in actual felt correspondence with things unseen and eternal.

The object of faith then, is always the supernatural; something that transcends nature, and is incapable of being reached in the way of mere sense and understanding.[76] In this respect, it differs materially from common belief, such as we exercise continually in human testimony. This remains bound always to the things of this world. No amount of authority, no simply outward word, can bring into the mind under any such form, a real inward persuasion of the truth of things that belong to a higher world. Let a prophet come, doing miracles in proof of his mission, and then reporting to us invisible heavenly realities; and let us be never so well satisfied with his credentials, still the report, such, can beget in us no actual faith.[77] It might be fully sufficient to assure us of earthly things; but it cannot assure us in the same way of heavenly things. These hold in a higher order of life, and can be apprehended accordingly only where the capacity is at hand for perceiving them in this form. The testimony of the prophet must be met with the power of faith on our side, as the true inward sense for the supernatural already in force, in order that it may be truly understood and received. By no possibility can faith in God, or in a divine word, be the consequence and product simply of faith in man, or faith in nature. The apprehension of divine things to be in any case real, must be in virtue of a direct and immediate communication with them, as something above nature and more than nature. This is faith; and in this sense it is, we suppose, that Abraham is made to say in the parable: "If they hear not Moses and the prophets, neither will they be persuaded though one rose from the dead [Luke 16:31]." Such an outward miracle could generate no faith, as men are apt to think it might. It would be no better for this purpose, we may say, than magic.

Faith looks at things unseen, things that transcend sense; eyes the supernatural; apprehends the divine. Its general object in this view, is the revelation of God; the being, and presence, and glory of God, as they are made manifest for the knowledge of men in his works and word. Such a revelation we have, to a certain extent, in nature itself. "The heavens declare the glory of God" [Ps 19:1], we are told; "the invisible things of him from the creation of the world, are clearly seen, being understood by the

---

76. [Again, the prevalence of the language of "the supernatural" and "the invisible" betrays the influence of Coleridge. See Coleridge, *Aids to Reflection* (1825).]

77 [A similar claim that belief cannot be based on the testimony of others was voiced in Ralph Waldo Emerson's (1803–1882) "Divinity School Address," (1838) even though Nevin and Emerson were diametrically opposed on many issues.]

things that are made, even his eternal power and Godhead [Rom 1:20]." But all this is no part of nature itself, as it exists for mere sense. The animal sees it not; and brutish men, as the Apostle tells us, "change it into a lie" [Rom 1:25]. It is only by faith we are enabled to discern the supernatural in nature, looking through the sacramental symbol and embracing the divine sense, which lies beyond.[78] "Through faith," it is said (Heb. xi. 3)," we understand that the worlds were framed by the word of God, so that things which are seen were not made of things which do appear." Some might think mere natural understanding, reasoning from experience, quite sufficient for this. But the philosophy of the Bible is deeper, and far more sound; the empirical understanding could never bring us to any such result; we come to it, before all ratiocination, and in spite of it we may say, by faith. We understand *through* faith; not in order to it, but by its means; our Creed precedes and underlies our intelligence. So in the case of history. God reveals himself here too gloriously, in the way of his providence. But the revelation is only for faith. "A brutish man knoweth not, neither doth a fool understand this [Ps 92:6]." God reveals himself still more fully in the Bible. This is made up of many parts; but the whole may be regarded as one vast act of self-manifestation, by which he unfolds himself more and more for the view of the world, till at last the whole process comes to its consummation in the mystery of the *Word made Flesh* [John 1:14]. Throughout, the general nature of faith remains the same. It is still the organ for the invisible and eternal, by which God and his relations to the world are apprehended, in the measure of the revelation actually at hand, at any given time, and under any particular form. It may have less or more range and horizon, but its relation to what this contains, is always the same; it remains throughout the *form,* in which the substance of what God reveals is apprehended; it is the light of the eye towards the higher world of the spirit, without which, emphatically, the whole body, the entire man, must be full of darkness.

Faith then admits of measures and degrees, from the bursting germ to the full corn in the ear [Mark 4:28]. It could not be under the Old Testament, in this respect, what it is required to be under the New; and we have no right to try it in the child by the same standard, that may be applied to it in the case of the full grown man.[79] With the same revelation, there may be very different measures of capacity (strong and weak faith) for its apprehension; and then the capacity must be conditioned objectively, by the amount of the revelation. Only a full revelation can make room for a complete faith. Thus it is, that true Christian faith goes beyond all that faith could

---

78. [Again, the impact of authors like Coleridge and Herder upon Nevin was pronounced and overt. Of course, Nevin did have reservations about them, for he feared that they might have reduced faith to a subjective feeling without an objective source or referent. See Nevin, "Faith," in *The Weekly Messenger*, February 12, 19, 23; March 4, 11, 18 (1840).]

79. [Such metaphors of organic growth as "child/man" and "seed/plant" were common in Romanticism, including the work of Herder, who influenced the young Nevin. The mechanical imagery of Newtonian physics that had dominated the Enlightenment was displaced by metaphors of animate vitality. See Herder, *Ideas on the Philosophy of the History of Mankind* (1784–1791).]

be under any other form, while at the same time it only completes the nature which belongs to faith universally. How could it be otherwise, if Christ be indeed the last and fullest revelation of God in the world, "the brightness of the Father's glory and the express image of his person [Heb 1:3]." The soul of man, brought into felt contact with the presence and truth of the world invisible under such form, must be more completely open to the light of that world, than it could ever be possibly by any inferior revelation; which is only to say, however, in other words, that it can in no other revelation have the same perfection of faith. Christ is the absolute and ultimate sense of all God's revelations; and so we say of Christian faith, that it is the end of all other faith, the only form in which finally our correspondence with the invisible world can be made complete. A fully developed faith, in our circumstances, can have place by the manifestation which God has made of himself in Christ, and in no other way. This is the end, towards which it struggles from the beginning, and without which it must remain forever incomplete. Any true *creed* must be in the end Christianity.

Christianity then, is the absolute creed. Its very form primarily is that of faith, in its highest and most perfect power, as called into exercise by the revelation which God has made of himself in his Son Jesus Christ. The revelation can have place only in this way; it could not be made to the senses or to the merely natural understanding; it must hold in the element of faith.[80] It belongs to the conception of the supernatural, as it appeared in Christ, that it should be apprehended, that it should come thus to a real and true *revelation,* by the form of existence we denominate faith, and in no other way. Aside from this form and out of it, Christianity might be objectively true in other respects, but it could not have any real existence in the world, it must be for men as though it did not exist at all. To such real existence it comes only and wholly through faith, or the receptivity which makes room for it in the actual order of the world's life. Others *saw* Christ in the days of his flesh, and had their *opinions* about him more or less shrewd; but to Peter it is said: "Blessed art thou Simon Bar-jona; for *flesh and blood* hath not revealed it unto thee, but my Father which is in heaven! [Matt 16:17]." The revelation was in the person of Christ himself, not as an outward fact for sense, but as the presence of a divine life for faith.

For Christianity, it deserves to be well laid to heart, is in a deep sense identical with the life of Christ itself. It is not the words he spoke, nor the works he wrought, as something sundered from his own person, but the living fountain of all these as introduced into the world in the mystery from which his person springs.[81] He is the

---

80. [Once again Nevin reveals his indebtedness to authors like Neander and Coleridge, both of whom distinguished "understanding," which Coleridge defined as the faculty of judging according to sense, from a higher form of knowledge, which he often called "reason." Reason, unlike the more empirical understanding, could intuit supersensible realities. The distinction of "understanding" and "reason" was rooted in Kant's critical philosophy, although Kant severely restricted the scope of reason, particularly in regard to metaphysics, and would have vigorously discounted the notion of supersensible intuitions. For Coleridge on reason, see, for example, *Aids to Reflection.*]

81. [The theme of the introduction of Christ's person into humanity as a source of new and higher

word itself made flesh; grace and truth enshrined in living *shekinah*;[82] the life of God disclosed, to the fullest possible extent of revelation, in the very bosom of man's life. Christianity unfolds itself into a whole world of divine realities (doctrines, promises and deeds) to the eyes of angels even glorious to behold; but the inward substance of all this new creation holds continually in the mystery of the incarnation. It is no abstraction, nothing primarily of thought and notion; but a divine supernatural reality, brought into the world, revealed, made accessible and available for men through faith, and this the faith of our Lord Jesus Christ, by whom and in whom only life and immortality are brought to light. All comes to apprehension first, and has its true reality thus, only as Christ himself is apprehended in the spirit and power of Peter's memorable confession; in virtue of which, as the living appropriation of what it owned and saw, he is proclaimed a *rock* indeed, truly answerable to his own name. Christianity in this way is just as much a *living* reality, as Christ himself; and being like him above nature, the revelation of God in the world, its presence can be apprehended primarily only in the living form of faith. So apprehended, it may be made the object of reflection and science; but its whole reality stands first in this apprehension.

So it was regarded by the Church, in the beginning. Independently of all theoretical and practical use to be made of Christianity, she knew herself to be in possession of its substance, as something real and constant, in a direct and immediate way. This was seen and understood to fall back on the person of Christ, as its ground. Not on this however, of course, as a mere outward historical fact; but on the mystery of the incarnation which it involved, and the world of truth and life here opened to the gaze of faith. Christianity in this form, was felt to be immediately and at once at hand, as a divine reality, which men were bound to admit and obey whether they might be able to understand it or not; just as the world of sense, made real to us by our senses, is to be accepted for what it is in such view, whatever may be required farther for its explanation in the way of science. This immediate substance of Christianity, as it comes to a real revelation in the first place directly for faith, forms the contents, and furnishes us with the true idea, of the ancient Creed. It was never intended to be a theory of religion; it was not exhibited as a formulary imposed by outward authority, nor as the result of any process of reflection. It presented itself to the world simply as a firm affirmation, on the part of the Church, of what Christianity was to her living consciousness in the way of direct and immediate fact. It embraces propositions, of course, for the understanding; which, moreover, it is quite possible to accept, and repeat with the lips, in a merely notional way; but the propositions themselves are no product of thought, comparison and deduction; they are the utterance only of what is immediately at hand in the proper consciousness itself; and they can be truly understood, only where this consciousness prevails. This is the *form* of the Creed. It has its very being in the element and sphere of faith; and it holds there, in the character of

---

life was common in the tradition of Schleiermacher. See Schleiermacher, *The Christian Faith*, 425–38.]

82. [Trans. "God's visible presence."]

a direct spontaneous witness, with the mouth, to the great central realities of faith as they are immediately felt in the heart.

It is as though one should stand forward, with the full free use of all his senses, in the midst of the world of mere nature, and proclaim his faith in it as a fact actually present in such immediate view: "I believe in the sun, moon and stars, and this solid earth on which I tread; I believe in these towering mountains, and wide extended plains, and gently flowing streams;" &c. We understand at once, without any difficulty, the nature of such a confession. It involves no reflection. It takes the realities of sense, as they are at hand, for the mind in their immediate primary form, and simply affirms their presence accordingly. So here. Faith turned towards Christ, as he stands revealed in his own life, finds itself filled with the sense of a new spiritual world, the proper consciousness of the Christian Church; and all this comes to its right expression, under such form, in the solemn language of the Creed. This is Christianity, that a man should stand in Christ, in the new world which Christ creates, and say, as in the other case: "*Behold* these heavens and this earth, wherein dwelleth righteousness and everlasting salvation [see 2 Pet 3:13], I believe in God, the Father Almighty, Maker of heaven and earth; and in Jesus Christ, his only begotten Son, our Lord; &c." The Creed affirms all this as a glorious reality, present not to sense, but to faith. It offers no problem, no hypothesis, no argument; but simply plants itself in the midst of the new order of things which is revealed in Christ, and proclaims its fundamental character and outline, with the force of an assurance that is felt to be identical with that of life itself. This, we say, is its constitution and form; this is its original meaning and force; to this it seeks to come always in the use of the Church. Its object is, not to lodge its articles as so many points of Christian orthodoxy in the mind; but so to bring this rather into the very consciousness of what they affirm, that they may be appropriated by it, and made one with it, as a part of its own life.

It would be a mistake, however, to conceive of the Creed, as springing in the form now described, at once and in full, from the faith immediately of every single Christian, separately considered. It owes its origin to the faith of the Church, as a whole; and it came to pass as we have seen, not at once, as a thing complete from the beginning, but in the way rather of free gradual progress and growth. These two points now require our consideration.

The Creed, we say, sprang in the beginning, not from the Christian faith as something individual and single, but from the faith of the Church as a whole.[83] It is

---

83. [Here Nevin introduces the crucial theme of the corporate nature of faith, another legacy of Schleiermacher and Romanticism. Herder had drawn attention to the corporate nature of language, including the language of faith, and its power to shape individual subjectivity. Employing a more Hegelian conceptuality, Friedrich Augustus Rauch (1806–41), Nevin's German émigré colleague at Mercersburg for one year, also reinforced for him the theme of the social nature of experience, without discounting the importance of individual selfhood. This more corporate understanding of faith differed dramatically from the standard Reformed view in America that the Holy Spirit nurtured faith by operating immediately upon individuals. Such a view had been entertained by Rauch's initial and

the product of the early life, in its general and collective capacity. We shall not stop here to show how it is, that a collective life may originate and produce, in this way, without any outward consultation or reflection, forms of existence, to which no part of it can be considered fully equal when singly and separately taken. The fact itself is abundantly established, on all sides. Our single life is always borne and carried in the bosom of a broader social and public life, whose contents are not simply the arithmetical aggregate of its several parts, but a true spiritual unity rather, which as a single power pervades the whole, and as such, is always something deeper and more comprehensive than any portion of it separately viewed.[84] So in the early life of nations, as it lies back of all history, we meet with creations continually, products of the spirit, that can be resolved into no single activity whatever and that come by no reflection, but seem to shoot forth spontaneously, by a sort of inward organic force, from the substance of the national mind itself. Language itself is such a production.[85] It comes by no outward gift or command; it springs from no invention or compact; the single life, as such, could never reach it; it grows out of our nature, in its collective or solid capacity. And yet what an amount of intelligence does it not involve, even under the rudest form, far beyond all that may enter into the consciousness of any who speak it, through many generations. How often it happens, that a deep philosophical idea lies hid in the very etymology of a word, which has been made to enshrine it in this way, for the undeveloped popular mind, from the earliest stage of its existence. Think too of the institutions generally, in which society starts, its customs, maxims, and laws; think of the world of wisdom embodied, no one can tell when or how, in the proverbs of a nation, its old saws, its legends, its myths. Are they the fabrication of any single mind, condensing the result of its observations into such artificial shape, and so handing it over to the community for general use? Or have they sprung, perhaps, from a number of minds working together, with common counsel and agreement? Not at all. The national life itself, as a collective power, has produced them; making use, of course, of single organs, here and there, to bring them to utterance and expression; but with a depth and wealth of sense, at the same time, which has seldom been clearly

---

sole colleague at the seminary, Lewis Mayer, and this difference in ecclesiologies contributed to the tension between the two faculty members. See Rauch's *Psychology*, the second edition of which Nevin edited and for which he wrote the introduction. Rauch's exploration of the power of different ethnic and national cultures to shape the experience of individuals in different ways could be extrapolated to explain the power of different religious cultures. (*Psychology*, 66–80). Rauch also used organic, collective language to describe the church in his posthumoulsy published "Faith and Reason," *Mercersburg Review* 8 (1856) 80-94]

84. [Here again the influence of Hegel, mediated to Nevin by Rauch, is evident. See Rauch, *Psychology*, 22–23.]

85. [In 1844 Nevin had emphasized the theme of the importance of the corporate nurture, worship, catechetical instruction, and discipline of church as a living force in *The Anxious Bench*, contained in *One, Holy, Catholic, and Apostolic*, Tome One, MTSS 5, ed. Hamstra, 54, 78, 87–89, 90–103. Nevin elaborated the concept of the organic nature of the church, and its priority to the faith of the individual, in his 1844 sermon "Catholic Unity," in MTSS 5, Hamstra, ed., 118–19.]

present, we may say, even to the consciousness of such individual organs themselves. In no other view, is it possible to do justice to such early creations of the human spirit. They are the spontaneous outbirth of mind itself, in its general or universal character. In some sense, this may be said of every production of true genius. Its proper ground lies back of its immediate authorship, in the power of a far broader and deeper life (the spirit of the nation, the idea of the age), which simply lays hold of this for the purpose of bringing itself to expression. Every true work of art is an outbirth, organically, of the general life to which it belongs.[86]

All this may serve to explain what we mean, when we speak of the general life of Christianity, in the beginning, as something more than the Christian life added to itself in its simply individual forms; and when we say that the Creed is to be taken, not as the product of such single Christianity separately considered, but as the full free outbirth rather of the Christian faith as a whole.

The notorious Dr. Strauss, in his *Leben Jesu,* the most ingenious and complete of all infidel books, has endeavored to account for the whole fact of Christianity itself, in this way.[87] The life of Christ, as we have it portrayed in the four gospels, is nothing more, he tells us, than an ideal of the church, the product of its joint imagination, a magnificent myth, or rather a series of myths like the labors of Hercules, made to cluster around the person of the man Jesus of Nazareth, and reduced to shape finally as they now stand, sometime during the second century. This, of course, is a most wild and extravagant hypothesis, which no amount of learning and ingenuity can ever rescue from contempt. The *idea* of Christ is itself something supernatural, and authenticates the reality of his life; and the main use of this work of Strauss, if it can be allowed to have any, is found just in this, that it serves, for a thoughtful mind, to make the mere letter of Christianity, even as it stands in the New Testament itself, something secondary to its living substance as exhibited in the actual mystery of Christ and his Church. So much of truth, however, may be allowed to it, that this mystery is actualized, or brought to pass in the world, through the medium of the general Christian life as such. It comes to its *revelation,* not to its creation, as a product only of human thought (the Hegelian dream of Strauss), but to its revelation as the supernatural in the form of faith, by means of the Church; and this through the activity of the Church, in its collective or universal character, the life as a whole.[88] The primitive form of this

---

86. [The concept that each nationality, ethnicity, and era possesses a unique "spirit" that informs all its productions was a common Hegelian notion, probably mediated to Nevin by Rauch's *Psychology,* in which that theme is pervasive.]

87. [David Friedrich Strauss (1808–74), a German theologian much influenced by Schleiermacher and G. W. F. Hegel, published his *Leben Jesu* (English title, *Life of Jesus Critically Examined*) in which he sought to discredit any historical basis for supernatural elements in the gospel narratives. See McKim, ed., *Major Biblical Interpreters,* 364–68.]

88. [In this somewhat obscure passage Nevin is arguing against Strauss that the concept of Christ is not the product of the human imagination, but is a supernatural revelation mediated through the life of the Church. Nevin did, however, cautiously appreciate the fact that Strauss drew attention to the importance of the personhood of Christ, even though Strauss regarded the incarnation as a mythic

revelation, is presented to us in the Creed. No man can be said to have composed it; it is no work of bishops or synods; it must be taken rather as the grand epos [ethos] of Christianity itself, the spontaneous poem of its own life, unfolded in fit word and expression from the inmost consciousness of the universal Church. It is the direct image and transcript in word, of what Christianity was as a living substance, at once historical and divine, for the faith and by the faith of the early world. It is Christianity proclaiming its own immediate presence, as the new creation in Christ Jesus. That presence is the power of a supernatural or heavenly life in the Church; and the primitive necessary form of this is the living Christian *Creed,* whose immediate utterance we have in this most ancient and venerable among all church symbols.

It will be seen then, that we are not disturbed in the least by the difficulty some urge against the Creed, on the ground of its outward history, as showing it to be vague und uncertain in its origin. Would it help the authority of what is called the Common Law of England, as we find it handled by Blackstone,[89] if we were able to trace it back to some single source, and could lay our hand on a particular authorship of given place and date, to explain its rise? Who does not see, that as the product of the English mind itself, collectively considered, it must be a much more faithful transcript of the very substance of the nation's life, than it could ever possibly have been under any other form? So in the case before us, that the first Christian symbol, the Apostles' Creed, should *not* spring from any particular source or authorship, but come down to us rather as the free spontaneous product of the life of the Church as a whole, the self-adjusted utterance of its faith, we may say, as it was felt to have stood from time immemorial; that no one can show exactly when or how it rose, and took its present shape; that its origin, in one word, is not mathematically definite, but confused and vague, and referable to no fixed time or place; all this, to our mind, is just as it ought to be, and rightly considered invests it with the highest title it could well have to our confidence and respect. It is in this character precisely of its organic relation to the life of Christianity as a whole, that its authority may be said primarily and mainly to stand.

And so, of course, we accept also, without any hesitation, the idea of a gradual expansion and enlargement of the Creed, the other point already noticed, as claiming our attention. The outward history of it shows clearly enough that it did not pass at once into the complete form in which it became finally established. It came, not suddenly and at once, but in the way of *growth*.[90] So come all such free creations, whose laboratory is the life of the spirit under a general and not simply individual form. It

---

projection of the speculative concept of the general unity of the transcendent and the immanent.]

89. [Sir William Blackstone (1723–80) was an authority on the history and substance of English common law. He was one of its premier interpreters whose legal commentaries were highly valued during his day and beyond.]

90. [The motif of "growth" as a pivotal and pervasive concept was common to both Romanticism and Hegelianism. It was also prominent in the later work of the German philosopher Friedrich Schelling (1775–1854), some of whose famous Berlin lectures of 1841 Schaff attended and appreciated. Nevin himself had read some of Schelling's works at least as early as 1840.]

lies in a just conception of the true nature of the Creed, that it should come precisely in this way, and in no other.

There are two kinds of growth, or rather two ways in which what is called growth in this case, may be considered as taking place; by outward accretion namely, or accumulation, and by inward development.[91] A stone grows in the first way; a plant, in the second. If the growth of the Creed had been by accumulation simply, one part added to another from time to time, without any inward reason, it might well be taken indeed, as a serious objection to its authority; for it would imply a mechanical production, the worth of which must depend, at every point, on the judgment and skill exercised in adding to it something new; and the process of its formation altogether would be felt to fall over in this way, into the sphere of common human reflection and contrivance. But we have seen already, that this is a false conception of the nature of the Creed. It represents, not a system of thought, but a system of life;[92] and it comes into being along with this, as its direct, immediate revelation or expression in the way of word. It is the free spontaneous externalization of the Christian consciousness, the substance of living Christianity as a whole, in its primary form of faith. Its growth accordingly corresponds with that of the inward world it represents, the gradual amplification of the Christian consciousness itself, or the determination successively of the grand facts it is found necessarily to embrace. This is no growth by mere outward addition or multiplication. It is such rather as belongs always to life, by its very nature; a growth from within; the evolution of hidden contents from a single root or ground, in which all have been comprehended from the beginning. Such growth implies no change, but is the argument rather of unity and sameness; it springs not from deficiency, but shows rather the presence of a complete whole. The Creed was not *made*, not manufactured like a watch; it *grew,* self-produced, we may say, out of the great fact of Christianity itself. The early Church was not the artificer that hammered it into shape, part by part, and one article after another; but the organ, through whose life as an actual fact it brought itself to pass. Its contents thus come from within, and not from without. In larger or smaller compass, it remains throughout the same. As uttered by Peter, in his rock-like confession; as it meets us in the simple baptismal formula; as "the answer of a good conscience," more or less full, in the apostolical churches; through all its variations in the second century; and in the round symmetrical beauty of its last settled form, as accepted formally by the universal Church; it is still always one and identical with itself, the same fundamental witness and monument of the

---

91. [The distinction of the two kinds of growth appeared in Rauch's *Psychology* and is indebted to Hegel. See Rauch, *Psychology*, 29.]

92. [The concept "life" was an essential component of Nevin's conceptuality. Appropriating it from Romanticism and Idealism, he used vitalistic language as a contrast to the mechanistic conceptuality of the Enlightenment. See, for example, Coleridge, *Aids to Reflection*, in which the poet proclaims that "Christianity is not a theory or a speculation, but a life. Not a philosophy of life, but a life and a living process." As early as 1834 Nevin had even published a series of articles entitled "Religion a Life" in the journal that he edited, *The Friend*.]

new creation revealed in Jesus Christ. All its articles gather themselves up at last into a single root, and are throughout but the evolution, more or less full, of what is found involved in this potentially from the beginning. No view of the Creed can be taken as just, no interpretation as sound and complete, in which this inward unity of organization fails to make itself felt.

The very circumstances then, which go with some to invalidate the credit of the Apostles' Creed, in what regards the manner of its origin, we hold to be of special weight in its favor. That it should be so free, as to outward form, and yet so fixed and true to itself always, as to its actual inward substance; that it should rise into view gradually, now one article, now three, and now twelve, and still show itself a single growth, the development of the same faith throughout; that it should appear under so many editions and phases, all more or less different in different regions and at different times, and be recognized notwithstanding on all sides as the one invariable *regula fidei* of the whole Christian world; that it should be so loose a deposit apparently in the hands of the Church, from the first century to the fourth, and alter all, without negotiation or authority, by the spontaneous voice of universal Christendom, assume in the end, the settled form it now carries, as its proper ultimate and constant type; could there well be, we may ask, a more convincing argument than all this, that the symbol is what it claims to be, a true tradition, not dead but living, of the primitive Christian faith, the fundamental consciousness of the Church, the *Creed of the Apostles*! A very real and fixed substance, most assuredly, the "rule" of Christianity must have carried in itself, in the midst of all its flowing freedom, to come at last in such free way to so fixed and solid a result; and we have no right, accordingly, to quarrel with the early fathers, Irenaeus, Tertullian and others, for appealing to it as they do, under this character, though their very appeal itself may be quoted in proof of the freedom now mentioned. They had no idea of a bound scheme of words, in the case, handed down from the Apostles; but they had a most distinct and strong sense of the actual contents of the Christian faith as historically or traditionally carried forward from the apostolical age in the life of the Church; and to this they boldly and confidently appeal, and we may add triumphantly too, in opposition to all heresies, as a sure unity and firm universal fact, which no one could pretend to call in question. It is this *living* character of the ancient *regula fidei*[93] precisely, its self-conserving and self-determining power, which clothes it with its chief title to respect. That such an apostolical rule, as to inward substance, existed and had force, as the unity of the universal Christian faith, in the early Church, no one who does not choose to put out his own eyes, can for a moment doubt; and yet it is just as clear that this living rule embodied itself finally, and became permanent and fixed, in the Creed as we now have it. However it may have reached this precise form, the Creed is still, at all events, that old living tradition, nothing more or less, expressing itself in the one sense of the Universal Church. To reject it, is to reject the ancient faith; to make light account of it, is to make light account of the very

---

93. [Trans. "rule of faith."]

substance of Christianity, as it stood in the beginning. If the *regula fidei* of Irenaeus and Tertullian, is to have any reality or be of any force for us whatever, we must own its presence in the Apostles' Creed. We shall have for it most certainly but a figment of our own minds, if we pretend to find it anywhere else.

The true nature and constitution of the Creed, as now explained, may assist us in understanding its material structure, the organization under which its contents are presented to our view; while the right apprehension of this, at the same time, will serve to confirm and enforce still farther the representation of its character already given. It remains then, to consider the architecture, as it may be called, of this ancient creation of the Church, for the purpose of comprehending more completely its plastic reigning spirit and idea.

III. Its Material Structure or Organism.[94]

The articles of the Creed, in its full form, gather themselves up, in the first place, into three parts; the first treating, as our Catechism has it,[95] of God the Father and our creation; the second of God, the Son, and our redemption; the third of God, the Holy Ghost, and our sanctification. Christianity rests throughout on the mystery of the Ever Blessed Trinity, as revealed for the apprehension of faith through the incarnation of our Lord and Saviour Jesus Christ.[96]

In this way, however, the three parts of the Creed now mentioned, fall back ultimately upon a single proposition, affirming the fact of the revelation thus made by Christ. The whole Christian faith, as we have had occasion to say before, finds its primary central utterance in the confession of Peter: "Thou art the Christ, the Son of the living God [Matt 16:16]." This accordingly must be taken as the foundation article of the Creed, on which its whole subsequent structure is to be regarded as resting from the beginning. This does not imply, of course, that Christ is in any way the ground or source of the Trinity itself, but only that the being and presence of God under this form come by him to an actual revelation in the world. He underlies in this way the entire mystery of the new creation, as it is in the process of being brought to pass through the Church; which is said accordingly to be built upon the foundation of the apostles and prophets, Jesus Christ himself being the chief corner-stone [Eph 2:20].

94. [(July 1849) 313–47.]

95. [The Heidelberg Catechism, in Schaff, *The Creeds of Christendom*, III:315–28.]

96. [The Trinity had become a focus of attention in German "mediating" theology. While Schleiermacher had relegated the Trinity to an appendix in his *Christian Faith*, theologians influenced by Hegel and Schelling had made it a foundational doctrine, for it located the cosmic drama of differentiation and reunion in the inner life of God. The mediating theologians had appropriated this Idealist view of the Trinity and added the proviso that the manifestation of this dialectic in the created world happened not by necessity but by God's transcendnet will. These theologians intent upon recovering a robust understanding of the Trinity included the German scholar Isaak Dorner (1809–1884) and the Danish bishop Hans Lassen Martensen (1808–84), whose works were introduced to Nevin by his colleague Schaff. Throughout their lives Schaff and Dorner maintained an active correspondence.]

Chapter 1: "The Apostles' Creed"

This confession of Peter is well suited to exemplify the true conception of the Creed, as it has been already represented and explained. It is no mere opinion, borrowed from others or the product of private reflection, to which utterance is thus solemnly given. It is the conviction of faith, as immediately exercised upon the living person of the Redeemer himself. Others might think him to be Elias [Elijah] or Jeremias [Jeremiah], or some other of the ancient prophets, but Peter *knew* him to be more than all this; the revelation of his higher nature, his immediate union with God, had made itself felt in the inmost soul of the disciple as a part of his own life; and so he was prepared to exclaim in the language, not of speculation, but of lively heart-felt creed, *Thou art the Christ, the Son of the living God.* That the confession carried in it this high character, we are expressly assured by our Saviour himself. "Blessed art thou, Simon Bar-jona," we hear him saying; "for flesh and blood hath not revealed it unto thee, but my Father which is in heaven [Matt 16:17]."

The confession utters, in the most immediate and direct way, the fact of Christianity, the new order of life it has brought into the world, as apprehended under its most general character in the person of Christ.[97] The object so apprehended by faith, and thus at once brought to utterance, is no doctrine or report simply concerning Christ, but the glorious reality of the incarnation itself, as exhibited in him under a historical and enduring form. Christianity resolves itself ultimately into this mystery. It has its principle and root in Christ's person. So are we taught most clearly and fully, in the New Testament. The Word reveals itself in him, not by outward oracle or prophecy, but by becoming *flesh;* he is the living comprehension of the truth he proclaims, the actual world of grace itself, which he unfolds and makes known. He is the way, the truth, and the life [John 14:6], by whom alone it is possible for anyone else to come to the Father. He is the resurrection and the life; not the proclaimer simply of the doctrine of a future state and the soul's immortality, but the very ground and medium of the whole fact. The new creation which is, at the same time, the end and completion of the old, starts from the mystery of his person, and holds from first to last in the power of the indissoluble union, thus established between earth and heaven, eternity and time. The incarnation is the deepest and most comprehensive fact, in the economy of the world. Jesus Christ authenticates himself, and all truth and reality besides; or rather all truth and reality are such, only by the relation in which they stand to him, as their great centre and last ground. In him are hid thus all the treasures of wisdom and knowledge [Col 2:3]. He is the absolute revelation of God in the world; the brightness of the Father's glory, and the express image of his person [Col 1:15]. As all this, he is no object primarily of intellection, but can be apprehended only by faith; and in this

---

97. [This focus on the coming together of the infinite and the finite in the person of Christ, and the consequent perfecting of human nature, was characteristic of the "right-wing" Hegelians, such as Philip Marheineke (1780–1846), and many of the German "mediating" theologians, such as Isaak Dorner (1809–84).]

form, he constitutes the sum and substance of Christianity, as it lives in the consciousness of the Church and finds its expression in the Creed.

It is easy to see here the difference between the contents of faith as actual, and its contents again as simply potential. Peter's Christianity, at the time of this confession, fell far short of the sense he had of the new creation in Christ Jesus after the day of Pentecost [Acts 2:1–36]. It included no apprehension of Christ's sufferings and death, of his resurrection and ascension, or of his glorious mediatorial kingdom. It brought with it no knowledge of the Holy Ghost as he works in the Church, no knowledge of the Church itself, or of its cardinal attributes, no distinct sense of the glorious prerogatives and privileges comprehended in its communion. We have no right to suppose, that the mystery, even of the holy Trinity, or the doctrine of our Saviour's true and proper divinity, as afterwards defined, came clearly into Peter's view, when he uttered his wonderful confession. It would have been hard for him probably, to say, what view he had precisely of Christ's person, or what exactly he expected from his life. He was simply overwhelmed with the felt power of God's presence, as it broke upon him, under a form transcending all other revelations, in the "glory of the only begotten of the Father, full of grace and truth [John 1:14]." And yet his faith, in this form of primitive and undivided simplicity, was, in its own nature, universal and complete. In its apprehension of Christ, as a living reality, it embraced in truth the entire meaning and power of Christ, as set forth afterwards in the full Creed. All its articles were there, though still to a great extent only under a latent or potential form. As the new creation grows forth actually from the mystery of Christ's person, being from first to last the evolution or development simply of capabilities, relations and powers, that are treasured up in him from the beginning; so the sense of what Christ is as the incarnate Word, when it enters the soul by faith, however circumscribed the horizon of its sight may be at the first, brings with it surely, in the end, by proper culture, all that the full idea of Christianity requires. The mere notion of Christ, or an abstract thought made to stand for him in the Unitarian sense cannot, of course, do this; but it is the very character of faith, as distinguished from all fancy of opinion, that it is called into exercise and determined in the nature of its action, by the supernatural object from which it is filled, as form, with its proper contents. As the *real* apprehension of Christ thus, it can embrace him only as he actually is, from the beginning, and must carry in itself thus an inward necessity of development always under the same form and no other.[98] Of all this we are indirectly assured, by the high honor put on Peter's confession when it was first spoken. This stands not simply in the marvelous and sublime benediction which was pronounced upon his faith, considered as his own, but still more in the proclamation made of its value and power for the future Church. "Thou art *Peter*" [Matt 16–18]—now, indeed, first worthy in full of thine own name—"and on this

---

98. [The theme of "necessary" development was a prevalent Hegelian theme that was probably reinforced for Nevin by Rauch. Nevin had encountered the more general notion of inward development in Neander while still at Western Seminary.]

Chapter 1: "The Apostles' Creed"

rock" (the living Creed here incorporated with thy life) "I will build my Church, and the gates of hell shall not prevail against it."[99] Narrow as the foundation might seem to some, this single article of the incarnation, "Christ the Son of the living God," really embraced by faith, bears up in the end the entire superstructure of Christianity. All Christian theology, as well as all Christian life, starts here, and flows forward from this as its all comprehending source. Here, as we have seen, the outward history of the Creed commences; and here also we find the power, from which is generated its entire structure, inwardly considered. This article, in the form of *creed,* or as made to be actually present in the life of the world by faith, is, in very truth, the Rock, on which rests the Church, and that may be said to support the new heavens and the new earth themselves, through this as "the pillar and ground of the truth [1 Tim 3:15]."

Out of this primary article grows, in the first place, generally, the faith of the holy *Trinity;* as it comes before us, for instance, in the formula of baptism: "Go teach all nations, baptizing them in the name of the Father, and of the Son, and of the Holy Ghost [Matt 22:19]." So we have it also in the apostolic benediction: "The grace of our Lord Jesus, and the love of God, and the communion of the Holy Ghost, be with you all [2 Cor 13:14]." This threefold view of the divine nature, proceeds from the apprehension of Christ, as the Son of the living God. This does not mean, of course, that the fact of the Trinity commences with the incarnation; the filiation of the Son, and the procession of the Holy Ghost, as they hold in the being of God himself, are from eternity. Neither does it mean, however, simply, that the doctrine of the holy Trinity has been published by Christ more clearly than before. We meet with no such outward proclamation, in his ministry and word. Some have objected to the doctrine on this very ground, that being so mysterious, and so fundamental as the Church pretends to her whole constitution, so little stress is laid upon it, in the way of clear categorical statement, in the New Testament.[100] And there must be allowed to be no small force

---

99. Nothing can well be more miserable in its way, than the shifts which have been resorted to here to wrest this great passage out of the hands of the Romanists. Some turn it into a sort of pun or ambiguous play on Peter's name, in which Christ *pointed* to his own person, as he spake, to show the true sense of his riddle. Others make the doctrine avowed in Peter's confession, to be the rock on which the Church is built. All in full disregard of the context, as well as of the special stirring solemnity of the whole occasion as presented in the evangelical narrative. It is, indeed, a contradiction, against which all religion revolts, to found the Church, in the Roman sense, on the person of Peter separately considered; but neither can it be said to rest on Christ, or on the thought and confession of his name, in any like outward and separate view. The idea of the *Church* requires the flowing together of our common human existence and the higher life revealed in Christ. So long as they stand apart, the new creation must be without effect in the world. It holds altogether in the mystery, by which, through the capacity of faith on one side and the wonderful power of the Holy Ghost on the other, the fallen weak nature of man is so linked with the very life of Christ, "God manifest in the flesh," as to become one with it in a living way. This fact it is, the passing over of Christ's life into the life of the world, the comprehension of the last in the sense of the first, which forms the soul of Peter's confession; and on this living ground, of a truth, as it was now laid in him and his fellow-apostles, the Church, which binds earth and heaven together, was to be built to the end of time.

100. [This objection had been raised in a dramatic way by the celebrated preacher William Ellery Channing (1780–1842) in his famous "Baltimore Sermon" delivered in 1819 at the ordination of Jared

in the objection, if the revelation of Christianity be taken, as it often is taken, to stand primarily in the form of word or thought for the understanding. It only shows, however, in truth, that such is not its original and fundamental form. It is not primarily a doctrine spoken by Christ, but a fact comprehended in his person; which as such, accordingly, is to be apprehended and appropriated by the world in the way of creed, before it can enter truly into its intelligence or outward life. Christ then, is neither the creator of the Trinity, nor simply its proclaimer; but the form of its explication in the economy of time, the medium by which it manifests itself for faith, and so for knowledge, in the consciousness of the world. The economical Trinity, as it is sometimes styled, in distinction from its immanent character, the Trinity in its relations to man, as it goes forth from eternity into time, for the accomplishment of our salvation—the only form in which the mystery can be said at all to have for us any *revelation*—comes fully into view only and wholly by Christ. There are indeed, adumbrations of the idea, what may be called a spiritual *nisus* [impulse] towards it in the depths of the human spirit, in the religion and philosophy even of the heathen world; and still clearer intimations of it are to be found in the revelation of the Old Testament, like streaks of light in advance of the rising day; just as in all respects Christianity completes the sense of our universal life, by which, at the same time, thus its advent is gloriously harbingered from the beginning. But still the absolute and proper revelation of the Trinity, is brought to pass at last only in the person of Christ, and by the mystery of the incarnation. So it is expressly affirmed in the New Testament. *He* is the brightness of the Father's glory, and the express image of his person [Heb 1:3]: No man hath seen the Father, the only begotten Son which is in the bosom of the Father, he hath *revealed* him [John 1:18]. No man knoweth the Father but the Son, and he to whom the Son shall *reveal* him [Matt 11:27]. God had manifested himself to a certain extent, came forth in some measure from the awful solitude of his own absolute being, in the work of creation, and in the course of history as it stood before Christ came. But all this fell short immeasurably of the self-manifestation which took place in the *act* of the incarnation, when the everlasting Word became flesh, and linked itself into one life with the life of the world itself, as raised to its highest power in man. God came forth in this act, manifested himself, laid himself open in the form of life to the view of faith, as never in all revelations before. Only so was it possible for the mystery of the Trinity to bring itself out clearly in the apprehension of the world; and in no other form, than as thus apprehended, can the doctrine be of any true value or force. Never was there a greater mistake, than to conceive of it as primarily an abstract theory or speculation. It is the most practical of all truths; for it lies, in the form of *fact,* at the ground of the whole Christian revelation, and is in truth the very form in which this revelation makes itself real, through faith, in the consciousness of the Church. This precisely is the mystery that faith finds in Christ. It lies at the foundation of Christianity. To be baptized into Christ, is to be baptized into the holy Trinity [Rom 6:3, see Matt 28:19].

Sparks. That sermon helped inspire the formation of the Unitarian denomination in 1825.]

Chapter 1: "The Apostles' Creed"

The faith and apprehension of God in three persons, Father, Son, and Holy Ghost, lie involved from the beginning, in Peter's confession—Thou art the Christ, the Son of the living God.

It is only by this view of the revelation of the Trinity, that we can at all maintain the credit of the doctrine as a part of Christianity. Infidels and Unitarians are able easily enough to show, not merely that no pains are taken to affirm it with clear doctrinal precision (after the fashion of our catechisms), in the New Testament; but also that the doctrinal statements of the early Church in regard to it, continue to be for a long time very indefinite and insecure.[101] We do not find the distinction of persons in the Godhead, and their several relations, clearly and fully apprehended from the beginning, in the form under which all was afterwards defined and settled. This has often embarrassed those whose conception of Christianity requires it to start in the form of doctrine rather than in the form of life. With any right view, however, of its true nature in this respect, the difficulty is made at once to vanish. The Trinity unfolds itself, discloses itself as a fact, only in the historical process of the incarnation, the mystery revealed by Christ's person; and in this way, of course, only as this mystery is made to pass over truly, through faith, into the living constitution of the world, so as to underlie it and take possession of it as the power of a new creation. Thus revealed and apprehended, the entire fact might be in the life of the Church, long before it could be brought to any satisfactory representation in the form of thought. So we have it proclaimed from the start, in the Apostles' Creed. The Trinity is there, not indeed in full theological statement as afterwards settled, but still in the overwhelming sense of its necessary substance, as it looks out upon the world through the glorious fact of the incarnation, and completes its presence in the Church, "the fulness of Him that filleth all in all [Eph 1:23]." The new creation stands throughout in the mystery of the Triune God, Father, Son, and Holy Ghost, historically brought to light by the union of the everlasting Word with our fallen flesh.

The Creed is the utterance of this mystery as it unfolds itself by Christ, in the consciousness of the Christian world. All forms a single revelation, which takes effect, however, in the way of magnificent process, starting in the bosom of the Father, and completing itself finally in the full glories of the new earth and new heavens. The end accordingly grows out of the beginning, and is comprehended in it from the start. The new creation commences with the Father, enters the world through the incarnation of the Son, and runs its course in the world's life subsequently, by the Holy Ghost constantly present and always active in the Church. Such is the order in which the three grand divisions of the Creed come into view; each forming a complete whole within itself, with more or less full utterance of its leading landmark facts; while the entire

---

101. [This was the contention of William Ellery Channing, who followed the general argumentation of the English Deists. Channing was much discussed by American Protestant church leaders in the decades during which Nevin theologically matured, ususaly polemically in the context of the spread of "infidelity."]

contents of the second are apprehended, as flowing in the way of derivation from the first; and then again, as coming to their full issue and last sense, only in the broad sea of glory which is thrown open by the third. In the case of each division, moreover, the characteristic points of fact which it is made to include, whether more or less full, follow each other to a certain extent, in the same way. They are not properly so many items of truth, separately propounded for our reception, as they are notes and characters rather that mark the onward progress of the great universal fact to which they belong, and by which they have place. The Creed rolls thus, like a lofty anthem, with continuous stream of music, rising and swelling throughout on the same key, from its commencement to its close. We may style it a panoramic view of the "pure river of water of life" [Rev 22:1], the moving process of the world's redemption, as it starts from the throne of God and of the Lamb, and flows forward by successive stages, with paradise on its banks, to the region of light and immortality in which finally the Holy Catholic Church shall become forever complete.

All begins in "God the Father, Almighty, Maker of heaven and earth." This is not to be taken, of course, as an article here, of mere natural religion, which may be supposed to go before the revelation of Christianity and to make room for its presence.[102] God does, indeed, reveal himself through nature, as the absolute ground of the universe. But Christianity does not simply take up this fact as thus previously at hand, and then go on to add to it new truths of its own. It goes beyond all previous revelations, and especially all merely natural religion, not only extensively in the amount of what it makes known, but also *intensively* in the depth and power of its apprehension. God in Christ is indeed the God of nature; but with such new self-manifestation of his interior life, as makes him to be, even in this last relation, a wholly different being for our faith, from all he seemed to be before. The revelation of nature is shadowy and superficial, as compared with that which has place in Christ; and it is only by means of this finally, that it comes to its own full significance and sense. Christianity then allows no simply natural religion in its bosom. "When that which is perfect, is come, then that which is in part shall be done away" [1 Cor 13:10]; the relative, as such, enters not into the composition of the absolute. So the Creed embraces God, even in his character of Creator, as he has now come to be known, not simply in nature, but in the person of his Son Jesus Christ; "by whom also he made the worlds" [Heb 1:2]; and through whom alone, "in these last days" [Heb 1:2], the full sense of that first creation is fairly brought to light. He is recognized thus, and worshipped, not merely as the author of nature, or as the supreme being, in the cold language of rationalistic deism, but as "the God and Father of our Lord Jesus Christ," who is disclosed to the vision

102. ["Natural religion" was a concept popularized by the English Deists, some Latitudinarians, French *philosophes*, and German "neologians." The phrase suggested a form of piety derived from human reason and the moral sense alone, without the aid of any special historical revelation. Usually the term was associated with the theory that the human intellect could discover the existence, justice, and benevolence of God, the basic principles of the universal moral law, and the immortality of the soul through its own powers, or that these concepts were innately present in human experience.]

Chapter 1: "The Apostles' Creed"

of faith, *through him*, as *our* Father also, the fountain and source of the new glorious creation revealed in his person. In this way it is, we are encouraged to approach him in the Lord's Prayer; and in no other view can he be the object of a truly Christian faith. It is through the apprehension of Christ, as the Son of the living God, in the sense of Peter's confession, that the Creed throws us back to this first article as its own everlasting ground and foundation. "He that hath seen Me," our Saviour himself says, "hath *seen the Father* [John 14:9]."

In the second section of the Creed, this sublime revelation is represented as going forward, to the actual apprehension of faith, in the historical person of our Blessed Redeemer, Jesus of Nazareth, from the point of his miraculous conception and birth, onward to the completion of his glory finally at the right hand of God in heaven; where he reigns head over all things to the Church, and from, whence he shall come at the last day to judge the quick and the dead. "The Life was manifested," says St. John, "and we have seen it, and bear witness, and show unto you that eternal Life, which was with the Father, and was manifested to us [1 John 1:2]." The mystery of the incarnation is not strictly a fact, which is to be considered as complete all at once from the point where it commences. In any such view, it would be more magical than real. Our human life does not hold at all under any such stationary character; but is, in its very conception, a fact that accomplishes itself only in the way of historical process and growth.[103] To become human at all then, to enter truly into the stream of man's life, it was indispensable that the Son of God should take humanity upon him, not suddenly and abruptly, but with progressive order, agreeably to the general law of all existence in time. His life as human, moreover, could not become absolutely complete, so as to display the full sense and meaning of its union with the divine nature, until it was brought, in the way of regular historical progress, to surmount in full the limitations of our present mortal state, thus triumphing over death and him that had the power of death, in the glory of the resurrection. Hence altogether, in the very nature of the case, the stupendous fact of the incarnation, resolves itself into a series or chain of events, a living historical process rather, by which the mystery enters more intimately and deeply always into the drama of the world's life; till finally it becomes complete, and is found to have its perfect work, when "Jesus was glorified," and the windows of heaven were opened thus (John vii. 39) for the power of his Spirit to descend in full measure upon the earth. Only under such view, can the faith, which the Creed requires us to exercise in Christ, be considered real and true. Hence the general fact comprised in his person, is drawn out in a succession of historical points, that mark once, might easily be more or less in number, without affecting the substance of the main article, or the general design with which they are brought forward. As the Creed now stands however, they are wonderfully pertinent and complete; as we shall see presently, when we come to speak more particularly of their significance as articles of faith.

103. [This focus on the spiritual maturation of Christ's humanity was typical of Schleiermacher and those whom he influenced. See Schleiermacher, *The Christian Faith*, 408–9.]

The mystery of the incarnation, as it stands before us in the person of Christ, includes two sides, which must both enter steadily into our faith, to make it complete. We must apprehend, in the first place, the presence of a truly divine life in the fact, the entrance of God into the world as he had not been in it before; in the second place, this life must be admitted under a true human form, and in such relation to the previous constitution of the world, that it shall not violate its order, but be felt rather to fall in with it organically and complete its sense.[104] Thus in Peter's confession, the power of his faith shows itself just in the firm combination of these two views. "The Son of the living God"—a new full manifestation of the divine life—"art *thou*" the living human Master, whom we follow and serve. This *felt* apprehension of the union of the divine and human, the infinite and the historical, in Christ's person, was that precisely which imparted to the faith of the disciple such high value in his Master's eyes.

So the Creed affirms first the full presence of God's life, in the awful fact which is here proclaimed. "I believe in Jesus Christ, his only begotten Son, our Lord." This is to be taken in direct continuation of what goes before; and asserts, in fact, that our faith in God the Father himself is conditioned by the real revelation, under which he is made known to us in Christ; as it is said in one place by the Saviour himself: "This is life eternal, that they might know thee, the only true God, and Jesus Christ whom thou hast sent" (John xvii. 3); and, again, by the Apostle John: "We know that the Son of God is come, and hath given us an understanding, that we may know him that is true; and we are in him that is true, even in his Son Jesus Christ. This is the true God and eternal life" (1 John v. 20). The Creed, in the strongest manner, asserts this identification of Christ with the contents of God's life, so far as this can be an object either of faith or knowledge for men; in full correspondence with what is said in the first chapter of St. John's gospel: The same Word which was in the beginning, which was with God, and which was God, in the fulness of time became flesh, and tabernacled among us, exhibiting his glory as of the only begotten of the Father, full of grace and truth; no man hath seen God at any time, the only begotten Son, which is in the bosom of the Father, he hath declared him.[105]

Then follows however, at length, the assertion, no less clear and firm, of the true human and historical character of all this revelation, in the person of Jesus of Nazareth. The Son of the living God, who is here embraced as the object of faith, "was conceived of the Holy Ghost and born of the Virgin Mary." So the supernatural in him links itself organically with the existing constitution of the world, and lays the foundation thus within it for a new and higher order of life. The miraculous conception becomes

---

104. [This theme that Christ's maturation occurred according to general human development principles was the position of Schleiermacher. Schleiermacher wrote, "Every outward activity of Christ, whether it be regarded as an activity of the intellect or one of the will, was in its aspect of human growth a result of the temporal development . . .", *The Chrisian Faith*, 408. Of course for Schleiermacher (and Nevin) this growth was perfect, for it was propelled by the presence of God in Christ (for Schleiermacher, in Jesus' perfect God-consciousness.]

105. [Nevin paraphrases John 1:1–18.]

a natural birth, making room and way for the coming of Christ in the flesh. Such a birth implies growth, development, progress in stature and wisdom (Luke ii. 52); and the life of Christ involves subsequently his full ministry and work.[106] In this way, the Creed might include other dates and facts in his history, such as his baptism, temptation, miracles, &c., and still not suffer any material alteration. It does include all these points in truth, though only in a latent way, and as comprehended in the general fact; while its utterance confines itself to the great and necessary outline simply of the Saviour's history as a whole. In this way, we are carried at once to the close of his life under its earthly form: "He suffered under Pontius Pilate; was crucified, dead, and buried; descended into hell." His existence in the world was human throughout, rounded in as a living process from the womb to the grave. As he came into the world by a real birth, notwithstanding the divine sublimity of his nature as the Son of the living God, so he went forth from it at last by a real death. His was no fantastic manhood only, that played itself off on the eyes of men as true, when it was only a Gnostic shadow, or vision, in fact. He suffered under a Roman magistrate, openly, publicly, and with solemn form, and this passion ran out into a most real and full dissolution of body and soul; it was no sleep or swoon, but death; his body was laid in the grave, while his soul went into Hades, the intermediate state. This last clause, as we have seen before, was introduced at a comparatively late period. It was, however, virtually a part of the Creed from the beginning; having no other object at last, than to affirm explicitly, what had been affirmed all along by implication, in the assertion of his death and burial. The descent to Hades is indispensable to complete the conception of a full obedience to the law of mortality, comprehended in the problem which Christ came to fulfill. Short of this, his death could not be regarded as a historical fact.

The death of Christ, however, as an object of faith, is far more than the termination simply of a common human life. The person, of whom all this holds, is still the Son of the living God, the everlasting Word in union with our weak mortal flesh. The *reality* of this conception requires then, that the higher nature here at work should not allow itself to be overwhelmed and crushed in the process, but so enter into it, as to assert in the end its own superiority in the way of universal triumph over its terrific power. The sufferings and death of the Son of God involve thus necessarily, for faith, the idea of a *conflict,* the issue of which is a full victory over death and the grave, as well as over the power of sin from which they come.[107] It was not possible, we

106. [This motif, mediated to Nevin by Schleiermacher and those influenced by him, was ultimately rooted in the understanding of Christ as "the Second Adam" articulated by Irenaeus. In a critical evaluation of Nevin's work, Charles Hodge noted the similarity of Nevin's view of Christ to that of Schleiermacher. See *Coena Mystica*, MTSS 2, ed. DeBie, 124.; see also *The Incarnate Word*, MTSS 4, ed. Evans, General Introduction, xxvii.]

107. [Here Nevin deviates from the typical scholastic Reformed understanding of the death and resurrection of Christ as a substitutionary atonement for sin, and concentrates on Christ's victory over death and sin as powers that afflict humanity. Although he contined to use forensic vocabulary to describe the power of the crucifixion, he more characteristically shifted to the "Christus Victor" language typical of Eastern Orthodoxy.]

are told, that he should be holden of death (Acts ii. 24); that he should sink to rise no more, in the catastrophe, which brought his mortal state to a close. This *impossibility* is perceived and felt by faith, even while it acknowledges his passion; the sufferings of the Son of God are proclaimed, as the very form in which he destroyed death, and him that had the power of death, that is, the devil, and thus brought in righteousness and immortality for all that believe in his name. So it follows immediately: "The third day he rose again from the dead; he ascended into heaven, and sitteth at the right hand of God, the Father, Almighty." All in continuation simply of the living process, on which he entered at his birth. The true universal significance of his life, as including in itself a deeper power than the law of mortality he came to abolish, now comes into view. The nature he had assumed, is made to surmount the limitations of its first state, and rises triumphant to the skies. Hades is shorn of its strength, the grave resigns its prey; he that descended into the lower parts of the earth (Eph. iv. 9, 10), is the *same* that is seen to ascend up far above all heavens, that he might fill all things. The old order of the world, in his case, is brought to an end; he leads captivity captive; man, in his person, finds himself exalted finally to his proper supremacy over the whole inferior creation. All things are placed under his dominion, and he is head over all things, to the Church. In this character, he must reign till all enemies are put under his feet, and the whole world subdued into harmony with the order of the new creation [1 Cor 15:27–28]. His mediatorial government extends, by the very nature of the case, from the hour of his exaltation onward to the end of time; and finds its necessary conclusion in the general judgment. So all is comprehended here again, as in the case of our Saviour's first state, within the extremes that bound the entire stadium on either side; and, with a single stroke, we have this part of the Creed complete: "From thence he shall come to judge the quick and the dead."

In all this representation of the Saviour's personal history, the outline of his life as it reaches from his introduction into the world on to the winding up of his mediatorial reign, we have, after all, it must be borne in mind, the evolution simply of the one single fact in which Christianity begins, as proclaimed in Peter's confession: "Thou art the Christ, the Son of the living God." The several specifications employed to set it forth, are not to be taken as so many independent propositions, asserted on separate evidence, and brought together in the way of collective sum; they might be more, or they might be less; but in any case they are to be taken as bound together in the constitution of one and the same great object of faith, out of which, in the end flows all their title to a place in the Creed. For instance, it would be a mistake to suppose that the miraculous conception, or the descent to Hades, or the resurrection and ascension into heaven, are exhibited as articles of Christian belief, which we may be expected to receive in the first place on their own proofs separately considered, and then lay away under this form in the general repository of our faith; as though the Creed were the accumulation merely of such theological conclusions and results.[108] The only *ground*

---

108. [Here again Nevin rejects the inductive, empirical approach to biblical interpretation typical

of all Christian faith, we have seen already, to be the person of the Lord Jesus Christ himself. To suppose now, however, that the miraculous conception, or the resurrection, might be made certain by themselves, in the first place, on proofs lying wholly out of Christ, is to contradict this conception in full. There is no such contradiction in the Creed. Every topic affirmed here of Christ's history, is an article of *faith* in the high Christian sense; a reality that belongs not to the world of nature and sense as such, but to the new creation, in which heaven and earth are brought supernaturally together by the mystery of the incarnation; no outward witnesses and no common human reasons, impart to it its ultimate credibility; this lies in the relation in which it is felt to stand to the fact of the Saviour's person itself. The grand argument after all, for the great distinctive *memorabilia of* Christ's theanthropic life, and that without which no evidence besides could make them certain, is comprehended in his own presence.[109] The first condition of all knowledge here, is an entrance, by faith, into the central fact of the Gospel, as we have it presented to us in the living and moving form of the Divine Word itself, incarnate for us men, and our salvation, in the Virgin's Son. Not as we stand on the threshold merely of this sublime and magnificent temple, but only as we pass into the awful bosom of the sanctuary itself, may we ever expect to apprehend as they are the forms and proportions of its true interior structure. Only in proportion as my faith is first overwhelmed with the sense of Christ's real divine majesty, as the Son of the living God made flesh, can I be brought to admit with firm faith, on any evidence, the astounding mystery of his birth, or the no less astounding mystery of his resurrection. The whole lies *beyond* nature, in the sphere of a new order of life which is revealed in Christ and nowhere else; how then should it be apprehensible at all, or creditable, under any other form of observation? But, on the other hand, let the sense of Christ's majesty so overwhelm the mind, in the first place, and these mysteries, astounding as they are, can no longer be repelled; they are felt to be indispensable to the conception of his person. *Such* a person could not come into the world by the ordinary course of nature; and equal violence is involved in the imagination of his yielding finally, like other men, to the power of the grave. The man Christ, as he stands before us there through the medium of Peter's faith, is felt to be a fact that transcends the whole course of nature, even while it discloses itself historically in its bosom; it is the presence and power of a higher supernatural order of existence in union with nature, which cannot, as such, be included and bound within its economy as it stood before, either first or last. Faith in Christ, as the revelation of a divine life in the world, cannot stand at all in connection with the supposition, either of his being born, or of his remaining in the grave, like other men. In any such view, it would cease to be

---

of Enlightenment empiricism and the Common Sense philosophy, and opts for a more holistic and organic understanding of texts. Holifield hails this as a break with the dominant "Baconian" tradition of American theology. *Theology in America*, 467–81.]

109. [Referring to Christ as "theanthropos" was a linguistic habit of the German mediating theologians.]

this faith altogether, and the Christ of the Creed would no longer exist, except as a phantom for the imagination.

Thus it is that all the points of this historical confession, however some of them might seem to be accessible to our knowledge at least, to some extent in a different way, yet in the true force and spirit of the Creed, are to be taken as supernatural truths, which can be rightly apprehended and uttered only by faith in full communication throughout with the grand primary fact to which they belong and from which they spring. Even the passion of the Saviour, his sufferings under Pontius Pilate, his bloody death and burial, are vastly more in this case than topics of natural intelligence; the apprehension of them, as entering into the life of Christ, the Son of the living God, lifts them at once into the supernatural sphere in which that life holds; and it requires accordingly the same sort of faith to say, "*Christ* died," which we need to add immediately, "and rose again." The fact of the resurrection witnessed by *sense,* that is as a mere phenomenon in the world of nature, would not be its truth as asserted in the Creed; just as little as the sight and acknowledgment of Christ's miracles, in the days of his flesh, amounted, with the Scribes and Pharisees, to any true apprehension of his divine glory. The idea of Christ is not of itself his history; but it is only through the power of it, as actually at hand, for faith, that his history becomes intelligible and enters also into our creed under a corresponding mode of existence.

The great fact of the Creed, the revelation of the Ever Blessed Trinity in the mystery of redemption, completes itself finally in the Holy Ghost, through whose presence in the world the saving power of Christ's life is carried over to his people. A new region of glory is thus thrown open to the vision of faith, including as before, a flowing process, whose commencement is here joined at once with its magnificent end. The whole however, as already intimated, is but a continuation of the one stupendous mystery that goes before. Our faith in the Holy Ghost is not drawn from some other quarter, and then made to range itself as a separate and independent belief, along with our faith in the Incarnation; it grows forth from this as its necessary and only sufficient ground; it can have no value, no reality in truth, save as it is made to enter our minds in this way. So too our faith in Christ completes itself legitimately only in the faith of the Holy Ghost. A true Christology, involving, as it must, a living sense of the true universal import of Christ's life, carries in itself a demand for the extension of its power, in some way, over to the race he came to redeem. The river of life which first opens upon our view in his person, must flow over these banks in the end, and become a sea of glory, filling the whole world.[110] This can be accomplished only through the living activity of the Holy Ghost; whose proper personality and work, accordingly, faith is thus brought to apprehend, as the necessary complement, we may say, of what it has

---

110. [The notion that the Holy Spirit works upon the church, the human race, and the world as collective entities was alien to most American Protestants, who tended to restrict the Spirit's work to the interior lives of individuals. For example, Charles Hodge wrote that divine guidance is promised to persons "in their personal and individual relation to Christ" (*Systematic Theology,* I:131). Equally shocking would have been Nevin's suggestion that the Spirit's work is an extension of the incarnation.]

previously apprehended as the presence of God in Christ. We read of God's Spirit as present with a certain kind of action in the world, before Christ came [e.g., Gen 41:38, 1 Sam 10:6, 1 Kings 18:12]; but it will not do to take this as identical at all with the form of his presence in the world since. We are plainly told, that the Spirit as he now works in the Church, could not be given till Christ was glorified; the mystery of the incarnation must complete its course in His person, before room could be made for the farther revelation of its power in the other form. This accordingly was the great promise for which his disciples were directed to wait, when he left the world; the fulfillment of which too, as we all know, took place on the day of Pentecost, and laid the foundations of the Christian Church. The article, "I believe in the Holy Ghost," has regard altogether to this revelation, the entrance of God's Spirit into the process of the world's life as the Spirit of Jesus Christ, under such form of existence and action as had no place before, and was first rendered possible only by the new creation brought to pass in his person. To accept the doctrine of the Holy Ghost as true on *other* grounds, and under a simply abstract form, cannot satisfy at all the sense of the Apostles' Creed. The only faith in the Holy Ghost it knows, is that which is conditioned by faith in the sublime Christology that goes before, and which grows out of this as its cause and ground.

Forth from this divine spring-head now rolls, in conclusion, the full tide of Christianity, as it is found still pouring itself forward, age after age, in the Church. The topics or heads that follow, stand related again to the primary article, much as we have found the several clauses in regard to Christ to be related to the general article of the incarnation. They serve simply to draw out and define graphically the contents of our faith in the Holy Ghost. The Holy Ghost is apprehended in the Creed, not as an abstraction or thought merely, but as a fact actually revealing itself in the world; and the form of this revelation expresses itself comprehensively in the "Holy Catholic Church," where the new creation is exhibited in grand outline, as "the communion of saints, the forgiveness of sins, the resurrection of the body, and the life everlasting."

The article of the Church, then, of course, is not made co-ordinate in any way with the articles of the Father, Son, and Holy Ghost. We are not to believe *in* the Church, as we are required to believe in God; we believe it simply, as we believe the resurrection of the body and the life everlasting; it is something sure to us, as the form under which the Holy Ghost is apprehended, as historically present and active in the world.[111] So the world itself may be an object of faith (Heb. xi. 3) when the revelation of God in it is truly seen and felt. It must be always kept in mind, however, that this involves far more than the knowledge of it by mere sense. The world does not properly beget our faith in God; but it is this faith, rather, which enables us to believe the world, as the true sacrament of his presence. And so the Church also, the

---

111. [Nevin's construal of the Church as the form of the Holy Spirit's activity in the world would have been unsettling for many American Protestants who tended to regard the visible church as a voluntary gathering of believing individuals.]

new creation in Christ Jesus, notwithstanding the subordinate character now assigned to it, is still altogether an object, not of sense and natural knowledge, but of faith. However accessible it may be under certain aspects to mere outward observation, its actual reality and substance, as affirmed in the Creed, are ever to be acknowledged as something divine, of which no proper assurance can be had in any such outward way. The entire Creed has to do with realities that hold in a world above nature (though not abstractly disjoined from it), and that can be apprehended, accordingly, as they are, only by faith. To believe the Church, then, is something far more than to believe the presence of some certain, tangible and visible organization in the world, like the British Parliament, for instance, of which we can take the measure and gauge by direct outward inspection. Such palpability in the case of the Church, even if it were fully at hand, would not of itself bring with it what this article requires; just as little as the *sight* of Christ after his resurrection, might be taken as equivalent to the sense of it by faith. The invisible and supernatural here, as throughout the Creed, must be apprehended as going before the outward, underlying it, and filling it with its true and necessary sense. We rise not from the region of sense here, into the region of spirit; but from the region of spirit itself, rather, as we have come to be in it already by the faith of our Lord Jesus Christ, we descend into the region of sense and actual life;[112] and by virtue of the same assurance with which we say: *Thou art the Christ, the Son of the living God*, are enabled and urged at the same time to exclaim: *We believe in the Holy Catholic Church.* The revelation of grace and truth which starts in the mystery of the incarnation, the great christological fact here disclosed to the view of faith, runs forward, of itself, into the mystery of the Church. We need no outward precepts and texts here to prop up our belief and make it rational; on this *rock,* the Church is built as a living necessary fact; and if it have no reality for our faith in such form, it is in vain to expect that it can ever be made an object of faith to us truly in any other way.

Thus apprehended in its ideal constitution, as the necessary outbirth of Christ's Mediatorial life, the Church waits for no definition from abroad, but proceeds at once to define itself, in the Creed, as One, Holy, and Catholic; which at once includes also the title Apostolical, as afterwards frequently introduced. These attributes come not from without, hang not at all on men's invention or consent, rest not primarily on any basis of empirical observation or induction.[113] They are the necessary conditions of

---

112. [The claim that in matters of faith the apprehension of the invisible and supernatural realm of spirit is prior to the proper cognition of the visible, natural, and sensory realm was typical of many German thinkers from Herder to the Romantics. This assertion stood in sharp contrast to the Enlightenment's effort to base religious knowledge upon the empirical data of nature and history and the rational procedures of induction.]

113. [Here Nevin was implicitly arguing against any theory that the apostolicity of the church was based upon the historical demonstration of an unbroken chain of apostolic succession in the episcopacy or any other organ of the church. In *The Principle of Protestantism*, Schaff had criticized the "Puseyite" (the Anglo-Catholic) location of the apostolocity of the church in the historical continuity of the episcopacy as being external and mechanical, as well as unverifiable and conducive to skepticism. See *The Development of the Church*, MTSS 3, ed. Bains and Trost, 144–45.]

Chapter 1: "The Apostles' Creed"

the *idea*, which is here laid hold of by faith, as something given and made sure through the mystery of Christianity itself. It will not do to cut and square this, with arbitrary violence, into our own shape; we must take it as it stands, and interpret it accordingly. To say that facts forbid such a construction of the Church, is only to say in other words, that the idea of Christianity presented in the Creed is a fiction, and along with this that its view of Christ's person is false; for the one conception flows with inward necessary deduction from the other. From the standpoint of the Creed, the attributes of the Church are just as fixed and certain, in its own sense, as the being which is felt to belong to it as the Body of Christ. It is this relation precisely in which it stands to his person, that fixes and settles its character in all the respects here under consideration. If it be in very truth the comprehension of a new and higher order of life for the world, the fountain of which is the Redeemer himself, it must require in its own nature, unity, sanctity and catholicity. It must be such a positive whole, as owns nothing beyond itself, and can allow no schism within itself. As it is the most perfect form of human life, so it must claim authority also as the most universal. It must be apostolical too, or in other words strictly *historical,* a real continuously active constitution from the time of the Apostles on to the end of the world. All this is implied, for faith, in the lively sense of what is comprehended in Christ's person; as all skepticism or indifference, on the other hand, in regard to these necessary attributes of the Church, is a worm which may be said to lie at last very near to the core of Christianity itself.

The mystical supernatural character of the Church, as now described, is expressed in one word as the "communion of saints." The Creed means not by this, of course, to resolve it into the ordinary fellowship of kindred minds. The object is rather to lift the conception distinctly into a higher sphere. Nothing can be more real than this new order of existence, though the law which underlies it, and the bond that holds it together, be "not of this world" [John 18:36] in the ordinary view. Its common universal character is membership in Christ, who is the one everlasting foundation of a life, more real, and deep, and solid, and enduring, than all that belongs to the world besides. To believe the *communion of saints,* as such a supernatural constitution in Christ, historically present in the world, binding all ages of the Church together as a single whole, reaching over into the intermediate state, and destined to break forth at last into the full triumph of the resurrection, amid the glories of the new heavens and the new earth, may well be counted something high and great, and worthy of the place it holds in the Creed. "*Fools* never raise their thoughts so high"[114]; mere flesh and blood can bring us truly to no such revelation.

Within this mystery now of the new creation, is comprehended the process by which individual souls, from age to age, are gathered from ruin and made meet for eternal glory. To a vast deal of our modern thinking, the order observed here by the Creed must appear careless, at least, and ill-advised. It would be led far more naturally to say: I believe in repentance and conversion, then in the communion of saints, and

---

114. [Isaac Watts' hymn, "Sweet is the work, my God, my King," stanza 4.]

finally, in some sort of holy catholic church; putting the individual isolated Christianity, in order of thought, before that which is general and collective.[115] The early Church, however, had a different way of looking at the matter; and the difference is here very plainly graven upon rock, in this old monumental symbol. The Church is taken to be the Holy Mother, from whose womb, as Calvin has it, we must all be born, and on whose breasts we must all hang, in order that we may grow up unto everlasting life.[116] The general, objective, universal side of Christianity, starting as it does in Christ, although it can never be sundered from individual religion in the Church, must not be viewed simply as the product and consequence of this, but is to be apprehended always by faith rather as the power that truly underlies and supports all its worth. The process of our salvation lies, not beyond the Church and out of it, but directly in its bosom. We have it measured here by its extreme ends, with all intermediate forms of experience quietly included, of course, as parts of one and the same historical fact. This starts in the "remission of sins," and becomes complete finally, with the completion of the Church as a whole, in the "resurrection of the body." The first clause is no doubt one in sense substantially, with the Nicene article, "one *baptism* for the remission of sins."[117] No one at all familiar with the life of the early Church, or in any way at home in the true genius of the Creed, can hesitate at all or feel much embarrassed, in regard to this point. The religion of the Creed is, throughout, sacramental and churchly, in the right sense of these terms. We may, if we choose, force into it a different meaning, to suit our own different taste; but the meaning of the period from which it springs, is abundantly clear, and we are bound to respect it, at least so far as history is concerned. The Church is here made an object of faith; a new divine economy is regarded as permanently at hand in her constitution; she is the mystical mother of saints; her sacraments convey grace, where the way is open for its reception; the remission of sins, in order to a Christian life, comes under God from her hand (Matt. xvi. 19, xviii. 18); and the act by which the grace is sealed is holy baptism, which it is the duty and privilege of all, accordingly, to embrace with full faith, as carrying in it this divine force. All this was liable to be greatly abused, and, as we very well know, was so abused in fact. But still, rightly understood, it expresses deep and sacred truth; the force of which *we* also must acknowledge and feel, if we would not forfeit all lot and part in the Creed of the ancient Church.

The whole winds up with "the life everlasting;" which is simply the triumphant issue of the process, as it is to reach its conclusion finally in the resurrection. To some, the doctrine of everlasting life appears to carry with it an independent certainty, on other grounds; so far at least as the "immortality of the soul" is concerned, it is felt to be comparatively easy to accept the idea of a future state, on what are supposed to be

---

115. [In making the collectivity prior to the individual Nevin was again manifesting his indebtedness both to the Romantics and to the Idealists.]

116. [John Calvin, *Institutes of the Christian Religion*, II:1016.]

117. [Schaff, *The Creeds of Christendom*, II:59.]

the merely rational evidences of its reality.[118] But the Creed knows nothing of any such abstract immortality. Its life everlasting is conditioned absolutely, by the resurrection of the body; it stands in the recovery of the man as a whole unity, from the law of sin and death which lies upon him in his present state; and all becomes real, only as a fact comprehended in the new creation which is brought to pass in Jesus Christ. Such plainly too is the view taken of it in the New Testament. The *immortality of the soul,* as it is called, in the common sense of the doctrine, is not taught in the Bible; on the contrary, it is heathenish, and tends to subvert the fundamental idea of Christianity. Life and immortality in the New Testament sense, are "brought to light" by Jesus Christ, as the result of his own mysterious union with our fallen nature, and in this form embrace at once body and soul together. To be in Him, is to have everlasting life, with the certainty of being raised up in virtue of it at the last day. He is the Resurrection and the Life. Thus it is that this article of the Creed as well as all the rest, is an object strictly and truly of *faith*; and this the same faith at last by which we assent to the mystery of Christ's person. To hold it on other grounds is not enough; we *believe* it truly, only when we embrace it as a fact which is felt to have its foundation and necessity in this living revelation, and in this alone.

IV. Practical Reflections.

Such we conceive to be the general scheme and structure of the Creed. It is no such fragmentary, disjointed production, as it is often imagined to be, by those who have little or no sympathy with its true sense and spirit. Take it as it is in its own constitution; let it be apprehended and estimated, not as a work of outward theological reflection, but as a transcript of what may be styled the intuitional consciousness of Christianity itself in its original fundamental form; let the true conception of Christianity be at hand as a new life, and not simply a new theory springing from Christ, and along with this the true conception also of faith as the very power by which it is substantiated and made to be present in the world; and it will be no longer difficult for anyone to feel the divine force of the symbol, the grandeur of its idea, the unity and harmony and complete wholeness of its architectural design. It is in all respects single, rotund and full, within the compass of its own orb. It is a majestic tree that grows forth from a single root. It is a grand oratorio of the Messiah, and of the Creation, in which the full harmony of heaven pours itself along, like the sound of many waters, from beginning to end. It is a vast Gothic dome, whose massive symmetry, poised upon a single centre, seems to swim with aerial lightness in a world of its own, piercing at last the very heavens. No work of art could well be more finished and complete. Each part becomes intelligible, nay, as an object of *faith,* becomes real, we may say, only by its inward organic union with the whole; while this, on the other hand, includes and requires all

---

118. [This was the position of many Enlightenment thinkers, including most English Deists.]

THE APOSTLES' CREED

the parts, from the beginning, as essential to its own constitution. Some have thought, that it would be an easy thing to *improve* the Creed, by throwing out some parts of it and adding to it various doctrinal propositions which are now wanting.[119] There is reason to suspect, indeed, as already intimated, that with no small portion of our modern Protestantism, the task would be felt comparatively light, to construct a much better new Creed altogether. All such thinking, however, turns of course, on a radically defective sense of its true nature and design, and betrays besides a most unsafe apprehension of Christianity itself; the very last that can deserve to be trusted, with all its imaginary orthodoxy, for the manufacture of any religious creed or confession whatever. The Creed, in its right conception, can admit no such improvement or alteration. There is no room to speak of different creeds as we may speak, for instance, of different catechisms or church covenants;[120] as though the fact of Christianity might be cast into several totally diverse schemes of thought, and yet remain true to itself in this character. To be truly a *Creed* at all, it must be the very movement of the fact itself, as disclosed to the vision of faith. It must be one thus, and not many. There is room, as we have seen, for variations in the filling up of the outline or scheme. This may be more or less full. But there is no room for different outlines or schemes. The Creed, in this respect, is as much one as Christianity itself is one. It determines its own contents, and it determines also its own form. It literally makes itself, and it will allow no man to turn it into any other shape. Whatever else our Christianity may include, in the way of doctrine or practice, it must start under the form here proclaimed, if it is to be at all legitimate and worthy of trust. This, at all events, is Christianity in its most universal character, the glorious fact of the new creation by Christ Jesus, under its broadest and most comprehensive features. Under such view, it is admirably complete; and it must be the wildest extravagance ever to dream of improving it by taking from it, or adding to it, or re-forging it into any new shape.

We close with the following reflections, flowing more or less directly, in the way of corollary or suggestion, from the whole subject:

I. The Creed does not spring from the Bible.[121] This is plain from its history. Its main substance was in use before the New Testament was formed. Peter's confession,

---

119. [It was feared that such emendations or the production of a new Creed might be contemplated by the more liberal factions in the Prussian Union Church.]

120. [Nevin is referring to the practice of many New England Congregational churches to develop their own unique church "covenants," which often included their own idiosyncratic modifications of the Westminster Confession.]

121. [Here Nevin is arguing against most American Protestant theologians, including Charles Hodge of Princeton, that the Creed's authority rests solely upon the fact that it is an apt summary of bibilical teaching. Rather, Nevin suggests that the authority of the Bible and the Creed are rooted in their capacity to communicate the "living sense of Christ's presence." The person of Christ is the ultimate source of the Creed's authority, as it also is of the Bible's. The church and its traditions, including the Bible and the Creed, through the power of the Spirit become the vehicle of the living presence of Christ. See also "Evangelical Radicalism" in *Mercersburg Review* 4, 511–12, and "Antichrist," in *One, Holy, Catholic, and Apostolic*, Tome One, MTSS 5, ed. Hamstra, 207–8.]

"Thou art the Christ, the Son of the living God," had no such origin. It was produced from the living sense of Christ's presence itself. And so, we may say, the whole Creed which lies involved in that confession, is derived through faith out of the same living ground. It is, of course, in harmony with the Bible; for it has to do immediately with its central revelation, the mystery of the Word made Flesh. It comes not, however, circuitously, in the way of reflection and study, through its pages. The early Church got it not from the Bible, but from the fact of Christianity itself, which must be allowed to be in its own nature older even and deeper than its own record under this form. Strange that there should be any confusion in regard to what is in itself so palpable and clear. The Bible is not the *principle* of Christianity;[122] nor yet the *rock* on which the Church is built. It never claims this character, and it can be no better than idolatry and superstition to worship it in any such view; as much so as though the same worship were directed towards a crucifix or the Roman mass. The one only principle of Christianity, the true and proper fountain of its being, is the person of Christ; not any written account or notion of his person, but the actual living revelation of it, as a fact in the history of the world. The Church rests immediately on this foundation, and no other. The Bible is of force, only as it proclaims this revelation. In such view, it is of indispensable account for the preservation and advancement of the Christian life; it is the divinely constituted rule, by which, through all ages, it must be measured and led. But still it is not this life itself; its relation to it is, after all, that of a condition, rather than that of a ground; and we are bound to see in Christianity always the presence of the Word under another form, as the true substratum at last of all its glorious power in the world. It is a Fact,[123] independently of the Bible and before it, which, as such, has a right to challenge our faith, whether we can show the Bible to be inspired or not. Indeed our ability to show the Bible inspired, must ever turn on our ability to prove in the first place, the reality of the revelation. So in all our systems of divinity, we begin, not with the inspiration of the sacred volume, as though this could be established in any wholly *ab extra* way, but with the truth of Christianity itself; feeling well assured that without this, it must be worse than idle to think of bringing the other question

---

122. [The notion that the Bible alone, apart from all ecclesial traditions and authoritative teachings used to interpret it, is the "principle" of Christianity was popularized by William Chillingworth (1602–1644), a somewhat spiritually unstable Anglican who had briefly become a Roman Catholic, in his *The Religion of Protestants*. This jettisoning of the ecclesial context for biblical interpretation was an extreme radicalization of Luther's theme of *sola scriptura*. By the nineteenth century the more nuanced description of the Bible (as read through the lens of church traditions) as the "formal principle" of Protestantism had become common. Schaff uses it prominently as a category to structure "The Principle of Protestantism," in *The Development of the Church*, MTSS 3, ed. Bains and Trost, 94.]

123. [The repeated use of the term "Fact" underscores Nevin's desire to distance himself from any theology that would regard Christianity as the product of human religious experience. For this reason he castigated the "subjectivity" of the evangelicals and even what he perceived to be Schleiermacher's inadequate attention to the objectivities of the faith. His repetition of "Fact" is also a function of his rejection of F. D. Strauss's and the Hegelian Left's tendency to describe the incarnation as a speculative concept (concerning the unity of the infinite and the finite) cloaked in mythic form.]

to any satisfactory issue. But what is this else than an acknowledgement that the Bible is not the principle of Christianity, but that this has its being in the world under another form, which is no less divine than the Scriptures themselves. Christianity is not only a written word, but a new creation in the form of life, starting from its founder Jesus Christ. In this last view, it *must* have, if it be what it claims to be, a real historical substance, which we are bound to respect as divine, no less than the Bible itself. There is not merely room thus, but an absolute necessity, for what may be styled a true Christian *tradition* in the Church; not as something against the Bible or foreign from it; but still not as a mere derivation either or efflux simply from its pages; a tradition which starts from the original substance of Christianity itself, as it underlies the Bible, and which in such form becomes the living stream into which continuously the sense of the Bible is poured, through the Holy Ghost, from age to age, onward to the end of the world. This divine tradition meets us under its clearest, most primitive and most authoritative character, in the Apostles' Creed.

II. The idea of the Creed, as now given, throws light on the true character of the Church, as related to Christ in one direction and to the Bible in another. The Creed represents the primary substance of Christianity, as it has passed over from Christ in the form of life, into the general consciousness of his people. This general life is the Church. It is of course, a divine fact in the world, and so of right an article of faith more immediately than the Bible itself. First the Church, and then the Bible. So in the Creed: "I believe in the Holy Catholic Church," instead of: "I believe in the Holy Inspired Bible"; not certainly to put any dishonor on this last; but to lay rather a solid foundation for its dignity and authority in the other article; for, after all, it is the Church, next to Christ, and not the Bible, save as comprehended in the Church, which according to St. Paul, is "the pillar and ground of the truth [1 Tim 3:15]." Is this to throw Christ into the shade, as the opposers of the Church sometimes pretend? Just as little, we reply, as faith in the divine authority of the Bible tends to throw him into the shade. The Church *may* be so magnified as to wrong Christ; but it is just as possible, and at this time also, just as common, to magnify the Bible in a like bad way, at Christ's expense; as where men, for instance, insist on sundering it from the objective fact of Christianity itself, the life of Christ in the Church, and force it to become instead the vehicle only of their own private judgment and proud self-will. Neither the Church, however, nor the Bible, can be held responsible for any such abuse. In their own nature, they do homage perpetually to Christ. The Church is but the living revelation of his presence and power, from age to age, in the world. The Bible is his written word. In this view, both are required to go together. Christianity is the proper union of both. Neither can fulfill its mission, apart from the other. The Church, to be true to her vocation, must be ruled by the Bible; if any pretend to follow her voice, without regard to this, they will be led astray. But the converse of this is no less certain. The Bible to be a true word of Christ, must be ruled by the life of the Church; if any pretend to follow it without regard to this, they too will most assuredly miss the truth. Will it be said that this is a circle? Be it so. In such circle precisely, is it the divine prerogative of faith, at all times firmly and serenely to move.

III. Christianity, as such a divine fact in the consciousness of the Church, is historical. The idea of history is opposed both to dead tradition and to dead change. It moves; it lives; it grows. So the Creed originally came to pass. In its very conception thus, it makes room for a continuous historical evolution of the Christian life on all sides. To take it as the end of all Christianity, is to mistake its nature entirely. It is only the form in which it begins. Christianity must be far more than such beginning. Its mission is, not merely to cover the earth with its outward presence, but to occupy and rule inwardly also the universal being of man. It must regenerate the thinking of the world and all its action; it carries in itself, accordingly, the possibility of becoming such a reconstruction or intensification of our universal life, from the start. The substance then which it exhibits primitively in the Creed, is by no means bound to that, either as a rigid shell or loose drapery; but widens itself continually, in the way of historical concrete growth, and unfolds its inward wealth in forms as manifold as the complex fact of humanity itself. So in particular it admits and requires a progressive theology; for why should not Christianity occupy our nature in the form of science, as well as in the form of action or feeling? Theology implies doctrines. These come, for the understanding, by gradual process. Hence each single doctrine has its history, and theology is historical as a whole.[124] The history in this case is not something outward only, but enters into the very substance of the fact itself; so that in any right view of the case, it is just as necessary for theology to be historical, as it is for it to be biblical. History is one of the factors, by which it is brought to pass and made to have in itself a real existence. True faith in the Creed then, does not require us to renounce all interest in theology, and fall back on the primary Christian consciousness as the *ne plus ultra*[125] of the new creation; on the contrary, it is just what we need to overthrow the idea of all such stability, and fit us for the right appreciation of theology as a continuously progressive science. To have faith in the Church, is to have faith at the same time in History. The spirit of the Creed is not radical. It is the spirit of Sect, ever violent and abrupt by its very constitution, that seeks to nullify the whole Christian process since the days of the Apostles. To a mind in sympathy with the Creed, that process is ever something sacred and divine, no less, we may say, than the primitive faith itself.

IV. With such historical character, all true theology, at the same time, grows forth from the Creed, and so remains bound to it perpetually as its necessary radix or root. History is not progress in the way of outward local remove from one point to another, but progress that carries the sense with which it is freighted onward and upwards always into new forms. It resembles the growth of a tree or the gradual evolution of our individual human life. It is a river, which carries itself forward with its own flow,

---

124. [Nevin was deeply indebted to Herder, Neander, Rauch, and Hegel for this understanding of the historically evolving nature of theology.]

125. [Trans. "ultimate."]

ever changing and yet ever the same. The relation of the Creed then to the forms of sound Christian doctrine which have since appeared, is simply this, that they are to be regarded as lying silently involved in it from the beginning, though some time was needed to bring them to clear and distinct utterance. The great articles of Christian theology come from the Bible; but, at the same time, they are *mediated* or brought to pass for the mind of the Church, only through the presence and power of the primitive Christian consciousness, expressed in the Creed, as something already at hand. It is no defect in the Creed, that it contains not several most important and necessary articles of a sound theology as the Church now stands, the inspiration of the Scriptures, for instance, or the doctrine of justification by faith. On the other hand, however, such articles lose no credit or authority whatever, by the fact of such omission. The only question is, do they flow from the substance of Christianity as given in the Creed, and do they hold in it and from it perpetually as their vital root. This, after all, is complete, under its own form, as an utterance of the primary *fact* of Christianity; and it only follows that other articles have their truth and importance, not in the same primary way, but all the more surely, for this very reason, in the way of derivation and outflow from what goes before. We reach thus this great practical conclusion, that the orthodoxy of every doctrine is fairly tested at last by its inward correspondence or want of correspondence with the Creed. It is not enough that it seem to be biblical from some other stand point; its biblicity must be evident, as seen *through* the fundamental substance of Christianity embodied in this universal faith of the Holy Catholic Church. It is not enough that a doctrine be sound in form; if it refuse notwithstanding to coalesce inwardly with the spirit of the Creed, it convicts itself of substantial falsehood. Take in illustration, the article of justification by faith, Luther's criterion of a standing or falling Church. It is not sufficient, surely, that it be accepted in a merely general and abstract way. Our sects, United Brethren, Albright Brethren, Winebrennerians,[126] and a score of others to the same general tune, readily meet for the most part, on this ground; one trying to outdo another, in its zeal for this particular side of religion. And yet Luther would have denounced the whole of them, as a worse plague than the locusts of Pharaoh. Do we ask, why? With Luther, the article had firm and fast root in the Creed, the historical substance of the old catholic Christian life; whereas, with these upstart sects, it is a mere abstraction or fancy, which makes no account of the old catholic faith whatever, and so proves itself to be the growth of some other soil,

---

126. [Nevin's examples of sects are the Church of the United Brethren in Christ founded by Philip William Otterbein (1726–1813) and Martin Boehm (1725–1812), the Evangelical Association (later Evangelical Church) founded by Jacob Albright (1759–1808), and the Church of God founded by John Winebrenner (1797–1860). He was especially irritated with Otterbein and Winebrenner both of whom had roots in the German Reformed Church. Winebrenner separated from that church over his use of the "New Measures" evangelistic techniques. Although Otterbein retained his clerical status in the German Reformed Church, he and Martin Boehm, an evangelical Mennonite, were co-founders of a new "sect." For Nevin's more elaborated critique of these groups, see "The Sect System," in *One, Holy, Catholic, and Apostolic*, Tome One, MTSS 5, ed. Hamstra, 238–71.]

the product simply of the human brain. These sects have no sympathy with the Creed; they do not stand in it with their inward life; their theology starts not out of it at all, as its primitive ground. *Thus* held, the article of justification by faith ceases to be true, and is no longer safe, but full of peril for all the interests of religion. So would all the Reformers say, with one voice.[127]

V. Regard for the Creed then, may be taken as a fair measure of sound church character, as distinguished from the spirit of sect and schism. In its whole conception and life, the Creed is catholic, inwardly bound to the true universal power of the Christian life, as it stood in the beginning. Hence it will be found invariably, that the sect spirit, whose essential nature it is to be abrupt, violent, unhistorical and upstart, lends, if not openly, at least quietly, always, to the abandonment of the venerable symbol altogether. Sect piety has no relish for the Creed; it cannot utter itself naturally in any such way; it makes no account, in truth of Christianity in that form. The genius of Puritanism, as we have already seen, is also strikingly at variance with the same rule. The fact admits no doubt. It stares upon us in the almost universal neglect into which the Creed has fallen, wherever Puritanism prevails. It will not do to say that this neglect is more apparent than real, and that the substance of the Creed is still in honor, though not its particular form. The difficulty is, precisely, that the form is such as will not easily allow another substance to be put into it, than that which belongs to it in truth; on which account, the use of it is felt to be uncongenial with the true life of Puritanism, as something which is, in fact, not inwardly harmonious with the life of the ancient Church. Hence such use in this case can never be easy, natural and free, but produces always some sense of awkward and stiff constraint. Puritanism must wrest the Creed into quite a different sense from its own original meaning, to be able at all to acquiesce in its several articles. Left to itself, it would fall on a very different scheme of fundamental and necessary truth. It can see no reason why the Creed

---

127. *Professor Tayler Lewis,* of the New York University, in his manly and truly able review of the Mercersburg School, as he calls it, published in Nos. 114 and 115, of the *Literary World,* expresses some apprehension of the danger there is of wronging the forensic side of our salvation, in trying to make too much of Christ as the bearer of life for us in a real way. He allows both, but seems to think that the first interest forms for our faith the safety of the second. "The incarnation and the crucifixion," he remarks, "are the fundamentals of our faith. It may be admitted too, that the first is the necessary ground of the value of the second; but all ecclesiastical experience has shown, that for us, and to us, in our unrecovered state, the latter is the nearest truth, that it has the most of moral power, and that when vividly sustained, it has ever sustained the belief in the coordinate mystery." This we cannot admit. The forensic interest is full as liable to run wild, as the other. So we see in the case of our unsacramental sects, on all sides. The true order is, the mystery of the incarnation first, and then the atonement, as growing forth from this, and *only in such view.* Such is the conception of the Creed. Peter's confession is the rock that must underlie, in our minds, all other divinity. Protestantism can be true and genuine growth, only as it grows forth from *catholicity,* the primitive substance of Christianity as a fact, made to break on the sense of the soul through the apprehension of Christ's person. A sound *christology,* involving always the idea of a sound church life, is indispensable, we more and more believe, to all true orthodoxy at other points. [Lewis (1802–77), a biblical scholar and theologian, was a graduate of Union College, Nevin's own alma mater, and later taught there. Lewis was especially interested in the relationship of science and religion.]

carries just its present form, or why so much should be left out of it, that Puritanism is apt to think of first, in its own abstract way. The orthodoxy of New England, for instance, can hardly be said at all to grow forth organically from the primitive mind or consciousness of the Church, as embodied in this symbol. Is not this strange and startling fact entitled to some consideration? We are firmly persuaded that it will be felt to be solemnly significant, in proportion exactly as it is made the subject of earnest thought. An orthodoxy which owns no inward fellowship with the Creed, and which feels itself complete in a wholly different way without it, deserves to be regarded with distrust, and may well be asked to give a reason of the hope that is in it under such abstract and unhistorical form. We are free to confess, that, in our view, any scheme of Christianity to which the voice of the Creed has become thus strange, labors under a most serious defect; and we need no other proof than the general fact here noticed, to show what is shown by so many proofs besides, that Puritanism, with all its great excellencies and merits, involves a material falling away from the faith of the sixteenth century as well as from that of the early Church.

VI. For the settlement of our existing theological and ecclesiastical difficulties, the first and most indispensable necessity is a true and hearty inward submission to the authority of the Creed, according to its original intention and design. Not that this is to be taken as of itself the sum and end of all theology; but all sound doctrine and true church life, must proceed forth from a common faith here, as their only sure ground, and it is vain to dream of their being prosperously advanced in any other way. It is mere loss of time, for instance, to argue the question of election, or that of infant baptism, with those who are not imbued, in the first place, with a true reverence for the Apostles' Creed. It is, in truth, of very little consequence, in such case, whether it be the affirmative or the negative of any such question that is maintained; as growing forth organically, not from the primary substance of the Christian faith at all, but from some other ground altogether, the opinion whether right or wrong in its notional and formal character, is sure to be in its inward material constitution, unchristian and wrong. So, as we have just seen, the doctrine of justification itself, in its right outward shape, may become, through such divorce from the life of the Creed, in the highest degree false and dangerous. Election, the atonement, imputation, &c., can have no validity as Christian doctrines, in an abstract view, but only as they can be developed from the concrete mystery here apprehended by faith. Theology in any other form, is always necessarily rationalistic, an effort to build faith on intellection, whereas the true order is just the reverse. This rightly understood and felt, would at once greatly narrow the field of theological controversy, as well as greatly facilitate the proper conclusion of its cardinal debates. How much, especially of our modern disputation, our *sect-fights*, we may say, generally, would be found by this rule to be little better than mere *skiomachy* ["shadow boxing"], the battling of phantom shapes projected on the air. The first condition of all sound theology is, active sympathy with historical Christianity, with the idea of the Church, with the catholic mystery of the

Creed. So also as regards all church questions; we do but run ourselves into endless talk, if we propose to settle them from any other ground, or in any other frame of mind. For instance, the question of using, or not using, a settled liturgy in public worship; how much of the argument on both sides, do we not find proceeding under a wholly different, and, therefore, wholly unsatisfactory form? The interest is vindicated or opposed on purely outward grounds, instead of being referred, as it should be, first of all, to the interior demands of Christianity itself, as embodied in the Creed. Or take the question of *Episcopacy.* It has been much the fashion to place it all round, on such *ab extra*[128] proofs and reasons, as though the point were to make out a simply external warrant for or against it, independently altogether of the contents of the life itself. Thus Episcopalians often try to find it outwardly prescribed in the New Testament; a vain and hopeless task, which only serves to countenance the equally vain and fruitless attempt, on the other side, to overthrow it in the same mechanical way. To make Episcopacy the necessary hedge of Christianity, which we are to be sure of first on outside reasons, whether biblical or historical, in order that we may then be sure of the enclosed truth, is just again to subordinate faith rationalistically to the lower authority of the understanding; for how can such a purely outward and mechanical authority be a whit better at last, than any other form of thought and will which is not ruled by the very substance of the truth itself. Who may not see, that if Episcopacy be indeed the *first* thing towards a sound faith, it ought to come first also in the Creed, or, at least, to follow immediately the general article of the Holy Ghost; whereas, in truth, as we all know, it has no place in the Creed whatever.[129] Are we then, at once, to infer from this, on the other hand, that Episcopacy is false, or that no definite organization is required as the normal form of the Church? By no means. Only this is not the way in which the question can ever be settled. What we need for that, especially just now, is a general hearty return to the catholic life of the Creed, as the necessary point of departure for coming to a true solution of all our church questions. This we firmly believe is something that *can* take place extensively, long before we are able to see at all to the *end* of the perplexing difficulties with which we are now surrounded; and that *must* take place, indeed, before a single step can be successfully made towards their proper practical resolution. It is the idea of the Church, the mystery of Christianity as it is made sure to us by faith in the Apostles' Creed, something older certainly, and deeper in its own nature, than any mere outward hedge surrounding it, which we are bound first of all to embrace; which alone is sufficient to draw after it any right theory or practice, as regards all other church interests; and which, therefore, we have it in our power to begin with, as an *a priori* foundation, for reaching in the end the results

---

128. [Trans. "from extra."]

129. [Nevin is undoubtedly thinking of the Oxford (or Tractarian) Movement which was prominent in the Church of England (1833–45). One of its assertions was that the Anglican Church could claim apostolic origin because of its traditional episcopal polity. See John Henry Newman, "The Episcopal Church Apostolical," Tract 7.]

that the case requires. A convention of sects to negotiate a federal Church, is much like a convention of the blind to settle the laws of light. We must be in the Creed, and so have faith in the Church, in order to find it, or to settle its exact form and limits. This is the true method for bringing to an issue the sacramental question, the liturgical question, the question of festival days. An active revival of the consciousness expressed in the Creed, would in due time restore all these great interests to their pristine authority. And we will just add, in the way of friendly hint to Episcopalians, that if their favorite system of church polity *could* be vindicated as necessary, in this way, to the conservation of the great catholic ideas that enter into the primitive faith, it would be, in our estimation, an argument of more weight and force in its favor, than whole tomes of learning employed to establish its authority in an outward and abstract view.

Chapter 2

"Puritanism and the Creed"

by John W. Nevin

Editors' Introduction

Nevin's third and final article in his opening series on the Apostles' Creed was published in Volume 1 of *The Mercersburg Review* in July 1849. The series was controversial and critical reviews were quickly forthcoming. The first appeared in a series of articles in *The Puritan Recorder*, the principal newspaper of New England Congregationalism, which began its treatment of Nevin's views in its July 26, 1849 issue. The series continued on a weekly basis until September 13, 1849. Other articles based on some of the *Recorder's* comments were printed in the *Lutheran Observer*[1] and also in a Presbyterian periodical.[2] Nevin's answer to the *Recorder's* attack was the following article in the November 1849 issue of *The Mercersburg Review*.

Although Nevin claimed that he was not interested in a polemical defense of his views on the Creed, he knew it was necessary to engage in a vigorous apologetic reply to the allegations leveled against him. It was clear to him that the *Recorder's* articles demanded a powerful response. He was especially incensed with the contention that the Creed taught some very anti-scriptural ideas. For example, it was alleged that the Roman Catholic doctrine of purgatory was inherent in the Creed's statement that Jesus descended into hell. Furthermore, the Creed's assertions of belief in the "Holy Catholic Church" could too easily be taken as authorizing the legitimacy of one organized visible church, namely that centered in Rome. Nevin's contention that any denial the Creed's affirmation of the oneness of the church was to legitimize the "sect system" (which he so vehemently rejected), was taken to be further proof of a Romanizing tendency. The Creed's stated belief in the "communion of saints," it was argued by his critics, may point to the Roman Church's practice of intercessory prayers to the saints or prayers offered

---

1. See *The Lutheran Observer* 17, no. 38 (September 21, 1849). *The Lutheran Observer* was a weekly denominational newspaper published under various names from 1840–1915. Benjamin Kurtz (1795–1865), one of its early and very influential editors, championed revivalism because he believed that the contemporary American evangelical fervor was fueled by the same spirit that had animated seventeenth-century Lutheran Pietism. Consequently he opposed the "Old Lutheran" party's attempts to buttress American Lutheranism by requiring subscription to the unaltered Lutheran confessional documents.

2. Research inquiries to the Presbyterian Historical Society in Philadelphia resulted in no further information regarding the precise issue in which Nevin's Apostles' Creed matter was addressed. This was confirmed by the Society's researcher in an email message dated February 16, 2016.

for the dead, and it was pointed out that such prayers were not legitimate for Puritan (American Congregationalist and Presbyterian) doctrine or practice.

The *Recorder* claimed that for many Puritans the Creed was outdated and outmoded. It was a product of the past and could justifiably be laid aside. What would take its place? The answer was that the Bible and the Holy Spirit would fill that ostensible void, of course. The *Recorder's* editor proudly proclaimed, "Puritanism draws its life directly from the Bible and the Holy Ghost" quite apart from creeds and traditions. Nevin, predictably, countered by writing, "We see no good reason . . . for divesting ourselves of the general consciousness of the ancient church, as expressed in the Apostles' Creed, and putting on in place of it the consciousness or creed of modern New England, as the only sure medium of access to the true sense of the Bible."[3] He doubted that the theological opinions of the New Englanders were simply the fruits of the interaction of the Bible and the Holy Spirit; rather, the theology expressed in the *Recorder* was itself the product of a tradition, although it was a tradition of recent origin and limited geographic scope. Nevin favored a broader and longer historical approach in which the centuries of the Christian church (Roman Catholic and Protestant) held the Apostles' Creed to be the authentic sense of Scripture and the groundwork of Christian faith.

Appended to this article is a "Postscript" in which Nevin commented on T. C. Porter's[4] review of J. P. Lesley's[5] book *Private Judgment* (1849) in *The Mercersburg Review* (September 1849). Nevin was concerned that exercising personal, private judgment in biblical interpretation was dangerous. According to Nevin, this was, indeed, one of the root causes of the unchurchliness of the sect plague which threatened to engulf the American continent and destroy authentic Christianity. For Nevin, the Bible should be interpreted not by individuals operating atomistically, but by a community of the faithful participating in the liturgical and creedal heritage of the church stretching across time and space.

---

3. Nevin, 114 (this volume). Many New England Congregationalist congregations were in the habit of formulating their own unique church "covenants," which often included a home-grown confession of faith.

4. T. C. Porter (1822-1901) served on the faculty of Marshall College from 1849 to 1866, teaching the physical sciences. He actively supported the liturgical reforms and theological vision of Nevin and Schaff.

5. J. P. Lesley (1819-1903) was a Presbyterian minister who converted to Unitarianism, left the ministry, and became a seminal geologist and a prolific cartographer, often exploring and mapping the topography of Pennsylvania.

Puritanism and the Creed

[by John Williamson Nevin]

The *Puritan Recorder*, one of the most respectable and widely influential religious papers in New England, has lately uttered itself on this subject, in a succession of short articles (called forth as it would seem, in opposition to our late view of the Creed) which we have no right entirely to overlook.[2] We trust at the same time, that our object in noticing them, will be rightly appreciated. We should be sorry to give way to mere polemical zeal, in such a case, for its own sake. We have no quarrel specially with the *Recorder*; and it is not in our mind at all, to challenge it to any sort of public argument or debate. That would require a common audience; which it is vain for us, of course, at this time, to ask or expect. Before the amphitheatre of the *Recorder's* public, we can be heard, for the most part, only in such form as the paper itself may see fit to allow; and we have had experience enough to know, that even where our denominational religious papers are least disposed to be consciously unfair, no sort of justice is to be hoped for, ordinarily, in this way. Our interest is in the subject, under its general aspect, and as related to theology in its broad view. We make use of the *Recorder* as an *occasion*, simply, for bringing home to the consideration of our readers a vastly significant interest, in a connection of actual life, near at hand, such as is suited to fix upon it their earnest attention. There is no good reason, at all events, why a review like ours should limit its critical interest to what is published in the form of pamphlets and books. A large part of our literature, at present, appears in the form of newspapers. The weekly religious press, especially, has come to be of far more account for our theology, so far as we can be said to have any that is living and not dead, than

---

1. [J. W. Nevin], *The Mercersburg Review* 1 (November 1849) 585–607.]

2 [*The Puritan Recorder*, published in Boston, Massachusetts between 1849 and 1858, was a weekly newspaper that carried religious news and opinion pieces that would be of interest to the Congregationalists of New England. The phrase "Puritan" here was used proudly as a term of approbation (unlike Nevin's use of it.) The first article in *The Puritan Recorder* series on the Apostles' Creed was "The Mercersburg Theology," July 24, 1849.]

Chapter 2: "Puritanism and the Creed"

all the books now produced in its service. These are in general so mechanical, that they carry in them very little power either for bad or good.³ To understand the actual religious life of the country, theoretic as well as practical, we must commune with the religious newspapers of the different sects. They, indeed, generally disclaim scientific theology; aiming simply, as they say, to be practical; but in their own way they show themselves ready enough, notwithstanding, to settle all theological questions in the most summary offhand style; and with the advantage of their position, the authority thus assumed is allowed very generally to prevail. We are bound, accordingly, to have regard to them, if we would deal with the theological life of the country in a living way. A newspaper paragraph may be of more account at times, as a text for religious discussion, than a whole sermon, or a large lettered duodecimo of three hundred and fifty pages, manufactured to order according to previous fashion and rule.

In writing upon the Creed, we ventured to say, not without hesitation in our own mind, that Puritanism is constitutionally at variance with this ancient rule, and if left to itself would fall on a very different formula to represent its faith.⁴ The hesitation we felt in saying this, arose not from any doubt of its being the truth, but from the apprehension of its seeming to be a hard saying to others, who might not see the truth of it at once, and so be led to think our judgment unkind and harsh; just as some have considered it harsh, that we should affirm a similar falling away from the faith of the sixteenth century in the case of the holy sacraments; as though the question were one of courtesy only, and had nothing to do at all with stern historical reality. We were afraid that many might consider it a slander to charge Puritanism with being in conflict with the Creed, when it is still willing to accept the form of it at times, as orthodox and good; the circumstance being overlooked, that in every such case the Creed is quietly filled with a new sense materially different from that which belonged to it in the beginning.⁵ We are now, however, happily discharged of all this concern.

---

3. [In this essay Nevin continues to employ and further develop his contrast of the "mechanical" (a hallmark of the Enlightenment) with the "organic" (a favored concept of Romanticism).]

4. [Throughout the article Nevin associates "Puritanism" with an ahistorical hermeneutic stance that assumes that the meaning of Scripture is clear to contemporary readers, or at least to contemporary Congregationalists in New England. He also linked Puritanism with the belief that the church is constituted by the commitments of like-minded individuals. He, on the other hand, was convinced that the church was constituted by the life of Christ that animates it and unites it as a corporate body through the centuries, prior to the decisions of any individual believers.]

5. "Dr. N., who appears to be chief cyclops, and forger of thunder-bolts for what is called the Mercersburg Theology, has turned his one eye, with vulcanian glare, towards us; and launched his lightnings at our heads, for a supposed want of respect for that venerable symbol, the so-called Apostles' Creed. In rebuking the flippancy of a sciolist ["one who pretends to know"], (Dr. Bushnell) who had spoken as if it were an undoubted fact, that this ancient form was drawn up by the Apostles, we had said that it 'was no more an apostolical invention, than was Christmas pie.' In the sense in which we used the words, Dr. N., like any man of ordinary learning, fully accords with us. And we hold, as firmly as he does, that the Creed is truly apostolical in regard to the 'divine substance of its contents,' and 'as representing from the beginning the one unvarying faith of the universal Christian world.' There are other creeds, which, in the same sense, are no less apostolical."—*Boston Christian Observatory, for Sept.,* 1849: This is well, as far as it goes; but it tallies badly with the *Puritan Recorder*. [The correct

The *Puritan Recorder*, in the name of Puritanism, and with intelligent insight, as it would seem, into the true nature of the question at issue, openly and boldly accepts our representation as fully correct. The Creed, in its genuine and original sense, is no true type, we are told, of the present *orthodoxy* of New England. Whatever traditional respect may have been allowed to it in the beginning, it has fallen on all sides into disuse, and is notoriously out of date. All this too is proclaimed an improvement in our general Christianity, for the Creed turns out, on close examination, to be at war with the Bible, and the use of it is perilous to the interests of evangelical religion. The *Puritan Recorder*, in this case, is no mean witness. We are bound to respect its testimony; we do respect it in fact; and we wish it to be listened to seriously and solemnly, throughout the length and breadth of the American Church.

"The experience of two centuries has shown," says the *Recorder*,

> that the Creed and Puritanism have not a kindred spirit. The first Puritans did not discard what is called the Apostles' Creed, but expressly allowed its use, and by a sort of courtesy, gave it a place beside their formularies and catechisms. It even had a place in the New England Primer. But its life and spirit never entered into the life of the Puritan churches. And, consequently, it now exists among us as some fossil relic of by-gone ages. And we look with a sort of pity upon those who are laboring to infuse life into it, and to set it up as a living ruler in the Church. We are free to confess, that this Creed has forsaken the Puritans, and gone over to become the idol and strength of all branches of anti-puritanism.
>
> And there are good reasons; for Puritanism builds on the Scriptures, and this Creed teaches, in several respects, anti-scriptural doctrines. It is true, that most of it is capable of a sense which harmonizes with the Scriptures, and so the Puritans received it, in a sense consonant with their theology—either leaving out, or putting a strained sense upon the passage which asserts that Christ descended into hell. But it is neither safe nor expedient to receive such a document, in such a perverted sense. For the document once being admitted, and its authority being made to bind the conscience, then the way is open for those who hold the errors held by its authors, to plead that we are bound to receive it in the sense which its authors gave to it, and this makes it an instrument of corrupting the faith of the gospel.
>
> But what are the heretical points of this Creed? We shall have space in this article for only one, and that is the doctrine of purgatory, as taught in the assertion that Christ descended into hell."—*Puritan Recorder*, August 23, 1849.[6]

reference for this publication is not the *Boston Christian Observatory*, but the *Christian Observatory* 2, no. 10 (October 10, 1848): 479. Horace Bushnell (1802–76) was a Congregational minister with a long pastorate in Hartford, Connecticut. His theological work paralleled Nevin's writings in some respects, for he argued that being nurtured by the church community should be the typical way for an individual to become a Christian, rather than by being converted through a dramatic emotional episode. He also maintained that spiritual truths could best be communicated through poetic language rather than through a deductive, logical doctrinal system. Nevin, however, was much more committed than Bushnell to remaining rooted in the historic creedal and liturgical traditions of historic Christianity, and much more intent upon stressing the centrality of the incarnation.]

6. [*The Puritan Recorder*, No. 34, August 23, 1849.]

Chapter 2: "Puritanism and the Creed"

This particular charge of teaching the doctrine of Purgatory, the article then goes on to substantiate and settle in its own brief way, without the least regard to true history, by a few hop-step-and-jump combinations, within the bounds of a paragraph measuring about one-fourth part of a single column of the paper in which it appears. Two other errors, one latent in the clause "Catholic Church," the other peeping forth from the "Communion of Saints," are laid over for subsequent dissection.[7]

In the *Recorder* of the following week, August 30, we have another article, nearly a column long, disposing of the second of these last mentioned errors in equally sweeping and summary style. Modern evangelical Christians, we are told, have no occasion for the clause "Communion of Saints," in their forms of belief. The meaning which they would fit to it, is not one sufficiently prominent to have a place in so brief a confession of faith. And it is very clear that the unknown authors of the Apostles' Creed had a meaning for it, and a use for it, which we have not." And then we have historical hypothesis again substituted for historical fact, to show that the true sense of it is to be found in the superstitions of the Roman Church. "If we suppose that the Romish doctrine of the intercession of departed saints for men upon earth, and of the efficacy of prayers addressed by us to the saints in heaven, and of the efficacy of prayers offered for the dead, had obtained at the time when this phrase was added to the Creed, then we see an adequate reason for its addition." This IF, made good by the violent assumption, that the article was no part of the primitive faith of the Church, but a device added to it somewhere along in the fourth century (a fact demanded, and so made sure, by the necessities of the hypothesis itself), proves strong enough to hurry us, by a few strokes of the pen, into the convenient conclusion, that it was brought in purely and solely for the purpose of covering this general Roman fancy. "And *if* so, the use of the Creed by us is a snare, since, though we may find a different and true sense, which will fit the words, the historic sense has superior claims, which will not fail to be felt by many minds, that attach an authority, not to say sacredness, to the venerated document."[8]

The first article in the *Recorder* of the next week, Sept. 6, calls our attention again to the "heretical points of the Creed," under the somewhat startling caption: The Holy Catholic Church a Figment.[9] In repeating the clause, *I believe in the holy catholic Church,* the early Puritan, we are told, wist not what he said. They suit not the faith of a Puritan. "Let him attach his own sense to the words, and he can utter them. But then the utterance comes from him with a sort of foreign accent and unnatural constraint. If the term 'catholic church' embrace all the elect or true believers, in all places and all times, the living and the dead, and those not yet born—that is, the spiritual or invisible church, the mystical body of Christ—very well. But if it means that the visible church is a 'holy catholic church'—an organic body, embracing all professing

---

7. [*The Puritan Recorder*, No. 34, August 23, 1849.]
8. [*The Puritan Recorder*, No. 35, August 30, 1849.]
9. [*The Puritan Recorder*, No. 36, September 6, 1849.]

Christians as one whole, in one organic brotherhood—it has no warrant in Scripture. In the light of the New Testament, the idea of a *catholic visible church* is intrinsically impossible and absurd." Christ himself, we are gravely informed, "organized no church," but committed the "organizing of *churches*" to the apostles. This they did after the day of Pentecost. The churches thus organized, however, were all equally original, independent, and complete in and by themselves.[10] "They were not splinters nor fractions of churches, but whole *churches*." In the *Recorder* for Sept. 13, the subject is resumed, under the caption: "The False Theory of the Visible Church a Hindrance to Christian Union."[11] Here the Creed is charged with teaching "the phantom of an organic catholicity of the visible Church"; on which account, says the *Recorder*, as such a church "exists not in fact, nor in the theory of the New Testament, it is not for us to recite such a creed." It kills "the principle of the essential independency of the churches," and makes sectarianism and schism to be a sin. Only let the public mind be well charged with this principle of atomistic Christianity, and the misery of our sect system is at once in a great measure brought to an end. It is the notion of catholicity, as we have it in the Creed, that leads men to declaim against what they call the "sect spirit." "Let that phantom go to the winds," and we shall see that individuals may form a new church at any time to suit themselves, without prejudice to Christ's house. "Let the principle of independency expand to its just proportions in the public mind, and the right of Christians thus to organize will be generally conceded." Then, too, the evils of sectarian division will in a large measure cease; "the mutual irritation and odium of the sects comes of this false assumption," that the Church should be outwardly one. The same false theory it is, which originates the reproach brought against the Church by the surrounding world, on account of its sectarianism. "Just remove the phantom which dwells in the imagination as some sacred thing, and no violence will be supposed to have been done to a sacred thing, when, like Abram and Lot, Christians separate for the avoidance of strife. Take away the idol, and no sacrilege will be committed in mutilating it, and no weak consciences will be defiled in eating what is offered in sacrifice to it." This may be taken, certainly, as a short and easy cure for all sorts of schism; though one can hardly fail to see in it a certain sort of analogy with the style, in which our Socialists and Radical Reformers generally affect to rid themselves of such ethical and religious obstructions as happen to come in *their* way. Remove, for instance, the phantom of holy matrimony, which now dwells in the imagination of men as some sacred thing, and no violence will be supposed to have been done to what is sacred, when, like Abraham and David, Christians multiply wives or concubines to suit themselves.[12] Take away the idol, and no sacrilege will hold against it in

---

10. [Many Congregationalists believed that each rightly ordered individual congregation possessed all the essential marks of a true church, quite apart from its relation to other congregations.]

11. [*The Puritan Recorder*, No. 37, September 13, 1849.]

12. [By pointing to the presence of polygamy and concubinage in the Bible, Nevin was arguing against the belief that Scripture was so perspicuous in itself that no communal hermeneutic was

the form either of adultery or fornication. But what if the "idol," holy matrimony in this last case, and the holy catholic church in the other, should prove to be, in the end, no phantom at all, but the very shrine of divinity itself, set up among men to be the object of their perpetual faith and veneration? The *argumentum ab utili* ["argument from use"] is then at an end. Marriage may not be set aside, to accommodate a community of libertines; the Church may not be shorn of its original inborn attributes, to suit the humor of sects.

The *Puritan Recorder*, of course, assumes throughout, that the Church is no divine institution, in the form asserted by the Creed. But this at last remains simply an *assumption*. It is not proved. The writer has a certain preconception of the nature of the Church, which he finds to be contradicted by the theory of the Creed; whereupon he expects us at once to accept *his* preconception, on the authority of his own word, as the true sense of the New Testament, and so to jump with him to the conclusion, that the theory of the Creed is unscriptural, fantastic and false. We are not prepared to bow to such logic as this. The whole assumption here taken against the Creed, is gratuitous and untrue. The *idea* of the Church presented in the Creed, falls back historically to the very cradle of the Christian faith; full as much so as the idea of the incarnation itself. The one mystery in truth grows forth from the other; the idea of the Church has its necessary root in the idea of Christ. And this entire faith, of course, then, meets us in the New Testament. The conception of the Church, as a new universal or catholic creation, starting in Christ, and destined to take up the world finally into its sphere, underlies the Christian revelation from beginning to end. This conception involves, too, throughout, all the attributes which are ascribed to the Church in the Creed; unity, sanctity, catholicity; for these come not from abroad, but have their necessity in the nature of the conception itself. The Church is by its constitution one and not many; and however it may fail to actualize its own interior sense in this form, in any given stage of its history, it can never renounce this sense as something false, but must still labor towards its full actualization as the only end in which it can be regarded as complete. So as regards holiness; and so also as regards catholicity. The Church can never, without infidelity, renounce her vocation and right to be the absolute mistress at last of all spheres of our human existence, however far short she may fall at present of the power that is needed to make good such universal pretension. This, of course, implies *visibility*; however the Church may be hindered for ages in her effort to come to a complete externalization of her divine life, as the true last sense of the world, yet to this it must assuredly come in the end, if she be indeed this last true sense; and the whole process of this effort itself, moreover, must include throughout the character of visibility as far as it goes.[13] All this, we say, lies in the New Testament, as well as in

---

necessary for its interpretation. With the rise of Mormonism and the proliferation of utopian communities, which were suspected of rejecting monogamy, Nevin's example of marital arrangements was culturally very apt.]

13. [The theme that the invisible spirit must be externalized and become visible was a standard

the faith of the primitive Christian world, expressed in the Apostles' Creed; and it is a mere play of fancy, accordingly, when the *Puritan Recorder* imagines the contrary, and so requires us to give up the article of the Creed as a pious figment.

This, however, by the way. It is not our business here, to interpret the New Testament, or vindicate the Creed. We wish simply, to fix attention on the general fact now in hand, the discrepancy which is acknowledged to hold between the true sense of this ancient symbol and Puritanism. It will be seen at once, that the difference, as presented by the *Recorder*, is very material. Three points are particularly singled out, in proof and illustration of its force, namely, the descent to Hades, the communion of saints, and the idea of the holy catholic church; but the difference itself is plainly of a general character, and must be regarded as extending to the entire Creed; for this is not made up of disconnected fragmentary parcels, but forms a single whole in harmony with itself throughout.[14] The *Recorder* indeed denies this, and declares itself out of patience with us (July 26) for assuming, without proof, that "the Creed is the product of the first ages of Christianity," and that it is to be considered at all "rotund and full" in its constitution; quoting Sir Peter King,[15] to show that it *was* a fragmentary production, after the third century. But there is no good reason here, we think, for getting out of patience on *that* side, however it may be on ours. We have never pretended that the Creed came round and full, as it now stands, from the age of the Apostles, or that it was not made to undergo some variations and additions, in the progress of its early history. We have taken pains to say just the contrary; for the purpose of planting its authority on better ground, in the conception of its organic derivation from a central principle, in the faith of the universal early Church. We have said that it *grew* forth from the primary Christian consciousness, the sense of Christ as the ground and fountain of the new creation; in which view, it might be of more or less volume, and admit many varieties of expression, without any change in its essential substance; just as the ten commandments gather themselves up at last into love to God and love to man. The Creed represents truly the faith of the universal Church in the first centuries; nobody pretends that the different forms of it before the Council

---

conviction in Romanticism. It was particularly evident in the poetry and literary theory of Coleridge that Nevin read as a young man. It also followed from Nevin's understanding of the incarnation, in which the infinite deity is manifested in visible finite form. See Appel, *Life and Work*, 668–69.]

14. [The idea that life and beauty is a function of the integration of disparate phenomena into a unique, harmonious whole was typical of Romantic aesthetics and metaphysics, as well as of the classicism of Goethe. See, for example, the German poet and philosopher Friedrich Schlegel's (1772–1829) *Transcendental Philosophy* (1801). Nevin lectured on German aesthetic theory in 1840 at Marshall College, and emphasized the organic unity of variegated parts as a fundamental aspect of beauty. See Appel, *Life and Work*, 668–69.]

15. [Sir Peter King (1669–1734), an English lawyer by profession and a successful politician who became England's Lord Chancellor, indulged his life-long interest in early church history as an avocation. He published *An Inquiry into the Constitution, Discipline, Unity and Worship of the Primitive Church* (London, 1691) as well as *The History of the Apostles Creed: with critical observations on its several articles* (London, 1703).]

Chapter 2: "Puritanism and the Creed"

of Nice [Nicea], involved any material divergences of belief; and the whole stands before us in the end as an inwardly symmetrical and complete system, shooting forth from a common root, and revealing in all its parts the power of a common life. This inward, constitutional unity of the Creed, which is something very different from the unity of a catechism or a watch, we have endeavored to establish by an actual analysis of its form and plan; and we have not met with any attempt yet to show our analysis wrong.[16] The Creed here speaks for itself. We need no outward testimony to prove its unity. All the case requires is, that we should rightly study the structure in its own forms and proportions. In this view, its roundness and wholeness are such as to make themselves felt by all serious persons. The *Recorder* itself, evidently feels this constitutional unity of the Creed, even while trying to make it out a bundle of fragments; and it is on this ground, accordingly, we have the candid and free admission, that the symbol, as a whole, falls not in with the proper life of Puritanism. This is undoubtedly correct. The variation may be more directly apprehensible at some points than it is at others; but it runs through the entire scope and structure of the Creed. Its genius is not that of Puritanism. The two "have not a kindred spirit." Their standpoint is different. The descent to hades, the communion of saints, the holy catholic church, we are told, belong not to the Puritan circle of thought, and must have a new sense forced upon them to sit even in a stiff way on Puritan lips. But they belong plainly enough to the circle of thought embodied in the Creed, and fall in naturally and easily with all its other articles. All these, then, must have a sense in the Creed, which is not fully owned in the same form by Puritanism. The christological confession holds under a different view. The forgiveness of sins, and the resurrection of the body, are thought of in different relations. The whole inward habit of the ancient faith, is not such as to fit at all the habit of the modern faith. Puritanism is not at home in the Creed: feels awkward in the use of it; prefers quietly to drop the use of it altogether. That is not the mould in which its faith has been cast. Its orthodoxy puts things together in another way.

But surely now the open acknowledgment of such a fact as this deserves attention. For only see how much it involves. The Creed expresses the faith, the primary religious mind or consciousness of the universal ancient Church. In this form, Christianity took its historical rise, in the living heart of the Christian world. The sense of the mystery ran into this fundamental shape from the beginning, and was made to underlie thus the whole subsequent life of the Church. All later symbols were held to be of force, only as they rested on the first. The old catholic Christianity throughout had its basis in the consciousness expressed by the Creed. Its fathers, martyrs, confessors and saints, would all have shrunk with dismay from the thought of holding it in any other form. The Reformation again planted itself professedly on the same ground, the faith of the New Testament, as set forth fundamentally in the Apostles' Creed. Both the Protestant confessions, in the beginning, the Reformed as well as the

---

16. [Again Nevin contrasts the mechanistic metaphors typical of the Enlightenment with the organic metaphors characteristic of Romanticism.]

Lutheran, stood here upon common ground. Protestantism was held to be, not a new faith extracted from the Bible, but the old Christian faith itself, purged from Roman corruptions; and the ancient symbols were taken, accordingly, as its necessary ground and rule, from which it was counted unlawful and unsafe to depart.[17] The confessions and catechisms of the sixteenth century, all do homage to the Apostles' Creed, as the primary text and outline of evangelical Christianity. What would Luther have said to the suggestion, that the Creed and Protestantism had not a kindred spirit? How would such an assertion have fallen on the mind of Melanchthon[18] or Calvin? Beyond all controversy, Protestantism in its original form, supposed itself to be of one mind with the Creed, and would have shuddered at the thought of treating it simply as "the fossil relic of by gone ages." Our modern *Puritanism*, then, by its own confession in the case before us, is something materially different from all previous Christianity, both Catholic and Protestant. The Creed does not suit it, and cannot be used by it without unnatural constraint. This, indeed, was not at once clear to the genius of Puritanism itself. It started with the idea that it still loved the Creed, and could frame its mouth easily enough to recite it on fit occasion; "by a sort of courtesy, gave it a place beside its formularies and catechisms;" allowed it even to figure, for a time, in the New England Primer. But the water and the oil refused at last to mix. The Creed lost its voice, and wasted gradually into a shadow. "Its life and spirit never entered into the life of the Puritan churches;" and now the secret is fairly out. "We are free to confess," says the respectable editor of the *Recorder*, "that this Creed has forsaken the Puritans, and gone over to become the idol and strength of all branches of anti-puritanism."

It is plain, then, that Puritanism, in this view, is at war at once with the Fathers and with the Reformers, with early Christianity and with the Christianity of the sixteenth century. However it may agree with them in many points of doctrine, abstractly stated, its apprehension of Christianity as a whole, the organism of its faith, the standpoint of its religious contemplation, and so, of course, the relations and bearings under which it sees all particular truths, come before us with a quite different character. Puritanism is not original Protestantism. It is an advance on this; a real breaking away from its first life; Protestantism, we may say, self-stimulated into a sort of "second growth." The simple fact that it allows no room whatever for the *Lutheran* principle, which in the beginning divided the interest of Protestantism with the Reformed, is of itself enough to prove this for any reflecting mind. It is proved here, also, however, by its want of affinity and sympathy with the Creed. Puritanism is ready to acknowledge

---

17. [Nevin was influenced here by the views of Neander and of his own colleague Schaff that the magisterial Reformation was not a total rejection of the patristic and medieval church, but rather an organic development from the early traditions and a purgation of papal corruptions. See Schaff, "The Principle of Protestantism," in *The Development of the Church*, MTSS 3, ed. Bains and Trost, 62–75.]

18. [Philip Melanchthon (1497–1560) was a Wittenberg theologian who worked closely with Martin Luther. His *Loci communes* (1521) functioned as the first Protestant theological system. He was the chief architect of the Augsburg Confession (1531), the most influential confessional document in Lutheranism.]

that the spirit of the Creed, which is the spirit of all earlier Christianity, is against it and not to its taste. It glories in setting history here at full defiance. It is *independent* in all respects, and able to stand without help on its own bottom.

We are reminded, however, that Puritanism in all this exercise of independence, is still the dutiful disciple of the Bible. What is history against the word of God; what is the voice of the Creed, in comparison with the oracles of inspiration? Why make account of Fathers and Reformers, in the presence of the Scriptures? "Puritanism," says the *Recorder*, "builds on the Scriptures, and this Creed teaches, in several respects, anti-scriptural doctrines." *We* are charged with denying that the Bible is a complete rule of faith, because we insist on the authority of the Creed: nay, the "main characteristic" of our theology, its "parent feature," is made to be an idolatrous devotion to this symbol, as a sort of rival to the written word. There would be full as much reason, by the way, to resolve our system into an idolatry to the idea of sacramental grace. We are quoted as saying: "The Bible is not the *principle* of Christianity, nor yet the rock on which the Church was built"; but what we say immediately after, is not allowed to follow: "The one principle of Christianity, the true and proper fountain of its being, is the person of Christ; not any written account or notion of his person, but the actual living revelation of it, as a fact, in the history of the world." This position, of course, is not to be contradicted. Still we have the same changes rung perpetually on the old string. "Puritanism draws its life directly from the Bible and the Holy Ghost," aside from all creeds or traditions. "No stopping place here between Puritan liberty and Romish inquisition; that is, between liberty to think, and the suppression of thought by force." All this, we are told, is fully and forever settled in New England. "So deeply has the conviction that the Bible is the only rule of faith, seated itself in the Puritan mind; so clearly have the reason and force of this principle been revealed to the descendants of the Pilgrims; and so fully are we all possessed of the right of private judgment in religion; that we should seem to be laboring the proof of self-evident truths, if we were to go into argument here" (*Puritan Recorder*, August 2).[19]

It is a blessed thing, certainly, and at times, too, saves much trouble, for "every man to be fully persuaded in his own mind." The case, however, is one that allows liberty and inquiry; and we do not ourselves find it by any means so clear, as these wholesale positions imply. We beg leave, respectfully, to reiterate our word: The Bible is not the principle of Christianity, nor its foundation; this is a fact, out of the New Testament, before it and beyond it, which has its principium in the living person of Christ; and which, in this form, must rule the interpretation of the Bible for every true believer, and not be itself ruled, through the Bible, simply by his own mind.[20] Will this be denied even in New England? We trust not. And yet, in the face of it, what becomes of all this talk about private judgment and the Bible, as the *sole* factors of the Christian

---

19 [No. 31, August 2, 1849.]

20. [See *The Mystical Presence*, in *The Mystical Presence*, MTSS 1, ed. DeBie, 174ff., the "Biblical argument," for a fuller development of this theme.]

faith? Christianity itself, as something far more than any private judgment, must assist me to the true sense of the Scriptures, or I shall study them to little purpose. The only question, then, is, where this help is to be found. Puritanism refers us for it at once to the Holy Ghost. Very good; we too say, only those who are taught by the Spirit can understand the things of the Spirit. But the question returns: Where and how are we placed in communication thus with the Holy Ghost? Puritanism, in the case before us, assumes that the mystery takes place in a purely private way,[21] each Christian being enlightened by abrupt illapses[22] for himself alone. This, however, we can by no means allow. It is against nature, against revelation, and against all sound philosophy. The agency of the Spirit on men, is conditioned universally by their living relations in the world, reaches them through the medium of their social and historical life, makes itself actual in and by the spiritual organism in which they are comprehended and carried.[23] The child is illuminated as a child, and not as a full grown man; the Hottentot[24] as an unlettered savage, and not as a graduate of Oxford or Cambridge. To read the Bible to purpose, then, requires still more than the momentary presence of the Holy Ghost. There must be previous education, a development of thought, an inward moral habit, in one word, a positive spiritual substance, to some extent, already at hand, as the fruit of history and growth, *through* which only the voice of the Spirit can ever be heard.[25] Will any sane mind dispute this?[26] We think hardly. The question, then, is not, whether the Bible shall be our sole rule of faith, but with what inward posture and habit we are to come to the study of the Bible for this purpose; for

---

21. [Nevin here rejects what he takes to be the implicit assumption of "Puritanism" (and contemporary revivalistic Protestantism) that the Holy Spirit's work is primarily devoted to the conversion and illumination of individuals, thereby ignoring the Holy Spirit's operations in the corporate and historical life of the church and the world.]

22. [An "illapse" is "a falling or flowing into."]

23. [For a similar assertion, see notes from Nevin's lectures in Erb, *Nevin's Theology*, 57–58: "There are some who think in their hatred of all tradition that God will make clear the Scriptures to every individual mind separately, without any previous instruction. This view is false. It presupposes that life can develop itself, but we know that physically considered a man could not even learn to speak without society, much less could his religious nature be unfolded without the surrounding atmosphere of morality and religion…There is no such thing as a blank mind—*tabula rasa*; and the mind that pretends to such a conclusion knows nothing of its own nature." Erb's volume is a synthesis of different versions of Nevin's lectures on theology; it was the product of a comparison of three different sets of notes from 1851 taken by three different students; the notes were remarkably similar. Nevin's rejection of Lockean empiricism and Scottish Common Sense philosophy is manifest.]

24. [Now generally considered offensive, this term probably originated with Dutch seamen who used it to refer to African natives.]

25. [Like the Romantics and Idealists who influenced him, Nevin stressed the themes that individual minds, including their religious capacities, must evolve gradually in a communal context, and that the moral and spiritual sensibilities of human communities must also evolve throughout history. See Erb, *Nevin's Theology*, 57–58.]

26. [Following Neander and Schleiermacher, and also Hegel and Rauch, Nevin embraced the notion that an individual's and a community's habits of interpretation are shaped by and presuppose participation in certain foundational cultural norms concerning how the Bible should be engaged.]

it is grossly absurd to suppose, that we can ever come to it without *some* such posture and habit. Puritanism has its spiritual habit, its tradition, its theological medium, its *a priori* governing religious consciousness, in this way, just as fully as any other section of the Christian world. The point here, accordingly, is in truth, not the Creed against the Bible; this last we all allow to be supreme; but the Creed against the inward habit and tradition of Puritanism, which, to our view, is something quite different. It is all idle, in such case, to raise the cry: The Bible, the Bible, the Bible of the Lord, are We. That is the very point which is to be settled. Other ages have had the Bible too, to study and follow; and it is not at once clear, why the use of it by modern New England is to be taken as infallibly right, and all other use of it, differing from this, as infallibly wrong. Every such assumption is suited rather to remind us of Paul's keen challenge to the Church at Corinth: "What! came the word of God out from you? Or came it unto you only [1 Cor 14:36]?" Christianity is older than Puritanism; and we see no good reason, in this case, why the elder should serve the younger, or the past become nothing to make all of the present. We see no good reason, in other words, for divesting ourselves of the general consciousness of the ancient Church, as expressed in the Apostles' Creed, and putting on in place of it the consciousness or creed of modern New England, as the only sure medium of access to the true sense of the Bible. We go for private judgment too, and Protestant independence; but for this very reason we wish to secure the conditions that are most favorable to their rational exercise; and it seems to us, in this view, we confess, vastly more safe to be in union here with the general mind of the ancient Church, than to be in conflict with it through the authority of any other system. Why may not private judgment stand in the bosom of the old faith, as fully as on the outside of it? Why should our homage to the Bible be less free and independent in the communion of the Creed, than when we substitute for this the theological habit of Puritanism? It comes to nothing, that Puritanism pleads in its favor the authority of the Bible, and charges the Creed with heresy. That is only its own word. Whole ages of Christianity, thousands and tens of thousands of God's saints, the noble army of martyrs, fathers and reformers, have thought differently, with one voice proclaiming the Creed as the true and proper sense of the Scriptures, the glorious ground type of the Christian faith. A mind in no sympathy with the Creed, will, of course, not find it in the Bible; just as the Unitarian fails to find there the mystery of the Trinity, and so appeals to it as *his* witness against all other orthodox authorities. But let such sympathy prevail, and at once the whole case is changed; the supposed heresies of the venerable symbol brighten into glorious truths; and the Bible is found, with easy interpretation, to speak the same sense from every page. When the *Puritan Recorder* claims the witness of the Bible against the Creed, it simply asks us to accept beforehand its own scheme of religion, through the medium of which the Bible is made to speak what it pretends. We, for our part, protest that we find in it no such meaning whatever. On all the points urged by the *Recorder*, the Creed is in full harmony with the Bible.

It would be strange indeed, if the sense of Christianity in the age when the New Testament was formed, were a less sure medium for its interpretation, than a later habit of thought altogether different. The presumption here, is at once powerfully against Puritanism. The true standpoint for understanding the Bible, is that of the Creed; and any view that may be taken of it from any different position is of small force, as weighed against the light in which it is seen and read from this position. "To the law and to the testimony" [Is. 8:20], by all means; but then to save the force of this appeal, we insist on coming to the rule in a right way. Let us have the Bible in the element of its own life. And where else can we rationally pretend to find this, if it be not allowed to start, at least, in the Apostles' Creed?

Whether any protest may be made against the declaration of the *Puritan Recorder*, on the part of the general Puritan interest itself, remains to be seen. We would fain trust, that there are many in New England as well as out of it, owning the power of this system, on whose feelings still the declaration must fall harshly, and who will be disposed to demur to its authority. It is of itself, however, something very significant, that so far as we have heard no such protest has been uttered as yet from any quarter. Is silence here to be construed into consent? Or does it imply, at least, indifference and apathy towards the whole subject, as one of comparatively small account in any view? Such a declaration, made from any respectable source in the name of Protestantism, during the sixteenth century, would have called out, most certainly, from all sides, a loud indignant rebuke. Now it is met, at best, with passive unconcern. Congregational New England has no voice to vindicate the authority of the Creed. Presbyterianism too is silent. Were the honor of its Shorter Catechism invaded in the same way, there would be no lack of remonstrance and complaint.[27] And yet the Creed is the *primary* Protestant symbol, of more sacredness and force, assuredly, than any catechism.[28] From other non-episcopal bodies, of course, (if we may except the Reformed Dutch), not even the most gentle protest was to be expected. It needs no proof that our sects

---

27. [The Shorter Catechism, composed between 1646 and 1647, was authorized by the Westminster Assembly of Divines and was intended to bring the Church of England into greater conformity with the Scottish Presbyterian church. Although it was never adopted by Parliament, it became very influential in both Presbyterian and Congregational circles (with some modifications), and was widely used as a model catechism by the New England Puritans.]

28. We have heard of one Presbyterian paper, in which the *Recorder's* vilification of the Creed was republished, without a word of exception or censure. [Research inquiries to the Presbyterian Historical Society in Philadelphia resulted in no further information regarding the precise issue in which Nevin's Apostles' Creed matter was addressed. This was confirmed by the Society's researcher in an email message dated February 16, 2016.] We meet the same portentous phenomenon in the *Lutheran Observer,* [17, no. 38 (September 21, 1849)]. It is still for this model of Lutheran orthodoxy, it seems, an open question, whether the *symbolum apostolicum* [Trans. "Apostles' Creed"] teaches false doctrine or not. While some assign it a place beyond its merits, "others as learned and pious as they," charge it with heresy, "when explained agreeably to its original design and import." On this issue, *"we are anxious that our readers should be made acquainted with both sides of the question, and therefore lay before them the following article on the subject, taken from the Puritan Recorder."* The *Observer* itself thus is *non liquet* [Trans. "not clear"].

Chapter 2: "Puritanism and the Creed"

generally, are without zeal for the Creed. Its historical, catholic, sacramental, mystical character, suits not their mind. There can be no veneration for the Creed, where there is no veneration for the Church.

It seems to us, however, that this is a case which is entitled to general serious consideration. We have no right to overlook it, or to pass it by as of only insignificant account. The question, whether the Apostles' Creed is of force for evangelical Protestantism, however it be answered, is a very great question, which ought not to go without a clear and full response, that may be heard and laid to heart on all sides. The Creed is a theological unit. It cannot be taken to pieces, without destruction. From its own standpoint and posture, all its articles flow with easy necessity as the proclamation of a single fact. In this form it is the primitive type of Christianity, the mould in which the faith of the gospel first took living shape in the Church. It was so acknowledged at the Reformation, as well as in all ages before. Now, we are told, it has become a fossil relic, with the spirit of which Puritanism owns no inward affinity or fellowship. Is this confession to be accepted as truth? If not, the occasion certainly requires that it should be met with some open contradiction. Puritanism should let the world know, that the Creed has *not* forsaken it, and is *not* still to be counted a dead letter only in its old confessional Primer. If, on the other hand, the confession be accepted as true, the occasion requires that a fact so strange and startling should be openly explained and made to appear right. Silence here is wholly out of place. A great theological interest is at stake. Here are two *minds,* two theological habits, the old catholic consciousness and the modern Puritan consciousness, "having no kindred spirit," each of which claims to be, not at once the Bible (neither the Creed nor the New England Primer[29] is *that*) but still the only true and safe preparation for coming to the sense of the Bible, the necessary "ποῦ στῶ"[30] for the right understanding of its divine contents. Which are we to follow? Puritanism acknowledges its own novelty, and yet requires us to quit the Creed, and cast ourselves upon its independent separate guidance instead, as the infallible rule and measure of Christianity. *I* build upon the Scriptures, it exclaims; the Creed is a human production, and teaches false doctrine; follow *me.* Truly, a very great and solemn demand! Let it be heard with all becoming seriousness and respect. Still, we tremble at the thought of such a deep rupture with the old Christian consciousness, and venture to ask: By what authority doest *thou* this thing, and who *gave* thee *such* authority? And this question, we say, demands a calm and clear answer; a scientific answer; an answer that may satisfy at once the yearnings of pious feeling, and the necessities of earnest theological thought.

---

29. [Originally published in Boston in the late seventeenth century the *New-England Primer* remained in use into the nineteenth century. The Westminster Shorter Catechism (1647) was appended to some editions of the *Primer.* For the text of the Shorter Catechism see Schaff, *The Creeds of Christendom*, III:676.]

30. [Trans. "vantage point."]

Again we say, in conclusion, we are anxious that the *animus* of this article should not be misunderstood. Our aim is not war, but God's free truth in the spirit of love and peace. We need no angry voice, to remind us of the vast achievements and high merits of Puritanism. All that is fully and constantly before our mind. We need no outward advocate, to urge the force of its peculiar claims. We know what they are, by inborn constitutional sense. The hardest Puritan we have to do with always, is the one we carry, by birth and education, in our own bosom. But the misery of it is, for our quiet, that the Catholic is there too, and will not be at rest. In other words, we are forced to do homage to *both* tendencies, and have no power, like many, to resign ourselves wholly to the separate beck of one.[31] According to the *Boston Recorder*, "there is no stopping place between Puritan liberty and Romish inquisition, between liberty to think and the suppression of thought by force." But just this we are by no means prepared to believe.[32] On the contrary, we are deeply persuaded that the sense of authority and the exercise of free thought go hand in hand together, and cannot be disjoined in the moral world without deep prejudice to truth. We are deeply persuaded too, in the case before us, that Catholicism and Puritanism both enter of right into the constitution of Christianity, and that neither can legitimately exclude the other. The problem of their true and proper union, is indeed one of no common difficulty; the great problem, as it would seem, for the new era of Christianity, which is now so generally supposed to be at hand.[33] The inmost wants of the time, however, cry aloud for its solution. Blind outward authority, and mere private judgment, are alike insufficient as a key to the Bible. What we desire is, that this should be acknowledged, and a true conciliation at least aimed at between the great tendencies, which are here placed in opposition and conflict. It is not by the simple assertion of its own life, but in *so* asserting this life as to leave no room for the other side of religion, that Puritanism seems to us to be too often at fault. When it claims to be at once the sum and substance and end of all Christianity, the absolute sense of the Bible, and requires that all other systems, the old Catholic, the primitive Protestant, the thinking of all other times and of all other lands, shall be tested and tried by itself or by the Bible to its particular mind, which is just the same thing, we cannot but feel that the claim is at war with all reason and right. Such exclusiveness involves vast wrong to the cause itself, in whose favor it is

---

31. [The theme that some dimension of truth is present in both polls of a dialectical tension was prevalent in the work of Hegel and those thinkers whom he influenced, including Friedrich Rauch.]

32. Romanism, in its genuine shape, takes the same ground; only planting itself on the contrary pole of the antithesis, and requiring us to accept our faith in an *ab extra* [Trans. "extra"] way from the hands of the Pope. Both poles, thus disjoined, come to very much the same falsehood in the end. This we hope to show more fully in our promised review of *Brownson's Quarterly*; and as many seem to be a little impatient with the delay of this article, we here take occasion to say, that it will appear, God willing, in our next number. Good reasons have stood in the way of its appearing sooner. [The promised article was finally published by Nevin, "Brownson's Quarterly Review," *Mercersburg Review* 2 (1850) 33–80.]

33. [This hope for the future of the church was strongly and persistently articulated by Nevin's colleague Philip Schaff.]

thus urged. Puritanism is bound to acknowledge the rights of other tendencies, the Catholic, the Lutheran, the original Reformed, for instance, if it would have its own acknowledged, and so cooperate efficiently in the great task of bringing Christianity to its last universal form. Let it do this, and we are ready always to sit respectfully at its feet, and drink in wisdom from its lips. We reserve to ourselves, of course, in this posture, the right of free contradiction, where it may seem to be needed; and we shall not insult it, by supposing its granite nature so soft that any such freedom can ever require an apology.

Postscript

Though in no very immediate relation to the subject of the foregoing article, we may as well notice here as anywhere else, if we are to notice at all, the sharp dissatisfaction expressed by the *Puritan Recorder*, and in another quarter also, with the article in our last number, referring to the case of Mr. Lesley.[34] It has been held up to reproach, as a direct vindication of this gentleman's opinions and course; and the attempt is made, on this ground,to insinuate against all connected, whether nearly or remotely, with the *Mercersburg Review*, a general sympathy with error and a wish to set aside church authority and the binding force of creeds!

We are sorry, that any occasion should have been furnished by this article, however innocently, for those who seek occasion, thus to pervert and misrepresent our true position, for the purpose of keeping out of sight the questions of deep practical concern, that are really at issue between us and themselves. Our interest in these, on the score simply of their general theological significance, is so sincerely honest and earnest, that we are always made to feel sick at heart, when we find any merely personal or party reference thrust forward into their place, and some accidental purely subordinate question allowed to run away thus with the attention that should be confined to the main interest in debate. We have no concern for the cause of Mr. Lesley whatever, and no wish, certainly, to endorse or vindicate his views in any way; we are very certain too, that nothing of this sort can be legitimately saddled on the particular article to which this notice refers; still we regret, for the reason just stated, that more care was not taken to anticipate and shut out more effectually the possibility of its being abused into any such wrong and injurious sense. We hope to profit by the lesson, and shall try to bear in mind that we need the wisdom of the serpent, no less than the simplicity of the dove, to keep at bay the *odium theologicum*,[35] with which unfortunately we are called too often to deal as the substitute of zeal for the truth.

---

34. [T. C. Porter, Review of *Private Judgment—Address to the Suffolk North Association of Congregational Ministers, with Sermons on the Rule of Faith, the Inspiration of the Scriptures, and the Church*, 515–19.]

35. [Trans. "theological hatred."]

It is not true that the article in question "enters with all zeal into the case of Mr. Lesley and his come-outer church," and makes common cause with the man and his measures. It explicitly says the contrary, and condemns the separatistic position he has allowed himself to take. The design of the article, as any candid mind may easily see, was not at all to support Mr. Lesley in his theological or ecclesiastical position; he is only an accident in the case; the true thing proposed, was to exemplify the inconsistency and contradiction of those, who cry *up private judgment* as a last authority in religion, and yet in this and similar cases, are not willing to let their principle prevail beyond certain metes [measures] and bounds of their own imposition. The very caption of the article is "Private Judgment," and its whole aim and scope is, not to magnify this, certainly, but to bring it into discredit. How should it be imagined, then, to go in favor of such individualism, under its most rampant form? It is throughout, an *argumentum ad hominem*.[36] It takes Puritanism, or Independency, on its own premises, and charges it in the case of Mr. Lesley, any similar case would have answered for illustration just as well, with palpable and gross self-contradiction. In this view the argument is of full force. If the Church of the Creed be a phantom, and Christianity the sense simply of the Bible, as every "Tom, Dick and Harry" in the land, *pax verbo*,[37] may choose to take it, we see not, certainly, on what ground any church censure can legitimately hold against the exercise of such independency in any form.

Such we take to be the drift and purpose of this offending article. If, however, it might be supposed by any to carry covertly a different sense, nothing could be more unfair, surely, than to lay the burden of such different sense on the general character of the *Review*, contradicted, as any child might see it to be, by the whole spirit and bearing of the *Review* itself, from the beginning. It has been asked, whether the Church in which *we* stand would not also exclude a man for grave confessional errors. We reply, it would do so certainly. The uniform doctrine, moreover, of this *Review* has been, that the right as well as the duty to preserve the faith once delivered to the saints, resides by divine appointment in the Church. Private judgment and independency, in the ultra Puritan sense, we do not allow, but consider rather to be in bad opposition to Christ and Christianity. The sect spirit thus we hold to be emphatically *Antichrist*.[38] It is all in order, therefore, for *us* to insist on church authority and the evil of schism. But it is not in order for those to do so, who profess to give full scope to the sect maxim: "No creed but the Bible and private judgment." When *they*, notwithstanding, in virtue of their associated judgment, pretend to lay bit and bridle on the principle of independency where it varies from themselves, and charge it with "come-outerism,"[39]

---

36. [Trans. "attack on one's character."]

37. [Trans. "literally."]

38. [See Nevin, "Antichrist," in *One, Holy, Catholic, and Apostolic*, Tome One, MTSS 5, ed. Hamstra, 163–232.]

39. ["Come-outerism" was a term that became popular in the 1830's to suggest anyone who left a church or political party because it was perceived to be ideologically or theologically impure,

Chapter 2: "Puritanism and the Creed"

as the word goes, for being independent in such separate style, they give the lie to their own principle, and may well be called upon to explain and justify the contradiction involved in their conduct.

The "Presbyterian," we understand, finds it a bad sign against us, that we are against creeds; on the familiar adage, that men do not oppose creeds commonly till creeds come to be in opposition first to themselves. The "Puritan," on the other hand, finds it a bad sign that we make too much of creeds. "Those," we are told, "who give to the creed and tradition an authority superior to that of the Scriptures, can hardly be inconsistent in endorsing for one who denies the plenary inspiration of the Bible." These two insinuations, of course, do not cohere very well together. For any fair reader of our *Review*, both must be taken as simple balderdash.

We are not opposed to creeds. No one can go against creeds, who goes for the Church as an article of faith. The difficulty with us here is, not in the too little of our faith, for the taste of the dissatisfied, but in its *too much*. To oppose sects, is not to oppose creeds; but just the reverse. What is needed above all things to upset their tyrannical arbitrariness, is the sense of a true catholic tradition springing from the life of the Church, in a real way, as it has stood from the beginning. This starts beyond all controversy in the Apostles' Creed; while on this foundation it makes room for much more, in the way of historical orthodox faith, comprehended with more or less success in later symbols, Catholic and Protestant, which the Church is bound to acknowledge and respect to the end of the world. For creeds, so called, that affect to set aside the foundation creed of Christianity, substituting for it some original scheme of their own, we do entertain, it is true, but small admiration or regard. But such upstart faith is itself at war with the true idea of a creed. It makes no account of history, but just fancies its own system from the skies. The sect spirit is universally unhistorical, and so, to the same extent, *creedless*. Those who oppose creeds, on the other hand, independents, radicals, come-outers, are always unhistorical. *We* go with all our might for the idea of the Church, for the Apostles' Creed, for catholic tradition, for historical Christianity; as the only refuge and help from the horrid evils, that seem to yawn upon us continually from the abyss of the unchurchly system.

Is this to wrong the Bible? So thinks the "Puritan"; but so think not we. We have full faith in its inspiration, and own its authority to be supreme in all questions of religion. But you "give to the Creed and tradition an authority superior to that of the Scriptures?" Not at all. We give to them only an authority superior, at worst, to that of the Puritan scheme of thought, the New England tradition, so far forth as this same may be found seeking to thrust the old faith out of the way. Forced to an election between two conflicting traditions, one resting in the Apostles' Creed, and the other charging it with *heresy*, we choose the first, as on the whole more rational and safe than the second. This is the only true issue in the case. To make the Puritan tradition *per se* the same thing with the Bible, is but an impudent begging of the whole question

---

particularly in regard to the issue of slavery.]

in debate. We do not believe that Puritanism, as distinguished from the old catholic sense of the Creed, expresses at all the true sense of the Bible; and we have yet to learn by what right we are to be shut up to its authority here, that is a whit better, to say the least, than that claimed to the same purport by the Church of Rome. Why should the fathers of New England be counted more infallible, as interpreters of the Bible, than the fathers of the ancient Church in Africa or Asia Minor? Did these last love the Bible less? Had Augustine less regard for its authority than Edwards?[40] *Why*, to show my obedience to the Bible, must I give up the Creed, and immerse my mind in the element of Puritanism only in its stead? To say: "Come to the Bible, without *any* medium," is pitiful nonsense. No man *can* come to it in that way: and the least really free in their approach to it ordinarily, are just those who are most forward to dream and talk of their freedom in any such fantastical style.

---

40. [Jonathan Edwards (1703–58) was a celebrated colonial American pastor, theologian, and philosopher. The various components of his complex thought were multiple, ranging from Lockean epistemology, to Platonic metaphysics, and to orthodox Calvinism. He was a defender of the Great Awakening, a critical analyst of religious experience, a theocentric ethicist, an amateur scientist, an apologist for predestination, and an evangelical preacher.]

Chapter 3

Nevin and Proudfit: Opposed Views of the Early Creeds

Editors' Introduction to John Williams Proudfit's "The Apostles' Creed" and to John Williamson Nevin's "The Anti-Creed Heresy"

John Williams Proudfit (1803–c. 1870), son of the prominent Presbyterian clergyman and author Alexander Proudfit (1770–1843), graduated from Union College, Schenectady, NY in 1821 and from Princeton Theological Seminary in 1824. He graduated from Union College the same year that Nevin graduated from that very school. There is no information whether the two future theologians, who later became antagonists, had much contact, social or otherwise, at their collegiate alma mater. At Princeton Proudfit would have been acquainted with Charles Hodge (1797–1878) whose early period of teaching at Princeton spanned 1822 to 1826.[1] When Hodge took a leave to study in Europe (1826–28), John Williamson Nevin, whose theological and exegetical abilities Hodge admired, was appointed to occupy temporarily his teaching post at Princeton. In their subsequent careers Proudfit would continue to follow Hodge's lead, while Nevin would not.

Proudfit, who was of Scots-Irish decent and hailed from a family of "Seceders" who had opposed lay patronage and lax discipline in the Church of Scotland, was ordained into the Presbyterian ministry in 1825 and served as a pastor in Newburyport, MA. He later taught Latin and Greek at New York University (1841–48) and at Rutgers College, New Brunswick, New Jersey (1848–67). While at Rutgers he often preached in Dutch Reformed churches in the Raritan Valley, where that tradition was prevalent. Proudfit even began to publish a literary and theological journal for the Dutch Reformed Church, *The New Brunswick Review*, in 1854, but it was discontinued after one year. During that year he attacked not only the works of Nevin, but also those of Schaff. In spite of his frequent displays of ire, Proudfit was much more than an acerbic polemicist, for his academic prowess with the two classical languages is abundantly clear in the text and footnotes of this essay. In recognition of his linguistic skills, in 1841 he was awarded an honorary Doctor of Divinity degree by Union College.

---

1. For more on the relationship of Hodge and Nevin see *Coena Mystica: Debating Reformed Eucharistic Theology*, MTSS 2, ed. DeBie, xiii–lvii.

Chapter 3: Nevin and Proudfit: Opposed Views of the Early Creeds

After reading Nevin's three 1849 articles on the Apostles' Creed published earlier in this volume, Proudfit penned a lengthy essay which appeared in *The Biblical Repertory and Princeton Review* in October 1852 (vol. 24. no. 4, 662–77) challenging Nevin's views on the Creed. The two also disagreed in print on the significance of the Heidelberg Catechism. Proudfit published an earlier article on the Catechism in the January 1852 issue of *The Biblical Repertory and Princeton Review* (vol. 24, no. 1, 91–184) and Nevin responded with an article on the Catechism in *The Mercersburg Review* in the March 1852 publication (vol. IV, no. 1, 155–86).[2] The rhetoric between the two became increasingly combative over the matter of both the Heidelberg Catechism and the Apostles' Creed, with Nevin denouncing Proudfit as a "Puritan." The title of Nevin's answer to Proudfit on the Creed provides a clue to the quarrelsome nature of Nevin's response, calling his critic's position the "Anti-Creed Heresy." The exchange between the two became so rancourous that Nevin began to fear that it was damaging the relationship between the Dutch and German branches of the Reformed family in the United States.[3]

First, we will consider the text of Proudfit's lengthy assessment and critique of Nevin's position on the Apostles' Creed and its signficance. After the Proudfit essay we will present the text of Nevin's reply to his detractor.

Proudfit began his essay with a large number of comments concerning what he considered to be the core of Christian faith, life, and true Christian doctrine, all of which he supported with numerous scriptural references. The remainder of the article which refers especially to the church's earliest significant theologians, the prime leaders of the Protestant Reformation, and more contemporary theologians are cited to show that while the Apostles' Creed is an important statement of Christian faith, in the eyes of the most esteemed ecclesial authorities throughout history it does not supersede Scripture as the earliest primary historical source and confession of Christian belief. That, he believes, is Nevin's erroneous viewpoint. Proudfit was convinced that Nevin "puts the creed in place of the Bible." He labels Nevin's position "philosophical Catholicism" and alleges, "It is a combination of the mystical philosophy of our own age with the Romish idea of the Church." If Nevin's stance is accepted, Proudfit argued, "The Church instead of singing, 'Thy word is everlasting truth,' must sing, '*My Creed* is everlasting truth.'"

In his retort "The Anti-Creed Heresy" Nevin opened his attack on Proudfit by repeating the emphases in his three earliest articles on the Apostles' Creed found at the beginning of this volume. Since Proudfit made great use of the early Christian fathers, Nevin argued that the "early fathers . . . could not possibly have dreamed of any such creed-less use of the Scriptures, as Dr. Proudfit has laid himself out to fasten upon their theology, turning all history topsy-turvy to carry his prodigious point."

---

2. Nevin's biographer Theodore Appel makes reference to the feud about the Catechism in *Life*, 405–9.

3. Nevin, "Dutch Crusade," *Mercersburg Review* 6 (1854) 67–117.

EDITORS' INTRODUCTION

According to Nevin, the early church writers and Protestant leaders did not contend for the unchristological, unchurchly, unsacramental, unhistorical theological system that Proudfit, the *Puritan Recorder*, and his others critics prefer. Nevin argued, "Our controversy then with Dr. Proudfit [and others] . . . regards the symbolical authority of the Apostles' Creed. Is it still of binding force for the universal church *in its proper historical sense*, the only basis of all other symbols, as it was held in the beginning . . . ?" Nevin's reply was an emphatic and uncompromising "yes."

The Apostles' Creed[1]

[by John Williams Proudfit]

[Bibliography]

[The following is Proudfit's introductory bibliography, in which minor changes have been made to correct it and to provide more information about the resources that he cites.]

Tyrannius Rufinus, Presbyter of Aquileia, *Commentary on the Creed* (Paris, 1580) Vol. I, 169–94.
Explicatio Symboli Apostolici, from Codice Seculi *circiter XI*. (Vatican: Scriptorum Veterum Collectio Vaticana) Vol. IX, 384, &c.
Robert Bellarmine. *Explication du Symbole des Apôtres. Catechismes Philosophiques, Polémiques, &c.* Annoted and Published by M. L. Migne. (Paris, 1842) Vol.II, 270, &c.
James Ussher, Archbishop of Armagh, *de Symbolis Diatriba. Works*. (Dublin, 1847) Vol. VII, 308 &c..
Gisbert Vöetius, *de Symbolo Apostolico. Disputationes Theologicae Selectae* (Utrecht, 1648).
Gerhard Jan Voss, *Dissertationes Tres de Tribus Symbolis. Theses Theologicae et Historicae* (Hague, 1658).
Johann Heinrich Heideggeri, *Dissertation de Symbolo Apostolico* (Zurich, 1680), Vol. II.
Herman Witsius, *Exercitationes sacrae in symbolum quod Apostolorum dictur* (Amsterdam, 1697), Volume IV.
Lord Peter King, *The History of the Apostles' Creed: with critical observations on its several articles* (London: 1702).
John Williamson Nevin, "The Apostles' Creed," *The Mercersburg Review* I (March, May, July 1849), 105–27, 201–21, 313–47.]

---

1. [John Williams Proudfit, *The Biblical Repertory and Princeton Review* 24 (October 1852) 602–77).

[Confession in Scripture]

The first act of the Christian life is, "I believe." In this act, the soul awakes to the consciousness of a new life. It enters on a new creation; old things are passed away, behold all things are become new. It passes from death to life. It is delivered from the power of darkness and translated into the kingdom of God's dear Son. It is pardoned, justified, has peace with God, through our Lord Jesus Christ, has access into this grace wherein it stands, and rejoices in hope of the glory of God. The love of God is poured out within it by the Holy Ghost. And now begins that marvelous inward history which, through sore conflicts, and "groanings which cannot be uttered" [Rom 8:26], finds its true consummation at last, in "the manifestation of the sons of God [Rom 8:19]."[2]

And as the Christian life begins in faith, so it is sustained, advanced, and completed by it. The Christian "walks by faith" [2 Cor 5:7], "works by faith" [Jas 2:17], "endures by faith" [1 Cor 13:7], and finally "dies in faith" [Heb 11:13]. As the first act of his inward life is, "I believe in the Lord Jesus Christ," its last is a recollection and re-affirmation of that faith, "I know whom *I have believed* [1 Tim 1:12]."

Heathenism had no faith, because it had no truth. Its notions of supernatural things were expressed by such terms as ἔννοιαι [Trans. "knowledge"] and γνῶμα [Trans. "opinion"]; but πίστις [Trans. "faith"] was unknown to its religious phraseology. Christianity was from the first distinguished as the Faith, the Faith in Christ, the Chrsitian Faith. This was at once, the reproach of its enemies and the glory of its disciples. They were called, and called themselves, *believers* and the *faithful*.[3]

As it stands in the Christian system and history, faith is truth apprehended and received on the testimony of God. When it is so apprehended and received, truth passes into the subjective form and becomes faith.[4] In both forms it is the gift and operation of God. "*Truth* is the word of God" [John 17:17] (to transpose the terms of our Saviour's declaration) and "faith is the gift of God [Eph 2:8]." Christ is at once, "the Truth" [John 14:6] and "the Author and Finisher of Faith [Heb 12:20]."

All the great deeds of holy history have been achieved, and all its renowned characters formed "through faith." (Heb. xi.)

---

2. [For Nevin it is significant that Proudfit identifies the work of the Holy Spirit with its operations on the soul of the individual and the initiation of the soul's inward journey. Little mention is made of the Spirit's nurturing work in and through the church as an objective, corporate, and historical body.]

3. The very use of these terms shows the general impression made on the world, and the consciousness of the church herself, that the essential claim of Christianity was to be derived immediately and wholly from God.

4. [Proudfit here describes the apprehension of the truth of Christianity as being prior to its subjective appropriation. Charles Hodge agreed, later condemning any "mysticism" that "assigns more importance to the emotions than to the intellect" (*Systematic Theology*, I, 64), and warning that "Without right apprehensions of the Supreme Being, there can be no right affections toward him" (*Systematic Theology*, I, 101). Nevin contested this epistemic sequence that privileged cognition.]

Chapter 3: Nevin and Proudfit: Opposed Views of the Early Creeds

To beget this faith is the distinct object of the history and all the various revelations of the Gospel. "These things are written that ye might believe [John 20:31]."

This faith, however, so "precious" [1 Pet 1:7], and of such wondrous might, is not a mere mental act. It must find its way forth in the form of utterance or confession. "With the heart man believeth unto righteousness, but with the mouth confession is made unto salvation [Rom 10:10]."

How large a part of the acts and teachings of our Lord, his precepts, rebukes, and commendations, his whole discipline in a word, had a distinct and special reference to the production, strengthening, and manifestation of faith! "Wherefore is it that ye have no faith? O thou of little faith, wherefore didst thou doubt? Be not faithless but believing. Verily I say unto you, have faith in God. Only believe; all things are possible to him, that believeth. Said I not unto thee, that if thou wouldst believe, thou shouldst see the glory of God? Believe in God, believe also in me. He that believeth in me hath everlasting life and shall never perish, but I will raise him up at the last day. He that believeth in me, the works that I do shall he do also, and greater works than these shall he do." [Quotations include Matt 8:26, Mark 11:22, Matt 19:26, John 14:1, 6:47, 14:12.] What vast blessings, what divine might in faith!

To draw out this faith into manifestation and confession, was also, on many occasions, his special and evident object. Thus, when he delayed and apparently slighted the prayer of the Syrophenician woman, till her faith showed itself too strong and persevering to be disheartened by slights and delays, and then exclaimed, (as if faith were an admirable spectacle to the Son of God himself) "O woman, great is thy faith! be it unto thee even as thou wilt" [Matt 15:28]; and when the centurion said that diseases waited on his omnipotent "word," even as disciplined soldiers on the command of their officer, "Jesus turned to his disciples, and said, Verily I say unto you, I have not found so great faith, no, not in Israel [Matt 8:12]!" And yet more distinctly, when he proposed such questions as these, "Believest thou this? believest thou on the Son of God? believest thou that I am able to do this? believest thou not that I am in the Father and the Father in me [John 11:26, Matt 9:28, John 14:10]?"

Each of these questions was intended to elicit a creed or confession of divine and saving faith. The responses to each was (where it is given) such a creed.[5] Of such creeds the Bible contains great store. Some of these are short and simple indeed. "Abraham believed God [Rom 4:3]." His creed was comprehended in one word. His faith embraced one fact, "that God was faithful who had promised." But what a mighty and prolific faith was that! "It was imputed to him for righteousness. He became the father of all them that believe" [Rom 4:3]; and "through" that "faith there sprang of one, and him as good as dead, so many as the stars of the sky in multitude, and as the sand which is by the seashore innumerable [Heb 11:12–14]." The creed of Peter (for which he was "blessed" and honoured to be the first to proclaim the rock on which the

---

5. [This view that the Bible implicitly contains a variety of short creeds in the form of personal verbal confessions was espoused by Charles Hodge of Princeton Seminary.]

church was to be built, and to receive his name from it) consisted of but one article, "Thou art the Christ, the Son of the living God [Matt 16:16]." On another occasion it was amplified by the additional clause, "Thou hast the words of eternal life [John 6:68]." Nathanael's creed was, "Rabbi, thou art the Son of God, thou art the King of Israel [John 1:49]." That of Martha, "Yea, Lord, I believe that thou art the Christ, the Son of God, which should come into the world [John 11:27]." That of the restored blind man, "Lord, I believe" [John 9:38] (i.e. "in the Son of God," see verse 35). That of the disciples, collectively, is thus expressed by our Saviour, "They have believed that thou didst send me [John 17:8]." All future sharers in the benefit of his intercession are described as "those who shall *believe on me* through their word [John 17:20]." And the award of the last day will bestow glory and honour and immortality on those who *confess Christ* before men.

In the Apostolic Church and ministry, we find the same necessity, virtue and power awarded to faith, the same importance attached to its confession, the same methods employed to elicit it. Philip said to the Eunuch of Ethiopia, "if thou believest with all thine heart, thou mayest." "And he answered and said, I believe that Jesus Christ is the Son of God. And Philip baptized him, and he went on his way rejoicing [Acts 8:37–39]." "King Agrippa," said Paul, "believest thou the prophets [Acts 26:27]?" Alas! that this noble interrogation and confiding solicitation to faith should only have called forth "almost" a confession of it! The Gentile world were [sic] admitted into the Church through "a door of faith." Acts xiv. 27. And here is Paul's statement of "the word of faith which we preach:" "If thou shalt confess with thy mouth the Lord Jesus Christ, and shalt believe in thine heart that God hath raised him from the dead, thou shalt be saved [Rom 10:9]."

Do we inquire into the philosophy of this divine energy and these incomparable virtues and benefits of faith? All must be finally resolved into this: "Even so, Father, for so it seemed good in thy sight [Matt 11:26]!"

> This faith in the promises of God, this relying and acquiescing in his word and faithfulness, the Almighty takes well at our hands, as a great mark of homage, paid by us frail creatures, to his 'goodness' and 'truth,' as well as to his 'power' and 'wisdom;' and accepts it as an acknowledgment of his peculiar providence and benignity to us . . . This oblation of a heart fixed with dependence on, and affection to him, is the most acceptable tribute we can pay him; the foundation of true devotion, and life of all religion. . . . This is the way that God deals with poor, frail mortals. He is graciously pleased to take it well of them, and give it the place of righteousness, and a kind of merit in his sight, if they believe his promises, and have a steadfast relying on his veracity and goodness.[6]

---

6. [John Locke, *The Reasonableness of Christianity, as Delivered in the Scriptures*, ed. John C. Higgins-Biddle, 136–37. John Locke (1632–1704) was a celebrated English philosopher and political theorist. He pioneered the central tenet of empiricism that the mind is a *tabula rasa* upon which experiences are recorded, articulated a powerful justification for religious toleration, formulated an influential version of social contract theory, and inspired many of the core values of classic republicanism.

Subjectively considered, the marvelous energy of faith lies in this, that it opens and first makes visible and real to the soul a new world of sublime and certain truth, invisible to sense and undiscoverable by reason, and therefore before unknown, but to the objects and persons of which, the believing soul finds that it stands even now in the most intimate relations, and that at the extinction of this mortal breath, it will enter on them fully, and leave all else behind. In the world which faith discloses, God stands fully revealed to the believer as his Father, Christ as his Redeemer, Advocate, Friend, Teacher, Brother, the Holy Spirit as his Sanctifier, angels as ministering spirits to him, life as a state of tuition and discipline, heaven as his home, glory and honour and immortality as the proper and only worthy objects of his ambition.[7] He sees at his feet the precipice over which he himself, till awakened and rescued by grace, was about to fall into endless misery. He sees his fellow men blind and unconscious as he once was himself, in danger of the same perdition.[8] These things may doubtless be professed by those who in works deny them; they may be preached with the tongues even of envy or strife, or for filthy lucre, or dominion over the flock of God; and though they be thus preached "with the tongues of men and angels" [1 Cor 13:1], and with such a confidence of their truth as "to remove mountains" [1 Cor 13:2], never send one transforming ray into the deceiving and self-deceived soul. But where they are seen and felt and "believed in the heart" [Rom 10:10], they must appeal to every faculty and energy of man with a power which will make "the things that are seen and temporal" fade away into utter insignificance before "those which are not seen and are eternal [2 Cor 4:18]."

With such ideas of faith and of its confession, bequeathed to her by her Lord and his inspired apostles, we are not surprised to find that the early Christian church turned all her thoughts and energies towards awakening faith in the minds of men, and drawing it forth in confession. In this work, she had all the wisdom, might, and magnificence of the world against her; its learning, its habits, its political organizations and religious establishments, its pride and sensuality. To all this array of material and intellectual power, she had nothing to oppose but the divine verities, and unconquerable energy of her faith. The weapons of her warfare were not carnal, yet were they mighty through God to the pulling down of fortresses, the overthrow of

---

It is noteworthy that Proudfit chose to quote this premier British empiricist of the late seventeenth century, thereby manifesting the partial reliance of his theology upon that tradition. Locke describes the confession of faith as a voluntary and meritorious human act of honoring God, based on probable evidences. Proudfit modifies Locke's scenario by emphasizing the necessary operation of the Holy Spirit in enabling the individual to affirm the veracity of the biblical data, and by asserting that the faith awakened by the Spirit involves every human faculty. Although Proudfit insisted that rationality cannot discover the truths of revelation by itself, he still described faith as beginning with cognitive conviction.]

7. [Here Proudfit expresses the disjunction of the natural and the supernatural that was typical of British empiricism and the "Common Sense" philosophy.]

8. [Proudfit tends to situate the inception and growth of faith primarily in the drama of the individual's movement from sin to repentance and sanctification.]

reasonings and every high thing that exalted itself against the knowledge of God. She was victorious in the conflict; and "this was the victory which overcame the world, even our faith [1 John 5:4]."

In this purely spiritual form of church extension, she had almost overspread the world and won to Christ all its centres and citadels of influence and civilization before a solitary church edifice had been erected on the face of the earth.[9]

Surely, then, her maxims and methods are worthy of our deepest attention. Have we not the same truth in our possession, the same objects before us, the same promises of Christ's presence? The work and conflict of the church is and ever must be, through all outward changes, substantially the same; the setting up of the kingdom of God, a purely spiritual and "inward reign" [Luke 17:21], the kingdom of righteousness and peace and joy in the Holy Ghost. The weapons of her warfare are the same, the sword of the Spirit, the armour of light, the armour of righteousness on the right hand and on the left. The processes by which this warfare are carried on must therefore be substantially the same. This is still the victory which must overcome the world, if it is overcome at all, "even our faith."

---

9. "The first instance recorded of the Christians assembling in what would now be called a church," is about a.d. 229. Barton, *Ecc. Hist.* 496. So little has the whole matter of "Ecclesiology"and church-finery to do with the true power and majesty of Christianity. Ἐκκλησία, says Chrysostom, οὐ τόπος, ἀλλὰ τρόπος. [Trans. "The church, not the place, but the character"] (temper, influence which it should form and exert.) Do walls make Christians? said Victorinus. (*Ergo parietes Christianos faciunt?*) [Victorinus quoted by Augustine, *Confessions*, ed. Albert C. Outler, *The Library of Christian Classics*, (London: SCM Press, 1955), VII:160. Gaius Marius Victorinus was a fourth century Roman rhetorician and Neoplatonic philosopher who converted to Christianity and articulated his faith in a Neoplatonic idiom.]

Chapter 3: Nevin and Proudfit: Opposed Views of the Early Creeds

[Confession in the Primitive Church]

By her preaching,[10] reading,[11] exposition,[12] catechesis,[13] and circulation of the word,[14] the primitive church laboured to impart to the souls of men that truth which is the seed of the new life, the mould of Christian character, the object and the life of faith. With equal solicitude, she sought, in the preparation of her converts and catechumens for baptism and at their admission to that initial seal of her communion, to elicit the "faith" which had thus "come by hearing," in the form of sincere, intelligent, individual and appropriative confession. It was this "utterance together," (ὁμολογία) with the church, (not only of such of her members as were then assembled with them, but of all the faithful dispersed over the earth, of the whole community, in fact, both militant and glorified) of her divine faith, which made them Christians. Nor did her labour and care end when they were thus "added to the church [Acts 2:37, 47]." They were still "nourished up in the words of faith and sound doctrine,"[15] warned and guarded against harmful fellowship with "the unbelieving" [Titus 1:15], called back with rebukes and discipline when they "erred from the faith" [1 Tim 6:10], exhorted to "hold fast to", and "stand fast in the faith" [1 Cor 16:13], to "abound in faith" [2 Cor 8:7], and to "*add* to their faith virtue, knowledge, temperance, patience, godliness, brotherly-kindness and charity" [2 Pet 1:5–7] aiming at nothing less than complete Christian knowledge and virtue.[16]

How exact was the conformity of these methods to the parting command of our Lord, "Go ye and *teach* (μαθητεύσατε) all nations, *baptizing* them in the name of the Father, and of the Son, and of the Holy Ghost, teaching them to observe all things whatsoever I have commanded you [Matt 28:19–20]."

---

10. Αὔξοντες εἴς πλέον τὸ κήρυγμα καὶ τὰ σωτήρια σπέρματα τῆς τῶν οὐρανῶν βασιλεὶς ἀνὰ πᾶσαν ἐπισπείροντες τὴν οἰκουμένην. [Trans. "(They) preached the gospel more and more widely, and scattered the saving seeds of the kingdom of heaven throughout all the world." (Schaff, tr.)] Eusebius, *The History of the Church*, III, section 37 [Eusebius (c 260–340), Bishop of Caesarea Maritima was an historian of the early church and an apologist for Emperor Constantine.]

11. *Scripturarum tractatio plenissima et lectio sine falsatione*. [Trans. "The most complete treatment/discussion of the Scriptures and reading without falsification."] Irenaeus, *Adversus Haereses*, IV:63.

12. Γραφῶν θείων ἐξηγήσεις. [Trans. "Exposition of sacred scriptures"] Dionysius (2nd century) quoted by Eusebius, IV, c. 23. M. J. Routh, *Reliquiae Sacrae* (Oxford, 1846), I:130. [Martin Joseph Routh (1755-1854), an English patristics scholar, was also a president of Magdalen College, Oxford. His revised *Reliquiae Sacrae* was published in five volumes (1846–48)]. *Secundum Scripturas Expositio legitimaet diligens*. [Trans. "According to the diligent exposition of the Scriptures, the foundation and pillar of our faith."] Irenaeus, *Adversus Haereses*, IV:63.

13. Ἡ μὲν γὰρ κατήχησις εἰς πίστιν περιάγει. [Trans. "And indeed the instruction in faith spread around."] Clement of Alexandria, *Paedagogus*, I. 6.

14. Τὴν τῶν θείων εὐαγγελίων παραδιδόναι γραφήν. [Trans. "To teach them the writing of the divine gospels."] Eusebius, III, section 37.

15. Routh, I:172.

16. Routh, Ibid.

THE APOSTLES' CREED

Here then was the type or delineation of Christian doctrine. Here was in brief form, the truth which, "believed in the heart," "confessed with the mouth" [Rom 10:10], and that confession sealed and publicly ratified by baptism, constituted a Christian. "He who" thus "believeth and is baptized, shall be saved [Mark 16:6]." He "enters into the kingdom of God," "born of water and of the Spirit [John 3:5]." He is "saved by the washing (laver λουτρῷ) of regeneration and the renewing of the Holy Ghost [Titus 3:5]." He is one of that Church for which Christ gave himself; which "having cleansed with the washing of water by the word" [Eph 5:26], it is his purpose "to sanctify and to present unto himself a glorious Church, having neither spot nor wrinkle nor any such thing, but holy and without blemish [Eph 5:27]."

Having become "a disciple" he was still under the tuition of the Church, whose faithful labours had made him so. Those who had "taught" and "baptized" him were still to "teach him all things whatsoever Christ had commanded [Matt 28:20]."

This was the faith into which the Church was to *disciple* the nations. This was the full course of Christian education, "teaching them to observe all things whatsoever I have commanded you [Matt 28:20]."

Here then was the original outline, or framework of the Christian Creed, "I believe in the Father, and in the Son, and in the Holy Ghost." Every expression of the Church's faith, every manifestation of her life was, in truth, a Creed. Her letters of mutual edification, her apologies to emperors and nations, her homilies, her hymns, her litanies, doxologies,[17] and benedictions, all were confessions of her faith; and all retained this original and divinely impressed form with surprising distinctness.

As particular aspects of heathenism pressed upon her, as Judaism sought to intrude its obsolete and abolished peculiarities into her faith, as heresies arose within her own bosom, other ideas and phrases were inserted or added, exegetical or completive of these great linear verities of the Creed.[18] These ideas or phrases were added on the authority and from the teaching of the Scriptures. They were such as to assert more fully or distinctly some particular truth of Christianity in the face of some particular error or corruption.

The only creed in full of Christians (and this idea we find most distinctly recognized in their earliest writings) was Christianity itself,[19] as delivered in the teachings

---

17. Clement of Alexandria, *Paedagogus*, III to end. [Clement (c. 150–215) was a Christian middle Platonist philosophical theologian who taught in the catechetical school of Alexandria.]

18. [This was the opinion of Jacque Basnage, a French Reformed theologian and linguist (1653–1723).]

19. Ἡ ἐν Χριστῷ πίστις. [Trans. "Faith in Christ"] Clement of Rome, "Letter to Corinth," i. 22, immediately and largely developed from the words which "himself spake to us by the Holy Spirit." Ἡ χριστιανή συντάξις. [Trans. "The Christian system"] Ἡ οὐράνιος πηγή τοῦ ὕδατος τῆς ζωῆς τοῦ ἐξίοντος ἐκ τῆς νηδύος τοῦ Χριστοῦ. [Trans. "The heavenly fountain of the water of life, which comes forth from the side of Christ."] It was to this the martyrs of Vienne and Lyons gave their ὁμολογία [Trans. "confession"] and which "refreshed and fortified" them amidst torture and death. See their deeply affecting letter chapter 6 and 11, and in fact throughout. Routh,. I:267, &c. [See also P. Nautin, "Letter of the Church of Lyons and Vienne," ed. Angelo Di Berardino, *Encyclopedia of the Early Church* (New York:

Chapter 3: Nevin and Proudfit: Opposed Views of the Early Creeds

of our Lord and in the inspired writings generally of the Old and New Testaments.[20] It was from this common source they derived their "one and the same faith" expressed in "dissimilar languages and phrases."[21] The divine beauty and truthfulness of the Church's early life is, in fact, chiefly discerned in the variety and freeness of manifestation and expression combined with unity of faith.

[Early Summaries of Faith]

The only recognized *formula* of that faith was, at first and for a long time, that which Christ delivered at the institution of baptism. This was undoubtedly "the immovable rule of truth" which Irenaeus says, the convert to Christianity "received by baptism."[22] Even as late as the fourth century (and the beginning the fifth) it was so recognized. Gregory of Nyssa (4th cent.) says, expounding "the faith of Christians,"[23] "We believe even as our Lord unfolded the faith to his disciples, when he thus spake,[24] 'Go ye and teach all nations, baptizing them in the name of the Father, and of the Son, and of Holy Ghost.' This is the word of the mystery,"[25] &c.

Chrysostom on Matt xxviii. 19, 20, says that in this passage, our Lord "gave a charge to his disciples, relating partly to doctrines and partly to precepts."[26] . . . "He commands them," he adds "to disperse over the whole globe of the earth, *and commits to them a compend of doctrine to be communicated through baptism.*"[27] To fulfil

---

Oxford University Press, 1992), I:483–84. Clement was Bishop of Rome in the late first century. He is primarily known through his letter to the Corinthians.]

20 *Dei voluntas in Scripturis tradita, fundamentum et columna fidei nostrae*. [Trans. "The will of God is handed down in the Scripture, the foundation and pillar of our faith."] Irenaeus, *Adversus Haereses*, I. 1.

21. *Loquelae dissimiles, . . . una et eadem fides*. [Trans. "Dissimilar utterances . . . one and the same faith."] Irenaeus, I. 3.

22. *Regulam veritatis immobilem quam per baptismum accipit* [Trans. "The immovable rule of truth which is received by baptism"]—and he adds on the same line, "the contents of the Scriptures" (*quae sunt ex Scripturis*) as the source and test of truth which he accepted by the adoption of this *regula*. Irenaeus, *Adversus. Haereses*, I:1—near the end.

23. *Fides Christianorum*. [Trans. "The faith of Christians." Gregory of Nyssa (335–95), a bishop of Nyssa, was one of the influential "Cappadocian Fathers." He is remembered for his speculations concerning the nature of the Trinity and the significance of the incarnation.]

24. *Credimus quemadmodum suis discipulis Dominus fidem exposuit, sic locutis, Euntes docete,* &c. [Trans. "We believe the faith as the Lord explained it to his disciples, as he spoke, Go teach," etc.]

25. *Hic est sermo mysterii*. [Trans. "This is the word of mystery."] Gregory of Nyssa, *Contra Eunomium*, I:253. See below. [Eunomius (d. c.394) was a proponent of radical Arianism. See M. Simonetti, "Eunomius" ed. Angelo Di Berardino, *Encyclopedia of the Early Church*, 297.]

26. *Partim de dogmatibus, partim de praeceptis mandans*. [Trans. "Commanding partly regarding doctrines, partly regarding precepts."] We have some of his commentary in the Latin version. [John Chrysostom (349–407) was a widely read theologian and Patriarch of Constantinople, lauded for his eloquent and edifying sermons.]

27. *Compendiariam quae baptismum fieret doctrinam*. [Trans. "A compendium which is to be conveyed in baptism."] Chrysostom on Matt. xxviii. 19, 20.

THE APOSTLES' CREED

this two-fold *charge,* he says, was "the whole apostolic work,[28] nor need the private Christian," he adds, "attempt (or look for) anything beyond it."[29]

Athanasius, (who in time preceded those just mentioned,) says, "The sum and body of our whole faith is contained in the words of baptism, and is founded in that Scripture,[30] 'Go ye,'" &c.

Basil (of Caesarea), in his two admirable books on Baptism, begins with this passage, and unfolds from it the whole Christian doctrine and life, without the remotest allusion to any other summary or formula.[31]

And Augustine, (early in the fifth century) says that "the creed consists of words of the gospel."[32] And, in his sermon on the Creed he adds,

> This norm of faith the Lord Jesus Christ himself drew up,[33] and none but an impious man doubts concerning that rule of the catholic faith, which he to whom the faith itself is owed, dictated. Our Lord Jesus Christ himself, therefore, when he rose, now glorified, from the dead, and was about to ascend to heaven to the Father, left these mysteries of faith to his disciples, that is, the Apostles. For he saith, "Go ye and baptize all nations in the name of the Father, and of the Son, and of the Holy Ghost."

Whether the candidate for baptism was required to repeat this passage aloud in the form of a creed, ("I believe in the Father," &c.) as a confession of his faith, or to give his assent to it in reply to certain questions, does not certainly appear. The latter

---

28. *Hoc opus est Apostolicum.* [Trans. "This is the apostolic work."]

29. *Nec plusquam tibi opus sit exquiras.* [Trans. "You need not inquire into any further work."]

30. Against Gregory Sabellius quoted by Voëtius, 66. *Summa et corpus totius nostrae fidei continetur in verbis baptismi, et fundatur in illa Scriptura, Ite &c.* [Trans. "The summary and body of our entire faith is contained in the words of baptism, and founded in that Scripture, etc." Athanasius (293–373) was a theologian and a bishop of Alexandria who, arguing against the Arians, defended the doctrine of the divine equality of the Father and the Son. Gisbertus Voetius was a Dutch Reformed theologian and a scholar of ancient Asian languages who vehemently opposed the Arminian party and also the philosophy of René Descartes.]

31. Basil of Caesarea, *Collected Works,* ed. J. Garnier and P. Maran with J. J. Gaume, III:887. He says, "The things which are here laid down by the Lord, in *the way of outline* (τῷ Κυρίῳ ὁριστικῶς προσταχθέντα), are in other places fully delivered." Lib. I, Chapter 1. Basil (c. 330–79) was the politically powerful bishop of Caesarea in Cappadocia. He was an ardent defender of Nicene theology and a pioneer of communal monasticism.]

32. *Symbolum constat verbis Evangelicis.* [Trans. "The creed consists of the words of the Gospel."] Augustine, *Against the Donatists,* Book 6, section 25, quoted by Voëtius.

33. *Hanc fidei normam ipse Dominus noster Jesus Christus instruxit.* [Trans. "The Lord Jesus Christ himself taught this norm of faith."] Augustine "Sermon de Symbolo," quoted by Voëtius, ibid.

method is implied by Cyprian[34] and Augustine,[35] and as respects the Roman Church, is distinctly affirmed by Rufinus.

In almost all the writings which remain to us from that early period, we meet with summaries, here and there, of Christian doctrine; as in Clement of Rome,[36] Justin Martyr,[37] Irenaeus,[38] and Tertullian.[39] These are simply given as *first aspects,* or prominent lines and points of truth. When such terms as *regula fidei, regula veritatis, lex veritatis* [Trans. "rule of faith, rule of truth, law of truth"], &c., or such epithets as *una, immobilis, irreformabilis,* ἀσάλευτος [Trans. "one, immovable, unchangeable, immovable"], and the like are applied to them, it is obvious that these names and epithets were meant for *the whole truth, from which these points stood prominently forth.* This is quite manifest from two facts: 1st. No one of these summaries is ever appealed to as an acknowledged and authoritative *formula,* having the sanction of the Church or any part of it, but its derivation from Christ or from the Holy Scriptures is asserted and proved, and thus its true ground and authority intimated: and 2d, *No two of these summaries are the same, either in contents, order, or phraseology, in any two writers, nor even in the same.*

The second century was the age, emphatically, of Apologies for Christianity. Quadratus[40] presented one to Adrian, about A.D. 126; Aristides,[41] to the same emperor, in the same year; Justin Martyr to Antoninus Pius, about A.D. 140, and a second

---

34. Cyprian, Epistle. 69 and 70. Cyprian's *Works,* ed. Bishop John Fell, 297 and 301. Some explanatory questions are there inserted. The whole is called in a general way, "*ipsa interrogatio quae fit in baptismo.*" [Trans. "this interrogation which is done at baptism." Cyprian (c. 200–258) was a bishop of Carthage and a subsequent martyr. He famously argued that those who had "lapsed" during a Roman persecution could be readmitted to the church, but only after an appropriate penance.]

35. *Si dixerimus catechumeno, Credis in Christum? respondet, Credo.* [Trans. "If we say to the catechumen, Do you believe in Christ, let him respond, I believe."] Quoted in John Ayre, ed. *The Works of John Jewel,* II: Article 16, 706.

36. *Works,* I "To Corinthians," Chapter 46.

37. *Works,* ed. J. C. T. Otto, (Jena, 1842–43) *Address to the Greeks* and twice in his *Apologia II for the Christians.* [Justin Martyr was a second century apologist for the Christian faith who defended its moral ethos, comparing it to Stoicism, and promoted the concept that the pre-existent Logos ("Word") had become incarnate in Jesus.]

38. *Adversus. Haereses.* Book I, Chapters 2 and 19, and Book IV, Chapters 52 and 62, the Greek of which latter is preserved in one of the *Fragments in Codice,* ed. Feu-Ardentii, (Paris, 1639).

39. *De Velandis Virginibus,* Chapter I. *De Praescriptione Haereticorum* Chapter 13, end. *Adversus Praxeam* Chapter 2, beginning. and other places. *P. Mos inibi servatur antiquus eos qui gratiam baptismi suscepturi sunt, publice, id est, fidelium populo audiente, symbolum reddere.* [Trans. "At that time they kept the old way who received the grace of baptism publicly, that is, rendering the creed in the hearing of faithful people."] Rufinus, 170.

40. [Quadratus of Athens was said by Eusebius to have been the first Christian apologist. According to what are probably apocryphal traditions in the Eastern churches, he studied under the apostles themselves.]

41. [Aristides of Athens was a second-century philosopher who converted to Christianity and, according to Eusebius, became an apologist for the faith.]

to Marcus Antoninus, about A.D. 162; Melito,[42] to Marcus Antoninus, A.D. 170; Apollinaris,[43] to the same emperor, probably a little later; Athenagoras,[44] to Marcus Antoninus and Commodus, about A.D. 177; Miltiades,[45] to Commodus, about A.D. 180. The Oration of Tatian[46] to the Greeks, about A.D. 172, and the Books of Theophilus [47]to Antolycus, about A.D. 180, belong to the same class. Tertullian addressed his Apology to the Roman Magistrates,[48] near the close of the second or beginning of the third century.

Most of these apologies have descended to us entire or nearly so.[49] Of the rest, we have only scraps or allusions, in Eusebius and Jerome.[50] Their express object was to exhibit, explain, and vindicate the Christian Faith; to correct misrepresentations, and to answer objections. Had any recognized formula or summary of that faith been then in existence, we could scarcely have failed to meet with it or hear from it, in some of these works. They contain, however, nothing of the kind.

[The First Creeds of Christianity]

An equally profound silence reigns through the third century in respect to any received symbol, or formula of the Christian Faith.

Nor do the early historians of the church, Hegesippus[51] in the second century, and Eusebius in the fourth, mention any.

In the course of the fourth century, some of the *first truths* of Christianity were collected and arranged in the form of symbola. There has been infinite dispute about the sense in which the Greek word, σύμβολον, was applied to these documents. The

---

42. [Melito (died c. 180) was a bishop of Sardis in Asia Minor and a major participant in the codification of the Christian Old Testament.]

43. [St. Apollinaris was a second-century bishop of Hierapolis in Asia Minor mentioned by Eusebius and Jerome. He is not to be confused with Apollinaris the Younger, who was a vigorous opponent of the Arians.]

44. [Athenagoras of Athens was a second-century convert to Christianity and an apologist for the faith, who may have been a Platonic philosopher.]

45. [Miltiades was another second-century apologist about whom little is known, except that he seems to have argued against the Montanists.]

46. [Tatian (c. 120– c. 180) was an Assyrian Christian teacher, most remembered for his *Diatessaron*, a harmonization of the four canonical gospels.]

47. [Theophilus was a second-century patriarch of Antioch and early apologist for Christianity.]

48. *Vobis, Romani imperii antistites.* [Trans. "To you, Roman imperial magistrates."] Chapter 1.

49. [Proudfit was mistaken about this. Most of the written apologies that he lists are only known through fragments quoted by Eusebius and Jerome.]

50. [Jerome (c. 347–420) was an historian and theologian best known for his translation of the Bible into Latin. His version became known as the *Vulgate* and was eventually adopted as the authoritative version of the Bible by the Roman Catholic Church.]

51. [Hegessipus (c. 110–180) was a chronicler of the early church whose works (now lost) were quoted by Eusebius.]

most general use of it by the ancients, and therefore the most probable application of it by the Christans, was in the sense of a *tessera* or badge of mutual recognition.[52] The acceptance of the formula marked a disciple of "the common faith," and distinguished him from those who took or kept the name of Christianity, while they rejected more or less of its truth.

These summaries, symbols, or creeds were all constructed on the frame-work of the original baptismal doctrine of faith, (Matt xxviii. 19). They varied largely as it respects fullness of detail, but "the first principles of the doctrine of Christ" were the same in all. The churches of Jerusalem, of Rome, and of Aquileia, at least, had each a creed of its own.[53] Rufinus specifies differences between the creeds of the Eastern[54] and Western churches. He points out several differences between the creed after which he had been baptized, in the Church of Aquileia, and that of the Roman Church. In fact he has one statement which is curious and interesting. "In other churches," he says (besides that of Rome) "on account of various heretics, certain articles seem to have been added (to the creed) by means of which, the tenets of the new doctrine might be excluded." How plain, therefore, that each church drew up its own summary of truth to suit itself, and altered it to meet its own exigencies! All this occasioned no suspicion of schism, no fear of damage to Christian unity—so long as the particular creed harmonized with "the common faith."

Ursinus,[55] in a learned historical notice of the early creeds, enumerates the following as "catholic or universal, that is, received by the consent of the whole orthodox Christian Church, namely, the Apostolic, Nicene, Constantinopolitan, Ephesine, Athanasian, and Chalcedonian."

Voss[56] and Heidegger, in their elaborate creed-histories, reduce the number received by the whole church, both Eastern and Western, to three, viz., "the Apostolic, Athanasian, and Nicene, or Niceno-Constantinopolitan."

The shortest, simplest, most comprehensive, and most strictly scriptural[57] of these is, without doubt, the Apostolic creed.

---

52. *Ut singuli fideles tesseram et indicium haberent*. [Trans. "So that each of the faithful might have the token and sign."] Heidegger, 679. [Johann Heinrich Heidegger (1633–98) was a Swiss Reformed theologian and ecclesiastical historian who often polemicized bitterly against the Roman Catholic Church.]

53. That of Jerusalem is given in the 18th Catechesis of Cyril. [His Catecheses were delivered during Lent and provide information concerning the preparation of candidates for baptism.] Those of the Churches of Rome and of Aquileia, are given by Rufinus.

54. E.g., He says of the article "He descended into hell," *non in orientis ecclesiis habetur hic sermo* [Trans. "The phrase is not found in the eastern church."], Rufinus, 179.

55. See Ursinus' *Admonitio Neostadiensium* (1581). [Trans. "Admonition to Neustad." Zacharias Ursinus (1534–83) was a German Reformed theologian celebrated for being the principal author of the Heidelberg Catechism.]

56. [Gerhard Johann Voss (1577–1649) was a Dutch humanist who argued against the apostolic authorship of the Apostles' Creed.]

57. Heidegger thinks he can find every phrase of it in the Scriptures. Voss says, *prae aliis symboiis,*

The term "Apostolic," however, was by no means exclusively applied to this particular creed. Cyril calls the creed of the church at Jerusalem "a confession of the holy and *Apostolic* faith."[58] Epiphanius[59] says, in introducing the Nicene Creed, "This faith was delivered from (or by) the holy Apostles."[60] "By the Western churches also," says Archbishop Ussher, "that longer form of the creed which went under the name of the Nicene, was also reckoned *Apostolic*."[61] And he quotes the "Ordo Romanus" before the institution of baptism, which calls it "inspired by the Lord, *instituted by the Apostles*."[62] "And in the celebration of the holy Supper," he continues, "the Latin Missal, which was in use about the beginning of the ninth century, speaking of the same (Nicene) creed, adds these words, '*the Apostles' creed* being ended, the priest shall say,'" &c.

So that the distinctive title of "the Apostles' creed" as applied to this symbol, is not of very high antiquity, even in the Roman Church. It has of late, however, become general.

When it reached its full form, as it now stands, cannot with certainty be determined. "The creed of the Roman Church,"[63] as it stood at the time of Rufinus, and is compared by him with that of his own church of Aquileia, differs in several phrases, from that which passes under the name of the Apostles' Creed, and is now claimed as the special and ancient creed of the Roman Church, being often thus appropriated under the title of "Credo (or Symbolum) Romanum." We give them in parallel columns, with marks to indicate the omissions in the earlier creed:

---

verbis etiam gaudet Apostolorum et Evangelistarum; [Trans. "more than other creeds, he rejoices in the words of the Aposles and Evangelists."] *Dissertation de Symbolo Apostolico*, 17. And Ursinus, *totum fere ex verbis Scripturae constat*. [Trans. "It consists fully in words brought forth from Scripture."] Zacharias Ursinus, *Expository Lectures on the Heidelberg Catechism*, trans. G. W. Williard, (1852), 2. 23.

58. Ἁγίας καὶ ἀποστελικῆς πίστεως [Trans. "Of the holy and apostolic faith"]. Ursinus, Ibid., 18th.

59. [Epiphanius (c. 310–403) was bishop of Salmis, Cyprus, and a relentless opponent of hersies.]

60. Αὐτὴ ἡ πίστις παρεδόθη ἀπὸ τῶν ἁγίων ἀποστόλων [Trans. "This faith was handed down by the apostles"], quoted by Archbishop Ussher, 314. [Ussher, *Works*, vol. VII.]

61. [Archbishop James Ussher (1581–1656) was the Protestant Archbishop of Armagh and a prolific writer about biblical history and the early church. He is most famous for his attempt to precisely date the creation of the universe.]

62. *A Domino inspiratum, ab Apostolis institutum*. [Trans. "Inspired by the Lord, instituted by the Apostles."]

63. *Ecclesiae Romanae symbolum*. [Trans. "The creed of the Roman Church."] Rufinus, 179.

"Symbolum Romana Ecclesia," in Rufinus.

Credo in Deum Patrem Omnipotentem .et in Christum Jesum, unicum Filium ejus, Dominu nostrum: . . . . . qui . . . . natus est de Spiritu Sancto ex Maria virgine, . . . crucifixus sub Pontio Pilato . . . . et sepultus, ... tertia die resurrexit a mortuis, ascendit ad coelos, sedit ad dexteram Dei Patris, ... inde venturus est judicare vivos et mortuos, . . . et in Spiritum Sanctum, sanctam. . . . . Ecclesiam . . . . remissionem peccatorum, . . . hujus carnis resurrectionem . . . .

Symbolum Apostolorum from the Roman Breviary*

Credo in Deum, Patrem Omnipotentem, Creatorem coeli et terrae, et in Jesum Christum, Filium ejus unicum, Dominum nostrum; qui conceptus est de Spiritu Sancto, natus ex Maria virgine, Passus sub Pontio Pilato, crucifixus, mortuus et sepultus; descendit ad inferos: tertia die resurrexit a mortuis: ascendit ad coelos, sedet ad dexteram Dei Patris Omnipotentis: inde venturus est judicare vivos et mortuos. Credo in Spiritum Sanctum, sanctam Ecclesiam Catholicam, sanctorum communionem, remissionem peccatorum, carnis resurrectionem, vitam aeternam. Amen

*Breviarium Romanum ex dec. S. S. Concilium Tridentini restitutum, St. Pius V Pontifex Maximus jussu editum, &c. (Paris, 1842).

THE APOSTLES' CREED

It will be seen by a comparison of the two that "the creed of the Roman Church" as it stood in the fifth century differed from "the Apostles' Creed," as follows. From the first article[64] the creed of the Roman Church omits "*creatorem coeli et terrae*;" from the third, "*conceptus*;" from the fourth, "*passus*" and "*mortuus*;"[65] from the fifth, the entire clause, "*descendit ad inferos*;"[66] from the sixth, omits "*omnipotentis*" after "*Patris*;" from the eighth, omits "*Credo*," before "*in Spiritum Sanctum*;"[67] from the ninth article, omits "*Catholicam*" after "*Ecclesiam*,"[68] and the latter clause entire, "*sanctorum communionem*;" and ends with "*hujus carnis resurrectionem*," omitting entirely the last or twelfth article, "*et vitam aeternam*."[69]

The question respecting the history and structure of this creed assumes a far higher than merely historical interest from the theory which the Church of Rome has put forth respecting it, and the pretensions which she has founded upon it.

That theory, as it stands in the highest authority known to the Roman Church,[70] is as follows:

---

64. We follow the *Catechismus Concilium, Tridentini*, [Trans. Catechism of the Council of Trent.] in the division and numbering of the articles. Part I, Chapters. 2–13.

65. It must be allowed that *passus* is sufficiently expressed by *crucifixus*, and *mortuus* implied in *sepultus*.

66. Rufinus says "this clause is not contained either in the Creed of the Roman Church, or in those of the Eastern Churches; the meaning of the expression, however, appears to be the same with this, that he was *buried*." *Sciendum sane est, quod in Ecclesiae Romanae symbolo non habetur hic sermo, vis tamen verbi eadem videtur esse in eo quod sepultus dicitur* [Trans. "It is to be known that this phrase is not found in the creed of the Roman Church, although the same sense of the words may be seen to be where it says 'He was buried'"], 179.

67. Voss remarks (p. 28), that this word was sufficiently *understood* from the beginning of the Creed, and that the insertion of it here tends somewhat to give it the appearance of another creed. But he adds, "*Cum initio solum sit, Credo in Deum Patrem et in Jesum Christum et in Spiritum Sanctum; postea etiam, multis insertis, remansit vetus formula, et in Spiritum Sanctum: cui posteriores τὸ credo quod ἀπὸ κοινοῦ antea erat supplendum, majoris claritatis causa, praemiserant.*" [Trans. "Since in the beginning it was only 'I believe in God the Father and in Jesus Christ and in the Holy Spirit'; later with many things having been inserted, the old formula remains, 'and in the Holy Spirit': to which later I believe that τὸ ἀπὸ κοινοῦ, ("in common") was added earlier, for greater clarity, they were put first.]

68. So the edition before us (Paris, 1580). Pamelius added Catholicam; against the authority of ancient copies, says Voss. *Aliter libri veteres*: and adds, *quid mirum si non legatur apud Rufinum, cum nee habuerit Augustinus? Nec adeo levis est momenti. Imo Apostolorum aetate nondum obtinebat consuetudo, ut Christiani dicerentur Catholici*. [Trans. "Other old books . . . would it be a wonder if it were not read in Rufinus, since Augustine did not have it? And this is not inconsequential. Indeed in the age of the Apostles, it was not yet the custom for Christians to be called 'Catholics.'" Jacobus Pamelius (1536–87) was a Flemish priest and prolific scholar who edited ancient Christian liturgical texts.] If Catholicism had stood in the original text of Rufinus, that prolix and churchly commentator would surely have expounded it in his commentary, which he has not.

69. And Jerome states that it stood there in his time. *In symbolo fidei . . . post confessionem Trinitatis et unitatem Ecclesiae, omne Christiani dogmatis sacramentum carnis resurrectione includitur*. [Trans. "In the creed of faith . . . after the confession of the Trinity and the unity of the Church, every mystery of Christian teaching ends with the resurrection of the body."] Hieronymus [Jerome] to Pammachius against the errors of Jovinian by Jerome, II:59. (ed. Erasmus.)

70. *Catechismus Concilium Tridentini* [Trans. "Catechism of the Council of Trent] issued with the

Chapter 3: Nevin and Proudfit: Opposed Views of the Early Creeds

> The doctrines which Christian men ought first to hold, are those which the guides and teachers of the faith, the holy apostles, inspired by the Divine Spirit, have marked out in the twelve articles of the Creed. For when they had received from the Lord a command that, in discharge of their commission from him, they should go forth into all the world, and preach the gospel to every creature, they determined to compose a formula of the Christian faith, to the end that all men might think and say the same thing, and that there might be no schisms among them whom they called to the unity of the faith; but that they might be perfect in the same mind and in the same judgment. This profession of the Christian faith and hope, composed by themselves, the Apostles denominated a creed (symbol): either because it was formed of the various sentences which each contributed, or because they used it as a mark or badge, whereby they might easily distinguish deserters or false brethren, privily brought in, who adulterated the gospel, from those who bound themselves by the oath of the warfare (army) of Christ.

This creed is thus propounded as the product of inspiration, the rule of Christian faith. It is constantly affirmed by the highest Roman authorities to contain *all that is essential for a Christian to believe.*[71] And as the creed is not contained in the canonical books, but has been handed down by church tradition, the Papacy founds thereupon its theory of *tradition* or the oral transmission of truth and law of Christ, in the bosom of the Church and under its auspices and control, and that the doctrine and precepts so handed down have the same authority with those revealed in the Scriptures.

This theory, therefore, simply puts the creed in the place of the Bible.

The illustrious Protestants whose names stand at the head of our article (with many others) have assailed this theory with an erudition which had left almost no document of ancient or mediaeval times unsearched or untaxed. To us their onset seems like a war of giants, to demolish a pigmy; so utterly destitute of historical basis is the Romish figment which they attacked. But the labour was by no means unnecessary in their day. Under the long and absolute sway of the Papacy, this notion had been so *drilled and soldered* into the minds of men, that even after the Reformation, not a few intelligent Protestants were found (as Voëtius assures us)[72] who could, with difficulty, be disabused of the impression which invested the creed *formally* with a sort of divine and inspired authority. And so long as this impression

---

bull of Pius V, and with the usual complement of Papal anathemas, threatening "the wrath of Almighty God, and of the blessed Peter and Paul against any man who should rashly dare to oppose it" (*Ausu temerario contraire*). Pars I. and bull at the end of the volume. We quote from the fine edition "*ad usum seminariorum*" [Trans. "for the use of seminarians."] (Lyons and Paris, 1848).

71. *Tous les mystères qu'il importe de croire.* [Trans. "All the mysteries essential to believe."] Robert Bellarmine, *Explication du Symbole des Apôtres* (Paris, 1842), I, Preface, 1. [Robert Bellarmine (1542–1621) was an Italian cardinal and Jesuit theologian who enumerated and analyzed the disputed points that divided Catholics and Protestants.]

72. [Gisbertus Voetius (1589–1676) was a Dutch Reformed theologian who participated actively in the Synod of Dort and throughout his long career opposed the views of the Arminians.]

lingered among men, how was it possible to restore the word of God to its primitive and just supremacy in the church?

[Who Composed the Apostles' Creed?]

If the creed was composed by the Apostles, why is it not mentioned among the "Acts of the Apostles?" Why never alluded to in the Epistles? If it was composed by the Apostles, under divine inspiration, it must have formed a part of the canonical Scriptures, which has never been pretended. If it was composed by the Apostles, it must have been in the Greek language, and of course would have been received and carefully preserved by the Greek churches, but they were not in possession of it (by the plain statement of Rufinus) some time after the beginning of the fifth century. If it was composed by the Apostles before their separation, it must have been drawn up at Jerusalem, and of course, the church of Jerusalem would have first received and ever retained the precious deposit, which it did not, but had a creed of its own, as we have seen. Of all the early ecclesiastical writers who have narrated the acts of Christ and his Apostles, and the Confessions drawn up by Synods, antisynods and councils, no one has ever mentioned a creed composed by the Apostles. Hilary[73] in his first book on the Trinity, appeals to the Niceno-Constantinopolitan creed, in support of the doctrine, but never mentions the Apostles' Creed. In his sixth book he enumerates all the Confessions of the Christian faith, but the list does not contain the Apostles' Creed. If it was composed by the Apostles, it would have been delivered to all the churches of the world; how then was it unknown to so large a part of them in the fifth century? How did it exist with so many variations for several centuries afterwards?[74] Why was it necessary for the fathers both of the eastern and western churches, to draw up so many symbols and confessions on the rise of various heresies, (which are quite inferior to it in simplicity and precision) if they could have fallen back on so venerable and unquestionable an exposition of the faith as an "Apostles' Creed?"

Such are some of the arguments by which "the might of" Voss, Ussher, and their compeers, have demolished the curtain which the Papal "builders" had been, for ages, erecting between the Church and the Bible.

Shall we add a mite of our own to a stock already so ample?

The ancient Christians were in the habit of reading, beside the Holy Scriptures, the pious remains of yet earlier times (as Eusebius and others tell us) not indeed as authority, but for edification in their religious assemblies; but neither among inspired

---

73 [Hilary of Poitiers (c. 310–67) became Bishop of Poitiers in Gaul where he vigorously opposed Arianism, which had spread to many of the Germanic tribes.]

74. Archbishop Ussher produces a creed which he found written in the Latin Psalter of King Ethelstane, and another from the end of an old ms. of the Acts of the Apostles, in the Oxford [Bodleian?] library, both of which differed not inconsiderably from "the Apostles' Creed." So did another cited by Etherius, a Spanish bishop, A.D. 785, mentioned by Heidegger, 642.

Chapter 3: Nevin and Proudfit: Opposed Views of the Early Creeds

nor ecclesiastical writings so read, is there any mention of an Apostles' Creed. There is the same unbroken silence respecting it alike in the assailants and apologists of the early church; in the heretics who forsook and afterwards attacked, and the orthodox who defended her faith.

One unquestionable fact concentrates the force of all these arguments, and is of itself sufficient to overturn the whole Papal theory and the vast structure of traditional imposture which has been built upon it; *"the Apostles' Creed," either in name or form, was unknown to the Christian Church, for at least four hundred years after Christ.*

Witsius,[75] speaking of Ussher, Voëtius, Voss, and Heidegger, remarks that "the almost measureless reading[76] which they all brought to the discussion of this subject has left nothing for other men to do." But no subject was ever yet exhausted. Truth and error alike change their aspects and relations as ages roll on. The whole front and issue of this question has, within a few years, so totally changed, that the artillery of these renowned defenders of the faith, sweeps over a now almost unoccupied field.

The new Creed Theory, forming a part of the system of "Development," as maintained by Moehler in Germany,[77] Newman in England[78] and Dr. Nevin in this country (and others in both) is so remarkable that we shall leave Dr. Nevin to state it in his own language.

With regard to the historical era of the completion of the creed, Dr. Nevin expresses himself as follows:

> His (Irenaeus's) whole manner may be taken as evidence that no fixed formula of this sort, as afterwards settled in our present Apostles' Creed, was then," (in the second century) "in ecclesiastical use."[79] He speaks of "all its variations in the second century,"[80] and expresses his admiration "that it should rise into view gradually, now one article, now three, and now twelve, . . . that it should appear under so many editions and phases, . . . that it should be so loose a deposit, apparently, in the hands of the Church, *from the first century to the fourth,* and after all, assume *in the end, the settled form it now carries, &c.*

And yet on the page opposite our first quotation, he says: "the probability is certainly strong that *early*[81] in the second century, *if not before,* nearly all the particulars

---

75. [Hermann Witsius (1636–1708) was a Dutch theologian who attempted to reconcile the newer "covenant theology" with Reformed scholasticism.]

76. *Maximi viri Ussher, Voëtius, Voss, and Heidegger, omnes immensen propemodem lecionis, &c.* [Trans. "Just about an immense amount of reading, etc."], 1.

77. [Johann Adam Moehler (1796–1838) was a Catholic theologian of the Tübingen School who argued that the church was primarily a living, growing community rather than a static institution.]

78. [John Henry Newman (1801–90) was a prominent leader of the Oxford Movement within the Church of England who converted to Roman Catholicism and became a priest and later a cardinal. He articulated a controversial theory of the historical development of church doctrine.]

79. John Williamson Nevin, "The Apostles' Creed," in this volume, 41..

80. Nevin, "The Apostles' Creed," in this volume, 69..

81. Irenaeus was *late* in the 2d century. Tillemont dates his work *Against Heresies* about 190, and

THE APOSTLES' CREED

now embraced in it (the Creed) were found more or less in current use." And again more distinctly, "we meet the several parts of the Creed under full revelation in the second century."

The reader is just as able to put these statements together in an intelligible and self-agreeing form, as we are.

As it regards the source of the Creed, however, Dr. Nevin is entirely clear.

> The Creed does not spring from the Bible. The early Church got it not from the Bible, but from the fact of Christianity itself, which must be allowed to be in its own nature older even and deeper than its own record under this form.[82] . . . The divine tradition, which starts from the original substance of Christianity itself, as it underlies the Bible, meets us under its clearest, most primitive and most authoritative character, in the Apostles' Creed.[83]

Nor is the Creed the work of the Apostles. It is not "a bound scheme of words, handed down from the Apostles."[84]

> The Creed is no work of mere outward authority, imposed on the Church by Christ or his Apostles. It would help its credit greatly in the eyes of some, no doubt, if it could be made to appear under this view. Their idea of Christianity is such as involves prevailingly, the notion of a given or fixed scheme of things to be believed and done,[85] propounded for the use of men, on the authority of heaven, in a purely mechanical and outward way. . . . It is plain, however, that no such origin as this can he asserted in its favour. . . . In no such form could it be the glorious Christian *creed*, which we now find it to be in fact.[86]
>
> In the next place, it is no product of *reflection*, . . . no result of joint deliberation and discussion. This last view, especially, would suit the taste of many; more particularly, if it could be made to appear that the Bible had been taken as the source and rule of all evidence in the case, and that the formulary was exhibited, throughout, as an extract simply, and summary, of what is to be found in its inspired pages; . . . if that famous synod at Jerusalem, for instance, or some other . . . were known to have taken the matter in hand, (after the fashion of the great *world convention* in London,) and to have produced . . . what they conceived to be . . . a truly *scriptural*[87] platform of Christian doctrine.

---

says he died in 202.

82. Nevin, "The Apostles Creed," this volume, 90.'
83. Nevin, "The Apostles' Creed," this volume, 91.
84. Nevin, "The Apostles' Creed," this volume, 70.
85. Tertullian seems to have had a very similar "idea." "This I lay down," he says, "among first principles; that there was *one fixed scheme instituted by Christ*, which all nations must, under all circumstances, believe." *In primis hoc propono: unum utique et certum aliquid institutum esse a Christo, quod credere omnimodo debeant nationes. De Praescriptione Haereticorum* IX: 205 [*Prescription Against Heresies*].
86. Nevin, "The Apostles' Creed," this volume, 55.
87. All the italics on this page are Dr. N's.

Chapter 3: Nevin and Proudfit: Opposed Views of the Early Creeds

"'The articles of agreement'" "of the *late* 'Evangelical Alliance'" are instanced, and that new creed lately originated for the use of the Protestant Armenian Church, in Constantinople. "We can see and understand easily how *that* was made; the missionary goes into his upper room, takes the Bible into his hands," &c., &c. . . . "All this we miss in the creed which bears the name of the Apostles. . . . It is not the work of any mind or set of minds . . . reducing [the contents of Christianity] to logical statement for the understanding."

Whence, then, *is* this "glorious Christian Creed," which is neither from the Bible, from Christ, nor from the Apostles, nor yet the "product of reflection" or "joint deliberation," nor even "the work of any mind or set of minds?" The reader may go through Aristotle's Categories of space, or Plato's world of "things movable and things immovable," or even range over "the things which are in heaven and on earth and under the earth," and not find it. We do not wonder that, after all these negations, Dr. Nevin says, "No one can tell exactly whence or how it comes."—He essays the difficult task however.

"The immediate substance of Christianity," he says,

> as it comes to a real revelation in the first place directly for faith forms the contents, and furnishes us with the true idea of the ancient Creed. . . . Its propositions are the utterance only of what is immediately at hand in the proper Christian consciousness itself. . . . It owes its origin to the faith of the church . . . in the way of free, gradual progress and growth. . . . The Creed, we say, sprang in the beginning, from the faith of the church as a whole. It is the product of the Christian life, in its general and collective capacity. . . . So in the early life of nations, we meet with creations continually, products of the spirit that seem to shoot forth spontaneously, by a sort of inward organic force, from the substance of the national mind itself. . . . This may serve to explain what we mean when we say that the creed is to be taken as the full, free outbirth of the Christian faith as a whole. . . .

"The mere letter of Christianity, even as it stands in the New Testament itself" he represents as ("for a thoughtful mind")

> something secondary to its living substance as exhibited in the actual mystery of Christ and his Church. . . . This mystery is actualized, . . . comes to its revelation as the supernatural in the form of faith, by means of the Church. . . . *The primitive form of this revelation is presented to us in the Creed.* . . . It must be taken as the grand epos [a grand theme uniting disparate material] of Christianity itself, the spontaneous poem of its own life unfolded in fit word and expression from the inmost consciousness of the universal Church.

It is

> the free, spontaneous product of the life of the Church as a whole, the self-adjusted utterance of its faith. . . . It is the free spontaneous externalization of

the Christian consciousness, the substance of living Christianity as a whole, in its primary form of faith.... The Creed was not *made;* it *grew,* self-produced, we may say, out of the great fact of Christianity itself.... Its contents thus come from within, and not from without.

Again he calls it "the ancient creation of the church."[88] On the *authority* of the Creed, Dr. Nevin is quite up to the highest point of Papal orthodoxy.

To reject it is to reject the ancient faith; to make light account of it is to make light account of the very substance of Christianity, as it stood from the beginning. If the *regula fidei* of Irenaeus and Tertullian, is to have any reality or be of any force for us whatever, we must own its presence in the Apostles' creed. We shall have for it most certainly but a figment of our own minds, if we pretend to find it anywhere else.[89]

This is philosophical Catholicism. It is a combination of the mystical philosophy of our own age with the Romish idea of the Church.[90] It is the helping hand stretched forth by the infidel philosophy to the Papacy, in the hour of her agony. It comes too late, it is true, to save her claim of infallibility. The Council of Trent, as we have seen, and the earlier Roman doctors (Bellarmine among the rest,) insisted that *the Creed was composed by the Apostles themselves, under divine inspiration.* This "old wife's fable" they were not ashamed to repeat to children, long after full grown men perceived its ridiculous inconsistency with history. But this figment is no longer necessary.[91] Romanism, since her marriage with the modern philosophy, is quite ashamed of it. Dr. Nevin distinctly repudiates it. He is "not disturbed[92] in the least by the difficulty some urge against the creed, on the ground of its outward history, as showing it to be vague

88. Nevin, "The Apostles' Creed," in this volume, 71.

89. Nevin, "The Apostles' Creed," in this volume, 71. [Throughout this long excerpt, changes have been made to quotation marks and ellipses for clarity and simplicity.]

90. ["Mystical philosophy" probably refers to Romanticism and/or Idealism, both of which were thought by conservative American theologians to lose themselves in fantastic theorizing, ethereal abstractions, and pantheism. The phrase also suggested the identification of religious knowledge with immediate intuition rather than with revealed propositions. See Hodge's lengthy critique of mysticism, including the views of Schleiermacher, in *Systematic Theology,* I:61–69.]

91. It is however, still taught in the Roman Catechisms. So Bellarmine. "*Les Saintes Ecritures ne pouvant être lues en entier, ni comprises dans toutes leurs parties, les apôtres,* établis *par Jesus Christ maitres de 1'univers, ont extrait du corps des Ecritures et réduit à douze courtes sentences tous les mystères qu'il importe de croire.... On l'appelle Symbole des apôtres parceque les apôtres, avant de se séparer pour aller prêcher l'Evangile dans tout l'univers, laissorent aux fidèles cet abrégé de la doctrine; et ce symbole est composé de douze articles, nombre* égal *a celui des douze apôtres qui composèrent.*"—This edition is 1842. [Trans. "The Holy Scriptures, not able to be read in entirety, nor understood in all their parts, the apostles chosen by Jesus Christ to be teachers of the whole world, abstracted the body of Scripture and reduced into twelve brief sentences all the mysteries important to believe.... It is called the Apostles' Creed because the apostles, before separating to preach the Gospel to the whole world, left to the faithful this summary of doctrine; and this creed is composed of twelve articles, the number equal to these twelve apostles who composed it."]

92. Nevin, "The Apostles' Creed," in this volume, 68.

Chapter 3: Nevin and Proudfit: Opposed Views of the Early Creeds

and uncertain in its origin.... The outward history of it shows clearly enough that it did *not* pass at once into the complete form in which it became finally established." (A cruel thrust at the infallibility of the Council of Trent, and of Pius V;[93] in fact, at the truth of the whole testimony of the Roman Church, including councils, popes, catechisms and doctors, as to the history of the creed, down to our own times.) "The very circumstances which go with some to invalidate the credit of the Apostles' creed in what regards the manner of its origin, *we hold to be of special weight in its favour.*"[94] Certainly, the modern doctrine of "development" is far more convenient and pliable for Papal purposes. The Creed *was,* according to the old Roman doctrine, "an extract from the Holy Scriptures"; it is now "a product of the Spirit," "shooting forth spontaneously, by a sort of inward organic force, from the substance of the church itself; the full, free outbirth of the Christian faith." It *was* a rigid formula uttered, perhaps penned, by inspired Apostles; but now it is itself "the primitive form of revelation," "the self-adjusted utterance of the church's faith," "the substance of living Christianity as a whole." It *was* held to a somewhat close and uncomfortable relation to the "mere letter of Christianity, as it stands in the New Testament itself"; now, that "mere letter of Christianity" is "made (for a thoughtful mind,) *secondary* to its living substance as exhibited in the actual mystery of Christ and his church," and "this mystery is actualized," "comes to its revelation as the supernatural in the form of faith by means of the church, and the *primitive form* of this *revelation* is presented to us in THE CREED." On the old Roman system, it was enough that the authority of the church, should be *co-ordinate* with that of the Scripture.[95] It is now held to be *above* it; "the mere letter of Christianity as it stands in the New Testament" being "(for a thoughtful mind,) something *secondary* to its *living substance.*" The Bible is thus *secondary,* the Creed "the primitive of the revelation of the supernatural." And this "Creed was not *made;* it *grew,* self-produced, the spontaneous product of the life of the church. Its contents come *from within,* and not *from without.*" It is "the ancient *creation* of the church." Antiquity was once regarded as the exclusive claim and necessary imprint of Catholicism. It is so no longer. Her own "substance," "spirit," "life," "faith," is the "womb unmeasurable and boundless breast" which "teems and feeds" an endless progeny of "outbirths" and "creations." Unwritten traditions handed down by mysterious transmission from the days and lips of the Apostles, were once affirmed as the warranty of Papal innovations; but "young Rome"[96] turns out of doors without ceremony that hoary imposture and

93. [Pope Pius V (1504–72) oversaw the internal reform of the Roman Catholic Church, standardized the Mass, played a leading role at the Council of Trent, and was an implacable enemy of Protestantism.]

94. Nevin, "The Apostles' Creed," in this volume, 70.

95. *Omnes (scriptores pontificii) parem illi (symbolo) authoritatem tribuunt cum Scripturis canonicis.* [Trans. "All the papal writers, 'like' the creed, share authority with the canonical Scriptures."] Voëtius, 67.

96. [The phrase "Young Rome" indicated the progressive movements within the Roman Catholic Church, such as the Tübingen School, which, influenced by the Idealism of Hegel and Schelling and

absurdity, or keeps its beard only to overawe children with; the creed is now claimed as her own "creation," "the externalization of her consciousness," "the free spontaneous product of her life," "the *self-adjusted* utterance of her faith," "the full, free outbirth of her life"; and of course, she can "create," "externalize," "produce," "adjust," and "bring forth" whenever, whatever, and how much soever she likes; for her *vis genitrix* cannot be other than inexhaustible, her "living substance" being as Dr. Nevin affirms, "divine."⁹⁷ The Χνοῦς ἀρχαῖος, the *antique mould* which of old time gave the Creed and other "products" of "the church" so much of their reverence and authority, is thus brushed away without hesitation, for lo! beneath it, under the magic touch of the modern philosophy, there appears the bloom of perpetual and self-renovating youth. "It is this *living* character precisely, its *self-conserving* and *self-determining* power which clothes it" (the Creed) with its chief title to respect.⁹⁸

One difficulty, however, meets us. As the Creed came to its present size "in the way of free gradual progress and growth,"⁹⁹ why may it not continue to "grow"? Why may not this "trunk" put forth more shoots, more "living branches"? Dr. Nevin decides that it cannot, at least that it will not; having reached "the round symmetrical beauty of its *last* settled form," "its proper *ultimate* and *constant* type."¹⁰⁰ By what authority he thus pronounces the process of "free growth" and "externalization" arrested, *ended, and determined,* he does not inform us. Is it because it has reached the apostolic number of twelve? But let us dispense with conjecture. It is quite needless that the Creed should "grow" any more. It is now large enough. That single article, "I believe in the Holy Catholic Church," with the Papal interpretation, is a gate large enough for "an army with banners" to pass through. What an interminable line of shaven monks, begging friars, lying Jesuits, and inquisitors keen on the scent of heretical blood—what rites, orders, and ordinances ("which the Lord commanded not, neither came it into his mind,") interdicts and indulgences, anathemas and canonizations have already emerged through that ample portal and are ever on the march, a new line defiling at every order from the Vatican. Verily, the "merchandise" that passes in and out at that portal, is great—"the merchandise of gold, and silver, and precious stones, and of pearls, and fine linen and purple, &c., and souls of men"—and all under the sacred auspices and unquestionable sanction of "the *holy* Catholic *Church.*"

Never was so bold a theory of church power and supremacy propounded before. Even the Jesuits, who paid divine honours to the Pope,¹⁰¹ held that the Creed was "an

---

the Romantic tendencies in Schleiermacher, embraced a view of the organic development of doctrine.]

97. Nevin, "The Apostles' Creed," in this volume, 68.
98. Nevin, "The Apostles' Creed," in this volume, 70.
99. Nevin, "The Apostles' Creed," in this volume, 65.
100. Nevin, "The Apostles' Creed," in this volume, 70.
101. "Gregory XV went to visit the dying Cardinal, (Bellarmine) who addressed him in these words, *Lord, I am not worthy that thou shouldst come under my roof,* (*Domine, non dignas sum ut intres, &c.*) words which prove to what point Cardinal Bellarmine carried his respect for the Vicar of Jesus Christ." *Vie de Bellarmine,* by M. Abbé Migne. Preface to his *Catholic Encyclopedia.* "Must not

Chapter 3: Nevin and Proudfit: Opposed Views of the Early Creeds

extract from the Holy Scriptures," "the commandments of the Church based on the law of God" and "the Pope the vicegerent of Christ upon earth." But here is "a *regula fidei*," "a primitive form of faith" "externalized from the inmost consciousness," "created from the substance" of the Church herself.[102] And yet, "to reject *it*, is to reject the ancient faith; to make light account of *it*, is to make light account of the *very substance of Christianity*." "If the rule of faith is to have any reality, or be of any force for us whatever, we must own its presence in *the Apostles' Creed*. We shall have for it" (Dr. Nevin warns us) "most certainly but a figment of our own minds, if we pretend to find it *anywhere else*"—even of course in "the mere letter of Christianity as it stands in the New Testament."

It is but little to say of this system that it antiquates the Scriptures, it nullifies inspiration,[103] it removes the Church from its ancient foundation "of the apostles and prophets, Jesus Christ himself being the chief corner stone," and hangs it, self-poised, in mid air. It makes it the source of law, faith and life to itself. What reverence does it leave, what significance even, for those glorious and precious revelations, "Thy word is truth. I am the Life. Lo, I am with you always, even unto the end of the world"; or what force in those precepts, "Search the Scriptures, for *in them ye think ye have eternal life*." "Let the word of Christ dwell in you richly." What shadow of respect for that divine communication, (appended alike to the "law which was given by Moses" and to "the grace and truth which came by Jesus Christ"); "Ye shall not *add* unto the word which

---

all serious believing Protestants," says Dr. Schaff, (*Principle of Protestantism*) "feel themselves more closely related in spirit to a Bellarmine . . . than to . . . a Bruno Bauer?" If we are called upon to choose between an idolater and an atheist, our hesitation is not long. We say neither. Blessed be God, we have a better alternative. ["The Principle of Protestantism," in *The Development of the Church*, MTSS 3, ed. Bains and Trost, 124. Bruno Bauer (1809–1882) was a student of Hegel who claimed that the New Testament was more indebted to ancient Greek philosophy, particularly Stoicism, than it was to Judaism.]

102. We cannot wonder then, that Dr. Nevin lays down the following order of precedence and in doing so, distinctly takes the side of Rome in the great central issue between her and Protestantism, "*First the Church, and then the Bible.* So in the creed, 'I believe in the Holy Catholic Church,' not 'I believe in the Holy inspired Bible.' Not, certainly, to put any dishonour on this last, but to lay rather a solid foundation for its dignity and authority in the other article" (91). To lay a solid foundation for the dignity and authority of the Bible, in the faith of the Church!!

103. It is well know that the Mystical Philosophy holds that a revelation being *ex necessitate rei*, made to the intuitional faculty, a verbal revelation is a sheer impossibility, and a transmission of the contents of a revelation from one mind to another, of course, yet more so,—and therefore the ideas that "holy men of God spake as they were moved by the Holy Ghost," and that "*all Scripture is given by inspiration of God*" are just to be regarded as among the myths of the world's childhood. (Dr. Nevin, however, holds to inspiration. He thinks that Ursinus was inspired. "In a deep and true sense," he says (*History and Genius of the Heidelberg Catechism* [(Chambersburg, PA: Publication Office of the German Reformed Church, 1847)], 129,) "we may even say he was inspired. He spake not of himself nor from himself simply: but *it was the life of the Church, which is always truly a divine life, that sought and found expression through his words.* It is this pre-eminently that imparts to the Catechism its power and glory." The Church, then, it seems, if she can "create," "produce from her own substance" and externalize from her own consciousness a creed, is quite competent to *inspire* a catechism. Whether Ursinus would have laughed at the nonsense or shuddered at the blasphemy of such "philosophy," we will not pretend to decide.)

I command you, neither shall ye diminish aught from it, that ye may keep the commandments of the Lord your God." "If any man shall *add* unto these things, God shall add unto him the plagues that are written in this book."[104]

The issue here is of no less magnitude than *the source and derivation of Christian truth*. The Papal theory, in whatever form, makes the "Apostles' Creed" a *separate, subsequent* and *sufficient* revelation of Christianity. Whether, with some of the eminent Papal writers, you hold it to be the composition of the "hundred and twenty" including the Apostles,[105] (Acts i. 15) or of the twelve Apostles, immediately after the descent of the Holy Spirit at Pentecost,[106] or of the twelve with Paul and Barnabas, making, of course, fourteen authors and articles,[107] or of the twelve in the second year of Claudius, before they fled to escape the persecution of Herod:[108] whether it was *written* by the Apostles, or orally delivered and committed to the memory of the faithful:—whether it was a collect from the Scriptures,[109] or given by the inspiration of God, apart from all previous or other revelations;[110] whether its sentences were contributed singly or severally by the Apostles, Peter, (of course) beginning, "believe in God the Father Almighty," John adding, "Maker of heaven and earth," James, &c., &c,;[111] whether it was drawn up to preserve its own unity,[112] or to serve as an invariable and perpetual

---

104. [John 17:17; Matt 28:20; John 5:39; Col 3:16; John 1:17; Deut 4:2; Rev 22:18.]

105. *Antonius Nebrissensis*, cited by Voss, 3. [Nebrissensis (1441–1522) was a noted Spanish biblical scholar and grammarian.]

106. *Ante conversionem Paulii*, of course. Bonaventura, cited by Voëtius, 66. [Trans. "Before Paul's conversion."]

107. Whose fourteen *sententiae*, like so many others, were woven into a holy *basket* by Peter [Lombard], *quasi cophinum contextuit Petrus* [Trans. "as Peter wove a basket"]. Albertus Patavius, quoted by Voss, 4.

108. Baronius, in Heidigger, 640, 1. [Caesar Baronius (1538–1607) was a Roman Catholic cardinal and an ecclesiastical historian.]

109. *Extrait du corps des Ecritures*. [Trans. "Extract from the body of the Scriptures."] Bellarmine, Preface to *The Catechism of Pachasius Radbertus*, also quoted by Voss, 4.

110. This is the general opinion of the Papal writers. *Sententia est Vulgatior* [Trans. "The sentence is more common,"], Voss, 4.

111. Each apostle contributing his *bolus* [Trans. "morsel"], and all together making a σύμβολον, or *epulum spiritual* [Trans. "spiritual banquet"], as they call it, with a ridiculous disregard of the meaning of the word, not σύμβολον but συμβολή, signifying such a *collation* [Trans. "gathering"]. And what, for four hundred years, became of half the *bolus* of Thomas ("he descended into hell") and for nearly the same length of time of the same portion of the *bolus* of James the son of Alpheus, "the Holy Catholic Church"? And yet this silly story has been adopted by Baronius; "*ex Augustino suppositito.*" [Trans. "from pseudo-Augustine."] Heidegger, 640, "a sermon falsely attributed to St. Augustine." Lord Peter King, 26. The passage is now given up on all hands.

112. So some after Rufinus "*normam sibi futurae praedicationis in commune constituunt ne forte alii adducti, diversum aliquid his qui ad fidem Christi invitabuntur, exponerent* [Trans. "they together constituted for themselves the norm for their future preaching, lest perhaps with others having been added, these who were called to faith in Christ, might set forth something different."], 1. As if the illumination of the Holy Ghost were not sufficient to secure Apostolic unity!

formula[113] of the faith to Christians throughout the world and to all future time, it is, through all these modifications, *an independent revelation of Christianity apart from and unknown to the inspired Scriptures, bearing in itself the contents of the Christian faith*—"the things which Christian men ought to hold," and is so finally ruled and settled by the supreme authority of the Papacy.

[Nevin's Theory of Development]

In the later and far bolder form of the Papal theory, advanced by Dr. Nevin and the men of the "development," that namely, which holds it to be neither "got from the Bible,"[114] nor "imposed on the Church by Christ or his Apostles,"[115] but "a growth from within,"[116] "a creation of the Church," "owing its *origin* to the faith of the Church," vivified, as she is, by the incarnation of the Son of God, and so made "the bearer" and "depository of supernatural powers,[117] and yet "the primitive form of revelation," to which "the mere letter of Christianity, even as it stands in the New Testament, is something secondary," "the substance of living Christianity as a whole, in its primary form of faith,"[118] in this form we say, there is a yet more distinct renunciation of all dependence of the Church on the Scriptures, and all necessary connection between them.[119] If this theory be true, the Creed ought forthwith to take the place of the Bible throughout the whole Christian economy. Instead of "searching the Scriptures," men must henceforth *search the Creed*. Instead of having the "word of Christ dwell in them richly," they must go *to the Creed created by the Church*, for "doctrine, reproof, correction, and instruction in righteousness." Instead of being "sanctified by the word of God," they must be *sanctified by the Creed of the Church*. All things must be changed to suit. Preachers, instead of taking a text from the Bible, must henceforth take a text from the creed.[120] The Church instead of singing,

---

113. *Certa et constans formula* [Trans. "A certain and consistent formula"]; such is the general account of its design.

114. Nevin, "The Apostles' Creed," in this volume, 70.

115. Nevin, "The Apostles' Creed," in this volume, 54.

116. Dr. Nevin, Antichrist, p. 52. [Nevin, "Antichrist" in *One. Holy, Catholic, and Apostolic*, Tome One, MTSS 5, ed. Hamstra, 204.]

117. Dr. Nevin, Antichrist, p. 52. [Nevin, "Antichrist" in *One. Holy, Catholic, and Apostolic*, Tome One, MTSS 5, ed. Hamstra, 204.]

118. "All Christianity starts in the realities of the Creed, and is of no force any farther than these continue to be felt in the way of faith." Antichrist, p. 67. [Nevin, "Antichrist," in *One. Holy, Catholic, and Apostolic*, Tome One, in MTSS 5, ed. Hamstra, 216, n59.]

119. So the Romanist Möhler, though by no means so boldly as Dr. Nevin, "when ecclesiastical education in the way described, takes place in the individual, *the Sacred Scriptures are not even necessary.*" *Symbolism*, p. 350. [Proudfit is alluding to Johann Adam Moeller (1796–1838), a leading member of the progressive Tübingen School of Roman Catholic theologians who argued that ecclesial doctrine had evolved over the centuries.

120. Rather scanty material, but by the wise men of this school, *preaching* is thought to have been

"Thy word is everlasting truth,"

must sing,

"*My creed* is everlasting truth!"

The change would greatly abridge the cost and labour of our Bible Societies, which would then have only to print creeds instead of Bibles. It would quite supersede the voluminous emissions of our Boards of Publication. How light would be the burden of the colporteur! It would effectually tame the restless energy of our republicanism, and prove an absolute panacea for "the virulence of the *sect-plague.*" Instead of the process ("full of peril") of *thinking* and *inquiring,* Christians would only have to *believe.*[121] In a word, in place of the Bible, through all the relations of Christianity, would be installed the Creed; from forth the ninth article of which, "the Holy Catholic Church" would "externalize" all matters of faith and practice, and (in the gateway of that article stands the Papal throne) would legislate[122] once more to Christendom and to the world.

Catholic instrumentalities, too, would be restored to full operation. Instead of an "Evangelical Alliance" to promote unity of faith, we should have an Inquisition; instead of gospel preachers, cowled monks and shaven priests; instead of "reasonings of righteousness, temperance, and judgment to come," racks and thumb-screws; for evangelists, begging friars; for "the Bible and God's Spirit,"[123] Papal bulls, anathemas, and indulgences. The citizen would become a *peasant* again, and the Christian a *Catholic.* The Church and the world would be replaced as they were under the midnight glories of the Dark Ages. This is "the great Millennium, the Church of the Future," after which Dr. Nevin tells us, "very many truly Catholic souls are *silently* breathing an impatient, *How long, Lord*?"[124]

Of all the millennarian schemes of our age, we like Dr. Nevin's millennium of darkness and retrogression, the least.

Is it not, in every aspect, a new Christianity—"another gospel?"

The theory may seem ridiculous, but it is a grave matter, associated and identified as it is, with this still vast and powerful Papacy. On that stock it has grown. If the germ of mysticism had been "grafted" into any branch of vital and scriptural Christianity, it would have withered and died at once: for the stock and scion being of different genera, the bud would not take. But inserted in "Catholicism," it has vegetated with

---

overvalued. [Scriptural allusions or citations: Acts 17:11; Col 3:16; 2 Tim 3:16; 1 Tim 4:5.]

121. "Faith," says Dr. Nevin "goes before *all thought* and lies at the ground of it." "Our creed *precedes* and *underlies* our *intelligence*."

122. "What a conception is that of Christianity, which excludes from its organic jurisdiction the broad, vast conception of the commonwealth or state!" Catholicism, p. 14. [Nevin, "Catholicism," in *One, Holy, Catholic, Apostolic*, Tome Two, MTSS 7, ed. Hamstra, 22.]

123. "Few seem to have the least fear of schism, if only they can lay claim in their own way, to *the Bible and God's Spirit.*" Ant. p. 84. [Nevin, *Antichrist*, in *One, Holy, Catholic and Apostolic*, Tome One, MTSS 5, ed. Hamstra, 229.] Cf. John v. 39, and 1 John ii. 20, 27, both from the *mystical* Apostle!

124. Antichrist, p. 71 and 76. [A patische and paraphrase of Nevin, "Antichrist," in *One, Holy, Catholic, Apostolic*, ed. Hamstra, 222 and 218. Nevin had not capitalized "Catholic."]

a prodigious luxuriance. It is, indeed, a vast advance on any earlier "stadium"[125] of that system. Yet it is strictly and legitimately a development of it. The Roman Church began her apostasy, by claiming powers which the word of God did not grant nor even permit to any part of the Christian Church; she next prohibited the Scriptures because they rebuked and exposed her corruptions of Christian truth, and encroachments on Christian freedom; the Creed was a great assistance to her in this matter, serving in her abuse of it to antiquate (as summaries often have done) the volume from which it had been compiled. She at length took courage to contradict and *nullify* the plain and acknowledged precepts of the word of God;[126] and now at last, if she betakes herself to the encampment prepared for her by German mysticism—and she seems on the march to do so—she fully and for ever *forsakes* and renounces the word of God, shakes off what slack allegiance she has hitherto professed to hold to it, and proclaims her Creed "the primitive revelation," and herself the "Creator of the Christian faith."

This is certainly, a new phase in the "revelation" of "the man of sin and the son of perdition." Never before has he so distinctly taken the position of Antichrist; never before so boldly "seated himself in the temple of God, boasting himself that he is God." For who less than God can (either in the objective or subjective sense) *originate and create faith*?

May God speed forward that revelation *in his time!* For "the day of Christ shall not come [. . .] till that wicked be revealed, whom the Lord shall consume with the Spirit of his mouth, and shall destroy with the brightness of his coming [2 Thess 2:3, 8 paraphrased]."

Dr. Nevin does not attempt to bring from the Bible any testimony to its own degradation below the Creed. But he does claim for his theory—a theory never heard of by Christian, Pagan, or Infidel, till the time of Strauss[127]—the sanction of every thing that is venerable in the history of that Christianity of which it strikes at the very foundation.

125. "The Church is never stationary, but always passing forward from one stadium of perfection to another." Antchrist, p. 35. [Nevin, "Antichrist," in *One, Holy, Catholic, Apostolic*, MTSS 5, ed. Hamstra, 190, n20.] What "Church" is that whose every successive *stadium* is a further departure from the word of God? What will be her last *stadium*?

126. So in the Council of Constance, "*Decretum est Sept. viii. circa S. Eucharistiae Sacramentum quod 'licet* Christus *sub utraque specie instituerit, eundemque administrandi modum Ecclesia Primitiva retinuerit,* his tamen non obstantibus, *consuetudo* Ecclesiae, *qua sub specie panis tantummodo a laicis suscipitur,* est observanda.'" [Trans. "It is decreed September 8, concerning the holy eucharist that 'although *Christ* instituted it under both species, and the primitive church retained the same mode of administration, *nevertheless these are not to be observed*; the custom of the *church*, by which it is received by the laity under the species of bread only, *is to be observed*.'"] William Cave (1637–1713), *Scriptorum Ecclesiasticorum Historia Literaria* (London, 1688), 150. What was this canon less than a declaration of open revolt from Christ, and at the same time repudiation of Christian antiquity? [William Cave was an Anglican theologian and patristic scholar, and one of Charles II's chaplains.]

127. Dr. Nevin acknowledges, in the following passage, ("The Apostles' Creed," 67) to what notable source the Christian church is indebted for the *first hint,* which, by "thoughtful minds," has been wrought out into this new theory. "The main use of this work of Strauss, if it can be allowed to have any, *is found just in this,* that *it serves,* for a thoughtful mind, to *make the mere letter of Christianity, even as it stands in the New Testament itself, something secondary to its living substance, as exhibited*

"It, (the Creed) forms," he says, "the basis of all sound Christian profession in the Protestant, no less than in the Roman Catholic Church."[128]

[The Creed in the Reformation]

"It lay at the foundation of all Christianity with Luther himself. . . . It was a necessary means of grace with him, he tells us himself, to repeat the creed with the Lord's Prayer, throughout his life." "*The creed with the Lord's Prayer!*" Here is Luther's own enumeration: "The Lord's Prayer, the Ten Commandments, the Articles of Faith, some of the Psalms,[129] &c., I recite with myself early in the morning, and as often as I have a little leisure;"—and he goes on to discourse of "the power of the word of God," and "the blessedness of daily meditation upon it," saying, that "no perfume is more precious, no odour more efficacious against devils and bad thoughts, than if thou handle by constant use the word and precepts of God, mixing therewith familiar discourses upon it, singing and meditating the same. This, verily, is that *holy water* and true *sign*[130] (of the cross) whereby Satan is put to flight, and which he dreads above all things."[131]

So much for Luther's "necessary means of grace" in private, which were somewhat more ample than Dr. Nevin's *abridgment* would seem to imply. "His (Luther's) sense," Dr. Nevin adds, "of the authority that belongs to the ancient catholic faith altogether, was very earnest and deep." Undoubtedly it was; but not of that "catholic faith" of which "the creed is the primitive revelation." Hear his own words:

"By what sign, then," he says,[132]

---

in the mystery of Christ and his church. . . . So much of truth, however, may be allowed to it, that this mystery . . . comes to its revelation . . . by means of the church. . . . The primitive form of this revelation is presented to us in the Creed." A fitting master, verily, to teach the Church of Christ such a lesson! When she goes to school to such "filthy dreamers" as Strauss, she may expect to come back with the discovery that the word of her Lord is "something secondary" to her own consciousness! [David Friedrich Strauss (1808–74) was a controversial theologian and biblical critic who attempted to reconstruct the history of Jesus by using the tools of left-wing Hegelianism. He provoked a vehement reaction to his work by discounting all elements of supernaturalism in the New Testament texts.]

128. Nevin, "The Apostles' Creed," in this volume, 50.

129. *Orationem Dominicam, Decem Praecepta, Articulos Fidei, Psalmos aliquot. &c.* [Trans. "Lord's Prayer, Ten Commandments, Articles of Faith, some Psalms. etc."] Catechism Maj. Preface, Karl August [von] Hase, *Symbolik*, 392. [Karl August von Hase (1800–90) was a German Protestant theologian and church historian who was known for his compendia of Lutheran doctrinal teachings. He was also great-grandfather of the twentieth century theologian Dietrich Bonhoeffer. See Martin Luther's *Large Catechism* for the sections to which von Hase refers.]

130. *Haec vere aqua illa sanctificata, verumque signum.* [Trans. "This truly is that sanctified water and true sign."]

131. Ibid., 393.

132. Nevin's response to the book of Ambrosius Catharinus, *Apologia pro veritate catholicæ et apostolicæ fidei ac doctrinæ, adversus impia ac pestifera Martini Lutheri dogmata*" [Trans. "Apology for the truth of the catholic and apostolic faith against the impious and pestiferous teachings of Martin Luther."] (Wittenberg, 1546) II:147. [Ambrosius Catharinus (c. 1485–1553) was Archbishop of Conza and a vigorous and prolific critic of Lutheranism.]

Chapter 3: Nevin and Proudfit: Opposed Views of the Early Creeds

shall I know a church? For some visible sign must be given, whereby we may be gathered together to hear the word of God. I answer, the necessary sign is Baptism, the Lord's Supper, and, most of all, the Gospel.[133] These are the three signs, badges, and characters of Christians.... Where thou seest that the Gospel is not, (as we see in the synagogue of the Papists)[134] there thou mayest not doubt, *there is no church,* even though they baptize and eat from the altar .... But there thou mayest know is Babylon, full of witches, owls, cormorants, and other monsters.[135] ... The Gospel, before Baptism and the Lord's Supper, is the one surest and noblest sign of a church, since by the Gospel alone, it is conceived, shapen, nourished, brought forth, brought up, fed, clothed, adorned, strengthened, armed, preserved,—in brief, *the whole life and substance of the church is in the word of* God,[136] even as Christ says, man liveth by every word which proceedeth from the mouth of God."

"The Reformed Church here," says Dr. Nevin, was of one mind with the Lutheran. Thus, in Calvin's Catechism," &c.

Calvin's intention in following the order of the Creed, and his view of the Creed itself is nowhere so fully stated as in his *Institutes*. "Thus far," he says, at the close of the second book,

I have followed the order of the Apostles' Creed; because, since it sketches in few words, the heads of redemption,[137] it may serve to us the purpose of an index,[138] in which we behold distinctly and severally, the Christian subjects which deserve our attention. I call it the Apostles' Creed, little concerned meanwhile, about its authorship.[139] ... The only point of importance, I hold to be placed beyond controversy, that the whole history of our faith is therein set forth succinctly and in clear arrangements, and that nothing is contained in it which is not sealed by solid testimonies of Scripture.[140]

And again, "A creed must be a complete summary of our faith, into which *nothing may be infused, which is not derived from the purest word of God.*"[141] And, "since we

---

133. *Omnium potissimum, Evangelium.* [Trans. "Among all, especially the Gospel."]

134. *Sicut in Synagoga Papistarum videmus.* [Trans. "As we see in the synagogue of the papists."]

135. *Babylonem ibi esse scias, plenam lamiis, pilosis ululis, onocrotalis, aliisque monstris.* [Trans. "There you may know Babylon to be full of witches, hairy owls, pelicans, and other monsters."]

136. *Breviter, tota vita et substantia Ecclesiae est in verbo Dei.* [Trans. "Briefly, the whole life and substance of the church is the word of God."]

137. *Capita redemptionis.* [Trans. "Heads of redemption."]

138. *Vice tabulae nobis esse potest.* [Trans. "It can serve as lists for us."]

139. *De auctore interim minime solicitus.* [Trans. "Concerning the author, nevertheless caring little."]

140. *Nihil autem contineri, quod solidis Scripturae testimoniis non sit consignatum.* [Trans. "And nothing is contained there, which is not attested by the solid testimonies of Scripture." Calvin, *Institutes of the Christian Religion*, I, 527.]

141. *Nisi ex purissimo Dei verbo petitum.* [Trans. "Nothing except what is asked from the most

see the whole sum of our salvation and even its several parts comprehended in Christ, *we must beware lest we derive even the minutest portion of it from any other source."*[142]

"So," continues Dr. Nevin, "in the admirable symbol of the Palatinate, the Heidelberg Catechism, it is 'the articles of our catholic and undoubted Christian faith,' as comprehended in the same Creed which are made to underlie the doctrine of salvation from beginning to end." And again,[143] "it" (the Heidelberg Catechism) "is based directly upon the Apostles' Creed, *with the sound and most certainly right feeling, that no Protestant doctrine can ever be held in a safe form, which is not so held as to be in truth, a living branch from the trunk of this primitive symbol in the consciousness of faith.*"

The Heidelberg Catechism consists of three parts. The *second* of these follows the order of the Apostles' Creed. What it is that *underlies the doctrine of salvation*, to the apprehension of the author of the Catechism, (Ursinus,) is best learned from his own words. He inserts the Creed in his Catechism, with these and the like preliminary cautions. "Faith is borne upon the whole word of God and firmly assents to it.[144] . . . *Human traditions*, edicts of popes and decrees of councils are excluded"[145] (from the ground of faith). *"For faith can rest on the word of God alone, as its immovable foundation.*[146] Christians therefore, are neither to form for themselves matters of faith, nor to embrace what is formed or handed down by men, but *to believe the gospel."*[147]

And with regard to this theory of a church-created creed, if Ursinus had been gifted with prescience to foresee that combination of Popery and mysticism, he could not have struck it with greater precision than he has done in the following words.

"Certain it is that no Church, whether of angels or of men, has power to frame new laws concerning the worship of God, or *new articles of faith binding the conscience*. For that belongs to God alone. Nor are we to believe God on the testimony of the Church, but the Church on the testimony of God."[148]

---

pure word of God."] Ibid., paragraph 8, 513.

142. *Cavendum ne vel minimam portiunculam alio derivemus.* [Trans. "Beware lest we derive even the smallest portion from another source."] Ibid., paragraph. 19, 527.

143. Introduction to George Washington Williard's Ursinus, [*The Commentary by Dr. Zacharias Ursinus on the Heidleberg Catechism*], 15.

144. *Fides igitur fertur in omne Dei verbum, eique firmiter assentitur.* [Trans. "Therefore faith is brought forth in every word of God, and firmly assents to it."]

145. *Excluduntur traditiones humanae, &c.* [Trans. "Human traditions are excluded, etc."]

146. *Solo Dei verbo tanquam immoto fundamento.* [Trans. "On the word of God alone as its immovable foundation."] Ursinus, *Exposition of the Heidelberg Catechism*, Question 22.

147. Supported by Mark i. 15. –1 Cor. ii. 5.

148. *Certum est, nee angelorum, nee hominum ecclesiam habere potestatem condendi novas leges de cultu Dei, aut novos articulos fidei obligantes conscientiam. Id enim est solius Dei. Neque Deo propter ecclesiae, sed ecclesiae propter Dei testimonium credendum est.* [Trans. "It is certain, neither the church of the angels nor of men has the power to compose new laws for the worship of God or new articles of faith binding on the conscience. That belongs to God alone. Nor is God to be believed on the witness of the church, but the church is to be believed on the witness of God."] Ursinus, Question 23.

Chapter 3: Nevin and Proudfit: Opposed Views of the Early Creeds

Dr. Nevin claims also the sanction of the "Gallican," "Belgic," and "Helvetic Confessions," and "the Articles of the Church of England"[149] in support of his creed theory. A short citation from each will show what these "good confessions" "witness before" the world to be the fountain of Christian truth and the rule of Christian faith.

The Gallican Confession,[150] (after the list of the canonical books) declares as follows.

"We recognize these books to be canonical and the certain rule of our faith,[151] not so much by the common harmony and consent of the Church, as by the testimony and interior persuasion of the Holy Spirit, who makes us to discern them from other ecclesiastical books, on which, though they yet be useful, no man can found any article of faith."[152]

"And since it" ("the word which is contained in these books and proceedeth from God"[153])

> is the rule of all truth,[154] containing all that is necessary for the service of God and our salvation, it is not lawful for men nor even for angels to add thereto, nor to diminish or change it. Whence it follows, that neither antiquity, nor customs, nor multitude, nor human wisdom, nor judgments, nor sentences, nor edicts, nor decrees, nor councils, nor visions, nor miracles, must be opposed to that Holy Scripture, but on the contrary, all things must be examined, proved and reformed according to it.[155] And in this view,[156] we acknowledge the three symbols, to wit, of the Apostles, of Nice [Nicea], and of Athanasius, because they are conformed to the word of God.[157]

---

149. Nevin, *Apostles' Creed*, in this volume, 51.

150. [The Gallican Confession (1559) was composed for the Reformed churches in France. Much of it was authored by John Calvin.]

151. *Règle certaine de nostre Foy*. [Trans. "Sure rule of our faith."] Schaff, *The Creeds of Christendom*, III:361.

152. *Sur lesquels (encore qu'ils soyent utiles), on ne peut fonder aucun article de Foy*. [Trans. "Upon which, however useful, we cannot found any articles of faith."] Schaff, III:361–62. Confessio Fidei Gallicana, Article IV. H. A. Niemeyer, *Collectio Confessionum in Ecclesiis Reformatis* (Leipzig, 1840), 314.

153. *Procédée de Dieu*. [Trans. "Proceeded from God."] Schaff, III:362.

154. *La règle de toute vérité*. [Trans."The rule of all truth."] Ibid.

155. *Ainsi au contraire, toutes choses doivent etre examinées, reiglées et reformées selon icelle*. [Trans. "... but on the contrary, all things should be examined, regulated, and reformed according to them."] Ibid.

156. *Suivant cela*. [Trans. "And therefore."] Ibid.

157. *Pour ce qu' ils sont conformés a la parole de Dieu*. [Trans. "For they are conformed to the word of God."] Article V. Ibid.

The Belgic Confession[158] is admirably full and clear "*de auctoritate*"[159] [Trans. "concerning authority"] and "*de perfectione*[160] [Trans. "concerning perfection"] *Sacrae Scripturae.*" We cite but one sentence: "Since the whole method of that divine *cultus* which God requires from the faithful,[161] is therein most exactly and copiously described;[162] for no man, though he be endowed with Apostolic dignity, nor even for any angel sent down from heaven, as holy Paul speaketh, is it lawful to teach otherwise than we have been already taught in the sacred Scriptures."[163]

In the article on "the most Holy Trinity" it says, "we freely receive those three symbols, namely, the Apostolic, Nicene and Athanasian."[164] The Helvetic Confession is particularly exact and full on the relation of church doctrine, whether brought out in the shape of interpretation, tradition or creed, to the Scriptures.[165]

"The Canonical Scripture," it declares,[166]

> which is the word of God, delivered by the Holy Spirit, and set forth to the world by prophets and apostles, is the most ancient, perfect and exalted philosophy[167] and alone contains all[168] that conduces to the true knowledge, love and communion of God, to genuine piety and to the ordering of a devout and holy life.
>
> This holy, divine Scripture, is interpreted by none other than itself, and is cleared up by the analogy (under the guidance) of faith and love.[169]

"So far as the holy fathers have not gone aside from this kind of interpretation, we not only receive them as interpreters of Scripture, but revere them as chosen vessels of God."[170]

---

158. [The Belgic Confession [1559] was an influential confessional document of the Reformed churches in the Netherlands, and was used in the seventeenth century to oppose the tenets of Arminianism.]

159. Articles III and V. [Schaff, III:384–85, 386–87.]

160. Article VII. Ibid., 387.

161. *Omnis divini cultus ratio, quam Deus a fidelibus exigit.* [Trans. "The whole reason of divine worship, which God requires of the faithful."]

162. *Exactissime et fuse descripta.* [Trans. "Exactly and expansively described."]

163. *Aliter docere quam jampridem in Sacris Scripturis edocti sumus.* [Trans. "To teach otherwise than what we have already been taught in the holy Scriptures."] Niemeyer, 361, &c.

164. *Recipimus libenter, &c.,* [Trans. "We receive freely, etc."] Article IX. Niemeyer, 365.

165. [The first Helvetic Confession was composed in 1536 and the second Helvetic Confession in 1562–64. Both were intended to be unifying documents for the Swiss Reformed churches, but their influence was felt well beyond Switzerland, shaping Reformed thought from Poland to Scotland.]

166. Article I, Niemeyer, 105.

167. *Die aller* älteste, *volkomneste und höchste leer.* [Trans. "The oldest, the most complete and best teaching."]

168. *Begrifft allein alles das, das zu warer erkantnüss, liebe und eer Gottes, &c.* [Trans. "Understand only that which leads to true knowledge, love, and the glory of God."]

169. *Erklärt werden durch die richtschnur des glaubens und der liebe.* [Trans. "Be explained through the measure of faith and love."] Article. II.

170. Article III. [Schaff, III:212.]

CHAPTER 3: NEVIN AND PROUDFIT: OPPOSED VIEWS OF THE EARLY CREEDS

"For the rest of the traditions of men, however specious and universal, which lead us aside from God and the true faith, we say in the words of the Lord, in vain do they worship me, teaching the doctrines of men."[171]

The doctrine of the Reformed Church of England[172] on the subject of "the Holy Scripture" and of "the Creeds" is as follows:[173] "Holy Scripture containeth all things necessary to salvation; so that whatsoever is not read therein, nor may be proved thereby, is not to be required of any man, that it should be believed as an article of the faith, or be thought requisite or necessary to salvation."

"The Nicene Creed and that which is commonly called the Apostles' Creed, ought thoroughly to be received and believed: for they may be proved by most certain warrants of Holy Scripture."

What then was the "warrant" by which the creeds themselves were to "be proved," what was the "basis" of Protestant doctrine, the "trunk" from which it grew and depended, the only "safe form" in which it could be "held," is abundantly evident from these citations. And every time the Reformed Church uttered her voice on this subject, whether it was among the mountains of Switzerland or in the Universities of Germany and England, or a century later, in the Synod of Dort[174] and the Assembly of Westminster, it was to proclaim that *the word of God is the sole and all-sufficient rule of faith and life to the Christian Church.*

[The Primacy of Scripture in the Church Fathers]

And her voice in this grand and unanimous utterance of it, was a distinct reverberation of that which came down to her, weakened and confused somewhat, but never extinct, through the lapse of ages, from her elder sister, who in *voice* as well as *feature*, bore a strong family resemblance to her, the Primitive Church. And yet Dr. Nevin claims the sanction of this too, for his theory of a "growing," "expanding," "self-adjusted," "church-created" Creed.

> That such an Apostolical rule, as to inward substance, existed and had force, as the unity of the universal Christian faith, in the early Church, no one who does not choose to put out his own eyes, can for a moment doubt; *and yet, it is just as clear that this living rule embodied itself finally, and became permanent and fixed, in the Creed* as we now have it. . . . If the *regula fidei* of Irenaeus and

---

171. Article IV, Ibid.

172. [Proudfit is referring to the Thirty-Nine Articles of the Church of England from 1562 which he considered to be a Reformed statement of faith.]

173. Articles VI and VIII. [Schaff, III:489–91, 492.]

174. [The Synod of Dort (1618–1619) was an international meeting of Reformed Protestants, held in the Netherlands, to settle disputed doctrinal matters between the Arminians and the high-Calvinist party. The belief that God's grace can be freely resisted and other Arminian doctrines that compromised the doctrine of divine election were rejected by the synod.]

THE APOSTLES' CREED

Tertullian, is to have any reality, or be of any force for us whatever, we must own its presence in the Apostles' Creed."[175]

Now, we should be sorry to "put out our own eyes," for this, among other reasons, that then we might *fall into the ditch* with this *blind guide*. But having our eyes open, and Irenaeus and Tertullian before them, we confess ourselves amazed at the temerity of this citation. Shall we summon Erasmus[176] to try conclusions with Dr. Nevin on this point? Here is his testimony: "Irenaeus fought against the troop of heretics with arguments (munitions) drawn *from the Scriptures alone.*"[177]

But let the good Bishop of Lyons, (or Presbyter, for as to the matter of fact, we firmly believe it is of no consequence which title we use, *since he uses both indifferently*), expound himself on this point.

Irenaeus mentions no *regula fidei*. The phrase does not occur in his writings. "*Regula veritatis,*" "*principia Evangelii,*" and the like expressions, he uses often; by these *objective* denominations of the substance or material of the Christian faith, denoting that, to his apprehension, the "contents" of that faith came *from without, and not from within.*[178] In what sense he uses these expressions, we shall allow the reader to judge for himself.

> He who has the immovable *rule of truth* in his possession, which he receives by baptism, will recognize the names, phrases, and comparisons, which are from the Scriptures; but the blasphemous reasoning of those men he will not recognize.... But reducing every one of their assertions to its proper rank, and *applying it to the indivisible substance of truth,* he will strip their figment and reveal its weakness.... And by this demonstration may we know that firm truth which is preached by the Church, and that falsification of it which is contrived by these men.[179]

175. Nevin, "The Apostles' Creed," in this volume, 70.

176. [Desideria Erasmus of Rotterdam (1466–1536) was the leading humanist scholar of the northern Renaissance who encouraged the reading of sacred texts in the original languages. While he sharply criticized many of the features of the Roman Catholic Church, particularly the venality of the clergy, the ignorance and moral laxity of the laity, and the superstitions surrounding the cult of the saints, he remained faithful to the Roman Church.]

177. *Irenaeus, solis scripturarum praesidiis, Adversus haereticorum, catervam pugnavit.* [Trans. "Irenaeus fought against the troop of heretics *with guards from the Scriptures alone.*"] Erasmus Epistle prefixed to the books of Irenaeus.

178. "From within, and not from without," says Dr. Nevin. "The Apostles' Creed," in this volume, 69.

179. *Qui regulam veritatis immobilem apud se habet, quam per baptismum accipit, haec quidem quae sunt ex Scripturis, nomina et dictiones et parabolas cognoscet: blasphemum autem illorum argumentum non cognoscet.... Unumquemque autem sermonum reddens suo ordini, et aptans veritatis corpusculo, denudabit, et insubstantivum ostendet figmentum ipsorum.... et ex ostensione [cognoscere est] eam firmam, quae ab Ecclesia praedicatur veritatem, et ab iis id quod fingitur falsiloquium.* [Trans. "He who has the immovable rule of truth before him, which he received in baptism, will recognize these names, words, and illustrations which are from the Scriptures, but their blasphemous arguments he will not recognize.... But returning every one of their words to its place, and applying the essence of truth, he will expose their fantasies, and reveal its flimsiness ... and by this showing, the truth which

Chapter 3: Nevin and Proudfit: Opposed Views of the Early Creeds

And again: "While we hold the *rule of truth,* that is, that there is one God Almighty, who formed and arranged all things by his word, and from that state in which there was nothing, has brought this, in which all things exist, *as the Scripture declares,* 'for by the word of the Lord were the heavens made,' &c. (where he cites Ps. xxxii. 6, and John i. 3) . . . "So long as we hold *this rule,* therefore, though they (the heretics) utter very many and various things, *we easily convict them of deviating from the truth.*"[180]

Once more for the *regula veritatis* of Irenaeus. "When they (heretics) are refuted from the Scriptures, they turn to the accusation of the Scriptures themselves, as if they were not well expressed, or not of authority which without doubt, is most impudently to blaspheme their own Creator."[181]

"These are *the first principles of the Gospel,* that there is one God, the Creator of this universe, the same who was announced by the prophets and gave the ordering of the law by Moses, the Father of our Lord Jesus Christ, and they know no other God nor any other Father."[182]

"The Gospel is the pillar and strength of that church which is scattered over the whole earth, and the breath of its life."[183]

"The Gospel lifts men up and bears them on its wings to the heavenly kingdom."[184]

> Those who side with Valentinus,[185] being destitute of all reverence, have gone to such a length of audacity, as to denominate that a true Gospel *which in nothing agrees with the Gospels of the Apostles,* so that the Gospel itself has not escaped their blasphemy.[186] . . . All who will, may perceive that it (their gospel)

is preached by the church is recognized, and that false lie deceitfully offered by them."] Irenaeus, *Adversus Haereses,* Book I, Chapter 1, near the end. It is scarcely necessary to remind the reader that we only have Irenaeus in an old Latin translation, which is rude and often obscure.

180. *Cum teneamus autem nos regulam veritatis, id est, &c. quemadmodum Scriptura dicit. . . . Hanc ergo tenentes regulam, licet valde varia et multa dicant, facile eos deviasse a veritate arguimus.* [Trans. "Since we hold ourselves to to the rule of truth, that is etc. just as the Scripture says . . . Therefore holding this rule, although they may say truly various and many things, *we easily prove that they have deviated from the truth.*"] *Adversus Haereses,* Book I, Chapter 19, beginning.

181. *Cum ex Scripturis arguuntur, in accusationem convertuntur ipsarum Scripturarum, quasi non recte habeant, neque sint ex authoritate. . . . Quod quidem impudentissime est blasphemare suum factorem.* [Trans. "When they are convicted from the Scriptures, they turn to accuse the same Scriptures, as if they were not right, nor authoritative . . . which is indeed most impudently to blaspheme their maker."] *Adversus Haereses,* Book III, Chapter 2, beginning.

182. *Haec quidem sunt principia Evangelii, &c.* [Trans. "These which are the *evangelical first principles,* etc."] *Adversus Haereses,* Book III, chapter 11.

183. *Columna et firmamentum Ecclesiae est Evangelium et Spiritus vitae.* [Trans. "The pillar and foundation of the church and the spirit of life is the Gospel."] Ibid.

184. *Evangelium, elevans et pennigerans homines in coeleste regnum.* [Trans. "The Gospel, lifting and bearing men on its wings to the heavenly kingdom."] Ibid.

185. [Valentinus (c.100–160) was a leading gnostic theologian who was a frequent target of Irenaeus' critiques.]

186. *Hi qui sunt a Valentino . . . in tantum processerunt audaciae, uti . . . Veritatis Evangelium titulent, in nihilo conveniens Apostolorum Evangeliis, ut nec Evangelium quidem sit apud eos sine blasphemia.* [Trans. "Those who belong to Valentinus . . . proceed to use with us audacity . . . labeling as the

is unlike those which have been delivered to us by the Apostles, since it is plain from the Scriptures themselves, that it is not that Gospel of truth which was delivered by the Apostles.

The following passage is as remarkable for its beauty as for the distinctness of its testimony. But for the barbarous Latin, it might easily be mistaken for Melanchthon's.[187]

> The church everywhere preaches the truth, and she is the seven-bowled candlestick, bearing the light of Christ.[188] Those, therefore, who forsake the preaching of the church, inveigh against the unskilfulness of holy presbyters,[189] not considering how much better is a religious simpleton than a blasphemer or an impudent sophist. Such, however, are all heretics, and those who think they have found out something beyond the truth, following ambiguous utterances, and making a bewildered and feeble progress, *not always having the tame minds on the same subjects*,[190] but blind themselves are led about by the blind. . . . The opinions of such we must avoid, and look well to it, that we be not inveigled by them; but we must betake ourselves to the church, and be brought up in her bosom, and *nourished by the Scriptures of the Lord*.[191] For the Paradise of the church has been planted in this world. "From every tree of Paradise," therefore, "thou shalt eat," saith the Spirit of God, that is, feed on all the Scripture of the Lord.[192]

And thus he expresses the transition in his argument from the Gospels to the Epistles.

Gospel of Truth, what in no way fits the gospels of the Apostles, so that even the Gospel is not without blasphemy among them."] Ibid.

187. [Melanchthon (1497–1560) was a close theological associate of Luther at Wittenberg and was the chief author of the Augsburg Confession. His *Loci Communes* of 1521 was the first systematic exposition of Lutheran theology.]

188. *Ubique Ecclesia praedicat veritatem, et haec est* ἑπτάμυξος ["seven branched"] *lucerna Christi bajulans lumen.* [Trans. "The Church preaches the truth everywhere, and this is the 'seven branched' lamp oil of Christ, bearing light."] An allusion to Exodus xxv. 31, &c.

189. *Imperitiam sanctorum Presbyterorum arguunt.* [Trans. "They assert the ignorance of the holy presbyters."] You will look in vain for this passage, (or any others of the many in which *Presbyteri* occurs in Irenaeus), in the Index locupletissimus of Feu-Ardentius. *Episcopi* is duly honored. It would not have been edifying, to be sure, to have directed the attention of good Catholics to Irenaeus's declaration that "the tradition from the Apostles is preserved in the church, *per successiones Presbyterorum.* [Trans. "through the succession of presbyters."] (Book III, chapter 2), or to the startling fact that he uses *Presbyteri* and *Episcopi* ["presbyter and bishop'] interchangeably. Cf., e.g., Book. V, chapter 20 with Book III, chapter 2.

190. *Multiforme et imbecille facientes inter, de iisdem non semper easdem sententias habentes.* [Trans. "Making a multifaceted and foolish journey, they don't always have the same understanding."]

191. *Confugere ad Ecclesiam, et in ejus sinu educari et dominicis Scripturis enutriri.* [Trans. "Flee to the Church, and be taught in her bosom and nourished by the Scriptures, the rule of God."]

192. *Id est, ab omni Scriptura dominica manducate.* [Trans. "That is, eat of all the Scriptures of the Lord."] *Adversus Haereses*, Book V, chapter 20.

"Having then examined[193] the sentiment of those who delivered the Gospel to us (from their own fountains[194]), let us now come to the rest of the Apostles, and inquire into their teaching—and to conclude all let us hear the very words of our Lord."

Thus does the champion of the church's faith in the second century muster the war against errorists of every badge and banner. With him the *regula veritatis* is identical with the *principia Evangelii*; the *nomina, dictiones, parabolae quae sunt ex Scripturis* are the *Corpusculum veritatis*, the contact of which, like a powerful talisman, distinguishes *the firm truth which is preached by the church* from *the falsifications of heretics. The preaching of the church* is *the light of Christ. The food of her members* is *the Scriptures of the Lord.* All the weapons of his warfare "against heresies," are included in this inventory—"*the doctrine of those Apostles who delivered the Gospel to us—that of the other Apostles—*and *the very words of our Lord.*"

Then, as to the *regula fidei* of Tertullian. He can surely be no great authority for any thing, who in his latter years departed and revolted from the Christian church, and fell into the incredible folly of Montanism.[195] But his authority, such as it is, is all against Dr. Nevin.

The phrases *regula fidei, lex fidei, regula fidei aut spei, regula Scripturaram, regula Dei*, often occur in his writings. And they are used to denote the same thing. But as Dr. Nevin is partial to the *regula fidei*, let us briefly notice the way in which Tertullian speaks of it. Unhappily for Dr. Nevin's argument, the books of Tertullian in which the *regula fidei* is mentioned, were principally written after he was thrust out of the bosom of the Catholic Church, and the sect-plague was fairly developed on him. But Dr. Nevin must look after that. As our faith is not derived from the Church, nor from "the Fathers," the authority of Tertullian the Montanist is with us much the same with that of Tertullian the Catholic, as far as determining the *regula fidei* is concerned.

The following passage occurs in his book *de Praescriptione Haereticorum*:[196]

> The *rule of faith*,[197] that we may at once declare what we defend, is that whereby it is believed, that there is one God alone, and no other beside the Creator of the world, who brought forth all things from nothing by his own Word first of all sent down; that this Word was called his Son, who under the name of God was variously seen by the Patriarchs, who was always heard in the prophets, was afterwards conveyed by the Spirit and power of God into the

---

193. Book III, chapter 11, end.

194. *Ex ipsis principii ipsorum.* [Trans. "From their first principles."]

195 [Montanism was a late second century movement, originating in the Christian churches of Phrygia in Asia Minor. The Montanists believed in new prophetic revelations, practiced an austere moral discipline, and developed very stringent criteria for church membership. Montanus, their leader, may have thought that he himself was the Paraclete or at least a Spirit-filled prophet. In his later years Tertullian affiliated with the Montanists.]

196. Tertullian, (Paris, 1664), 206.

197. *Regula est autem fidei.* [Trans. "And it is the rule of faith."]

Virgin Mary, was made flesh in her womb, was born of her Jesus Christ,[198] thereafter preached a new law and a new promise of the kingdom of heaven, wrought miracles, was fastened to the cross, on the third day rose again, was taken up to heaven and sat down at the right hand of the Father, sent forth the vicarious power of the Holy Spirit to actuate all who believe, will come again with glory to take his saints to the fruition of eternal life and the promised joys of heaven, and to award the wicked to eternal fire, both being resuscitated with the resurrection of the flesh. *This rule, instituted by Christ*, as will be proved, has no questions among us, but those which heresies introduce and which make heretics.[199]

Again in his book *Adversus Praxeam*[200] we have a *regula fidei* different in form and order from the former, and less full, but *containing the article of the Paraclete*.[201] He immediately adds, "*this rule has descended from the beginning of the gospel.*"[202] There too, occurs the famous maxim, that "what was ancient and original in Christianity was true; what was later, was corrupted."[203]

Again, in his book *de Virginibus Velandis* [*On the Veiling of Virgins*], written also *post lapsum* [Trans. "after the fall"], we meet with the following *regula fidei*.

The rule of faith, indeed, is assuredly *one, only, immovable, incapable of change*[204] namely, that of believing in one Almighty God, the former of the world, and in his Son Jesus Christ, born of the Virgin Mary, crucified under Pontius Pilate, raised from the dead on the third day, received into heaven, to come again to judge the living and the dead through the resurrection also of

---

198. *Ex ea natum egisse (al. exisse) Jesum Christum*. [Trans. "From her was born (or came forth) Jesus Christ."] So, Theophilus of Alexandria, "*de virginali utero, quem sanctificavit*, egressus homo." [Trans. "'from the virginal uterus, which he sanctified, *man came forth*.'"] Jerome's *Works*, ed. Erasmus (Basel, 1516) at the end of Erasmus's *Jerome*. [The Renaissance scholar Desiderius Erasmus was the editor of the earliest edition of the collected works of Jerome (Basel, 1516).]

199. *Haec regula a Christo, ut probabitur, insitiuta*, [Trans. "This rule was by Christ, as will be proved, instituted."] Ibid., 207.

200. Ibid., 501.

201. This was after Tertullian had embraced the strange delusion that Montanus was the Paraclete, whatever sense he attached to that name.

202. *Hanc regulum ab initio evangelii decucurrisse*. [Trans. "This rule came down from the beginning of the Gospel."]

203. *Id esse verum quodcunque primum; id esse adulterum quodcunque posterius*. [Trans. "Whatever was first, that was true, whatever was later, that was corrupt."] A Maxim which in itself includes his testimony against a "growing and expanding creed." This maxim is memorable for having stirred up the soul of the immortal Usher to patristic studies. "He determined to read *through* the fathers and ascertain whether the claim of Stapleton (the defender of Romanism) was founded on fact. The task employed him eighteen years, from the 20th to the 38th year of his age." *Life*, preface to his *Works* (Dublin, 1847) [vol. I:9.] The conclusion to which the search led him is well known. [Thomas Stapleton (1535–1598) was an English Roman Catholic controversialist, living in exile, who opposed the Elizabethan Settlement.]

204. *Regula quidem fidei una omnino est, sola, immobilis, irreformabilis*. [Trans. "The rule of faith is indeed entirely one, only, immovable, unchangeable."] p. 173.

the body. *This law of faith abiding,*[205] other things, pertaining to discipline and conversation, admit of change and amendment;[206]

(This looks a little, it must be allowed, like the modern doctrine of *development.* Let it be observed however, that Tertullian learned this after he had fallen into "sect and schism." Observe, too, of what sort were the *first fruits* of this doctrine of development, for to the above words, Tertullian immediately adds,)

"the grace of God operating and advancing even to the end. For while the devil is ever active, and suggests daily to wicked minds, how can we suppose that the work of God should cease or halt in its progress? *The Lord has therefore sent the Paraclete, that as the limited capacity of man could not take all things at once, Christian discipline might, by degrees, be directed, shapen, and carried to perfection, by that vicarious Holy Spirit of the Lord.*[207]

Thus the first attempt at *innovation,* and *amendment* ("*novitas correctionis*") in Christianity, even in secondary matters ("*discipline et conversationis*") produced the blasphemous *ineptiae* of Montanism. It was the doctrine of *development* that made the good Catholic Tertullian a "sectary," a "heretic," and a Montanist. He advances the doctrine however, cautiously. ("Strauss" had not yet appeared to help him out with it.)

205. *Hac lege fidei manente.* [Trans. "This remaining law of faith."]

206. *Admittunt novitatem correctionis.* [Trans. "They admit the newness of correction."]

207. *Ab illo vicario Domini Spiritus Sancto.* [Trans. "From that vicar of the Lord, the Holy Spirit."] The treatise *de Virginibus Valandis* is reckoned among the writings of Tertullian after he became a Montanist. The subject and strain of it favour that supposition. If it be so, the above passage alone shuts out the charitable suggestions of Mosheim, that "the Paraclete which Montanus pretended to be, was not the Holy Ghost," that "however weak this heretic may have been in point of capacity, he was not fool enough to push his pretensions so far;" and that "this will appear with the utmost evidence to those who read with attention the account given of this matter by Tertullian who was the most famous of all the disciples of Montanus." (*Ecclesiastical History*, I:192. Note.) On the contrary, in the above sentence, Tertullian speaks of the *Paracletus* as identical with the *ille vicarius Domini Spiritus Sanctus*. We do not see how the learned Chancellor relieves the case much by supposing Montanus to have given out that he was ("not the Holy Ghost") but a divine teacher pointed out by Christ under the name of *Paraclete* or Comforter, who was to perfect the gospel by the addition of some doctrines omitted by our Saviour and to cast a full light upon others which were expressed in an obscure manner. Did Christ point out any other *paraclete* or *comforter* which is the Holy Ghost? Were not all *his* operations to be divine? Was he not to "teach *all* things" and to "abide with Christians *forever*?" In our humble opinion, the man who undertook "to perfect the Gospel" &c. and "to cast a full light upon" things already illuminated by the Light of the world was "fool enough" for anything—as much later instances than that of Montanus abundantly show. Few things have been more harmful to Christianity than the palliation of manifest departures from the truth of God. That Tertullian, who was undoubtedly one of the most splendid and powerful intellects of his age should have fallen into the delusion of "this ignorant fanatic" (as Mosheim calls him,) is indeed, a matter of equal grief and wonder. It teaches in fact, not more the sanity of his *faith* than that of his *reason.* But it only proves (and the whole History of the Church scarcely affords a more affecting lesson of the fact) that when a man steps off the *rock* of God's word, there is no telling whither the waves of error may toss him. [Johann Lorenz von Mosheim (1694–1755) was a German historian of the church who sought to investigate ecclesiastical history according to objective principles. In the critical view of Schaff and Nevin he had little sense of historical development, or of the underlying spirit that animated various movements and cultures.]

THE APOSTLES' CREED

The *law of faith, (a Christo instituta)* must *abide*. It is only in matters of "discipline and conversation" that *development* is admissible; and even in these it must be carried forward by "the operation of *the grace of God*," not of the "life," "the organic force," "spontaneously shooting up" of "the Church." Even in his wildest aberrations, Tertullian never dreamed of such folly. His very Montanism was far more sober and reverential than the "Catholicism" of Dr. Nevin.

While in the full communion of the Catholic church, his glowing pen recorded the following sentiments, (and many more like them) on the source and authority of Christian doctrine.[208] "To us (Christians) it is lawful to introduce nothing from our own mind. We have the Apostles of the Lord as our examples, who derived nothing which they taught from their own mind, but *faithfully made over to the nations the system received from Christ*.[209] Therefore, if an angel from heaven should preach otherwise, he must be called accursed by us."

Of heresies he says,

> these are the *doctrines of men* and of devils,[210] born with itching ears from the wisdom of this world, which the Lord pronouncing folly, has chosen the foolish things of the world to the confusion of its own philosophy. For that (philosophy) is the material of worldly wisdom, a rash interpreter of the divine nature and government.[211] The heresies themselves derive their substance from philosophy.[212] . . . The same material is worked up by heretics and philosophers, the same doublings (self-contradictions[213]) involved. . . . What is there in common with Athens and Jerusalem? What has the Church to do with the Academy? What have Christians to do with heretics? *Our institution is from Solomon's porch*,[214] and Solomon himself had taught that the Lord must be sought in simplicity of heart. Let them beware who have brought forward a Stoic, a Platonic and a Dialectic Christianity.[215] *To us there is no need of*

---

208. *De Praescriptione Haereticorum*, 202, &c. It is surprising that any should doubt (as Moreri seems to do) whether this book was written before his lapse. In the 52nd chapter he distinctly calls the tenets of Montanism *blasphemy*.

209. *Nobis vero nihil ex nostro arbitrio inducere licet. Apostolos Domini habemus auctores, qui nee ipsi quiequam ex suo arbitrio, quod inducerent, elegerunt: sed acceptam a Christo disciplinam fideliter nationibus adsignaverunt.* [Trans. "It is not allowed for us to introduce anything from our own thinking. We have the Apostles of the Lord as authorities, who chose not to introduce anything from thier own thinking, but faithfully distributed among the nations the discipline of Christ."]

210. *Doctrinae hominum et daemoniorum.* [Trans. "The doctrines of men and demons."]

211. *Temerarius interpres divinae naturae et dispositionis.* [Trans. "Rash interpreter of the divine nature and order."]

212. *Ipsae haereses a philosophia subornantur.* [Trans. "These heresies are equipped by philosophy."]

213. *Retractatus.* [Trans. "withdrawn, taken back."]

214. *Nostra instituto de porticu Solomonis est.* [Trans. "Our institution is from the porch of Solomon."]

215. *Viderint qui Stoicum et Platonicum et Dialecticum Christianismum protulerunt.* [Trans. "Let them consider/be aware who have offered a Stoic, Platonic, and Dialectic Christianity." "Dialectic" here probably refers to Aristotelianism.]

*curiosity, after Christ, nor of inquiry, after the gospel.*²¹⁶ When we have believed (that), we desire nothing more to believe.

[...]

All things spoken by our Lord were laid down for all. Through the ears of the Jews they have passed to us.

[...]

Thou must, therefore, seek till thou find, and believe when thou hast found:²¹⁷ and nothing more must thou do but keep what thou hast believed;²¹⁸ believing this too, that nothing else is to be believed, and therefore nothing to be required, since thou hast found and believed what was established by him who commands thee to *look after nothing else than what he has established.*

[...]

This limit has he himself fixed for thee who will not have thee to believe *anything else than what he has laid down.*²¹⁹

[...]

What Christ has taught, what must be sought after, what is necessary to be believed.²²⁰

[...]

Heretics themselves treat of the Scripture, and reason from the Scripture. Could they, in fact, speak *of the things of faith* from any other source than from *the letters of faith?*²²¹

[...]

It is evident, therefore, that the whole doctrine which harmonizes in faith with those Apostolic, maternal and original churches is to be reckoned a part of the truth; containing as it does, without doubt, *what the churches received from the Apostles, the Apostles from Christ, Christ from* God; and that all doctrine is to be prejudged of falsehood, which is contrary to the truth of the churches and of the Apostles and of Christ and of God. . . . This doctrine of ours, *the rule of which* we have given above, &c.²²²

The masterpiece of his genius, also, his noble "Apology"²²³ abounds in passages of the like import.

---

216. *Nobis curiositate opus non est post Christum Jesum, nee inquisitione post Evangelium.* [Trans. "For us there is no need for curiosity after Jesus Christ, nor of inquiry after the Gospel."]

217. Could there be a plainer expression, at once of the *right* and the *duty of private judgment?*

218. *Custodiendum quod credidisti.* [Trans. "Guard what you believe."]

219. *Hanc tibi fossam determinavit ipse qui te non vult aliud credere, quam quod instituit.* [Trans. "He who does not want you to believe otherwise, has set this boundary for you, that which he instituted."]

220. *Quod Christus instituit,* quod quaeri oportet, *quod credi necesse est.* [Trans. "What Christ instituted, what is necessary to seek, what is necessary to believe."]

221. *Aliunde scilicet loqui possent de rebus fidei quam ex litteris fidei?* [Trans. "Namely, could they speak of the things of faith from anywhere else than from the letters of faith?']

222. [*De Praescriptione Haereticorum,* 7, 8, 9, 10, 14, 21; http://www.tertullian.org/latin/de_praescriptione_haereticorum.htm, accessed 19 March, 2020.]

223. *Apologeticus adversus Gentes.* It stands at the head of his works and was by the consent of all, written before his heresy. [See http://www.tertullian.org/latin/apologeticus.htm, accessed 19 March 2020.]

He holds out to "the rulers of the Roman empire,"[224] and to "the nations"[225] the Scriptures as the sole fountain of the Christian doctrine, and their divine origin as the sole authorization of the Christian faith. In a masterly contrast between them and the pagan mythologies and philosophies (with which he shows himself profoundly acquainted,[226]) he demonstrates the antiquity, majesty, purity of the "Holy Scriptures," "our letters," the "divine letters," the "holy voices," the "voices of God," "the teaching of God our Master."[227] Of the Old Testament, he says,

> whosoever betakes himself to it will find God: he who contrives to *understand* it, will be compelled to *believe*" it too.[228] The highest antiquity claims for those documents the first authority. The latest of them are found to be not later than the earliest of your sages, lawgivers, and historians. . . . We present a yet higher claim, the majesty of the Scriptures, if not their antiquity. We prove them *divine*, even if you deny them to be *ancient*.[229]
>
> [. . .]
>
> The disciples scattered over the world, obeyed the teaching of their Master, God.[230] [. . .] The Son of God, the Arbiter and Master of our discipline, the illuminator and guide of the human race.[231]
>
> [. . .]
>
> We come together to refresh our remembrance of the divine letters. *With the holy voices we feed our faith*, we exalt our hope, we confirm our trust. . . .

---

224. *Romani imperii antistites*, [Trans. "Roman imperial magistrates."] Chapter 1.

225. *Apologeticus adversus Gentes*.

226. It is not too much to say, that the early Christian apologists discover a far deeper knowledge of the ancient system, in history, thought, and life, than the Pagans themselves. Where among the ancients, shall we find such profound expositions of these as in the "Apologeticus" of Tertullian, and Justin Martyr's ΛΟΓΟΣ ΠΑΡΑΙΝΕΤΙΚΟΣ ΠΡΟΣ ΕΛΛΗΝΑΣ and ΑΠΟΛΟΓΙΑΙ [Trans. "*Exhortation to the Greeks*" and "*Apologies*"] The higher ground of Christianity gave them a *wider* as well as *juster* view of these systems. [For Tertullian, *Apology*, http://m.ccel.org/ccel/schaff/anf03.toc.html (accessed July 22, 2014). For Justin Martyr, "First Apology," ed. and trans. Edward Rochie Hardy in ed. Cyril C. Richardson, *The Library of Christian Classics* (London: SCM Press, 1953), I:242–89.]

227. *Scriptae Sanctae*, [Trans. "Holy Scriptures"] Chapter 39, *litterae nostrae*, [Trans. "Our Letters"] 23, litterae divinae, [Trans. "Divine Letters"] 39, *Sanctae voces* [Trans. "voices of the saints] ibid, *voces Dei*, [Trans. "God's voices"] 31, *praeceptum magisteri Dei*, [Trans. "teaching of God the master teacher"] 21.

228. *Qui adierit inveniet Deum. Qui etiam studuerit intelligere, cogetur et credere*. [Trans. "The one who approaches will find God. The one who tries to understand will be compelled to believe."] Chapter 18. Very different from Dr. Nevin's statement that "our creed *precedes* and *underlies* our intelligence." "The Apostles' Creed," *The Mercersburg Review*, (May 1849). [Nevin, in this volume, 62.]

229. *Majestatem Scripturarum, si non vetustatem. Divinas probamus si dubitatur antiquas*, [Trans. "The majesty of the Scriptures, if not the antiquity. We prove their divinity, even if their antiquity may be douted."] Chapter 20.

230. *Discipuli quoque diffusi per orbem, praecepta Magistri Dei posuerunt*. [Trans. "The disciples indeed were spread over the world, they established/offered/put forth the teachings of God, the master/teacher," 21]

231. *Disciplinae arbiter et Magister, illuminator atque deductor generis humani, Filius Dei*, [Trans. "The arbiter and master of discipline, the illuminator of humankind, the Son of God."] 21.

Chapter 3: Nevin and Proudfit: Opposed Views of the Early Creeds

Your brethren we are too, by the law of nature, our common mother. But how much more worthily are they entitled and esteemed brethren, who acknowledge one Father, God; who drink one spirit of holiness, and *feed on one light of truth!*[232]

The reader has long ago been satisfied that Tertullian, quite as little as Irenaeus, is inclined to dispute with "Strauss" the paternity of the idea which "for a thoughtful mind, makes the mere letter of Christianity, even as it stands in the New Testament itself, something secondary to its living substance as exhibited in the actual mystery of Christ and his Church—which mystery comes to its revelation as the supernatural by means of the Church—the primitive form of which revelation is presented to us in the Creed." Of all the "Heresies" attacked by Irenaeus, none wore a front of so deadly hostility to the Christian faith. Among all the follies into which Tertullian fell, he never wandered so far, nor fell so low, as to conceive of a "Creed," "the primitive form of revelation," "unfolded in fit word and expression from the inmost consciousness of the universal Church!" No other parentage than "Strauss" and "the Papacy" could have generated such a progeny.

We have drawn largely on the reader's patience by citations from Irenaeus and Tertullian, because Dr. Nevin appeals to them by name. But every link in the "*Catena Patrum*" is just as distinctly against him.

"Clement," says Irenaeus,[233] "saw the Apostles themselves and conversed with them, and had in his view the yet audible preaching and tradition of the Apostles." . . . "Under this Clement, the Church which is at Rome wrote a powerful letter to the Corinthians—declaring the traditions which they had lately received from the Apostles." Let us turn then to this "powerful letter" written, if Irenaeus be correct, from one Christian Church to another in the first century.[234] It contains not one word or hint of any other tradition or *regula fidei* than the Scriptures, the study of which it enjoins with affectionate urgency as "the true utterances of the Holy Spirit." "Thus saith the

---

232. *Qui unum patrem Deum agnoverunt, qui unum spiritum biberunt sanctitatis, qui ad unam lucem expaverunt veritatis*, [Trans. "Those who knew the one Father God, who drank of the one spirit of holiness, who were refreshed at the one light of truth."] 39. A beautiful conception at once of the unity of the Church ("the brotherhood" 1 Pet ii. 17) and of the source of that faith, life, and love, which make them *one*! It is impossible to read so fine a passage without a sigh that one who was so *egregie Christianus* [Trans. "excellently Christian"] should ever have been *developed* into a Montanist. We cannot but hope that some kind historical Coroner may find this *felo de se* [Trans. "self-seducer"] the result of *mental aberration*.

233. *Adversus Haereses*, Book III, Chapter 3.

234. That fact has, it must be allowed, a very Puritan look. So has the "powerful epistle" itself, which is addressed, "From the presence of the Church of the Romans." Ἐκ προσώπου τῆς Ῥωμαίων ἐκκλησίας γραφεῖσα. [Trans. "From the presence of the Church of the Romans."] Cot. Pat. Apost. Vol. I, 145. [Manuscript of the Apostolic Fathers held in the collections of the Cottonian Library, now part of the British Museum, London.]

holy word,"²³⁵ "thus saith the wisdom which includes all virtue,"²³⁶ and similar formulae introduce its citations from the Sacred Volume, and support alike its statements of truth and its exhortations to duty.

From the second century, we have heard Dr. Nevin's own authorities. Nor is the testimony of Justin Martyr, (earlier in the same century) at all less clear or explicit. He takes his ground and weapons in his controversy with Trypho the Jew,²³⁷ in these few words, "I am going to cite the Scriptures to you,"²³⁸ and distinctly declines any "apparatus of argumentation," "for," he adds, "I have no skill of that sort, but grace from God alone has been given me for the understanding of *his Scriptures*"²³⁹ of which grace I exhort all to become free and unstinted partakers." And to the Greeks he says, "*the teachers of our religion have delivered to us* nothing of their own human understanding, but *all things from the gift bestowed upon them by God from above*."²⁴⁰

The testimony of Origen will doubtless be accepted in behalf of the third century. It is delivered in the beginning of his book "on First Principles," with a clearness and force which has never been surpassed. "All who believe and are sure that *both grace and truth are by Jesus Christ* and who know that Christ is truth, according to what he himself has said, 'I am the truth,' *receive the knowledge which guides men to a holy and happy life, from no other source than from the very words and teaching of Christ.*"²⁴¹

He speaks of the "miserable audacity"²⁴² of those who attempt to "rectify the Scriptures and to add or take away such things as may seem good to themselves."

His fourth book "*De Principiis*," treats expressly of "the Inspiration of the Divine Scripture and how it is to be read and understood." And he enters on this demonstration for the following reason. "Forasmuch as in the treatment of so important subjects, we are not satisfied to rely on general ideas and the operation of visible things,²⁴³ we

235. Chapter 56.

236. Οὕτως γὰρ λέγει ἡ πανάρετος σοφία [Trans. "Thus says the all-virtuous Wisdom."] Chapter 57.

237. [Trypho the Jew was probably a fictional character invented by Justin to present arguments against the validity of Christianity, arguments that Justin then sought to refute.]

238. Γραφὰς ὑμῖν ἀνιστορεῖν μέλλω [Trans. "I am going to inquire into the Scriptures for you."] *Dialogue with Trypho the Jew*, p.281.

239. Εἰς τὸ συνιέναι τὰς γραφὰς αὐτοῦ [Trans. "In order to understand his Scriptures."]

240. Ἐκ τῆς ἄνωθεν αὐτοῖς παρὰ θεοῦ δοθείσης δωρεᾶς [Trans. "Of the gift from above, given to them by God."]

241. *Omnes qui credunt et certi sunt quod et gratia et veritas per Jesum Christum facta sit et Christum veritatem esse norunt, secundum quod ipse dixit: "Ego sum veritas," scientiam quae provocat homines ad bene beateque vivendum non aliunde quam ab ipsis verbis Christi doctrinaque suscipiunt.* [Trans. "All who believe and are certain that both grace and truth came through Jesus Christ, and know Christ to be the truth, according to what he said: 'I am the truth,' receive the knowledge which urges men to good and happy living from nowhere else than the words and teachings of Christ himself."] (We give the translation of Rufinus as the original Greek is here incomplete.) Περί Ἀρχῶν (*On First Principles*). Origen, *Works*, ed. C. de La Rue (Paris, 1740), I:47.

242. Τόλμης μοχθηρᾶς [Trans. "Miserable audacity."] Ibid., in Matth. xix. 16, & c. III:671.

243. Περὶ τοῦ θεοπνεύστου τῆς θείας γραφῆς [Trans. "Concerning the inspiration of sacred Scripture"].

Chapter 3: Nevin and Proudfit: Opposed Views of the Early Creeds

must draw the proofs of those things which we affirm from those Scriptures²⁴⁴ which are believed by us to be divine, &c. Let us therefore state some of the reasons which lead us to the belief that they are divine."

> *The one Guide*²⁴⁵ of those things which are truly agreeable to reason,²⁴⁶ *is the Word,* the teachings of which, to those who have no ears to hear, seem to manifest discrepancies,²⁴⁷ but they are, in truth, most harmonious. For as the chords of a psaltery or harp, each of which has its own sound, and one which seems to be at variance with that of another, appear to one who is unskilled in musical harmony to be discordant on account of the dissimilitude of sounds, so, those who are not capable of hearing the harmony of God in the sacred Scriptures²⁴⁸ think that the Old Testament is out of tune²⁴⁹ with the New, the Prophets with the Law, the Gospels with one another, or an Apostle with the Gospel, or with himself or another Apostle. But whosoever draws near, taught in the harmony of God,²⁵⁰ and wise in deed and speech, . . . he shall draw forth from them a strain of divine music, having learned to strike in time,²⁵¹ now the chords of the law, then those harmonious²⁵² ones of the Gospel, at one time the prophetic strings and again the like-toned²⁵³ apostolic, and so the apostolic with the evangelical. For he knows that *the whole Scripture is the full-toned and harmonious organ of God, giving forth from many sounds one saving strain to all who will apprehend it.*²⁵⁴

"The fourth and fifth centuries," are Dr. Nevin's especial boast. "The fathers of this glorious period" he assures us, "knew nothing of the view which makes the Bible and private judgment the principle of Christianity or the only rule of faith.²⁵⁵ . . . *The order of doctrine for them was the Apostles' Creed.*"

---

244. Οὐκ ἀρκούμενοι ταῖς κοιναῖς ἐννοίαις καὶ τῇ ἐνεργείᾳ τῶν βλεπομένων [Trans. "Not being content with the ordinary ideas and operation of what is visible"]; which shows his conviction that men have no alternative but these and the teachings of Scripture.

245. Literally "Shepherd" [Ποιμήν].

246. Τῶν λογικῶν [Trans. "That which is reasonable"].

247. Δόξαν μὲν ἐχόντων διαφωνίας [Trans. "Seeming to have discordancies"].

248. Οἱ μὴ ἐπιστάμενοι ἀκούειν τῆς τοῦ θεοῦ ἐν ταῖς ἱεραῖς γραφαῖς ἁρμονίας [Trans. "Those not capable of hearing the harmony of God in the Scriptures"].

249. Ἀνάρμιστον [Trans. "Out of tune"].

250. Πεπαιδευμένος τὴν τοῦ θεοῦ μουσικήν [Trans. "Schooled in the music of God"].

251. Κρούειν ἐν καιρῷ [Trans. "To strike in time"].

252. Συμφώνους [Trans. "Harmonious"].

253. Ὁμοτόνους [Trans. "Single-toned"].

254. Ἐν γὰρ το τέλειον οἶδε καὶ ἡρμόσμενεν ὄργανον τοῦ θεοῦ εἶναι πᾶσαν τὴν γραφήν, μίαν ἀπατελοῦν ἐκ διάφοραν φθόγγων σωτῆρα τοῖς μανθάνειν ἐθέλουσι φωνήν [Trans. "For he knows that the whole Scripture is the full-toned and harmonious organ of God, giving forth from many sounds one saving strain to all who apprehend it."] Ibid.. Commentary on Matth. v. 9, III: 441.

255. Thus does Dr. Nevin *misstate* what he is labouring to undermine and render odious. Whoever held "the Bible *and private judgment*" to be "the principle of Christianity" and "the only rule of faith;"

The distinct and manifest voice of history, never met a more flat and palpable contradiction, than the above assertion.

To accumulate citations is a wearisome task, and to read them scarcely less so. But the generous reader must have a little patience in this matter. These good "fathers of the fourth and fifth centuries," have had hard usage at the hand of Dr. Nevin for some time. They have had all sorts of things laid to their charge; such as *not holding the Bible to be the only source and rule of faith, denying the right of private judgment, looking directly towards Romanism, standing in the very same order of thought that completed itself afterwards in the Roman or Papal Church, acknowledging,* in fact, *the central dignity of the Bishop of Rome,*[256] (which might about as well be affirmed of the seven sages of Greece). They have, in the meanwhile, been in no case allowed to speak for themselves, (though few men ever lived who were better able to do so). It is right, therefore, that some of them should be allowed to give their deposition, in their own language, in relation to the source of truth, the ground and rule of faith, the supreme and sole tribunal before which all controversies pertaining to the Christian doctrine and life, must be tried and decided.

Athanasius thus commences his "Synopsis of the Sacred Scripture." "The whole Scripture of us Christians is inspired of God."[257]

---

or, as Dr. Nevin elsewhere charges in the same piece, "the only source and rule of faith?" The doctrine of the Protestant and Primitive Church (for they are indeed one, and in no respect is their unity more clearly and beautifully revealed than by their unanimity on this point,) is simply this, that the inspired and written word of God is the only source and rule of the Christian faith—that the truth revealed in it shines by its own light, and needs no ecclesiastical or popish spectacles to behold it; that to apprehend and imbibe that heavenly light requires only the open eye of the soul, the spiritual apprehension; and that this is the gift of God, by the operation of his Holy Spirit. Here lies the *controversial summa,* as Melanchthon expresses it, the very pith and point of the dispute between Rome and all true, free and living Christianity, whether it lived before the corruption of the Papacy, struggled and gasped under its dark dominion, or broke forth again into glorious and powerful life at the Reformation. Melanchthon's own words taken from the same passage will be accepted, we doubt not, as a fair exposition of this doctrine. "Here is, as I think, the sum of the controversy. And now I ask you, my masters," (he addresses the *theologasters,* as he terms them, of the Parisian University), "has the Scripture been given in such form that its undoubted meaning may be gathered without exposition of Councils, Fathers, and Schools, or not? If you deny that the meaning of Scripture is certain by itself, without glosses, I see not why the Scripture was given at all, if the Holy Spirit was unwilling to define with certainty what he would have us to believe. Why do the Apostles invite us at all to the study of the Scripture, if its meaning is uncertain? *Wherefore do the fathers desire us to believe them no farther than they fortify their statements by the testimonies of Scripture?*" (A sufficiently plain evidence of what Melanchthon considered the *regula fidei* in the early Church!) "Why too did the ancient councils decree nothing without Scripture, and in this way we distinguish between true and false councils, that the former agree with plain Scripture, the latter are contrary to Scripture? Since the word of God must be the rock on which the soul reposes, what, I pray, shall the soul apprehend from it, if it be not certain what is the mind of the Spirit of God?"—Philip Melanchthon, *Apologia pro Luthero, adv. furoisum Parisiensium Theologastrorum Decretum* (1521).

256. Nevin, "Early Christianity," *The Mercersburg Review,* III (1851), 461–90, 513–62; IV (1852), 1–54.

257. Πᾶσα γραφὴ ἡμῶν Χριστιανῶν θεοπνεύστος ἐστίν [Trans. "The whole scripture of us Christians is inspired by God"]. Athananasius, II:61. Greek text, *Ex Officina Commeliniana* (Heidelberg,

Chapter 3: Nevin and Proudfit: Opposed Views of the Early Creeds

In his Oration against the Gentiles, he says, that "the whole science of piety and of truth shines forth (manifests itself) more brightly than the sun, through the teaching of Christ,"[258] and that "the holy and divinely inspired Scriptures are sufficient of themselves to the annunciation (indication) of the truth."[259]

And thus he concludes that noble discourse: "Rejoice, O thou that lovest Christ,[260] and be of good cheer, for immortality and the kingdom of heaven is the fruit of faith and piety towards him, *only if thy soul be adorned in conformity with his laws.*"[261]

In his disputation with Arius before the Council of Nice [Nicea],[262] when challenged by Arius to the controversy, he replies: "There are great men in the house of God, but if you wish to discuss the matter with me, who am only the least,[263] I will cheerfully meet you in this inquiry, only let us enter on it in the love of truth, and not act contentiously towards *the inspired words*[264] alleged by one another." (A sufficient indication of the rule and arbiter of faith to which both were expected to appeal in that august council, composed of bishops assembled from every part of the world within the jurisdiction of Constantine, who sat in its deliberations as a private Christian.)

Athanasius then lays down the Christian doctrine of God, the Father, the Son, and the Holy Ghost, which he maintains, unfolds and defends against the objections of Arius, solely by by Scriptural authorities, appealing to no rule, formula, or tradition, but to the word of God alone.

When he attests the unity of the Son with the Father, Arius retorts, "You are a Sabellian."[265] Athanasius replies, "Is our Lord then, a Sabellian, when he says, I and my Father are one?" "There appears to me," said Arius, "much discordance[266] in the Scriptures on this point." "God forbid," replied Athanasius, "that man should accuse the divine and inspired Scriptures[267] of not uttering all these things with mutual harmony; for as an even balance,[268] so do all the Scriptures agree to one another."

1600–1).

258. Ἡ μὲν περὶ τῆς θεοσεβείας καὶ τῆς τῶν ὅλων ἀληθείας γνῶσις . . . ἡλίου λαμπρότερον ἑαυτὴν διὰ τῆς Χριστοῦ διδασκαλίας ἐπιδείκνυται [Trans. "The whole science of piety and truth shines forth more brightly than the sun through the teachings of Christ"]. Ibid., I:1.

259. Αὐτάρκεις γάρ εἰσι αἱ ἅγιαι καὶ θεόπνευστοι γραφαὶ πρὸς τὴν τῆς ἀληθείας ἀπαγγελίαν [Trans. "The holy and divine Scriptures are sufficient of themselves to the annunciation of the truth"]. Ibid.

260. Ὦ φιλόχριστε [Trans. "lover of Christ"].

261. Μόνον ἐὰν κατὰ τοὺς αὐτοῦ νόμους ἡ ψυχὴ κεκοσμημένη γένηται [Trans. "Only if they should be adorned in conformity with his laws"]. Ibid., 36.

262. I:82–110.

263. Μοι τὸν συμικρότατον μόνον [Trans. "with me, who is only the least"].

264. Τὰ θεόπνευστα ῥήματα προσφερόμενα [Trans. "the inspired words alleged"].

265. Αὕτη ἡ αἵρεσις Σαβελλίου ἐστὶν [Trans. "This is the sect of Sabellius"].

266. Ἀσυμφωνία [Trans. "discordance"].

267. Μὴ γένοιτο ἵνα ἄνθρωπος κατείπῃ τῶν θείων καὶ θεοπνεύστων γραφῶν [Trans. "God forbid that man should accuse the divinely inspired Scriptures"].

268. Ζυγός ὥσπερ δίκαιος [Trans. "as an even balance"].

"On what authority," demanded Arius, "do you call the Son eternal?" *"I have learned,"* answered Athanasius, *"from the divinely inspired Scriptures that the Son of God is eternal."*[269]

When he defends acts of direct adoration of the Holy Spirit against the objections of Arius, he neither appeals nor alludes to any church rule, tradition, nor usage, but reasons solely from the Scriptures.[270]

In his letter to the bishops of *Egypt* and Libya against the errors of Arius, he says, "Our Lord himself has said 'Search the Scriptures, for they are they that testify of me.' *How then shall* men confess the Lord who have not, before-hand, searched the Scriptures?"[271]

Hilary (of Poitiers) reasoning against the Manichaeans[272] on the person of Christ, says, *"If the church knows from herself,* then bring against her the charge of rashly claimed knowledge; but if she has *learned from her Lord,*[273] allow to the Son a knowledge of his own nativity. Now, *these things have been so made known to her by the only-begotten God,*[274] that the Father and the Son are one."

Of the Manichaean system, he says, "This aberration of human folly has come of men's knowing from themselves rather than from God.[275] . . . Have done, have done, nor falsify the heritage of the church's faith by deceptive fancy and agitating assertion."

"Those churches within which the word of God has not been wakeful,[276] have been shipwrecked."

---

269. Ἀπὸ τῶν θεοπνεύστων γραφῶν ἔμαθον, ὅτι ἀΐδιος ἐστιν ὁ υἱὸς τοῦ θεοῦ [Trans. "I have learned from the inspired Scriptures that the Son of God is eternal"].

270. Ibid., I:109, citing, with many other passages the θεῖαι ὑμνῳδίαι [Trans. "sacred singing"] in Isaiah vi. 3.

271. Πῶς οὖν ὁμολογήσουσι τὸν κύριον μὴ προερευνῶντες τὰς γραφάς [Trans. "How therefore shall men confess the Lord who have not searched the Scriptures beforehand?"]. Ibid., I:113. Could the authority of the Scriptures, and the duty and necessity of private judgment be more plainly asserted?

272. [Manicheaism was a dualistic religion that arose in Persia in the third century. It regarded life in the world as a dramatic struggle between the forces of light and the forces of darkness.]

273. Hilary of Poitiers (c.315–67/8), *De Trinitate*, ed. P. Coustant (Paris, 1693), Book VI: 883–84. *Si ex se seit (ecclesia) infer calumniam temerariae usupatae scientiae; si vero de Domino suo didicit, &c.* [Trans. "If the church knows from herself, bring the claim of rash usurped knowledge; but if she learned from her Lord, etc."]

274. *Haec uta ei a Deo unigenito comperta sunt.* [Trans. "Thus these things have been make known to her by the only-begotten God."]

275. *Dum quod sapiunt, ex potius quam ex Deo sapiunt,* [Trans. "Since what they know, they know from themselves, rather than from God."] Ibid., 886.

276. *Intra quas verbum Dei non vigilaverit* [Trans. "Among which the word of God had not kept watch"] –Though the remark occurs in his commentary on our Lord's miracle, Matt. viii. 23, yet it is not easy to tell whether he speaks of the *Word* in a personal way or not. This is often the case with the early writers, especially Origen. See above.

Chapter 3: Nevin and Proudfit: Opposed Views of the Early Creeds

"To corrupt the purity of the Gospels, and to deflect the straight rule of the Apostles," he uses as equivalent phrases,[277] so that it is quite clear what *he* regarded as the true and only *Apostolorum regula*.

Victorinus (of Africa) by no means stood in the first rank among the writers of the fourth century. But his testimony is interesting, because he was not converted to Christianity till far advanced in life, and, as Jerome says,[278] was so inveterate a philosophizer as to be an unintelligible writer and commentator. Yet the Christian sentiment and habit which acknowledged the word of God as the only rule of faith, as yet universal in the church, appears in no writer of the age, more evident than in this philosophizing Christian. "*Edocet Scriptura*" [Trans. "Scripture teaches"], with him, announces an authority to which he reverently bows himself and anticipates no opposition from others. After a series of quotations from Scripture, in support of what he asserts of the works and attributes of God, he adds, "*This, spoken as it has been by the divine Spirit, must be believed. The rest of our positions we shall maintain by reasons drawn from nature.*"[279]

Cyril (of Jerusalem) gives his testimony on this subject in so many and such impressive forms, that the only difficulty his works present is that of selection. One of the topics of his Fourth Catechesis is "concerning the Divine Scriptures."[280] The good father states that he "founds his instructions on the divinely inspired Scriptures of the Old and New Testaments. "For," says he, "there is one God of both Testaments, who preannounced Christ in the Old Testament and revealed him in the New." And then adds this counsel to his catechumens: "*Read, therefore, the Divine Scriptures.*[281] *Read not the Apocrypha. Have thou nothing to do with the Apocrypha.*"[282]

---

277. *Evangelorum sinceritatem corrumpere et rectam Apostolorum regulam depravare*. [Trans. "To corrupt the integrity of the gospels and to distort the straight rule of the Apostles."] Augustine, Letter to Constantius Augraustus. Book I, 3:1220.

278. *Catalgus Scriptorum Ecclesasticorum* (Süstermanni, 1722). "*Victorinus Afer*" [Gaius Marius Victorinus, a rhetorician and theologian, was converted from paganism to Christianity in the fourth century. He polemicized against the Arians, expressed his faith through a Neo-Platonic idiom, and was an influence upon the development of the spiritual life of Augustine.] Augustine, *Confessions*, VIII:2, has given a very interesting account of the conversion of Victorinus, from the relation of Simplicianus. He calls him *"doctissimus senex, omnium liberalium doctrinarum pertissimus . . . doctor nobilium senatorum,"* &c. [Trans. "the most learned old man, most experienced in all the liberal teachings . . . the teacher of our noble senators,"] He says, "the Holy Scripture" was the first means of leading him to Christianity and God." The work from which we quote is entitled "*Pro religione Christiana contra philosophos physicos.*" It is contained in the magnificent *Scriptorum Veterum collectio Vaticana*, III. It certainly is not liable to the charge of obscurity on the part of Jerome. His account of our Lord's early life is especially just and beautiful.

279. *Hoc a Divino Spiritu dictum credendum est; cetera physicis rationibus paucis comprobemus.* [Trans. "This, spoken by the Divine Spirit, is to be believed; other things we will prove from a few natural reasons."] Chapter 27: 161.

280. Περὶ τῶν θείων γραφῶν [Trans. "Concerning the divine Scriptures"].

281. Ἀναγίνωσκε τάς θείας γραφάς [Trans. "Read the sacred Scriptures"].

282. Πρός δὲ τὰ ἀπόκρυφα μηδὲν ἔχε κοινόν [Trans. "Have thou nothing to do with the Apocrypha"]. These counsels, be it remembered, were addressed to catechumens, just receiving baptism. How

And yet, if possible, more positively, in his 18th Catechesis. "We declare to you candidly, that we use not human and modern inventions; for it is unprofitable. But we recall to your minds *only the things which are drawn from the Divine Scriptures*. For that is infallible: after the example of the blessed Apostle,[283] who also saith, which things we speak, not in words which man's wisdom teacheth, but which the Holy Ghost teacheth."

Gregory of Nazianzum, in his funeral oration on Basil,[284] (his intimate friend and companion of his retirement in Cappadocia) tells us that "Basil profoundly studied the Holy Scriptures in his solitude, and *drew from thence* the weapons with which he intrepidly and indefatigably contended for the refutation of errors."

The same discourse contains a fine eulogy of classical and various learning,[285] which, he says, "many Christians reject as delusive and misleading, but which Gregory defends for this especial reason, that 'we learn from the worse to appreciate the better[286] and on the very weakness and imperfection of those systems, to maintain the power of the word which is in our possession,[287] even as the divine Apostle says,[288] 'bringing every thought (all intellect[289]) into captivity to Christ.'"

Gregory Nyssa gives his deposition with no less clearness and force.

"The faith of Christians," he says, "which by the command of the Lord, was preached to all nations on the whole globe of the earth, is 'not from men, neither by men, but by our Lord Jesus Christ'; who is the word of God, and the Light and the Life and the Truth and God and Wisdom.[290] . . . We believe, therefore, '*credimus*,' here then, is *his* creed, with its Author, ground and rule) "even as the Lord put forth the faith to his disciples, when he thus spake," (quotes Matt. xxviii. 19)[:]

---

do they bear on the question, not only of the necessity and sufficiency of the Scriptures, but of *private judgment and Church-tradition*, aside from Scripture?

283. Τὰ ἐκ τῶν θείων μόνον ὑπομιμνήσκοντες ἀσφαλέστατον γὰρ κατὰ τὸν μακάριον ἀπόστολον, ὅς καὶ φησίν [Trans. "Recalling to your mind only those things which are drawn from the divine Scriptures. For that is infallible: after the example of the blessed Apostle, who also saith"]—1 Cor. ii. 13.

284. Or Septuagint, Εἰς βας. ἐπισκ. καις. κατ. ἐπιταφιος [Trans. "Funeral Oration on Basil, Bishop of Caesarea, Cappadocia"].

285. Τὴν τῶν ἔξωθεν παίδευσιν [Trans. "The system of learning set forth"].

286. Ἐκ τοῦ χείρονος τὸ κρεῖττον καταμαθόντος [Trans. "Learning from the worse to appreciate the better"].

287. Τὴν ἀσθένειαν ἐκείνων, ἰσχὺν τοῦ καθ' ἡμᾶς λόγου πεποιήμενοι [Trans. "On account of that very weakness, maintaining the power of the word in our possession"] (*fulcientes*, Lat. trans.).

288. Ὁ φησίν ὁ θεῖος ἀπόστελος, &c [Trans. "Which the divine apostle says"].

289. Πᾶν νόημα [Trans. "All intellect"].

290. *Christianorum fides, quae secundum Domini mandatum a discipulis omnibus gentibus in toto terrarum orbe praedicata est, neque ex hominibus, &c., sed per Dominum nostrum Jesum Christum; qui est Dei Verbum, et Vita, et Lux et Veritae et Deus et Sapientis.* [Trans. "The faith of the Christians, which according to the command of the Lord was preached by the disciples to all the nations in the whole round earth, and came not from men, etc., but through our Lord Jesus Christ; who is the Word of God, and Life, and Light and Truth and God and Wisdom.] Or, Bishop Gregory Nyssa, *Contra Eunomium*, (Coloniae, 1617), 253. We quote from the Latin version, not having the original at hand.

Chapter 3: Nevin and Proudfit: Opposed Views of the Early Creeds

This is the word of the mystery, in which, by a birth from above our nature is transformed into a better, since from corruptible it is renewed to incorruptible, from the old man it is renewed after the image of him who in the beginning created the divine similitude. *Of this faith, therefore, delivered by God to the Apostles, we make neither subtraction nor change (which is but perversion) nor addition;*[291] clearly knowing, that he who dares to pervert the divine voice by any cavilling and sophistical interpretation, is of his father the devil:[292] since it was by forsaking the words of truth, and *speaking of his own*, that he became the father of lies. For whatsoever is spoken beyond the truth is absolutely a mere lie, and not truth.[293] . . . *We have once learned from the Lord*,[294] *what it is that we must contemplate with thought and mind;* through which a transformation of our nature is wrought, from mortal to immortal. This is *the Father, the Son, and the Holy Ghost.*

He then goes on to develop the Christian faith on this basis, proving and explaining all points, and meeting all objections, from the Holy Scripture.

This is conclusive. There is, however, a short specimen of *exegesis* by this churchly father of the fourth century, which we add with peculiar satisfaction. It occurs in the last of his "*Testimonia delecta*" [Trans. "choice witnesses"].[295]

Jesus Christ, our Lord and our God, is called the Rock of life and the Rock of faith . . . the Rock of life, as he is the fountain, root, principle, and cause, imperishable and eternal; the Rock of faith, as he is the foundation, even as the Lord himself says to the chief of the Apostles, "Thou art Peter, and on this rock will I build my Church," *on the confession, that is, of Christ*,[296] because he said, 'Thou art the Christ, the Son of the living God.'"[297]

291. *Hujus itaque a Deo Apostolis traditae fidei neque subtractionem, neque immutationem sive perversionem, neque additionem facimus.* [Trans. And so, we make of the faith handed down from God to the Apostles, neither subtraction nor change (rather perversion) nor addition."]

292. *Ex patre diabolo esse.* [Trans. To be from his father, the devil."]

293. *Quidquid praeter veritatem dicitur, merum est prorsus mendacium et non veritas.* [Trans. "Whatever is said beyond the truth, is utterly a sheer lie and not the truth."]

294. *Semel a Domino discimus, ad quod nos cogitatione et mente perspicere oportet.* [Trans. "Once we learn from the Lord what it is we ought to perceive in thought and mind."]

295. *Contra Eunomium*, 252.

296. *Super Confessionem videlicet Christi.* [Trans. "Upon confession, namely of Christ."]

297. Dr. Nevin's exegesis is on this wise. "'Thou art Peter,' &c. Not on Peter's person, apart from his confession, of course, was the Church to be built; but not on Peter's confession, either, apart from his person. *Peter in Christ,* (Dr. Nevin thus italicises; it was never, we believe, affirmed to be *Peter out of Christ*) as the representative especially of the whole Apostolic college; the personality of Peter, as centered and poised now on the supernatural fact, which had entered into his consciousness . . . this was the *rock* on which, from this time onward to the end of the world, the Church should continue to rise," &c. . . . The confession of Peter represents the universal Christian consciousness. . . . *That consciousness expressed itself in the Creed.*" *Antichrist*, 21–22 [See "Antichrist," in *One, Holy, Catholic, and Apostolic*, MTSS 5, ed. Hamstra, 183–84].

We decidedly prefer the exegesis of Gregory Nyssa and of the fourth century. We believe the Church

Dr. Nevin mentions "Ephraim the Syrian"[298] among the Romanizing fathers of the fourth century, who "knew nothing of the view which makes the Bible the principle of Christianity," &c. We should not otherwise have thought of mentioning him. Gregory Nyssen thought quite otherwise of him, since he states that "nurtured from childhood in the meditation of the Sacred Scriptures,[299] and growing up and drinking from the perennial fountains of grace,[300] he (Ephraim) strove to attain, in the words of the Apostle, 'to the measure of the stature of Christ.'"

But the good and humble Syrian "deacon" will in a very few words vindicate himself from the charge.

In his discourse "Concerning Faith"[301] (which consists to a great extent of portions of Scripture linked together with a very simple exposition) he says,

> he who desires to become a Christian, . . . must form himself to a virtuous habit and a holy life by the word of God . . . and holding on his way by the guidance of the word of God such an one becomes a foundation and a pillar by the grace of God and an occasion of life to many souls and is able to bear the infirmity of many.

To a " young convert,"[302] among other "counsels pertaining to the spiritual life," he says, "if thou seest thyself ill affected towards the reading of the divine oracles,[303] know that thy soul has fallen into a grievous disease: for this is the beginning of mental disorder, the end of which is death." Advice which a *puritan pastor* would readily adopt, but not, we think, a *popish* confessor.[304]

---

is much safer built on the "Rock of faith, Jesus Christ, our Lord and our God," the object of Peter's "*confession*," than on Peter's "*personality*" however "poised," &c.

298. [Ephraim the Syrian (306–73) was a deacon and a celebrated composer of hymns and exegetical works.]

299. *Inde a pueritia in Sacrarum Scripturarum meditatione educatus.* [Trans. "Raised up from youth in meditation of the Holy Scriptures."]

300. *Ex perennibus gratiae fontibus bibens*, [Trans. "Drinking from the perennial fountains of grace"] &c. Gregory of Nyssa, *Encomium in Sanctum patriarch Ephraem Syrus*, 508.

301. *Ephraem. Syrus, Graece* (Oxford, 1609), last discourse.

302. Πρός νεόφυτον, περί πνευματίκου βίου. [Trans. "To a new convert, concerning spiritual life"], Ibid., 179.

303. Κακουχοῦντα περὶ τὴν ἀνάγνωσιν τῶν θείων λογίων. [Trans. "Ill affected toward the reading of the divine oracles".]

304. "Were the fathers who then lived to return to the world in our time, they would find themselves more at home in the Papal than in the Protestant communion." Nevin, "Early Christianity," *The Mercersburg Review*, Article III, IV (1852), 3. "Ephraim the Syrian" scarcely would. For to this same "young convert" he speaks of "communing with the Supreme God through prayer and eating the body and drinking the blood of the only begotten Son of God" (πίνων αὐτοῦ τὸ αἷμα. p. ρπ. γ –[Trans. "drinking the blood"]) He would hardly "find himself at home" in a "communion" where the latter is denied to "young converts." "Reading the divine oracles" and "drinking the blood" of the Saviour are not "Papal" means of promoting "the spiritual life," at least, "in our time."

CHAPTER 3: NEVIN AND PROUDFIT: OPPOSED VIEWS OF THE EARLY CREEDS

But of all the "fathers of that glorious period," none seems to have more of Dr. Nevin's admiration than Basil (of Caesarea) whom he often appeals to, duly decorating him with his later title of "the Great,"[305] but never allowing the eloquent father to utter a word in explanation of his own sentiments.

We, therefore, (sparingly, as our limits compel us) will indulge him with an opportunity.

Dr. Nevin says of him with the rest, "the order of doctrine for them was the Apostles' Creed," and asserts in a general way, that he with them "stood in the bosom" of the Papal system.

The Apostle's Creed is not mentioned in all the writings of Basil.

As for "the order of his doctrine," we infer it from his own language.

Against Eunomius[306] he says, "there is no sublimer *doctrine in the gospel of our salvation* than faith in the Father and the Son."

He objects to a phrase used by Eunomius (in speaking of the manner of the Divine existence) that "though it seems extremely congruous to our mode of conceiving things,[307] it *nowhere occurs in Scripture*,[308] and ought therefore to be suppressed."

In his homily on Ps. xlv.[309] which may be called a discourse on the church, he premises, "the oracles of God were not written for all, but for *those who have ears after the inner man*,[310] for *those who strive after progress, for those, as I think*,[311] *who take care of themselves*,"[312] (we must be literal here) "and ever, by the exercises of godliness,[313]

---

305. He stands a century after in Rufinus' translation of Eusebius, *The History of the Church* (402/3) Book II, c. 9) without either the *affix* or *suffix* (St. or *the Great*) which later superstition and adulation attached to his name. His friend Gregory too, sine *titulo* [Trans. "without a title of honor"]. A saint and a great man too Basil undoubtedly was; and for both reasons would have rejected both titles. Erasmus was of opinion that in strength and majesty of genius he was no way inferior to Demosthenes. Gregory (Or. Fun.) says that he was not more remarkable for his greatness of soul than for his lowliness of temper. Some of his writings (e.g. his books on Baptism) would furnish an admirable corrective of the notions lately ventilated of "sacramental" and "organic grace," "baptismal regeneration," and the like Papal ideas. Certain it is that his soul would have abhorred the fine things said of him by Dr. Nevin ("Early Christianity," *The Mercersburg Review*, Article III, IV (1852), 3. Even that "sporting bishop" of the fifth century, Synesius, would have exclaimed, as he did on another occasion, μὴ ὦ Σῶτερ, μὴ, ὦ Ἐλευθέριε. ("Never, O my Saviour, never, O my Redeemer!" *Epistle to his brother*, 81.) *He* too, could hardly have "found himself at home in the Papal communion in our time," for *he had a wife and four children.*

306. I:292, &c. [Eunomius (d. 393) was a leader of the extreme Arians.]

307. Κἂν μάλιστα δοκῇ ταῖς ἐννοίαις ἡμῶν συμβαίνειν. [Trans. "Though it seems extremely congruous to our mode of conceiving things".]

308. Οὐδαμοῦ τῆς γραφῆς κειμένην. [Trans. "It nowhere occurs in Scripture".]

309. Basil of Caesarea, *Collected Works*, ed. J. Garnier, P. Maran and Gaume (Paris, 1839), I:226, &c. It is numbered Ps. xliv. in the Septuagint.

310. Τοῖς ἔχουσιν ὦτα κατὰ τὸν ἔσω ἄνθρωπον. [Trans. "For those who have ears after the inner man".]

311. Ὡς οἴμαι. [Trans. "As I think".]

312. Τοῖς ἑαυτῶν ἐπιμελομένοις. [Trans. "Who take care of themselves".]

313. An allusion to the Septuagint translation of the title of the Psalms.

THE APOSTLES' CREED

are advancing to a higher ground. This is that noblest *change*[314] which the right hand of the Most High graciously bestows, which also blessed David experienced, (Ps. lxxvii. 11,) when having tasted the joys of goodness, he reaches forth unto those things which are before."

"The prophet," he says,

> yielding to the energy of the Holy Spirit which came upon him, says, "my heart venteth a good matter." . . . This venting is the inward effervescence of the food,[315] &c., so he who is nourished on the living bread which came down from heaven and giveth life to the world, and is filled with every word that cometh out of the mouth of God, (after the wonted tropology of the Scriptures,) the soul, that is, which is nourished by the divine teachings, emitteth a breath agreeable to the food it has taken. . . . Let us, then, seek, ourselves,[316] to be nourished from the Word, to the utmost capacity of our souls, (quotes Prov. xiii. 25,) that, after the nature of the food on which we live, we may not vent every chance word, but that which is good . . . *Seest thou what eructations come from the mouths of heretics? how offensive and ill-savoured, showing a very diseased condition in the bowels*[317] *of the unhappy men?* (Matt. xii. 35.) Do not thou, therefore, having itching ears, heap up to thyself teachers, who are skilled to create disorder in thine inner man, and cause the venting of evil words, &c. (Matt. xii. 37).
>
> This word, "I speak of the things which I have made, touching the King, *completely guides us to the meaning of the prophetic personage.*[318]
>
> "'My tongue is the pen of a ready writer.' As the pen is the graphic instrument, the hand of the expert moving it to the showing forth of the things to be

---

314. Διὰ τῶν γυμνασίων. [Trans. "Through the exercise".] Not a word of church, creed, "sacramental" or "organic grace." Free, individual aspiration and self-culture by all "the exercises of godliness," (including, of course, church, creed, and sacraments,) is the very soul of this fine passage. All progress is "graciously bestowed by the right hand of the Most High." This looks very much like "bringing one's separate subjectivity to the case," which Dr. Nevin deplores as "sectarian." (*Antichrist*, 46) [See "Antichrist" in *One, Holy, Catholic, and Apostolic*, Tome One, MTSS 5, ed. Hamstra, 208.]

315. We shall be excused from giving in full the good father's exegesis, which is founded on the Septuagint translation ἐξηρεύξατο, eructavit (spews forth/empties itself). This will explain what follows.

316. This, be it remembered, was a Congregational homily, ὁμιλία συνήθης [Trans. "usual homily"].

317. Ἐν τῷ βαθεί. [Trans. "In the depths"]

318. Πάνυ προσάγει ἡμᾶς τῇ διανοίᾳ τοῦ προφητικοῦ προσώπου. [Trans. "Completely guides us to the meaning of the prophetic personage."] Very like the Protestant principle of *the Bible interpreting itself.* So Tertullian, "The words of the Lord are put forth to *all*. . . . To *all* be it said, 'Seek and ye shall find.' Still it is of importance to labour with the sense by the help of interpretation. (*Sensu certare interpretationis gubernaculo.*) There is no divine word so disconnected and diffuse, that the words alone can be maintained, and the relation of the words (ratio verborum) not taken into account." *De Praescriptione. Haereticos* [*Prescription Against Heretics*], Chapter 9. beginning. If this is addressed as it is, "*to all*" and concerning "all the words of Christ," be not a recognition of *private judgment*, it would be difficult to find words for it.

written, *so the tongue of the just, the Holy Spirit moving the same, inwardly writeth the words of eternal life in the hearts of believers!*[319]

"Grace is shed upon thy lips" (v. 2.) They who are strangers to the word of truth call the preaching of the Gospel foolishness, despising the simplicity of the style of the Scriptures: but we who glory in the cross of Christ, to whom the things which are freely given unto us of God, have been made known by the Holy Spirit, not in the words which man's wisdom teacheth, know how rich is the grace which God has poured over the words of Christ. It was for this reason the preached word overran in a little time almost the whole world, because a rich and plenteous grace was shed over the preachers of the Gospel, whom the Scriptures have termed the lips of Christ. Therefore the preaching of the Gospel, even in despicable style, has a mighty power to guide and draw men to salvation. And the whole soul is subdued by its unchangeable doctrines, being established through grace, in an unwavering faith towards Christ. Whence the Apostle saith, &c. Rom i. 5; 1 Cor xv. 10.

"V. 2. Since the church is the body of Christ, and he is the head of the church, as we have said that those who minister to the heavenly word were the lips of Christ, (even as Paul, who had Christ speaking in him, 1 Cor. xiii. 3, and *whoever else resembles Paul in virtue,)* so also, *we who have believed* are severally the other members of the body of Christ."

"Gird thy sword upon thy thigh," v. 3. This we understand to refer tropically to *the living word of God,* (quotes Heb iv. 12.)

"Hearken, O daughter," v. 10. He summons the church to *hear and keep the things commanded her.*[320] "And consider." He teaches her to have her intellect practised to contemplation by that word, *consider.* "Incline thine ear." Run not away after strange fables, but *receive the lowly instruction of the voice which speaketh in the Gospel word.*[321]

V. 11. He teaches the church the necessity of subjection[322] by that word, "He is thy Lord." . . . It is not the church to which our homage is paid, but Christ the Head of the church.

"So shall the King greatly desire thy beauty." "Cast away, for me," he says, "the doctrines of devils, *forget sacrifices;*[323] . . . if by utter oblivion, thou blottest out the spots of unholy teachings and assumest thine own proper beauty, then shalt thou appear an object of desire to thy Spouse and King."

---

319. Ἐγγράφει τὰ ῥήματα τῆς αἰώνου ζωῆς ταῖς καρδίαις τῶν πιστευόντων. [Trans. "Inwardly writeth the words of eternal life in the hearts of believers".]

320. Προσκαλεῖται τὴν Ἐκκλησίαν ἐπὶ τὴν ἀκρόασιν καὶ τὴν τήρησιν τῶν προστασσομένων [Trans. "He summons the church to hear and keep the things commanded her"], not to "externalize" and "create" the contents of her own faith.

321. Τὸ ταπεινὸν τῆς ἐν τῷ εὐαγγελικῷ λόγῳ φωνῆς. [Trans. "The lowliness of the voice in the Gospel word".]

322. Τὸ ἀναγκαῖον τῆς ὑποταγῆς. [Trans. "The necessity of subjections".]

323. Ἐπιλάθου θυσιῶν. [Trans. "Forget sacrifices".]

V. 13. "All the glory of the King's daughter, that is, the bride of Christ, is *within*."[324] . . . "Obedience to the word,"[325] "interior purity," Basil here makes to constitute this "inward glory of the bride of Christ." "The word exhorteth us," he adds,

> to aspire to the inmost mysteries of the glory of the church, the beauty of the bride being wholly *within*. For he who beautifieth himself to the Father, who seeth in secret, and prayeth, and doeth all things, not to be seen by men, but to be manifest to God alone; this man hath all interior glory, even as the daughter of the King. The very golden tasselings,[326] with which her whole person is draped and adorned, are *inward. Look for nothing in outward gold, and material variety,* but understand a drapery worthy of one renewed after the image of him that created him, as the Apostle saith. (Col iii. 9, 10) . . . Paul also exhorteth us to "put on the Lord Jesus," not after the outer man, but that the *remembrance of God may enrobe the soul*.[327] The queen (that is *the soul* clad in the Bridegroom's word) stands on the right hand of the Saviour, in garments inlaid with gold, that is to say, clothed in holy dignity and beauty, with *intelligent doctrines*[328] interwoven and variegated. . . . The perfumes (v. 8) plenteously shed over the garments of Christ, (these are *the concomitants of discourses and diffusion of instructions*) are wafted back, however, from the whole edifice. For he speaketh of a great "edifice" here, and that too, built of "ivory,"[329] the prophet thereby showing forth, as I think, the *richness of the love of Christ* towards the world.
>
> Now, I think the spiritual drapery is woven *complete*, when an *answerable practice is intertwined with the word of doctrine*. For, as the bodily garment is finished when, the warp being first set up, the woof is inserted therein, so when the word has gone before, if conformable actions follow thereupon, there would then be a most glorious vesture of the soul, having attained, in word and act, a life complete in virtue.

In his exposition of v. 14, "the *virgins* her companions," we should expect, if anywhere, that Basil would "stand in the very same order of thought that completed itself afterwards in the Roman or Papal Church." For here was the precise point of divergence for Basil and many other leading minds[330] of the fourth century, from the Scrip-

---

324. Ἔσωθεν. [Trans. "Within".]

325. Cf. Dr. Nevin, "The Bible, to be a true word of Christ, must be *ruled by the life of the Church !!*" Apostles' Creed, in this volume, 91.

326. So the Septuagint Κροσσωντὰ. [Trans. "Tasselings".]

327. Περισκεπτάζη, literally *circumvest*. Dr. Nevin would have "the mind of the Holy Catholic Church to *circumfuse* his private thinking." *Antichrist*, 46 [See "Antichrist" in *One, Holy, Catholic, and Apostolic*, Tome One, MTSS 5, ed. Hamstra, 208. Here as elsewhere, Proudfit capitalized "Catholic," although Nevin had not.].

328. Ἐν δόγμασι νοεροῖς. [Trans. "With intelligent doctrines".]

329. "Ivory palaces." English Trans.

330. Not for all of them, however. St. Gregory Nyssa, the brother of Basil, rejoiced in his pious and

tural and Primitive into the Ecclesiastical system. We, therefore, give the exposition of that clause entire.

> Certain souls follow the bride of Christ, who receive not the germs of strange doctrines: these "shall be brought unto the King," in the train of the bride. Let those who have promised virginity to the Lord hear this, that "virgins shall be brought to the King": those virgins, however, who are near to the Church, who follow after her and stray not away from the discipline of the Church. But with mirth and gladness shall the virgins be brought and enter into the King's temple. Not those who constrainedly enter on virginity, nor those who, from sorrow or necessity, addict themselves to a chaste life, but those who, with mirth and gladness, *do so*, rejoicing in such rectitude—these "shall be brought to the King" and "they shall be conducted into no common place, but into the temple of the King." For, sacred vessels, which human use hath never denied, they shall he brought into the holy of holies, and shall have the privilege of access into the innermost sanctuary, where profane feet shall never walk. But what this "being brought into the temple of the King" is, the prophet signified, when in his own behalf he prayed and said, "One thing have I desired of the Lord, that will I seek after, that I may dwell in the house of the Lord all the days of my life, to behold the beauty of the Lord and to inquire in his temple."

To such virginal aspirations, we believe, even "a Puritan" would not object. If this is "glorifying celibacy,"[331] let Basil rest under the charge.

On v. 16, "'Instead of thy fathers have been born thy sons.' . . . Who, then, are the sons of the Church? *Without doubt, the sons of the Gospel.*" May God multiply such "sons of the Church," and daily enlarge and glorify the Church which consists of "sons of the Gospel!"

This entire Homily on the Church, if translated into English, and preached to "a congregation in Connecticut or Massachusetts" (with the one exception noted, and how far, even that is an exception we leave the reader to judge) would create no surprise, except by its somewhat fanciful expositions, its surpassing beauty and its high

---

affectionate Theosebeia. Even that rigid churchman Jerome kept pretty close to the Pauline theory on this subject, and, among many other exceptional cases, conceded matrimony to those *qui propter nocturnos metus dormire soli non possunt* [Trans. "who on account of nocturnal fears are unable to sleep alone"] (Against Jovian). No such concession to *weak nerves*, "in the Papal communion" since Gregory VII. Synesius, even after it became a decided *disqualification* for a "bishop" to "be the husband of one wife," being *rogatus episcopari* ["elected to the episcopate"], replies [*Works*, ed. D. Petavius (Paris, 1612)], (Epistle 105) "God and the holy hand of Theotimus gave me my wife, and I can neither forsake her nor *live with her as a harlot.*" He too, would not have been "*at home* in the Papal communion in our time." His eloquence and "pure manners," however, induced them to waive the objection, and Synesius was "ordained bishop," but never rose, (probably on account of his *domestic incumbrance*) to the rank of a "saint" in the Romish Calendar. Basil decides [*Works*, ed. J. Garnier, P. Maran, and Gaume (Paris, 1839] (Epistle, 199) that "matrimony must not be prohibited, but that a *man is better if he so abide.*" [Synesius (c.370–c.413), a native of Cyrene, was a bishop of Ptolemais. He wrote a number of short works and composed hymns. A number of his important letters survive.]

331. Nevin, "Early Christianity," *The Mercersburg Review* III (1852), 3.

spirituality. But how strange and startling would be its effect if delivered amidst the sights and sounds and fumigations of a Popish cathedral!

Let us suppose that "St. Basil the Great, Archbishop of Caesarea"[332] should according to Dr. Nevin's supposition, "return to the world in our day," and be requested by Cardinal Wiseman[333] or Archbishop Hughes[334] to "say mass" and preach in one of their cathedrals. In the first place, he would make an awkward mistake by calling "the mass" the "Lord's supper."[335] He would proceed to "fence the tables" in the downright style of what Dr. Nevin calls "hard and bony Presbyterianism," saying, they are his own words,[336] "He that *cometh to the communion*[337] is nothing profited without a consideration of the word after which the participation of the body *and blood* of Christ is given to us." "Let a man therefore *examine himself* and so let him eat of that bread *and drink of that cup*,[338] for he that *eateth and drinketh* unworthily, eateth and drinketh to his own condemnation." Yet

> unless ye eat the flesh and *drink the blood* of the Son of Man ye have no life in you. But through faith we are cleansed by the blood of Christ from all sin, and being baptized by water into the Lord's death, we become dead unto sin and the world, and are made alive unto righteousness, and so being baptized in the name of the Holy Ghost, we are born again; and being born again, we put on Christ, being clothed with the new man, &c. And therefore we must be nourished with the food of eternal life which the only begotten son of God hath given us.[339]

He would then proceed to lay down "the words of institution" from the gospels and 1 Cor. xi.[340] and go on to distribute *both kinds* to the astonished *faithful*, saying, with the precise introductory formulae[341] now used in the "Protestant sects," "take, eat, this is my body broken for you," and with the presentation of the cup, "this cup is the

332. So Roman authorities call him. He calls himself a "co-presbyter," with his brethren (συμπρεσβύτερος).

333. [Cardinal Nicholas Wiseman (1802–65) was the first Archbishop of Westminster after the restoration of the Roman Catholic hierarchy in England and Wales, which happened in 1850.]

334. [Archbishop John Hughes was the Roman Catholic archbishop of New York and founder of Fordham University.]

335. Τὸ Κυριακὸν δεῖπνον ["The Lord's Supper"]. Ερωτ. 310. Vol. II, 752. Athanasius too calls it ἡ ἅγια τράπεζα [Trans. "The Holy Table"]. *Epistle to Orthodox Everywhere*. And yet Dr. Nevin is very hard on our unchurchly selves for "degrading it by this appellation to the level of a common Supper." Nevin, "The Heidelberg Catechism," *The Mercersburg Review*, III, Number 2 (March 1852), 172.

336. Ὅρος 21. Vol. ii, 354, and more fully in his 2nd book on Baptism [Basil of Caesarea, *A Treatise on Baptism*, ed. Francis Patrick Kenrick (Philadelphia: M. Fithian, 1843), 225–41].

337. Προσερχόμενος τῇ κοινωνίᾳ [Trans. "Coming to communion"].

338. Καὶ ἐκ τοῦ ποτηρίου πινέτω [Trans. "And drink of that cup"]. Discipline on the holy Mysteries applied to his books on Baptism.

339. Basil of Caesarea, *De Baptismo* in *Works*, ed. J. Garnier, P. Maran, and Gaume (Paris, 1839).

340. He does so, quoting them in full.

341. Ibid.

Chapter 3: Nevin and Proudfit: Opposed Views of the Early Creeds

New Testament in my blood, which is shed for many for the remission of sins, *drink ye all of it*.[342] For thus eating and drinking, we perpetually *commemorate*[343] the love of our Lord Jesus Christ, who died for us and rose again and let us learn that it is thus we must preserve in the presence of God and of his Christ the doctrine delivered to us by the Apostle,[344] when he saith 'the love of Christ constraineth us,'" &c. (2 Cor v. 14, &c.).

Having thus "said Mass," the Archbishop would proceed (if he happened to select for the occasion, his Homily on Ps. xlv.) to deliver a good long discourse "on the Church," which would utterly leave on the outside of it, not only the Cardinal and Archbishop, but the Pope himself. And would then, in all probability, wind up with an extempore prayer, "selected from the Holy Scriptures," a practice which he fervently recommends in his beautiful observations on prayer.[345]

We doubt if the "*Archepiscopus Redivivus*" would be called upon a second time to *exercise his gifts* "within the Papal Communion."

May God *raise up* many such "Saints," and "Great" men as Basil to proclaim his everlasting Gospel;—endowed with the most splendid natural talents, enriched with all learning, animated by an indomitable spirit of Christian freedom, yet bowing with profound humility to "the lowly instruction of the Gospel voice." If they should not "find themselves at home," as they certainly would not, "in the Papal Communion," we will insure them a joyful reception in the Protestant Church.

We have an extraordinary revelation of the inward life of Basil, in a long letter[346] to his bosom friend Gregory, written from his religious retreat in Cappadocia. It bears, as might be expected, something of the monastic tinge. Let the reader, however, judge whether the *religious experience* it discloses, and the ideas of the means of spiritual proficiency it expresses, are of the Protestant or Papal stamp. Dr. Nevin says that Basil, &c. "glorified monastic life." Of what sort was the monastic life which they thus "glorified?"

> What I am doing night and day in this remote place, I am ashamed to tell thee. I have forsaken, it is true, my pursuits in the city, as the occasions of innumerable ills, but *I have not been able to leave myself behind*. On the contrary,

---

342. πίετε ἐξ αὐτοῦ πάντες [Trans. "drink all of it"]; Ibid.

343. The Archbishop would here be stricken on the spot by a papal thunderbolt, "Whosoever shall say that the sacrifice of the mass is simply a *commemoration,* is accursed (anathemate fulminari.) III. Anath. de Sac. Miss. Conc. Trid. PaoL Sarpi. p. 521. [For the "Canons and Dogmatic Decrees of the Council of Trent," see Philip Schaff, *The Creeds of Christendom*, 6th ed. (1931, ed. David S. Schaff; repr. Grand Rapids, Michigan, Baker Book House, 1990) II, 77–206, and for the "Profession of the Tridentine Faith" see Schaff, II:207–10. Paolo Sarpi (1552–1623) was a celebrated scholar, theologian, and canon lawyer.]

344. A very remarkable passage. It stands thus in full, on the page last cited.

345. Sarpi, II:769, "not using vain repetitions like the Greeks, but *making* a *collect from the Holy Scriptures,*" (ἀπὸ τῶν ἁγίων Γραφῶν ἐκλεγόμενος). He subjoins a specimen.

346. Basil of Caesarea, *Works*, ed. J. Garnier, P. Maran, and Gaume (Paris, 1839). Epistle II. Classis I. Nov. Ordo. III: 99.

I am like those who are tossed about on the sea, and sea-sick from being unaccustomed to navigation. They are dissatisfied with their ship, as if its size caused the greater agitation, and so get down into a little skiff or shallop, and yet are none the less seasick and ill at ease, for their bile and nausea go along with them. My case is much the same. For, carrying with me the *disorders that dwell within*,[347] I am everywhere alike disquieted: so that *my benefit from this seclusion is not great.* There are things, however, which we must do in order to press on the footsteps of him who is guiding us to salvation. (For if any man, saith he, will come after me, let him deny himself, and take up his cross and follow me.) These are some of them.

"We must try to maintain serenity of mind. . . . The undistracted mind *turns upon itself, and through itself ascends to God.*" . . . "Prayers," "hymns, and songs of praise to the Creator," and "labour," cheered and sanctified by these, are added.

"But," he continues, "the principal path[348] to the discovery of duty, is the meditation of the divinely inspired Scriptures," and dwells largely on the perfection of its precepts and examples. "Prayers again, *succeeding these readings* find the soul more fresh and active, stirred and awakened by desire towards God."

When we find the great Basil speaking in this letter of the sort of clothes, shoes, diet, &c., most conducive to detachment from the world, and fixedness of soul on divine things, we feel that he sinks below the element in which he generally moves, and approximates "the order of thoughts which completed itself afterwards in the Papal church." Still, as long as he keeps to "the principal path," he cannot "Romanize" in anything material, and *he does not.*

The above letter was written when he was about twenty-eight years old, and probably before he entered the ministry. In another, written about ten years later,[349] consisting of counsels to those who were in religious seclusion, he says, "I have thought proper briefly to advise you *as I have learned from the inspired Scriptures.*" Almost all these counsels are expressed in the very words of Scripture. His first remark is, that "a Christian should have a spirit worthy of his heavenly calling, and a conversation as it becomes the Gospel of Christ."

In neither of these letters, is there an allusion to any means of grace other than the word of God, prayer, praise, self-communion, and communion with God, and pious converse; and all these joined with useful labour.

In a letter of spiritual advice to an individual,[350] he exhorts him to "take upon himself *the easy yoke of the Lord.*"

---

347. Τὰ ἔνοικα πάθη, which might be neatly rendered by the *Puritan* phrase "indwelling sin."
348. Μεγίστη ὁδός [Trans. "The principle path"].
349. Basil, Ibid., Epistle 22.
350. Basil, Ibid., Epistle 23.

Chapter 3: Nevin and Proudfit: Opposed Views of the Early Creeds

Basil advises "young men,"[351] apparently under his own educational care, to study the writings of the ancient Greeks, because the mental discipline thus acquired would better enable them to apprehend the sublimer revelations of the Scriptures, and compares the perception of truth in the former to *looking at the image of the sun in water*;[352] in the latter, to *directing our view to the light* itself."[353]

During a long absence from his flock at Caesarea, he addressed them a pastoral letter,[354] containing this among other like counsels. "Take heed, O divine and most beloved souls, of the shepherds of the Philistines, lest some one of them stealthily fill up your wells and make turbid the pure knowledge of the things of faith. For this is ever their care, not *to teach simple souls from the divine Scriptures,* but to *sophisticate the truth from a science which is foreign to it . . .* bewitching the sheep that they drink not of that pure water which springeth up unto everlasting life, but that they bring on themselves that oracle of the prophet, 'they have forsaken me, the fountain of living waters, and have hewn out for themselves broken cisterns which can hold no water.'"

Do such counsels breathe the spirit of a creed or church religion? Do they not send every one of these "beloved souls" to the "fountain of living waters" to draw thence and drink for itself? How were these "souls" to detect the stealthy and bewitching arts of the "Philistine shepherds," but by comparing their doctrines with the "divine Scriptures"—in plain words, by reading their Bible, in the exercise of free, intelligent, *private judgment*. This is good Protestant advice. But Papal pastors do not, "in our time," write such letters to their flocks.

About the year 368, the people of Neo-Caesarea lost their bishop by death. Basil addressed a consolatory letter to them.[355] Whether it bears most of the Puritanic or Papal type, let the reader judge.

After many expressions of sympathy, and dissuasives from excessive grief, he continues:

> Shall we not shake off our sorrow? Shall we not bestir ourselves? Shall we not look up to the common Lord, who having permitted each of his saints to minister to their own generation, calls them back again, at fitting times, to himself? Call now seasonably to mind the counsels of him who, while yet ministering in your church, admonished you, "beware of dogs, beware of evil workers." . . . These you must beware of under the care of some watchful shepherd. *It is yours to seek for him*[356] laying aside all strife and love of pre-eminence. *It is the Lord's to point him out to you,* who from the time of Gregory, that great leader

---

351. Basil, Πρὸς τοὺς νέος. [Trans. "To the young men."] Chapter 2, to end, II:243.
352. Ἐν ὕδατι τον ἥλιον ὁρᾶν. [Trans. "Looking at the sun in the water".]
353. Αὐτῷ προσβαλοῦμεν τῷ φωτὶ τὰς ὄψεις. [Trans. "Looking at the light itself".]
354. Basil, Epistle 8.
355. Basil, Epistle 28.
356. Ὃν ὑμέτερον μὲν αἰτῆσαι. [Trans. "It is yours to seek for him."]

of your church, down to him who has just departed,[357] hath added one to another, and always with such fitness, that he has graciously bestowed a wondrous ornament, even as it were a string of most precious stones, upon your church. You must not, therefore, despair of successors. For the Lord knoweth them that are his; and *may lead into the midst of us those who, perchance, are quite unlooked for by us.*

I beseech you by your fathers, by the true faith, by the departed, arouse your spirit, *let every man judge the business in hand to be his own proper concern,*[358] and considering that he must himself be first affected by the issue of this transaction either way, not, as too often happens, throw off upon his neighbour the care of your common interests, and so, each one neglecting the matter in his own mind, all of you bring upon yourselves the sad consequences of your indifference. Receive these advices, with all good will, whether as expressions of neighbourly sympathy, or of the communion of those who hold the same faith, or, which is nearer the truth, of obedience to the law of love, and fear of the danger of being silent; resting assured that ye are our glorying, as we are also yours, in the day of our Lord, and that, by the pastor who is to be given to you, we shall be bound together yet more firmly in the bond of love, or utterly separated: which may God forbid!

This would be very *seasonable* advice from a New England pastor to a neighbouring church, mourning the death of an eminent minister, and *every word of this letter might be so addressed* without infringing on that "parity and rank democracy" which Dr. Nevin deplores as one of the great mischiefs and afflictions of "Puritanism." But do "Catholic" Bishops address such missives "in our time" to *vacant congregations*?

And the people not only "sought for" and elected their own bishops, pastor is the name [Basil] uses in this letter, in the "glorious period of the fourth century," but they called them to account roundly too, when they thought either their conduct or their faith deserved it. See Basil's apologetic letter to his own flock when they were dissatisfied at his long absence,[359] and to "all" the Christians of New Caesarea,[360] when they were alarmed by his monastic tendencies and certain changes which he made in the music of the Church, which he defends solely by the congruity of the thing to the Gospel and to the worship of the Church, and the like considerations, and never by any appeal to *tradition* or *sacerdotal* or *ecclesiastical authority.*

357. He commends especially the faithfulness and diligence of "the deceased" in *preaching,* and adds, "on *this account,* (ταύτῃ) not by reason of his *age,* he was esteemed worthy of higher honour in the assemblies of *his equally honoured brethren* (τῆς προτιμήσεως ἐν τοῖς συλλόγοις τῶν ὁμοτίμων) through the superior venerableness of his wisdom, taking the precedence by the common concession." (ἐκ κοινῆς συγχωρήσεως τὸ πρωτεῖον καρπούμενος) Did "Basil the Great stand in the bosom of the prelatical and high church system *at all points*?"

358. Οἰκεῖον ἕκαστον ἑαυτοῦ τὸ σπουδαζόμενον κρίναντα. [Trans. "Let every man judge the business in hand to be his own proper concern."]

359. Basil, Epistle 2nd.

360. Basil, Epistle 207.

Chapter 3: Nevin and Proudfit: Opposed Views of the Early Creeds

How close and intensely individual was the preaching of Basil, the most cursory glance at his homilies will show. We instance that "On the Soul."[361] He certainly did not bring out truth with the full-orbed brightness of a Howe,[362] or as Robert Hall,[363] send the *lucid arrows* to the conscience with the inevitable precision of a Baxter[364] or a Davies,[365] a Payson[366] or an Alexander;[367] what forbids us to say, "God having reserved some better thing for us that they without us should not be made perfect?" But he did bring his hearer to deal alone with his God and with himself. He held up to him no other aim than holiness of heart and life, and no other means of attaining it but the word and the grace of God. This alone would have utterly prevented him from "finding himself at home in the Papal communion in our time." The same lofty intrepidity of soul and "valour for truth" which led him to confront the tyrannical Valens, would surely have driven him to defy the Pope. And if the vigour of that "system" were equal to its spirit, we have not the slightest doubt that it would speedily bestow upon him, in addition to all his other titles, that of *Martyr*.

"We must have a full persuasion that every word of God is true and possible, even though nature fight against it. For *herein lies the very strife of faith.*"[368]

Such is the eighth rule of the *Moralia* of "Basil the Great,"[369] and with one allusion more, we end our *Basiliana*. For, when we unseal the "*exundans fons ingenii*" [Trans. "abundant source of intelligence"] of the "Christian Demosthenes," it will pour itself out inexhaustibly, unless we abruptly shut off its flow.

The death of Basil, exhibited in connection with that of Moehler, one of the most highly cultivated philosophic and devout Catholics "in our time," will form our last point of contrast. Basil, as Gregory tells us, met death with these words on his lips, "Into thine hands, O Lord, I commend my spirit; thou hast redeemed me, O Lord God of truth."

The last scene of Möhler is thus drawn by his biographer.

---

361. Περὶ ψυχῆς [Trans. "On the Soul"]. Basil, III:833. Σεαυτῷ μόνῳ πρόσεχε [Trans. "Take heed only to thyself"] is one of its leading counsels.

362. [John Howe (1630–1705) was an English Puritan theologian who had studied under the Cambridge Platonists and had served briefly as one of Oliver Cromwell's chaplains.]

363. [Robert Hall (1764–1831) was an English Baptist renowned for his oratory.]

364. [Richard Baxter (1615–91) was an English Purian pastor, spiritual writer, hymnologist, and theologian.]

365. [Samuel Davies (1723–1761) was a Presbyterian minister from Virginia who served as the president of the College of New Jersey (Princeton) from 1759–61. He was also an evangelist to the enslaved population and was a popular poet and preacher.]

366. [Edward Payson (1783–1827) was an American Congregationalist minister and a popular preacher.]

367. [Archibald Alexander (1772–1851) was an influential professor of theology at Princeton Theological Seminary and a well-known homiletician. He pioneered the popularity of the Scottish Common Sense philosophy at Princeton.]

368. Ἐνταῦθα γὰρ καὶ ὁ ἀγὰν τῆς πίστεως. [Trans. "Herein lies the very strife of faith."]

369. Basil, II:336.

THE APOSTLES' CREED

On the seventh of April he felt himself better, and desired that for his entertainment a favourite book of travels might be read to him.... At the beginning of Holy Week, feeling his end approach, he prepared by the reception of the sacraments, for appearing before his Almighty Judge.... The heavy icecold sweat-drops gathered about his brow and temples; the last struggle had come on. His confessor never left his side. At one o'clock in the afternoon, he awoke from a gentle slumber, clasped both hands to his head, ... gasped violently three times, and the soul, bursting her fetters, sprang upwards to her God.[370]

Thus closes the life-drama of scriptural and of "sacramental," "organic" (Catholic), Christianity. The former, at the approach of the last enemy, repeats its *first faith* in the very "letters of faith," commits itself once more to the hands of its mighty and loving Redeemer, and its last glance is a *look towards Jesus*. The latter "entertains" as it may, its easier intervals, and when the inevitable moment comes, "receives the sacraments" and *"gives up the ghost."*

Let me die the death of the Christian, rather than that of *the Catholic*.

Of Chrysostom, whom Dr. Nevin groups also with the "Romanizing fathers," we must not speak at any length, and we need not. For the beautiful monograph of Neander is before the world in an English translation, and shows how eminently scriptural were both his personal culture and his ministry.

But when in his Homily on 1 Cor i,[371] he defines the unity and ubiquity of the Christian Church to consist in this, that it comprehends "all who, in every place, call upon the name of our Lord Jesus Christ, both theirs and ours, and that its members are those who are "sanctified in Christ Jesus," "called to be saints," and explains at length, how each of these clauses reveals a *mark* and *distinction* of the true Church, and that the inclusion of all such makes the Church *one* and *universal*; and when, in his Homily on Col iii.[372] in the exposition of the words, "let the word of Christ dwell in you richly," (what a text for a "Romanizing" preacher!) he unfolds the exhaustless richness of the divine word, pointing out how "doctrine, opinions, exhortation,"[373] may all be drawn from it, and fervently exhorts his people to read the Scriptures, not carelessly nor occasionally, but with much diligent endeavour;[374] we feel sure that this style of preaching does not bear "a *very* near resemblance in all material points to the later religion of the Roman Church,"[375] that in fact it very nearly "corresponds with

---

370. Memoir of Johann Adam Möhler prefixed to his *Symbolik* (Mainz, 1832), 84, 85. [J. A. Möhler (1796–1838), a Roman Catholic theologian and historian, taught at Tübingen and Munich. In addition to his *Symbolik* he published a study of Athanasius (1827).]

371. Chrysostom, *Works*, ed. Montfaucon (Paris, 1718–38), X:4.

372. Ibid., XI:390.

373. Ἡ διδασκαλία, τὰ δύγματα, ἡ παραίνεσις. [Trans. "Doctrines, opinion, exhortation."]

374. Μή ἁπλῶς, οὐδέ ὡς ἔτυχεν, ἀλλὰ μετὰ πολλῆς τῆς σπουδῆς. [Trans. "Not carelessly nor occasionally but with much diligent endeavor."]

375. Nevin, "Early Christianity, Third Article," *The Mercersburg Review*, IV, Number 1 (January, 1852), 2.

the modern ecclesiastical life of Connecticut and Massachusetts."[376] At least it is clear that Chrysostom could not have agreed with Dr. Nevin that "*all* true theology grows forth from the creed, and so remains *bound* to it perpetually as its necessary radix *or root.*"[377]

Dr. Nevin cannot endure that "invisible" sort of unity which is manifested by "an occasional shaking of hands fraternally on the platform of a Bible Society, or a melting season of *promiscuous!* communion now and then around the sacramental board." It "falls immeasurably short," he says, "of the true idea of Catholic unity." "It has *no tendency whatever, however remote,* towards *true Catholicity.* It is *the very opposite* of all organic Christianity."[378] Now what *organic* Christianity is, it would probably have puzzled Chrysostom to conceive, but his "idea of true Catholic unity" is precisely that which Dr. Nevin charges upon the "sect-system."

One declaration we add, grand and impressive, like the genius and the faith of him who uttered it—"The apostolic writings are the fortifications of the churches."[379]

Could he then have "found himself at home," in a "Church" which is not only *without* those "fortifications" but which, with the aid of such a master mason as "Strauss," has undertaken "in our time, to shoot up spontaneously," independent fortifications of its own? No, the princely Archbishop of Constantinople would rather have betaken himself to the humblest "Puritanic" quarters *within* those fortifications, exclaiming, as he once did, when he stemmed alone the wrath of the emperor and the fury of the multitude, "*We are servants of the crucified!*"[380]

[Conclusion]

If we had time to descend to the fifth century and gather the suffrages of its eminent divines, great as the development of sacerdotal and ecclesiastical ideas during that century undoubtedly was, we should find that they were of one mind with the Reformers on the great points at issue between them and Romanism. If we should consult all the councils of the Church from that first consisting of inspired Apostles (Acts xv) which appealed to "the words of the prophets" as the ground of their decision, down to the time when the Papacy gained the ascendant and "made void the word of God by her traditions," if we should appeal to the early historians and hymn-writers of the

---

376. Nevin, "Early Christianity [First Article], *The Mercersburg* Review, III, Number 5 (September, 1851), 490.

377. "The Apostles' Creed," in this volume, 92.

378. Nevin, *Antichrist*, 61–62 [See Nevin, "Antichrist" in *One, Holy, Catholic, and Apostolic*, Tome One, MTSS 5, ed. Hamstra, 222].

379. Τειχῆ τῶν ἐκκλησιῶν ἔστιν. [Trans. "They are the fortifications of the church."] Chrysostom, Homily on 2 Tim iii. 1, *Works*, VI:282.

380. Οἰκέται ἐσμὲν τοῦ ἐσταυρωμένου. [Trans. "We are servants of the Crucified."] Ὁμιλ. εἰς Ἐυτροπίον. [Homilies on Expression] Chapter 4.

Church, we should derive from all one harmonious testimony to the fontal source and authoritative test of the Christian faith.

All these, with a harmony as perfect as the unity of the faith, and a variety as wonderful as the language and the imagination of man, proclaim the holy and inspired Scriptures to be "the bread" on which the Church feeds, "the garment" in which she is arrayed, "the breath of her life," "the light" by which she walks, "the sword" with which she fights, "the root" from which she grows, "the foundation" on which she stands, "the walls" which surround her, "the wings which bear her to heaven."

But we dismiss the subject and release the reader, (if indeed he has stayed with us through this long discussion) with the fervent hope that he may so apprehend *the first aspects* of truth as they stand forth in *the creed,* as to become possessor of the whole ample and glorious (as good Hilary calls it) *Patrocinium Ecclesiae* [Trans. "patronage of the Church"], as it is revealed in the Bible.

The Anti-Creed Heresy [John Williamson Nevin's Response to Proudfit][1]

[by John W. Nevin]

We have had ample opportunity already to expose the opposition, in which much of our Christianity at this time stands to the true sense and spirit of the Apostles' Creed.

Unitarianism rejects it as a matter of course. So also the whole Baptist body. But the case is not materially better with Puritanism in general. The *Puritan Recorder* has boldly avowed the fact that the Creed and Puritanism have not a kindred spirit, that in truth they mutually exclude each other, and cannot stand together, except as the first is taken in a wholly *non-natural* sense, and made to mean just the contrary of what it was taken to mean in the ancient church. We have found the *N. Y. Observer* denouncing also the principle and theory of this ancient faith, in similar radical style, as the beginning of an apostasy which is supposed to have turned the whole church into a synagogue of Satan.[2]

In the last number of the *Princeton Repertory*, the Rev. Dr. Proudfit,[3] of New Brunswick, has a long and labored article on the Apostles' Creed, which we are sorry to say falls into substantially the same heretical depravity. Our limits here will not allow us to notice it at much length. Nor is that necessary. Enough, that we bring into view simply its leading points, drawing them forth from the mass of irrelevant learning in which they are buried and hid. The article needs no other exposure.

Dr. Proudfit tries hard in the first place to make something dreadful out of the light in which the Creed is presented by our articles in the first volume of the *Mercersburg Review*. He will have it, that we make the intuitional consciousness of the Church the fountain of a Divine revelation in some way, independently of the word

---

1. [J. W. N[evin], *The Mercersburg Review* 4 (November, 1852) 606–20.]

2. [Rev 3:9.]

3. [Having taught Greek and Latin at New York University (1841–48), Proudfit accepted a call to teach at Rutgers College, New Brunswick, NJ, established in 1766 with roots in the Dutch Reformed Church in America.]

of God which is contained in the Bible; and with his characteristic dishonesty goes so far even as to insinuate that we follow Strauss[4] as a master, because we had said somewhere that his work shows the necessity of looking for the ground of Christianity in something deeper than the mere outward text of the sacred books, which give us an account of what it was in the beginning. Had we said that Gibbon's[5] abuse of Church History shows the necessity of looking beyond its external facts and persons to the Divine life which was in them, in the style for instance of Neander,[6] there would have been precisely the same room for charging us with taking lessons of an infidel. It is wonderful however how much of this nasty sort of art and trick our Brunswick Professor has. It seems to be part of his nature.

The view we have taken of the Creed is simple enough. We have granted, that it was not from the start, as to letter and form, just what we find it to be in the fourth century. In spirit and substance however it was always the same, any modifications it experienced being nothing more in fact than the bringing out of the sense which had been in it from the beginning. In this view it dates from the time of the Apostles. To say that it was drawn from the New Testament Scriptures is simply absurd; because these were not in existence when the faith of the Church started, and came not into their present canonical form for at least a hundred years after. During all this time however the Church had a rule of faith, a fixed and settled norm of doctrine, everywhere acknowledged and received. This had its seat of course in the life of the Church itself, in the fact of what Christianity was to the consciousness of her actual faith; but we have never dreamed certainly of making it for this reason the product of this subjective consciousness as such. It had its origin and ground in the objective revelation of Christianity itself, as an outward supernatural fact. This was primarily Christ himself, as in Peter's great confession [Matt 16:16]. Afterwards we have it in full outline in the preaching of the Apostles; from which it passed into the consciousness of the Church; where under the promised guidance of the Spirit it was kept afterwards to its true and proper form, as already mentioned. The Church exercised no other intuition in the case, than that of apprehending and holding fast in such way, under this promised guidance, the real objective supernatural mystery of godliness which

---

4. [David Friedrich Strauss (1808–74), a German theologian influenced by F. D. Schleiermacher and G. W. F. Hegel, was the author of *Das Leben Jesu, kritisch bearbeitet*, which questioned the historicity of the miracle stories of the gospels. See also, Robert C. Morgan, "David Friedrich Strauss," in McKim, 364–68.]

5. [Edward Gibbon (1737–94) was a British historian whose major work *The Decline and Fall of the Roman Empire* (1788) challenged the role of the supernatural in the establishment and development of Christianity.]

6. [Johann August Wilhelm Neander (1789–1850), Jewish by birth, was an important German church historian. He published a widely celebrated history of the Christian church, *Allgemeine Geschichte der christlichen Religion und Kirche* . (*General History of the Christian Religion and Church*) and a reply to D. F. Strauss' *Leben Jesu—Das Leben Jesu Christi, in seinem geschichilichen Zusammenhang und seiner geschichtlichen Entwickelung* (*The Life of Jesus Christ in its Historical Connexion and Historical Development*). Neander was highly regarded by both Nevin and Schaff.]

had thus been committed to her by the living Christ and his living Apostles in the beginning, and long before the authoritative publication of the N. T. Scriptures, as a more ample record of the same glorious revelation, under her auspices and care; a work for which, as well as for her most faithful guardianship of these "oracles of God," through the long night of the dark ages, when she was herself so completely sold as some tell us to the powers of hell, we owe her a debt of filial gratitude and love greater than can be well expressed.

Let Dr. Proudfit and all others whom it may concern, make themselves easy on this point. We have no sympathy with the intuitionalism of Schleiermacher[7] or Morell.[8] We hold Christianity to be a strictly objective supernatural revelation, a mystery in this view wholly above nature both logical and material, which can be apprehended only through faith and by a new understanding given to us for the purpose by the Son of God alone.

But let *our* view of the Creed now pass. What we have to do with here is the view taken of it by Dr. Proudfit. His object in trying to set aside our representation, is to make room for another conception which may snip the symbol of its binding authority altogether. It came not in full form as we have it now from the Apostles; it abounded at first in variations; it underwent some additions; *therefore* it is of no Apostolical necessity for faith. So Puritanism is wont to argue. We undertook to show, that these premises rightly understood led to no such conclusion; because the variations and additions were never such as to change at all the proper unity and sameness of the Creed, in its essential constitution. The *regula fidei*[9] on which the Church stood from the first, was just the substance of this glorious confession, handed forward from age to age in the life of faith. The Creed is the mirror of this faith as it had been received from the Apostles; and no other form of words can be said to represent truly and rightly the original fact of the Christian revelation. Against this Dr. Proudfit, we say, tries to fight as he best can. He wishes to have it thought, that the Creed had no fixed character in the beginning; that it was formed loosely at first from the Scriptures according to the private judgment of separate churches; that its variations prove the churches to have been much in the same state with our modern Independent ecclesiastical organizations, each of which claims the right of making its own creed in its own way; and that

---

7. [Friedrich Daniel Ernst Schleiermacher (1768–1834), influential German theologian, is often called the "Father of Modern Protestant Theology." His major works are *Reden über die Religion* (*Religion: Speeches to its Cultured Despisers*) and *Der christliche Glaube nach den Grundsätzen der evangelischen Kirche im Zusammenhang dargestellt* (*The Christian Faith*). Schleiermacher defined religion as the feeling of absolute dependence upon the source of our being.]

8. [Nevin is probably referring to John Daniel Morrell (1816–91), a British Congregational pastor, philosopher, and educator, who was the author of several books including *The Philosophy of Religion* which was much influenced by J. G. Fichte's idealism.]

9. [Trans. "rule of faith." A rule of faith was a brief statement of the core principles of Christian belief. There were a variety of rules of faith in the early church, but they held to a common theological core and were the predecessors of the early church's creeds. Philip Schaff, *The Creeds of Christendom*, I:3–11 and J. N. D. Kelly, *Early Christian Creeds*, 30–61.]

it is injurious to the Bible accordingly to attribute to it any binding authority whatever in determining the true sense of Christianity. If this be not what the article means, we know not how to find in it any meaning whatever.

Here then we have the heresy of the *Puritan Recorder* openly paraded in the pages of the *Princeton Repertory*,[10] by a learned Professor of the Reformed Dutch Church![11] For let it be observed, the question is not at last whether our theory of the rise of the Creed is to be considered correct or not; but whether the Creed, *however it may have risen,* is to be regarded as still truly and really the norm, as far as it goes, the fixed doctrinal matrix and mould of the Christian faith for all ages. It was so regarded, we know, in all ages before the Reformation. It was so regarded also by the first Protestant Churches. Dr. Proudfit makes a show indeed of proving the contrary, by quoting passages from their Confessions that make the Bible to be the rule of faith against all human traditions. But this is pitiful quibbling. They professed notwithstanding to hold fast to the Creed as a true exposition of the Christian faith. They never dreamed of sundering the Bible from the mind of the Church as it had stood in previous ages in every form and shape, and turning it over to the judgment of any and all persons for such interpretation as might happen to seem fit. They owned the necessity of a confessional *norm* for the right use of the Bible; and the necessary beginning of this, the archetypal and primitive symbol of Christianity, they acknowledged to be the Apostles' Creed. However it might have come to its present settled form, they held it to be a true expression of what the Christian faith was as received by the Church in the first ages from the Apostles, from which as a rule of belief the same Church in later times had no right to depart. But this is just what the article before us is not willing to admit; for the admission would be at once fatal to its whole argument.

True, the article affects to speak respectfully of the Creed. Ursinus, Vossius, Heidegger, we are told p. [140 in this volume], enumerate as catholic or universal the Apostolic, Nicene, and Athanasian creeds; and among these "the shortest, simplest, most comprehensive, and most strictly scriptural is without doubt the Apostolic." But then the drift of the whole discussion notwithstanding is to make this acknowledgment of no force. There is no conflict among these catholic creeds. They are strictly the *one* faith of the primitive church; and one must be interpreted by the rest to be of any real force. This fact however Dr. P. seeks to hide. His art is to throw all as much as possible into uncertainty and confusion. Then the Creed is for him a mere bundle of received maxims, brought together in a simply outward way; than which no conception can be more false or more contrary to sound faith. It is a most perfect unit; an organism, in which every part is true only as it grows forth from the whole. It is a mirror reflecting thus at every point the original life of the universal church. This Dr. P. has no power

---

10. [The correct title of the periodical is *The Biblical Repertory and Princeton Review*.]

11. [At this stage in his career, it is unclear whether Proudfit's denomination affiliation was Presbyterian or Dutch Reformed. In any case, by the time of his controversy with Nevin, much of his preaching and writing was being done under the aegis of the Dutch Reformed Church.]

to see; and so he will not allow it to be of true symbolical authority, in its own whole and only true original sense, for the interpretation of the Bible. He shows throughout a strong dislike to this sense, especially as it comes to view in the article of the church as the organ and medium of salvation; and openly repudiates as contrary to the Scriptures the whole sacramental and mystical side of Christianity, without which the Creed for the first Christians would have had no meaning whatever.

But what need is there of analysis to make out the point, that Dr. Proudfit rejects the authority of the Apostles' Creed, as the fundamental rule and norm of the Christian faith? In no other view, can his article be taken to have any sense. Is not this just what he finds fault with in the *Mercersburg Review*, that it seeks to bind the interpretation of the Bible by the Apostles' Creed? Either he honestly holds the Creed, as we have it and however it came, for such a symbol, or he does not. If he does so hold it, what ground of quarrel can he have with us for allowing to it the same authority? If not, what farther proof is wanted to fix upon him, in common with Unitarians and Baptists, the stigma of the Anti-Creed heresy?

To sustain himself in his desperate position, he finds it necessary in the next place to contend that the faith of the first ages was based upon the independent use of the Bible, without any other standing rule of faith, in the pretended style of the modern sect system; and he has the hardihood to think of forcing this outrageous misrepresentation, not only upon the times of Irenaeus and Tertullian, but even upon the Nicene period itself!

Is it asked now, by what *hocus-pocus* this feat of historical legerdemain is performed? We answer, it is done in the simplest and most *characteristic* way imaginable. The whole art and mystery of the thing consists in shifting the point in debate, so as to make it turn on the question only whether the early church regarded and used the Holy Scriptures as of Divine authority in matters of religion; about which, so far as we know, there never has been any sort of doubt. Will it be believed, that so learned a man as the Rev. Dr. Proudfit of New Brunswick lays himself out systematically to prove, by quotation upon quotation, first that Irenaeus, Justin Martyr, Tertullian, Origen, &c., and then that Athanasius, Chrysostom, Basil, the Gregories, &c., of a later day, all held and taught the inspiration and binding authority of the Scriptures in the Christian Church; and that this should then be gravely taken by him as proof that they owned and acknowledged no guiding rule, no governing norm, for determining *the true sense of these Scriptures,* but left it to private judgment to settle their sense as it best could on the outside of the Church?

The thing is absolutely ridiculous. Who does not know that the Fathers all held the Bible in the highest veneration? The Catholic Church has always honored it as of Divine authority. We owe the sacred deposit altogether to her care. She formed the canon of the New Testament, deciding what it should contain and what it should not contain, and affixing to it the stamp of inspiration. And what she produced in such form, she has most religiously and faithfully preserved through all ages.

Without her *imprimatur* and seal now, all would be thrown into loose uncertainty and doubt. There can be no firm faith in the inspiration of the Scriptures, where there is no faith in the mystery of the Church. So Augustine teaches;[12] and so too we are taught by the Creed. And yet here we have the champion of Puritanism holding up the faith of the early fathers in the inspiration of the Scriptures, as in and of itself a conclusive argument that they had no sense of any Divine authority in the Catholic Church. Could nonsense well be more egregious!

Only think of Tertullian's tract on *Prescriptions* being quoted, to prove just the opposite of the whole argument in which it deals; that is, to make it appear that the Bible is the rule of faith, aside from the tradition of the Church, in the hands of the faithful and of all sorts of heretics alike! What then *was* his famous argument against heretics? Who does not know, that his whole object is to reduce the determination of what is Christianity, and so of course the interpretation also of the Bible, to a standard of faith already actually at hand in the church, which was supposed as such to have come down from the time of the Apostles?[13]

The use made of Irenaeus is equally absurd. For the object he aims at, Dr. Proudfit's quotations absolutely stultify themselves. For instance: "We must betake ourselves to the Church," writes this Father, "and be brought up in her bosom, *and nourished by the Scriptures of the Lord.*" What does this mean, but that the right use of the Bible is confined to the Church; which he compares immediately after with a paradise in the world, within which the Scriptures as trees bear fruit, for such only of course as are *there* and not on the outside—the very same thought that we find so familiar afterwards to Cyprian? Yet this passage Dr. P. quotes, italicising the last clause, to prove these trees of salvation *not* confined for their right use to the garden of the Lord's planting; or to show, in other words, that Irenaeus made the Bible the source of Christianity without the Church.

But what shall we say of his attempt to Puritanize the Nicene Period, in the same violent style? Our statement, that the fathers of this time "knew nothing of the view which makes the Bible and private judgment the principle of Christianity or the only

---

12. Witness his memorable word: "*Ego vero evangelio non crederem, nisi me Catholicae ecclesiae commoveret auctoritas.*" [Trans. "I would not have believed the gospel had I not been moved by the authority of the Catholic church." Augustine, *Against the Epistle of Manichaeus, Called Fundamental*, Chapter V.]

13. In dealing with heretics, Tertullian tells us in *De Praescriptione haereticorum* [Prescriptions Against the Heretics], Chapter 18, the right order of controversy requires that we should settle first: "*Quibus competat fides ipsa! Cujus sint scripturae! A quo, et per quos, et quando, et quibus sit tradita disciplina qua fiunt Christiani!*" [Trans. "Among whom is this faith rightly kept? Whose are the scriptures? By whom and through whom, and when and to whom is the teaching handed down by which Christians are made?"] And then he adds: "*Ubi enim apparuerit esse veritatem et disciplinae et fidei Christianae, illic erit veritas scripturarum et expositionum et omnium traditionum christianarum.*" [Trans. "Indeed wherever Christian truth and discipline and faith may be found, *there will the truth of the scriptures and the explanations and all the Christian traditions be.*"] [Ibid., Chapter 19.] This is certainly plain enough. The only true sense of the Bible is that which agrees with the mind of the Church; and where is this norm to be had primarily if not in her established universal creed or scheme of faith?

rule of faith[14]—that the order of doctrine for them was the Apostles' Creed," he flatly denies; and anon sallies forth, in true Don Quixote style, to accumulate citations from Athanasius, Hilary, Victorinus, Cyril of Jerusalem, the Gregories, Ephraim the Syrian, Basil, and Chrysostom, page piled upon page, to make good the temerarious contradiction. He does prove indeed triumphantly that these worthies speak in the most exalted terms of the Bible, as the Catholic Church has always done, and that they made much account of inward personal religion also, as distinguished from dead outward forms; and so he draws what he conceives to be his invincible ergo: That they owned no Divine tradition of faith, no fixed creed, in the living Church as such, and knew nothing of Divine sacraments and true priestly functions in the style of the later Catholic system! It would be a pity to disturb the self-complacent serenity of such a notable *non sequitur*, by any show of serious resistance. We leave it alone in its glory.

We have never pretended to quote testimonies from the Nicene Period, for the purpose of proving that it was prevailingly Catholic and not Puritan. Why carry coals to Newcastle or Mauch Chunk?[15] That is a fact too well settled certainly for any *honest* controversy or debate. We have referred before to Isaac Taylor's *Ancient Christianity*. It is enough now to refer to it again. Much as we dislike the theological animus that reigns in it, its simply historical positions on this point are of unanswerable force. Let Dr. Proudfit meet them fairly if he can. Till he does so, it is breath spent in vain, to think of making good Puritans out of the fathers of the fourth and fifth centuries. They were as far as they well could be from anything of that sort.[16]

14. Here he charges us with *misstating* the case we oppose, by joining *private judgment* with the Bible. We beg leave however to retort the charge on himself and his school. To talk of the Bible as a principle or rule, *aside* from all judgment or interpreting sense, is downright childishness. The whole question regards the mind or judgment by which it is to be interpreted. Without some such mind, it never can become a principle or rule of anything. What *we* maintain is, that it must be read with the mind of the Church, which starts in the Apostles' Creed. Not so, says Dr. P. & Co.; that is to put it under the church; it must be read by some *other* mind, by *our* mind, by the mind of this or that sect; by every body's mind to suit himself. And what is this, we ask now, but to make the Bible *and* private *judgment* the principle and rule of Christianity!

15. [Newcastle, a city in northeastern England, was well known for its coal production. It would have been useless and foolish to carry coal to a community where coal was already readily available. Mauch Chunk, a town in eastern Pennsylvania, now named Jim Thorpe for the great 1912 America Olympic champion, is to that area what Newcastle was to England, a place rich in coal deposits. Nevin wished to illustrate a point commonly known to all.]

16. We are glad to find that *Dr. Ludlow*, associated with Dr. P. now in the New Brunswick Institutions, in his late *Inaugural Discourse*, has taken the true view of facts here, directly in the face of his learned colleague. He quotes with approbation Taylor's judgment concerning the Romanizing tendencies of the Early Church back even to the second century, and then adds: "The candid inquirer after truth will be amazed to find upon what a slender, precarious, visionary foundation the most strenuous endeavors were made in the ancient Church to create for her an all-absorbing, overpowering hierarchy. He will mark with surprise how soon new offices, forms, rites, ceremonies, were introduced. He will learn with no less astonishment that the custom of praying for the dead was universal; a custom of as high antiquity as any part of Christian worship which is not authorized by the inspired writings. Indeed, it is wanting no kind of support except from the holy Scriptures. Not much less may be said of the doctrines of celibacy and virginity, which seemed stealthily to make their way from the very days

"I firmly believe," says Taylor, "that it were on the whole better for a community to submit itself, without conditions, to the well known Tridentine Popery, than to take up the Christianity of Ambrose, Basil, Gregory Nyssen, Chrysostom, Jerome, and Augustine. Personally, I would rather be a Christian after the fashion of Pascal[17] and Arnold,[18] than after that of Cyprian or Cyril."[19] We confess ourselves to be very much of the same mind.

When Dr. P. is done with Isaac Taylor, he may try his polemical hand, if he see proper, with the masterly work of Richard Rothe,[20] entitled *Die Anfänge der christlichen Kirche*. This leaves little to be done, in the way of learning, for settling the view taken of the *Church* in the second and third centuries. When Dr. P. shall have answered it, we will begin to think that his vain babbling about the Christianity of this early time, is entitled to some little respect.

The case is abundantly clear. The faith of the Early Church is eternally imbedded in the Apostles' Creed. So, and not otherwise, the fact of Christianity was understood and embraced in the first ages. So the Bible was read, and not in any different *private* sense. This was the ground form in which the Christian consciousness, the universal mind of the Church, met and embraced by faith the corresponding substance of the Christian revelation, as it was preached by the Apostles and so passed over into the Sacred Writings. The Church had, it is true, different Creeds. But these were all in their fundamental conception and scheme one and the same; and this outline we have faithfully presented to us in the Apostles' Creed. There is no disagreement at

---

of the apostles, and were gradually growing into favor, until they received the sanction of the Synods of the Church, a little more than two centuries after the last of the apostles had departed. These doctrines, so pernicious to the morals and piety of the Church, so far from being opposed, were inculcated and lauded by all the Nicene fathers with scarce an exception. To these doctrines must be added the appointment of numerous days of feasting and fasting; rules and regulations in regard to meats and drinks; various appendages to the ordinances of baptism and the Lord's Supper; veneration for relics; the worship of martyrs; pilgrimages to holy places, and the formal establishment of Monachism. And all this within the period of those three centuries from which we are to derive the model of a perfect Church. [John Ludlow (1793–1857), was a clergyman and a theologian. He held the position of Professor of Biblical Literature, Ecclesiastical History and Church Government for two different stints (1819–25, 1852–57) at New Brunswick Theological Seminary.]

17. [Blaise Pascal (1623–62) was a French Catholic scientist, philosopher, and theologian. He adhered to the Jansenist theological party, which was suspected by the Jesuits of being too sympathetic to certain Protestant doctrines. He wrote in such a way as to evoke confusion and despair in readers so that they would be receptive to the offer of God's grace.]

18. [Gottfried Arnold (1666–1714) was a German Lutheran Pietist, who in his early days was exceedingly critical of the established church. He was also an influential ecclesiastical historian and author of devotional literature.]

19. [Isaac Taylor (1787–1865), English philosopher, historian, and writer, published *Ancient Christianity and the Doctrines of the Oxford Tracts* questioning the contentions of the Oxford Movement (the Tractarians) regarding the development of early Christian theology.]

20. [Richard Rothe (1799–1867), German Lutheran theologian influenced by F. D. E. Schleiermacher and J. A. W. Neander, published a highly respected book on the history of the early church, *Die Anfänge der christlichen Kirche*.]

all between it and the Nicene Creed for instance, or that of Athanasius. The proper identity of the symbol is not just in its so many clauses or words, but in its reigning idea rather, its grand *projection* of the primary facts of the "Mystery of Godliness." In this view, it gives us undoubtedly the true *regula fidei* of Primitive Christianity; and has always been regarded accordingly as of *oecumenical* or universal authority; not of course as excluding other symbols more extensive and full, but still in such a way as to require that these should grow forth from it, have their root in it and be a true carrying out of its sense, in order to be of any like oecumenical right and force.[21] The scheme of faith it presents is, for any honest and tolerably well informed person, sufficiently plain. It is the same that we meet with on every page of the ancient Fathers, and in all the institutions of the early Church. It is constructed throughout on the Catholic, as distinguished from the modern Puritan habit, of mind. Its articles are all mysteries. They set before us an order of things above nature, which is yet taken to be really at hand, as the presence of a new creation in the world, accomplishing its own supernatural ends. The scheme is sacramental, in the very sense which is so distasteful to the Gnostic spiritualism of the present day. This is felt at once in the article of the *Holy Catholic Church,* with its communion of saints and remission of sins. The article may be indeed construed to mean an invisible church simply, where grace works without sacraments. But then it is forced out of its proper historical sense. It had no such meaning for the early ages; and no such meaning falls in fairly with the scheme and scone of the symbol as a whole. The *Church* here spoken of is a real mystery derived through the Holy Ghost from the fact of the Incarnation—the Body by which Christ as Head works in the world—the ark of salvation—an object in this view of faith—just as it comes before us in the writings of Irenaeus, Cyprian, and all the fathers of the fourth and fifth centuries. Through her is the forgiveness of sins accordingly, the communion of saints, the resurrection of the body and life everlasting. The forgiveness of sins thus refers immediately to baptism; as we have it explicitly

---

21. Dr. P. affects to be scandalized at our saying, that "the article of justification by faith itself is turned into a perilous lie," if it be sundered from the scheme of truth exhibited in the ancient creeds. This only shows, however, the weak sense he has of the organic nature and true objective reality of the Christian faith. There is no such thing as getting to the doctrine of justification, or any other doctrine, legitimately and so that it shall be truly a part of the "One Faith" originally delivered to the saints, without beginning with the elementary form of this faith as it lies before us in the Apostles' Creed; for that can be no true fruit of Christian thought and feeling certainly, and so no true sense either of the Bible, which is not produced from the root of all Christian doctrine as it has entered into the very life of the Church from the beginning. Even what may be a sound doctrine in word must become false and dangerous in fact, if it be not apprehended under such felt relation to the unchangeable *incunabula* of Christianity, as they are here presented to our view, but be held as something brought in from a wholly different sphere of thinking. And there is no doubt whatever, that the article of justification by faith, as it is practically carried out by some of our unsacramental sects, which despise the Creed and resolve the Church into a Gnostic fiction, is just in this way converted into a fearful falsehood, that is doing more mischief on all sides than can easily be told. No theology can be orthodox, no religion safe, no faith more than spiritual fancy we fear, that does not breathe throughout a filial unconstrained and unaffected veneration for the *Symbolum Apostolicum*, in its original and only proper use.

brought out in the Nicene Creed: "I confess one baptism for the remission of sins." In all this we are offering no doubtful speculation. We simply state a fact which allows no contradiction. This is the system of Christianity taught in the Apostles' Creed, and held in the beginning by the whole Church.

But now just this scheme of Christianity Dr. Proudfit, with the whole spiritualistic school to which he belongs, has no mind or heart to accept. Everything like a churchly, priestly, sacramental religion, is for him the abomination of Romanism itself. He can subscribe to the Creed, if he be allowed to do so with vast mental reservation, in a non-natural sense, "foisting into" it a meaning to please himself; but not otherwise. He believes in no descent to hades, no continuation of the glorified resurrection life of Christ εν μυστηριω[22] here below, no supernatural church, no remission of sins, no communion of saints living and dead, in *the sense of this primitive symbol.* This implies a want of harmony with the symbol throughout. For these points are not in their place by accident. They belong to the life of the symbol as a whole. Not to see and feel this, is itself not to own the mystery of the faith it proclaims. It is only in keeping then with such unbelief, that the Puritanism of Dr. Proudfit refuses to see in this ancient oecumenical symbol the necessary matrix of all true Christian theology, and so the only sure primary norm and analogy of faith for the true understanding of the Scriptures. He will have it, that we are bound now by no such rule, but have a perfect right to re-cast the entire fact of Christianity in a different mould, as to *our own judgment* construing the Scriptures may seem best; so that the fact shall be to us something wholly different from what it once *was,* for the mind of the Church just after the time of the Apostles, and yet all be right and safe notwithstanding because we pretend to have found it in the Bible!

This is monstrous certainly. But it is no caricature. It does not, we think, exaggerate Dr. Proudfit's error in the least. If the interpretation of the Bible is to be set free from the authority of the Apostles' Creed, it is vain to talk of its being bound by any other symbolical authority derived from the ancient church. And how then can any modern symbol be allowed to have any such force? What right can the Belgic Confession or the Heidelberg Catechism now have to govern our theology, or be-spectacle our reading of the Holy Scriptures, where the first mirror of the Christian faith itself, the root of all symbols, the underlying foundation of all that is oecumenical in the belief of the Christian world, is thus roughly required to stand back, and make room for the glorious, divinely sacred rights of Private Judgment! To such gross monstrosity, most plainly, the precious theory must necessarily come at the last. In nothing short of this can it possibly pause or rest for a single moment.

What can be more preposterous in these circumstances, than to pretend, as Dr. Proudfit does, to make common cause in any way notwithstanding with the theological life of the ancient fathers? That *their* religion was cast throughout in the mould of the Apostles' Creed, is just as clear as the fact that the sun shines. They magnified the

22. [Trans. "this mystery."]

CHAPTER 3: NEVIN AND PROUDFIT: OPPOSED VIEWS OF THE EARLY CREEDS

Scriptures undoubtedly, as God's word, and found no terms too strong to set forth their heavenly authority; but they understood the Scriptures at the same time in the sense only of the great outline of doctrine that is contained in the Creed, and considered it heresy to think of forcing them into any other sense. Whatever may be thought of the way in which the symbol came into its present form, on this point no true scholar can have any sort of doubt. From the fifth century back to the second, all doctrine and faith may easily be seen to run in the channel of this scheme and no other. All the other oecumenical symbols include it, with one unvarying voice. All the oecumenical councils recognize it as the only true platform of Christianity, with one and the same witness, echoing from age to age like the sound of many waters. And are we to be told now, by such a man as Dr. Proudfit, that the fathers even of the fourth and fifth centuries, the bishops who sat in the Councils of Nice [Nicea], and Constantinople, and Ephesus and Chalcedon, knew nothing of the binding authority of this common settled scheme of faith, but held the naked text of the Bible, without the voice of the living Church, to be a sufficient warrant and rule of doctrine for all men, in the exercise simply of their own judgment, and over against the judgment of the whole Christian world; if need be, back to the earliest times—in the pretended style of the Cumberland Presbyterians, Campbellites, Winebrennerians,[23] Baptists and Puritans generally of the present day?

We say *pretended* style; for there is no such thing in truth as this sort of unsymbolical independence in the interpretation of the Bible; and those who promise liberty in this way, only bring in always a real bondage of spirit in the room of the lawful and just authority they dare to set aside. No man reads the Bible without a theological habit of some sort, even if it be that of a Voltaire or Paine only, which goes to determine for him the sense of its words. Every sect has its symbol, its tradition, written or unwritten, generally both, for the most part poor, harsh, hard, and dead—under whose iron yoke, is sung the melancholy song of freedom all the day long. Of all conceivable forms of spiritual vassalage, the most dismal surely is to be estranged from the oecumenical faith, the catholic creed, of God's Church as it has stood from the beginning, and to be adopted into the glorious liberty of some paltry sect, which has manufactured a new edition of Christianity for its own use, fresh from the mint of the Bible, in the most approved Puritan style—and now requires you, on pain of sore heresy if not actual perdition, to read the Bible and do up all your religious thinking

---

23. [Cumberland Presbyterianism was formally organized in 1810. Its origins are in the Kentucky frontier revivals of 1800. It was a schism from the Presbyterian Church in the U.S.A. The Cumberland Presbyterians attempted to design a theological middle way between Calvinism and Arminianism. The Cambellites were a movement organized by Thomas Campbell (1763-1854) and his son Alexander Campbell (1788-1866) who were key figures in the formation of the Christian Church (Disciples of Christ) in 1832. Winebrennerians, or the Church of God, were founded by John Winebrenner (1797-1860), who separated from the German Reformed Church over his use of New Measures revivalism. Nevin was antagonistic toward these and other "sectarian" groups who believed that they were called to restore Christianity in America to its primitive forms.]

in this same fashion precisely and no other. For our part, we think it infinitely more safe, as well as vastly more respectable, to take the sense of the inspired volume, with such men as Irenaeus, Cyprian, Athanasius, Chrysostom, Augustine, and the ancient fathers generally, from the standpoint of the old oecumenical councils and creeds, than to sit for the same purpose at the feet of any modern sect whatever, presuming to set up now any new scheme of faith, *not rooted in the Apostles' Creed,* as a better and surer version of what the Scriptures actually mean.

This, however, by the way. What we wish to press just now is, that the early fathers themselves at all events, along with the universal church in the first ages, could not possibly have dreamed of any such *creed-less* use of the Scriptures, as Dr. Proudfit has laid himself out to fasten upon their theology, turning all history topsy-turvy to carry his prodigious point. The oecumenical symbols ruled their whole faith. It will not do therefore, to quote their authority against themselves, by pretending to set them in opposition to their own age. There are two horns in this whole dilemma. One is, to contend that the modern unchurchly and unsacramental system is the same that prevailed in the beginning. The other is to give this up as a desperate position, and take refuge in the convenient hypothesis of a mystery of iniquity, working from the start and soon carrying all in its own way; in which case, the Apostles' Creed, together with all the oecumenical creeds and councils, must be included in the diabolical apostasy—since the sacramental system clearly underlies the whole scheme of thinking here brought into view. On one or the other of these horns every man must rest, who undertakes to vindicate Protestantism without the idea of historical development, or growth *through the old Catholic Church* into this later system viewed as a higher stage of Christianity—a view that cuts up by the roots the vulgar anti-popery notion of a total triumph of Satan over the Church, contrary to Christ's promise, in the middle ages. Neither of the alternatives affords a comfortable resting place. The horns of the dilemma are both sharp. Hence we see a disposition on the part of modern unchurchliness, to make use as much as possible of both; which, as the first is in truth just the contrary of the second, can be done only by hopping inconstantly backwards and forwards from one to the other, or by trying with wide straddle to gain a ticklish harlequin semblance of footing on both at the same time. This will not hold. We must either be true to the one horn or to the other—make the faith and religious life of the early church to be of force for settling the sense of Christianity, or else carry out in earnest the "mystery of iniquity" hypothesis. The two views cannot stand together. For there is no room to imagine here a distinction of tendencies in the same system, of any such sort as might suit the purposes of this unsacramental school. The whole theology and piety of these first ages are conditioned by the view of the Church that is presented to us in the old oecumenical creeds. All must go together. If we pretend to be on good terms with the fathers, we must not turn their universal creed into a diabolical lie. Antiquity cannot be both true and false here at the same time.

Chapter 3: Nevin and Proudfit: Opposed Views of the Early Creeds

One of the strangest phenomena in the theological world, it seems to us, is the readiness with which, in this whole controversy so many otherwise sensible people gravely pretend to plead for the credit and authority of the Bible, simply because they are bent on having it construed in their own way rather than in that of the ancient church. As though the whole question were not just this in the end, whether the ancient church took not the sense of the Scriptures more truly, than the version for which it is thus proposed to make room! The unsacramental school to which Dr. Proudfit considers it a merit to belong, continually take it for granted that Christian antiquity, wherever it differs from themselves, cannot have the Bible on its side, and that it is the easiest thing in the world to correct it now from the plain sense of the sacred volume as *read by this school.* And yet a child may see, what a perfect nose of wax they themselves make the sacred text to be, in accommodation to their own theory. A few doubtful passages, in the face it may be of the whole drift of God's word, are enough to prove for them this or that particular hobby, which they pretend then to pass off as the same thing with the Divine word itself; while the plainest passages against their general system make no impression upon them whatever. When Dr. Proudfit, in the name of this unchurchly school, makes himself and his system the exponent at once of the true sense of the Scriptures, we beg leave to say to him that the pretension is palpably and monstrously false. It would be easy to quote passage upon passage, the simple plain sense of which his whole standpoint must make it impossible for him to receive. The sixth chapter of John, the terms employed in the institution of the Lord's supper, the foundation of the church on Peter, the Apostolical commission, the giving of the keys, and the numerous passages which directly or indirectly ascribe the power of a new birth to baptism, and make the church the organ and vehicle of salvation, may be noticed as instances. All such passages his theological scheme compels him to misinterpret in the most outrageous style. And yet by this same scheme he undertakes to rule out of court the mind of the ancient church, as though in varying from such arbitrary rule it must of course vary to the same extent also from the Bible!

Our controversy then with Dr. Proudfit, we repeat, as heretofore with the *Puritan Recorder*[24] and the Baptists, regards the symbolical authority of the Apostles' Creed. Is it still of binding force for the universal church *in its proper historical sense,* the only sure basis of all other symbols, as it was held to be in the beginning; or has it run itself out into an obsolete fiction? That is the question, which brings fully into view the deep solemnity of this whole subject. What nonsense to prate of orthodoxy and heresy by other standards, where the original mould of the Christian faith is thus rudely dashed to pieces! *We* take no lesson here from any man, who constructs his whining homily on a formal repudiation of all the old oecumenical symbols, with the venerable Apostle's Creed at their head. We say to him rather, in the withering words of the Saviour: "Why beholdest thou the mote that is in thy brother's eye, but considerest not

---

24. [For more on Nevin's contention with the *Puritan Recorder* see his article "Puritanism and the Creed" earlier in this volume.]

the *beam* that is in thine own eye? Or how wilt thou say to thy brother, Let me pull out the mote out of thine eye, and behold *a beam is in thine own eye*! Thou hypocrite, first cast out the beam out of thine own eye, and *then shalt thou see clearly* to cast out the mote out of thy brother's eye."[25]

---

25. [Matt 17:3–5.]

Chapter 4

"The Athanasian Creed"

(by Philip Schaff)

Editors' Introduction

Born in Switzerland and theologically educated in Germany, Philip Schaff (1819–93) became a colleague of John Williamson Nevin at the German Reformed Seminary at Mercersburg in 1844 where he was appointed to be Professor of Church History and Biblical Literature, a position that he held until 1863. Schaff had been taught by or conversed with many of the most prominent mediating theologians, confessionalists, and right-wing Hegelians of the 1830's and 40's, including Tholuck,[1] Neander, Hengstenberg,[2] Gerlach, and Dorner.[3] Schaff and Nevin, who became close colleagues, became the leading creators of the movement that became known as the Mercersburg Theology. In the United States Schaff matured into a distinguished church historian and theologian whose writings were widely influential. He was also a biblical translator and commentator, liturgical authority, ecumenical theoretician and activist, and organizer of the American Society of Church History, which he founded in 1888. Among his most important works were the three volumes of *The Creeds of Christendom* which were first published in 1877. During his Mercersburg years he was also coeditor of *The Mercersburg Review* in which the following article on the Athanasian Creed appeared in the April 1859 issue.[4] By this time John Nevin had already left the Seminary, and much of the theological instruction was being done by Schaff. Notice the comment at the end of the first footnote in which Schaff pled for funds for the seminary library to buy the resources necessary for the professors to do their academic work.

Schaff believed that the Athanasian Creed stood in the company of the Apostles' and Nicene creeds as a fundamental statement of the central faith of the Christian

---

1. Friedrich August Gottreau Tholuck (1799–1877) was a neo-Pietist theologian and biblical scholar, teaching at Halle, who had been influenced by Schleiermacher. He was widely regarded as one of the leaders of the "mediating" school.

2. Ernst Wilhelm Hengstenberg (1802–69) was a German Lutheran biblical scholar who taught in Berlin. Although he had initially supported the union church of Prussia, after the mid-1840's he began to sharply critique it and to defend Lutheran confessional orthodoxy against its dilution by Reformed doctrines.

3. See Klaus Penzel, *The German Education of Christian Scholar Philip Schaff*.

4. For a chronology of Schaff's life and writings see Penzel, *Philip Schaff*, 351–65.

church. In the article's first footnote he listed ten writers who, in his estimation, published valuable and insightful comments and interpretations of this creedal statement.

In his article he printed the complete text of the Creed's forty-four articles in three columns—the Latin Original, the Old Translation, and a Revised Translation. The main body of the article continues in five sections: Name; Origin; Reception and Authority; Character and Contents; and Value and Use.

Name

While it is usually named the Athanasian Creed, sometimes thought to be the work of St. Athanasius (c.296–393), Bishop of Alexandria, or at least to reflect his theology, it is occasionally called the *Symbolum Quicunque, Quicunque vult* being the first two words of the Creed. For those unfamiliar with Athanasius, Schaff provided a brief biographical sketch of his life and ministry, much of it surprisingly drawn from Edward Gibbon (1737–94) whose critical historical assessment of the role of Christianity in the Roman empire in his *Decline and Fall of the Roman* Empire (1776, 1781) generated considerable hostility among church historians and theologians.

Origin

Schaff asked, while the Creed historically carried the name of St. Athanasius, is it really his work? He cited the findings of several reputable scholars who found Athanasius' authorship to be dubious. Schaff offered five reasons why this conclusion appears reasonable. Among them is the fact that Athanasius himself never mentions the Creed in any of his works nor do any of his contemporaries or early biographers. Even "internal evidence" in the Creed itself does not bear the mark of Athanasian authenticity.

If the Creed does not originate with Athanasius, who is its author? Schaff observed that various suggestions have been offered, but that no consensus has emerged. All that can be said is that while the Creed may reflect a "germ" of the thought of Athanasius, its final form was probably determined between the end of the fourth and the end of the fifth centuries. Like the Apostles' and Nicene creeds, Schaff argued, the Athanasian Creed is not to be credited to any individual, but is the creation of the common spirit of the catholic church.

Reception and Authority

Schaff observed, "As soon as the Athanasian Symbol [Creed] clearly appears in history, we find it in high esteem and quietly assuming its position among the authoritative doctrinal and liturgical standards of the *Latin* Church . . ." It never achieved the same status in the Eastern church as it did in Western Christendom, mostly because of the Creed's assertion that the Holy Spirit's procession was from both the Father *and* the

Son whereas the Eastern Church held that the procession was from the Father alone. From the Roman Church the Creed was adopted by the main Protestant churches. Lutheranism, Anglicanism, and the continental Reformed churches recognized its significance and value, although its liturgical and doctrinal use in the lives of some of the American congregations was often sporadic and anemic.

Character and Contents

Obviously, in Schaff's mind the theological content of the Athanasian Creed is central to its importance to the church and its use of it. He stated, that it is the "epitome of ancient Catholic theology and sets forth, in clear logical statement, the orthodox faith concerning the fundamental articles of the triune God and the divine-human Saviour . . ." Although Schaff was of one mind with Nevin in his high regard for the Apostles' Creed, he was also cognizant of the Creed's theological lacunae. The Apostles' Creed, he suggested, is especially worthwhile for catechetical and liturgical usage, but it is "defective" in that it does not teach the full trinitarian nature of the Godhead, including christological specifics (Jesus' divinity and humanity) and the nature and role of the Holy Spirit. The Athanasian Creed should be valued because it addresses these deficits. Moreover, it provides supplementary theological instruction that probes the mysteries of the faith even more deeply than does the Nicene Creed.

Value and Use

Schaff was convinced that the Athanasian Creed should take its place with the Apostles' and Nicene creeds in a new liturgy which had been proposed for the German Reformed Church. He admitted that it was not of equal importance with the Bible, however. The authority of Scripture is "absolute" while the authority of the church's official creeds and confessions is always dependent on their agreement with Scripture. Three creeds and confessions of the Church (Apostles', Nicene, and Athanasian) occupy the highest place among other creeds and confessions because the three are closest to the apostolic source of the basic message of the faith. According to Schaff, these three documents remain worthy of a significant place in the liturgy of the church.

Nevin also wrote essays on Athanasius[5] and the Athanasian Creed,[6] both of which were published after his Mercersburg years while he was President of Franklin and Marshall College, Lancaster, Pennsylvania. The former is mainly a biographical account of Athanasius. The latter mostly deals with questions regarding the Creed's authorship and circulation in the church. He agreed with Schaff and others that Athanasius did not compose the Creed and that questions about it its authorship remain

5. Nevin, "Athanasius," *Mercersburg Review*, July, 1867, 445–57.
6. Nevin, "Athanasian Creed," *Mercersburg Review*, Oct., 1867, 624–27.

Chapter 4: "The Athanasian Creed"

unresolved. He said of the significance of the Creed, "As the Apostles' Creed gives us in summary form the fundamental facts of Christianity as they were held to be derived from the Apostles themselves, so the Athanasian Creed is the doctrine of Athanasius in regard to the Trinity . . . "[7] He appended a brief bibliography which included authors cited by Schaff (Voss,[8] Montfaucon,[9] Heidegger,[10] Walch,[11] Köllner,[12] Waterland,[13] and Harvey[14]). To this list he added John Dennis[15] and, of course, Philip Schaff's article located in this volume.

---

7. Nevin, "Athanasian Creed," *MR*, Oct., 1867, 624.

8. [Gerhard Johann Voss (1577–1649) was a Dutch humanist scholar teaching at Leiden who, among many other interests, studied early Christian texts, including the creeds.]

9. [Bernard de Montfaucon (1655–1741) was a Benedictine patristic scholar and paleographer who did much work on the earliest texts of Athanasius.]

10. [Johann Heinrich Heidegger (1633–98) was a Swiss Reformed theologian and anti-Catholic controversialist.]

11. [Johann Georg Walch (1693–1775), a professor at Jena, was a Lutheran historian of the Reformation and the editor of Martin Luther's works and various theologically significant Reformation era texts and documents.]

12. [Wilhelm Heinrich Dorotheus Eduard Köllner (1806–94) was a Lutheran theologian and church historian whose work concentrated on the origins and transmission of the creeds and confessions.]

13. [Daniel Waterland (1683–1740) was an Anglican theologian who defended the orthodox doctrine of the Trinity against the Latitudinarians. One of his chief works was *History of the Athanasian Creed*.]

14. [William Wigan Harvey (1810–83) was an Anglican cleric, linguist, and scholar of the ancient church. His *magnum opus*, for which he received much academic acclaim, was a critical edition of the works of Ireneaus.]

15. John Dennis, *The Athanasian Creed*. [John Dennis was an Anglican vicar who polemicized against Unitarians and delivered a notorious speech in 1827 opposing the extension of full legal rights to Roman Catholics.]

The Athanasian Creed[1]

[by Philip Schaff]

We propose in this article to discuss the name, origin, authority, contents, value and use of the so called *Athanasian Symbol,* which, next to the Apostles' Creed and the Nicene, or rather Nicaeno-Constantinopolitan Creed, is the most generally received Confession of faith in the Christian Church, and presents to us a succinct and clear summary of ancient Catholic theology concerning the fundamental articles of the holy Trinity and the person of Christ.[2]

For the convenience of the reader, we give first the symbol itself in three parallel columns, in the original Latin, the old English translation of the sixteenth century,

---

1. [P. S[chaff], *The Mercersburg Review* 11 (April 1859) 232-71.]

2. The necessary information on this subject may be found in Louis S. Tillemont, *Memoirs pour servir à l'histoire eccles.* (Brussels: Fricx, 1693-1712), Vol. VIII:667 sqq. [*Ecclesiastical Memoirs of the First Six Centuries* (London, 1733-35)], Bernard Montfaucon, *Diatribe de Symbolo Quicunque* in the *Works of Athanasius* (Paris, 1698), Vol II:719 sqq.; James Bingham, *Antiquities of the Christian Church* (Oxford, 1855), Vol. IV:118 sqq.; J. G. Walch, *Introductio in libros ecclesiae Luth. symbolicos* (Book I, Chapter 2, *de tribus symbolis oecumenici*), 36 sqq.); and E. Köllner, *Symbolik aller christlichen Confessionen*, Vol. I:53 sqq. We have consulted more particularly Walch and Köllner, who have made good use of all their predecessors. Besides there are a number of special dissertations on the Athanasian Creed, to which, however, we have unfortunately no access just now. The best of them are the following: Gerhard Jan Voss (a Dutch Reformed divine), *De tribus symbolis*, (Amsterdam, 1642); Johann Heinrich Heidegger (German Reformed), *De symbolo Athanasiano* (Zurich, 1680); Daniel Waterland (Anglican), *A Critical History of the Athanasian Creed*, representing the opinions of the Ancients and Moderns concerning it: with an account of the Mss, Verss, and Comments and such other particulars as are of moment for the determining of the Age, and Author, and Value of it, and the Time of its Reception in the Christian Churches (Cambridge, 1724); Dominicus M. Speroni (Roman Catholic), *De symbolo vulgo S. Anthanasii* (Patavii. 1751); and William Wigan Harvey (Anglican), *History and Theology of the Three Creeds*, (London. 1854), 2 vols. The last (from the learned editor of Irenaeus, *Adversus haereses*) is probably the fullest, to judge from its size and some notices I have seen in English Reviews. (Who will have mercy on the Seminary Library at Mercersburg, and furnish it with a sufficient working apparatus for the industry of poor professors?) [Changes have been made to this bibliographic note to include additional information and clarification.]

Chapter 4: "The Athanasian Creed"

and the revised translation *prepared* for the new Liturgy of the German Reformed Church in the United States.

We give the old translation precisely as it is found in the Common Prayer Book of the Church of England, and in the old Dutch Reformed Liturgy[3]; but we italicize those words which have been changed in the revised translation for reasons of taste, clearness and closer adherence to the original.

---

3. [See Harry Klaasens, "The Reformed Tradition in the Netherlands," 463–68.]

THE ATHANASIAN CREED

Latin Original.	*Old Translation.*	*Revised Translation.*
1. *Quicunque vult salvus esse, ante omnia opus est, ut teneat catholicam fidem;*	1. Whosoever will be saved: before all things it is necessary that he hold the Catholick Faith;	1. Whosoever will be saved, before all things it is necessary that he hold the Catholic faith;
2. *Quam nisi quisque integram inviolatamque servaverit, absque dubio in aeternum peribit.*	2. Which Faith except every one do keep whole and undefiled: without doubt he shall perish everlastingly.	2. Which faith except every one do keep whole and undefiled, without doubt he shall perish everlastingly.
3. *Fides autem catholica haec est, ut unum Deum in trinitate et trinitatem in unitate veneremur;*	3. And the Catholick Faith is this: That we worship one God in Trinity and Trinity in Unity;	3. And the Catholic faith is this: that we worship one God in Trinity, and Trinity in Unity:
4. *Neque confundentes personas, neque substantiam separantes.*	4. Neither confounding the Persons: nor dividing the substance.	4. Neither confounding the persons, nor dividing the substance.
5. *Alia est enim persona patris: alia filii: alia spiritus sancti.*	5. For there is one Person of the Father, another of the Son: and another of the Holy Ghost.	5. For there is one person of the Father, another of the Son, and another of the Holy Ghost.
6. *Sed patris et filii et spiritus sancti una est divinitas: aequalis gloria, cooeterna majestas.*	6. But the Godhead of the Father, of the Son, and of the Holy Ghost, is all one: the Glory equal, the Majesty coeternal.	6. But the Godhead of the Father, of the Son, and of the Holy Ghost, is all one; the glory equal, majesty coeternal.
7. *Qualis pater, talis filius, talis spiritus sanctus.*	7. Such as the Father is, such is the Son: and such is the Holy Ghost.	7. Such as the Father is, such is the Son, and such is the Holy Ghost.
8. *Increatus pater: increatus filius: increatus spiritus sanctus.*	8. The Father *uncreate*, the Son *uncreate*: and the Holy Ghost *uncreate*.	8. The Father uncreated, the Son uncreated: and the Holy Ghost uncreated.
9. *Immensus pater: immensus filius: immensus spiritus sanctus.*	9. The Father *incomprehensible,* the Son *incomprehensible*: and the Holy Ghost *incomprehensible.*	9. The Father unlimited, the Son unlimited, and the Holy Ghost unlimited
10. *Aeternnus pater: aeternnus filius: aeternus spiritus sanctus.*	10. The Father eternal, the Son eternal: and the Holy Ghost eternal.	10. The Father eternal the Son eternal and the Holy Ghost eternal.

Chapter 4: "The Athanasian Creed"

Latin Original.	Old Translation.	Revised Translation.
11. *Et tamen non tres aeterni; sed unus aeternus.*	11. And yet *they are* not three *eternals*: but one eternal.	11. And yet not three but eternal, but one eternal
12. *Sicut non tres increati; nec tres immensi; sed unus increatus et unus immensus.*	12. As also there are not three *incomprehensibles*, nor three uncreated, and one incomprehensible.	12. As also, not three uncreated, nor three unlimited but one uncreated, and one unlimited
13. *Similiter omnipotens pater: omnipotens filius: omnipotens spiritus sanctus.*	13. So likewise the Father is Almighty, the Son Almighty: and the Holy Ghost Almighty.	13. So likewise the Father is almighty, the Son almighty, and the Holy Ghost Almighty.
14. *Et tamen non tres omnipotentes; sed unus omnipotens.*	14. And yet *they are* not three *Almighties*: but one Almighty.	14. And yet not three almighty, but one almighty.
15. *Ita deus pater: deus filius: deus spiritus sanctus.*	15. So the Father is God, the Son is God: and the Holy Ghost is God.	15. So the Father is God, the Son is God, and the Holy Ghost is God.
16. *Et tamen non tres dii; sed unus est Deus.*	16. And yet they are not three Gods, but one God.	16. And yet not three Gods, but one God.
17. *Ita dominus pater: dominus filius: dominus spiritus sanctus.*	17. So likewise the Father is Lord, the Son Lord: and the Holy Ghost Lord.	17. So likewise the Father is Lord, the Son Lord, and the Holy Ghost Lord.
18. *Et tamen non tres domini: sed unus Dominus.*	18. And yet not three Lords, but one Lord.	18. And yet not three Lords, but one Lord.
19. *Quia sicut singulatim unamquamque personam Deum ac Dominum confiteri, christiana veritate compellimur:*	19. For like as we are compelled by the Christian verity: to acknowledge *every* Person by himself to God and Lord;	19. For like as we are compelled by the Christian verity, to acknowledge each person, by himself to be God and Lord;
20. *Ita tres deos, aut tres dominos dicere, catholica religione prohibemur.*	20. So are we forbidden by the Catholick Religion: to say, There be three Gods, or three Lords.	20. So are we forbidden by the Catholic Religion to say: There be three Gods or three Lords.

THE ATHANASIAN CREED

Latin Original.

21. *Pater a nullo est factus, nec creatus; nec genitus.*

22. *Filius a patre solo est: non factus; nec creatus, sed genitus.*

23. *Spiritus sanctus a patre et filio: non factus; nec creatus; nec genitus, sed procedens.*

24. *Unus ergo pater. non tres patres: unus filius, non tres filii: unus spiritus sanctus, non tres spiritus sancti.*

25. *Et in hac trinitate nihil prius; aut posterius: nihil majus; aut minus.*

26. *Sed totae tres personae coaeternae sibi sunt et ceaequales.*

27. *Ita, ut per omnia, sicut jam supra dictum est, et trinitas in unitate; et unitas in trinitate veneranda sit.*

28. *Qui vult ergo salvus esse, ita de trinitate sentiat.*

29. *Sed necessarium est ad aeternam salutem, ut incarnationem quoque domini nostri Jesu Christi fidelitur credat.*

Old Translation.

21. The Father is made of none: neither created, nor begotten.

22. The Son is of the Father alone: not made, nor created, but begotten.

23. The Holy ghost is of the Father and of the Son: neither made, nor created, nor begotten, but proceeding.

24. So there is one Father, not three Fathers; one Son, not three Sons: one Holy Ghost, not three Holy Ghosts.

25. And in this Trinity *none is afore, or after other: none is* greater, *or* less *than another;*

26. But the whole three Persons are coeternal *together;* and coequal.

27. So that in all things, *as aforesaid:* the Unity in Trinity, and the Trinity in Unity, is to be worshipped.

28. He therefore that will be saved: must thus think of the Trinity.

29. Furthermore it is necessary to everlasting salvation: that he also believe *rightly* the Incarnation of our Lord Jesus Christ.

Revised Translation.

21. The Father is made of none, neither created, nor begotten.

22. The Son is of the Father alone, not made, nor created, but begotten.

23. The Holy Ghost is of the Father and of the Son, neither made, nor created, nor begotten, but proceeding.

24. So there is one Father, not three Fathers; one Son, not three Sons; one Holy Ghost, not three Holy Ghosts.

25. And in this Trinity there is no before, nor after; no greater nor less.

26. But the whole three persons are coeternal, and coequal.

27. So that in all things, as already said: the Unity in Trinity, and the Trinity in Unity is to be worshipped.

28. He therefore that will be saved, must thus think of the Trinity.

29. Furthermore, it is necessary to everlasting salvation, that we also believe truly the Incarnation of our Lord Jesus Christ.

Chapter 4: "The Athanasian Creed"

Latin Original.	*Old Translation.*	*Revised Translation*
30. *Est ergo fides recta, ut credamus et confiteamur, quod dominus noster Jesus Christus Dei filius, deus et homo est.*	30. For the right Faith is, that we believe and confess: that our Lord Jesus Christ, the Son of God, is God and Man;	30. For the right faith is, that we believe and confess, that our Lord Jesus Christ, the Son of God, is God and man;
31. *Deus ex substantia patris, ante secula genitus, et homo ex substantia matris, in ecsulo natus.*	31. God, the Substance of the Father, begotten before the worlds: and Man, of the Substance of his Mother, born in the world;	31. God, of the substance of the Father, begotten before the worlds; and man, of the substance of his mother, born in the world;
32. *Perfectus deus: perfectus homo, ex anima rationali et humana carne subsistens.*	32. Perfect God and perfect Man: of a reasonable soul and human flesh subsisting;	32. Perfect God, and perfect man, of a reasonable soul and human flesh subsisting;
33. *Aequalis patri secundum divinitatem: minor patri secundum humanitatem.*	33. Equal to the Father, *as touching* his Godhead: and inferior to the Father as *touching* his Manhood.	33. Equal to the Father, according to His Godhead, and inferior to the Father, according to His manhood.
34. *Qui licet Deus sit et homo; non duo tamen, sed unus est Christus.*	34. Who although he be God and Man; yet he is not two, but one Christ;	34. Who although he be God and man, yet he is not two, but one Christ;
35. *Unus autem, non conversione divinitatis in carnem; sed assumptione humanitatis in Deum.*	35. One; not by conversion of the Godhead into flesh: but by *taking* of the Manhood into God.	35. One, not by conversion of the Godhead into flesh, but by assumption of the manhood into God;
36. *Unus omnino, non confusione substantiae; sed unitate personae.*	36. One altogether; not by confusion of Substance: but by unity of Person.	36. One altogether, not by confusion of substance, but by unity of person.
37. *Nam sicut anima rationalis et caro unus est homo; ita deus et homo unus est Christus.*	37. For as the reasonable soul and flesh is one man: so God and Man is one Christ;	37. For as the reasonable soul and flesh is one man; so God and man is one Christ.

| *Original Latin* | *Old Translation* | *Revised Translation* |

38. *Qui passus est pro nostra salute: descendit ad inferos: tertia die resurrexit a mortuis.*

39. *Ascendit ad coelos: sedet ad dexteram dei patris omnipotentis.*

40. *Inde venturus est judicare vivos et mortuos.*

41. *Ad cuius adventum omnes homines resurgere habent cum corporibus suis;*

42. *Et reddituri sunt de factis propriis rationem.*

43. *Et qui bona egerunt, ibunt in vitam eternam; qui vero mala, in ignem aeternum.*

44. *Haec est fides catholica, quam nisi quisque fideliter firmiterque crediderit, salvus esse non poterit.*

38. Who suffered for our salvation: descended into *hell*: rose again the third day from the dead.

39. He ascended into heaven, he sitteth on the right hand of the *Father God* Almighty.

40. From *whence* he shall come to judge the quick and the dead.

41. At whose coming all men shall rise again with their bodies,

42. And shall give account for their own works.

43. And they that have done good shall go into life everlasting: and they that have done evil into everlasting fire.

44. This the Catholick Faith: which except a man believe *faithfully*, he cannot be saved.

38. Who suffered for our salvation, descended into Hades, rose again the third day from the dead.

39. He ascended into heaven, He sitteth at the right hand of God the Father Almighty.

40. From thence He shall come to judge the quick and the dead.

41. At whose coming all men shall rise again with their bodies;

42. And shall give account for their own works.

43. And they that have done good shall go into life everlasting, and they that have done evil, into everlasting fire.

44. This is the Catholic faith, which except a man believe truly and firmly, he cannot be saved.

Chapter 4: "The Athanasian Creed"

[I.] Name

The third ecumenical or universal Creed of the Christian Church bears a double name.

It is sometimes called the *Symbolum Quicunque* or simply the *Quicunque*[4] from its beginning in Latin: *Quicunque vult salvus esse*, Whosoever will be saved.

But more generally it goes by the name of the *Athanasian Creed*[5] from the supposed authorship of St. Athanasius, or its agreement with his theology. This makes it necessary to say a few words on this distinguished father.

Athanasius was the leading champion of the orthodox doctrine on the divinity of Christ and the holy Trinity in the Nicene age. He was born towards the close of the third century at Alexandria, the capital of Egypt. His youth fell in that remarkable transition period of the Christian Church from oppression and persecution to victory and power in the Roman Empire. He made his first appearance on the stage of history at the first general Council, convened by Constantine the Great at the city of Nice [Nicea] in 325, for the purpose of settling the Arian controversy, i.e., the question whether Christ is strictly divine or not; whether he is the eternal Son of the Father and equal in essence with him (ομοουσιος)[6] or whether he be a creature of God, though made before the world, and consequently of a different substance (ετεροουσιος) . Although at that time merely an archdeacon and secretary of Bishop Alexander of Alexandria, Athanasius occupied by his talents and zeal the most prominent place in that Council among the defenders of the strict divinity of the Saviour against the Arians who denied it, and materially helped the triumph of the orthodox view, as embodied and symbolically fixed in what has since been called the Nicene Creed. Soon afterwards he became the successor of Alexander in the first episcopal see of Egypt. From this time on, during the long continued Arian and Semi-Arian conflicts which soon followed the temporary settlement at the Nicene Synod, he stood forth as the acknowledged leader of the Nicene or orthodox party, beloved by his friends, feared by his enemies, admired and respected by all. He devoted his whole life, with unwavering consistency in prosperity and adversity, at home and in exile, to the defense of the true Godhead of Christ. This was the one great idea of his mind, the ruling passion of his heart, the all-absorbing object of his will. For this he suffered five times deposition and exile. For this he was willing at any time to shed his blood. He was a man of one idea, indeed, but an idea which he firmly and justly believed to be absolutely fundamental to the

---

4. First by Hincmar, Archbishop of Rheims, about A.D. 852, who calls it also "*Sermonem Athanasii de fide, cuius initium est: quicunque vult salvus esse.*" [Trans. "Athanasius' sermon on faith which begins, whoever wishes to be saved." See Hincmar, *Hincmarii rehemensis archiepiscopi,Opera omnia*. Hincmar (806–82) was an archbishop of Reims and a politically powerful apologist for the Frankish king Charles the Bald. He was an implacable enemy of predestinarian theories, which he persuaded Frankish church councils to condemn as a heresy.]

5. It first bears this name in the oldest complete manuscript copy extant, called *Codex Usserius* [Ussher] *secundus*, ascribed to the year 708. It has the title: *Fides Sancti Athanasii Alexandrini*. [Trans. "The faith of St. Athanasius of Alexandria." See Ussher, *The Whole Works*.]

6. [Trans. "of one substance."]

Christian system and the salvation of the world. To the violence and intrigues of the imperial court, to the passions and fanaticism of heretical parties, he uniformly opposed the overwhelming force of a commanding genius and a holy life. Although he died several years before the final settlement of this great controversy by the second ecumenical council, held at Constantinople in 381, the triumph of the orthodox view must, under God, be mainly attributed to him. Athanasius was unquestionably the greatest man of his age, and one of the purest and noblest in the history of the Church. He is justly called *the Great* and *the Father of Orthodoxy.*

Even [Edward] Gibbon, with all his strong prejudices, has pronounced an eloquent eulogy on him in the XXI chapter of his celebrated work. "We have seldom," says this Deistic historian,

> an opportunity of observing, either in active or speculative life, what effect may be produced, or what obstacles may be surmounted, by the force of a single mind, when it is inflexibly applied to the pursuit of a single object. The immortal name of Athanasius will never be separated from the Catholic doctrine of the Trinity, to whose defense he consecrated every moment and every faculty of his being. Educated in the family of Alexander, he had vigorously opposed the early progress of the Arian heresy: he exercised the important functions of secretary under the aged prelate; and the fathers of the Nicene council beheld with surprise and respect the rising virtues of the young deacon. In a time of public danger, the dull claims of age and rank are sometimes superseded; and within five months after his return from Nice, the deacon Athanasius was seated on the archepiscopal throne of Egypt. He filled that eminent station above forty-six years, and his long administration was spent in a perpetual combat against the powers of Arianism. Five times was Athanasius expelled from his throne; twenty years he passed as an exile or a fugitive; and almost every province of the Roman empire was successively witness to his merits and his sufferings in the cause of the Homoousion, which he considered as the sole pleasure and business, as the duty and as the glory of his life. Amidst the storms of persecution, the archbishop of Alexandria was patient of labor, jealous of fame, careless of safety; and although his mind was tainted by the contagion of fanaticism, Athanasius displayed a superiority of character and abilities, which would have qualified him, far better than the degenerate sons of Constantine, for the government of a great monarchy.... The archbishop of Alexandria was capable of distinguishing how far he might boldly command, and where he must dexterously insinuate; how long he might contend with power, and when he must withdraw from persecution; and while he directed the thunders of the Church against heresy, he could assume, in the bosom of his own party, the flexible and indulgent temper of a prudent leader. The election of Athanasius has not escaped the reproach of irregularity and precipitation; but the propriety of his behavior conciliated the affections both of the clergy and of the people. The Alexandrians were impatient to rise in arms for the defense of an eloquent and liberal pastor. In his distress he

always derived support, or at least consolation, from the faithful attachment of his parochial clergy; and the hundred bishops of Egypt adhered, with unshaken zeal, to the cause of Athanasius. In the modest equipage which pride and policy would affect, he frequently performed the episcopal visitation of his provinces, from the mouth of the Nile to the confines of Ethiopia; familiarly conversing with the meanest of the populace, and humbly saluting the saints and hermits of the desert. Nor was it only in ecclesiastical assemblies, among men whose education and manners were similar to his own, that Athanasius displayed the ascendency of his genius. He appeared with easy and respectful firmness in the courts of princes; and in the various turns of his prosperous and adverse fortune he never lost the confidence of his friends, or the esteem of his enemies.[7]

[II.] Origin

But is Athanasius really the author of the creed which has so long been identified with his distinguished name? This question must now be decided in the negative, as much so as the question of the strictly apostolic origin of the first ecumenical creed. And yet in both cases there is a certain propriety in the name, if we leave out of view the form of words and actual composition, and look merely to the contents and their essential agreement with the faith and teaching of the supposed authors.

It is probable that the designation was first given to this document with the view simply to characterize its doctrinal tone, as the expression of the faith of Athanasius,[8] (hence the oldest titles: "*fides Athanasii,*" "*fides Catholica*"[9]) and not to indicate the literal authorship and thus to clothe it at once with the authority of a great and universally revered name. At all events there is no room here for a willful pious fraud. An innocent mistake explains the matter sufficiently, especially in an uncritical age. The real author of this trinitarian creed being unknown, it was naturally traced, first by way of mere conjecture and supposition, to the great representative of the received doctrine of the holy Trinity, whose very name was identified with orthodoxy as regards this particular article. For the terms Athanasian, *homoousian*,[10] Nicene, orthodox, are used synonymously in the history of the Arian and Semi-Arian controversies of the Nicene

---

7. [Edward Gibbon, *The Decline and Fall of the Roman Empire,* I: 697–99. Edward Gibbon (1737–94) was an extremely popular English historian and also an influential politician. His classic *The History of the Decline and Fall of the Roman Empire* was noteworthy for its use of primary sources and its controversial thesis that the spread of Christianity in the empire, which diverted funds to ecclesial use and subverted the Roman martial spirit, was responsible for its demise.]

8. This was the view of Weber, *Symbolik*, 17: *Ab Athanasio nomen habet, non quod ab illo viro vere scriptum sit, sed quod cum sententia Athanasii maxime conveniat.* See W. H. D. Eduard Köllner, *Symbolik*, Ibid., 55. [Trans. "It is named for Athanasius, not because it was truly written by that man, but because it fits especially well his thought."]

9. [Trans. "Athanasius' faith," "Catholic faith."]

10. [Trans. "of one substance."]

Age. This conjecture was, however, by no means generally received at first. Several manuscript copies of the Creed give either no name at all,[11] or ascribe it to a different author, Anastasius.[12] We find doubts yet as late as the twelfth century.[13] But after this time the belief in the Athanasian origin became general and prevailed, without examination, down towards the middle of the seventeenth century,[14] when Gerhard John Vossius, a Dutch Reformed divine, made it the subject of a critical dissertation in 1642, and turned the current. Since that time it is almost universally given up by historians and critics, not only by Protestants,[15] as Vossius, Heidegger, Ussher, Jeremy Taylor, Pearson, Cave, Bingham, Waterland, Buddeus, Walch, Schroeckh, Meander, Gieseler, Köllner, but also by Roman Catholics, as Petavius, Quesnel, Pagi, Tillemont, Montfaucon, Muratori, Natalis Alexander, Du Pin, Speroni, and even Pope Benedict XIV. The arguments against the authorship of Athanasius are so strong indeed that it is impossible to resist them. Köllner enumerates nineteen. We will mention only the principal ones.

1.) Athanasius himself never mentions this symbol in any of his works, and had no occasion to compose it, being satisfied with the Nicene Creed and bent upon explaining and maintaining it against every opposition. Yea, he says distinctly, in one passage[16] that the Nicene Creed was sufficient, and that no other profession of faith should be issued.

2.) It is not found in any of the older manuscripts of the works of Athanasius, and those which have it, either deny it to him or express a doubt as to his authorship.[17]

11. Codices: Usserius [Ussher mss.], Treves [mss. Trier], Ambrosian [mss., Milan], Colb. 1 [Colbetine mss., Paris], Regius, Benet C. 2, Benet C. 8. Cotton 3 [Cottonian mss., London], Cambridge [mss. Bodleian Library], St. James 2. Compare Waterland, 24, and Köllner, 72.

12. So the German manuscripts. Daniel Waterland, *A Critical History of the Athanasian Creed*, however, supposes that this is a mere orthographical mistake for Athanasius.

13. In 1138 by Otho in the words: *Athanasius a quibusdam dicitur edidisse* [Trans. "Athanasius is said to have edited it by some"]; and in 1190 by Jean Beleth in the words: *Quod ab Athanasio Patriarch A. compositum est: plerique eum Anastasium fuisse falso arbitrantur.* [Trans. "It was composed by Athanasius, Patriarch of Alexandria, and many judged him falsely to be Anastasius."] [Bernard] Montfaucon, Diatr. [*Diatribe de Symbolo Quicunque* in the Works of Athanasius,] II:722.

14. The last distinguished defendants were the Roman Catholic divines, Baronius, Bona and Bellarmine. [See Baronius, *Institutes of Ecclesiastical History* (New York, 1839), II:11.]

15. [Among the Protestants named by Schaff are Gerhard Jan Voss (1577-1649), Johann Heinrich Heidegger (1633-98), James Ussher (1581-1656), Jeremy Taylor (1613-67) John Pearson (1613-86), William Cave (1637-1713), Joseph Bingham (1668-1723), Daniel Waterland (1683-1740), Johann Franz Buddeus (1667-1729), J. G. Walch (1693-1775), Johann Matthias Schröckh (1733-1808), August Herman Wilhelm Neander (1689-1850), Johann Karl Ludwig Gieseler (1792-1854), and Wilhelm Heinrich D. Eduard Köllner (1896-94). Roman Catholics named by Schaff are Dionysius Petavius (1583-1652), Pasquier Quesnel (1634-1719), Antoine Pagi (1624-99), Louis Sébastien Le Nain de Tillemont (1637-98), Lodovico Antonio Muratori (1672-1750), Alexander Natalis (1639-1724), Louis Ellies Dupin (1657-1719), Dominicus Maria Speroni, and Pope Benedict XIV (1675-1758).]

16. Athanasius, "Epistle to Antioch." Compare Köllner, 73, and J. G. Walch, Ibid, Book I, 149. [See also Johannes Quasten, *Patrology*, III:55.]

17. Abraham Scultetus, *Medulla theologiae Patrum*, Part 2, on Athanasius, 40, says: *In nullo codice*

Chapter 4: "The Athanasian Creed"

3.) It is not mentioned by any contemporary of Athanasius, nor his biographers and eulogists,[18] nor by any of the fathers and councils of the fourth and fifth centuries, although during the all absorbing trinitarian and christological controversies, they had frequent occasion to allude to this important document if it existed, and although they frequently appeal to the authority of Athanasius and mention his other writings. Under these circumstances the silence is absolutely conclusive against the very existence of the Athanasian Creed, unless we choose to suppose that it was concealed for nearly three hundred years, and then suddenly turned up in the sixth or seventh century, which would imply an almost miraculous preservation.

4.) The symbol under consideration was evidently first written in the Latin language and seems to have been unknown among the Greeks before the eleventh century. There are but few Greek manuscript copies extant,[19] and they differ so much, that they unmistakably point to several and rather unskilled translators. Now it is very improbable that Athanasius, even if he knew Latin sufficiently to write so well, should have composed such an important document in a foreign tongue, instead of his own vernacular Greek, which was then the prevailing language of the Church and used even by the early Western fathers, as Clement of Rome, Irenaeus of Gaul, and Hippolytus of Rome.[20] (The report, that Athanasius composed it during his exile at Treves, about 340, and submitted it to Pope Julius of Rome, in proof of his orthodoxy against the charge of heresy, or that he wrote it at Rome, and that it remained concealed there for a long time, is utterly worthless, since it is not even mentioned before

---

extat quos ego quidem vidi, inter Athanasii opera. In uno legitur; sed auctoris nomine suppresso. [Trans. "In no codex exists that which I have seen among the works of Athanasius. It is read in one, but with the name of the author suppressed."] [Dominicus M.] Speroni, *De Symbolo*, (quoted by Köllner, *Symbolik*, 72) says more distinctly: *At multi codd. Mss. sunt, qui non modo non habent hoc symbolum, quamquam opera omnia comprehendant Athanasii; sed negant omnino his verbis: Symbolum vulgo Athanasii, Symbolum quod non est Athanasii, Symbolum perperam Athanasio tributum.* [Trans. "And many codices are manuscripts, which not only do not have this creed, although they encompass all the works of Athanasius, but they deny it entirely with these words: The creed, popularly called 'of Athanasius,' which is not Athanasius's creed, but the creed wrongly attributed to Athanasius." Scultetus (1566–1625), a German theologian, exchanged his Lutheranism for Calvinism and then taught at Heidelberg.]

18 The only allusion which former writers have been able to find, is a passage of Gregorius Nazianzus, in his laudatory oration on Athanasius, where he speaks of him as having confessed (ομολογησας) the Godhead and essence of the three (την τριων δεοτητα και ουσιαν). But it is now universally conceded that this does not refer to a particular creed at all, or if so, to one of the two other confessions still extant, in which he likewise speaks of the Godhead and essence of the three Persons.

19. Four according to Montfaucon, eight according to Waterland. The former asserts that none of them was written before 1300. "*Nullum vidimus Graecum huius symboli codicem, qui trecentorum sit annorum; nec antiquum alium a quopiam visum fuisse novimus.*" *Diatribe de Symbolo Quicunque* in the *Works of Athanasius*, II:727. [Trans. "We have seen no Greek codex of this symbol that may be three hundred years old, nor do we know of another old one that anyone has seen anywhere."]

20. [Hippolytus of Rome (170–235) was a prolific theologian and biblical commentator, often referred to in the writings of other ancient Christian authors. Exactly what works can be ascribed to him is a matter of dispute. He seems to have been a moral rigorist and to have functioned as an alternative pope.]

the twelfth century (1130), and is evidently one of the many falsehoods which were manufactured in the Middle Ages for the supposed benefit of the absolute papacy. No Roman divine of any weight, since Baronius and Bellarmin, has dared to give it credit.)

5.) To these external arguments, though mostly of a negative and indirect character, must be added the internal evidence of the Creed itself, which alone is conclusive. For while it omits the favorite expressions of Athanasius, especially the term *homoousios*, on which the whole Arian controversy turned, it contains the later Latin addition *et filio*,[21] concerning the procession of the Holy Ghost,[22] which the Greek Church never admitted, and generally goes beyond the Athanasian theology and the Nicaeno-Constantinopolitan Creed, not only in the Trinity, but still more in the Christology, evidently presupposing the Nestorian[23] and Eutychian[24] controversies, which were not concluded till the Council of Chalcedon in 451, about eighty years after the death of Athanasius. We fully admit that he had already substantially the same faith, but by no means the same logical consciousness or scientific comprehension of it, as is here implied.[25] He nowhere in his writings speaks so clearly and definitely of the personality and divinity of the Holy Spirit, and as to the two natures of Christ, he even uses expressions which in a *later* age would have been justly liable to a Monophysite or Eutychian construction,[26] while the Creed which bears his name, is as clear and distinct on this subject as the Council of Chalcedon.

---

21. [Trans. "and the son."]

22. [Schaff, *The Creeds of Christendom*, II:66–71] vs. 23: *Spiritus Sanctus a Patre et Filio, non factus nec creatus nec genitus, sed procedens*. [Trans. "The Holy Spirit comes from the Father and the Son, neither made nor born, but proceeding."]

23. [Nestorianism, which was named after Patriarch Nestorius of Constantinople (386–450), was a Christological movement that denied the concept of a personal union of the divine and human natures of Jesus, and argued instead for a union of divine and human wills.]

24. [Eutychianism, named after Eutychus (380–456), an archimandrite (superior abbot) in Constantinople, was a Christological theory that believed that Christ's divine nature was totally absorbed by his human nature. Consequently, they believed, it is not appropriate to ascribe "two natures" to Christ. Because of this, Eutychianism was considered to be a variety of Monophysitism, the view that Christ had only one nature.]

25. This is honestly admitted even by his learned Benedictine editor, Montfaucon, Diatribe, 723: *Licet enim una eademque semper fuerit ea de re Ecclesiae doctrina, nondum tamen hae formulae in Ecclesia receptae vel in confesso erant*. [Trans. "Indeed although it was always one and the same concerning the essence of the doctrine of the church, nevertheless these formulas were not received in the church or generally acknowledged."] He asserts an entire difference of style between the *Symbolum Quicunque* and genuine Athanasian writings.

26. Especially in one passage "*De incarnation Verbi*" ["On the enfleshment of the Word"] (Montfaucon, *Diatribe*, II:1) where he says: "We profess also that there is one Son of God who is God according to the Spirit, and Son of man according to the flesh; not two natures, the one to be worshipped, the other not, but one nature of the God Logos which became incarnate (αλλα μιαν φυσιν του θεου λογου σεσαρκωμενην) and is to be worshipped together with his flesh in one worship." This, and similar passages of Hilary and even Pope Julius I, have given great trouble to such Roman divines who deny all development and change in the doctrine of their Church. Compare [Johann Karl Ludwig] Gieseler, [*Lehrbuch der*] *Kirchengeschichte* I:2, § 88, 133 seq.

Chapter 4: "The Athanasian Creed"

But the more difficult question now arises, who is the real author of this remarkable production? Here is a wide field for critical conjecture. Quite a number of persons have been proposed with more or less plausibility, but without sufficient evidence in any case, viz: Vigilius, Bishop of Tapsus in Africa, about 484,[27] Vincentius Lirinensis, about 434,[28] Venantius Fortunatus, Bishop of Poitiers, about 560,[29] Hilarius Arelatensis, about 429,[30] Hilarius Pictaviensis, about 354, Eusebius Vercellensis, 354, Pope Anastasius I, 398, Athanasius, Bishop of Speier, in Germany, 642. Others assign the symbol indefinitely to some Gallican divine,[31] or to Spanish origin,[32] others less indefinitely to a Latin father;[33] while still others leave the authorship entirely doubtful.[34]

This very diversity of opinion shows that we do not know the real author. Even the arguments in favor of the claims of Vigilius Tapsensis, which are the most plausible, prove only the possibility, not even the probability, of his authorship.

The case seems to us almost parallel with that of the Apostles' Creed, and in a less degree also with that of the Nicene Creed, and we are surprised that none of the numerous writers on this subject, as far as we can see, has directed attention to this fact.

---

27. By Pasquier Quesnel, *Sancti Leonis Magni, romani, pontificis*, diss. xiv, 884 seq., Natalis Alexander, Pagi, Dupin. So also J. A. W. Neander, in his posthumous work on Doctrine History [*Lectures on the History of Christian Dogmas*, I:828] where he says that this Symbol was made most probably in the fifth century in the North African Church by Vigilius Tapsensis, during the renewal of the Arian controversy under the rule of the Vandals. The principal argument for this view is taken from the similarity of thought and style and the occurrence of the passage: "*Deus Pater, Deus Filius, Deus Spiritus S.; Dominus Pater, Dominus Filius, Dominus Spiritus S.; Omnipotens Pater, Omnipotens Filius, Omnipotens Spiritus S.*" [Trans. God the Father, God the Son, God the Holy Spirit; Father is Lord, Son is Lord, Holy Spirit is Lord; Almighty Father, Almighty Son, Almighty Holy Spirit.] Vigilius is supposed by some to be the author of the twelve books *De Trinitate* which go under the name of Athanasius, and also of the Dialogue between Athanasius, Arius and Probus; but this is rather uncertain. [The North African Bishop Vigilius Tapsensis cited by Schaff is undoubtedly Vigilius Thapsus (c.470–500). See M. Simonetti, "Vigilius Thapsus," in *Encyclopedia of the Early Church*, II:870.]

28. By Joseph Anthelmi, on the ground especially of some resemblance between the Athanasian Creed and the Commonitorium of Vincentius. [Anthelmi (1648–97) was a French church historian. The Commonitorium of Vincent of Lerins was a document written by Vincentius to assist his remembering true doctrine from false.]

29. By L. A. Muratori. [Lodovico Antonio Muratori (1672–1750), an Italian historian and theologian, is best known for discovering the Muratorian Canon, the ancient list of New Testament writings. His collected works were published at Arezzo, 1767–73.]

30. By Daniel Waterland. [*A Critical History of the Athanasian Creed*.]

31. So Pithoeus, Voss, Köllner. [Pierre Pithou (1539–96) was a French historian and jurist. Originally a Calvinist, he converted to Roman Catholicism after the St. Bartholomew's Day Massacre made being a Reformed leader exceedingly dangerous in Paris.]

32. Gieseler.

33. Pearson and Johann A. Fabricius. [J. A. Fabricius (1668–1736) was a Lutheran scholar, teacher, and bibliographer.]

34. Petavias, Taylor, Cudworth, Tillemont, Baddeus, Walch. [Dionysius Petavius (1583–1652), was a Jesuit teacher, historian, and theologian; Jeremy Taylor (1613–67) was an Anglican bishop and scholar; Ralph Cudworth (1617–88) was a Cambridge University teacher and philosopher, strongly influenced by Platonism; Johann Franz Buddeus (1667–1729) was a Lutheran theologian and devotional author.]

The Apostles' Creed, it is now universally admitted, cannot be traced to the Apostles,[35] nor to any particular author, age or country, but must be regarded as the production of the ancient Catholic Church. Its living root and substance goes back, indeed, to the Apostolic age, to the baptismal formula (Matth. 28:19) and the confession of Peter (Matth. 16:16). But its present form is the result of a gradual and imperceptible growth which can be traced through the various and yet essentially identical rules of faith or baptismal creeds of the second and third centuries, as found in the writings of Justin Martyr, Irenaeus, Origen, Tertullian, and Cyprian, and which attained its maturity towards the end of the third, or at all events at the beginning of the fourth century, before the Council of Nice [Nicea] in 325, the Nicene Creed being an expansion and more explicit definition of the Apostles' Creed.[36]

As to the origin of the Nicene or rather Nicaeno-Constantinopolitan Creed, we can speak more definitely. "We know the precise time of its composition: it was formed at Nice [Nicea] in 325 and completed at Constantinople in 381, with the exception of the clause *filioque*, which is a later addition of the Latin Church and became a bone of contention between it and the Greek Church. We can go further and say that the formula proposed by Eusebius of Caesarea at Nice [Nicea], was, in all probability, made the basis of the first draft. But this was shaped into a far more definite, anti-Arian character, especially by the insertion of the famous predicate of the Son: *homoousios*, or *consubstantialis, coequal, of one substance* with the Father, which Eusebius wished to avoid in the interest of peace. Half a century afterwards the Constantinopolitan Council made several omissions and an important addition concerning the Holy Ghost, called forth by the intervening doctrinal controversies. Thus even this symbol, though less catholic than the Apostolicum, can by no means be traced to any individual author, but must be regarded as the joint product of the Nicene age or of the first two ecumenical Synods.[37]

We may illustrate the formation of the Nicene Creed by alluding to the official reports and acts of our ecclesiastical and political assemblies. Important matters are

---

35. As was done first by the presbyter, Rufinus of Aquileia, about 400, in his *Exposition of the Creed*. He represents it as the joint production of the twelve Apostles before leaving Jerusalem, each contributing one article, and thus explains the word συμβολον taking it in the sense of συμβολη, *collatio* [Trans. "while in fact it means sign, distinctive mark, form of confession.] This tradition became soon current in the fifth century and obtained to the fifteenth, when Laurentius Valla and subsequently Erasmus undermined it. [Lorenzo Valla (c.1406–57) was an Italian Renaissance humanist scholar who critiqued many traditions, legends, and apocryphal documents of the medieval church.]

36. On the particulars of the origin, history and character of the Apostles' Creed, we must refer to the following treatises; Rufinus, *Expositio in Symbolum Apostolicum* (in the works of Hieronymus). Augustinue, *De Fide et Symbolo*, Heidegger, *De Symbolum. Apostolicum*. Gisbert Vostius, *De Symbolum Apostolicum*. J. Pearson, *Exposition of the Creed*. P. King, *The History of the Apostles' Creed*. Köllner, *Symbolik aller Christlichen Confessionen*, I:6 sqq. J. W. Nevin, "The Apostles' Creed," three articles in *The Mercersburg Review* for 1849.

37. The origin and history of the Nicene Creed is more fully discussed by Voss, Ussher, Bingham, Heidegger, Walther, Baier, Blanchini, Suicer, Walch, Köllner, and others. See the literature in Walch, *Introductio in libros symbolicos*, 121 sqq., and in Köllner, *Symbolik*, etc., I:6, 28.

Chapter 4: "The Athanasian Creed"

generally first referred to a committee of three, five or more persons, with a responsible chairman. He draws up a report, submits it to the other members of the committee for approval, rejection, or revision, which may result in a radical reconstruction. Then it is brought up before the general body for action, and there it again undergoes, in many cases, a variety of changes before it is finally adopted. At all events, if adopted, it ceases to be the work of an individual, or even a committee and becomes the property of the whole body, clothed with all the weight and authority which it may possess.

Now, as the Apostles' Creed is the work of the ante-Nicene age, and the Nicene Creed the work of the Nicene age, so the Athanasian Creed may justly be called the work of the post-Nicene age, or of the Catholic Church from the close of the fourth to the close of the fifth century. Its germ may indeed be traced back to Athanasius, and so far it may still go under his name; single words and passages may be found in the writings attributed to Vigilius Tapsensis, and others. But its final shape and form evidently presupposes the Arian, Semi-arian, Nestorian and Eutychian controversies, and the first four general councils, none of which alludes to it, although such allusion, if the work existed already, could not possibly be avoided. Its composition, therefore, must be placed after the year 451, when the Council of Chalcedon settled that very doctrine of the two natures in Christ's person, which is so distinctly expressed in this Creed. On the other hand it cannot be carried down to a much later period, since it contains no allusion yet to the Monothelite[38] controversy concerning the two wills of Christ, which commenced in 633 and was finally settled by the sixth general Council in 680. We assign it, therefore, to the second half of the fifth century, or the beginning of the sixth.[39] It must have proceeded, moreover, from the Latin Church, for reasons already stated, and more particularly from the school of St. Augustine, who insisted more clearly and emphatically than any of the preceding fathers, on the strict equality and coordination of the Son and *Holy Ghost* with the Father, and represented the creation, redemption and sanctification as the work of the one undivided Divinity. The place of composition cannot be decided with any degree of certainty. It may have been written in North Africa, the country of Augustine, or in Spain, but more probably in Gaul, where it first spread and found favor.

This view of the case is sustained by the manner in which the Athanasian Creed comes to notice. It appears not in full at once, but gradually as it were. We meet first single words and passages of it in several writers of the fifth and sixth centuries, as

---

38. [Monothelitism was a Christological theory arising in the seventh century that asserted that although Jesus possessed two natures, he only had one will. This view was condemned as a heresy in 680 or 681 at the Third Council of Constantinople.]

39. We cannot agree with Dr. Gieseler *(Kirchengeschichte,* fourth ed., II:§12, 109, note 7) who thinks that the Athanasianum cannot be traced beyond the eighth century, and regards all the earlier allusions to it uncertain. He inclines to the opinion that it originated in Spain, where the conflict between the Athanasian and the Arian party continued longer than in any other country. But the majority of critics assign it to an earlier period and to Gaul.

Vigilius Tapsensis, of Africa (484),[40] Avitus Viennensis, of Gaul (500),[41] Caesarius Arelatensis, of Gaul (520),[42] Venantius Fortunatus, of Gaul (560),[43] and also in acts of councils, especially the Councils of Toledo in Spain, of the seventh century.[44] Then we have it in full in a number of Latin manuscript copies, the precise age of which, however, it is impossible, in most cases, to fix with any degree of certainty. The oldest, which is now lost, is assigned to the year 600,[45] the next to 660,[46] the third to 700,[47] the fourth to 703,[48] etc. The last mentioned is the first copy which ascribes, though in somewhat equivocal way, by calling it "*Faith* of St. Athanasius."

40. In the passage already quoted.

41. Who uses the terms *nec factus, nec creatus, nec genitus* [Trans "neither made, nor created, nor born"], of the Holy Ghost. Alcitus Ecdicius Avitus (c.460–518) was born in Vienne and was a Latin poet, antiArian, opponent of semipelagianism, and archbishop of Vienne, France.]

42. In a sermon which found its way among those of St. Augustine *Works*, V:399 but which the Benedictine editors of Augustine, also Oudin, Waterland, and Köllner, (*Symbolik*, I:60) ascribe to Caesarius of Aries (503–48). There occurs the first clear allusion which sounds like a direct quotation from the *Anthanasianum*, as Gieseler admits, who, however, doubts the authorship of Caesarius. It reads thus, (we italicize the words corresponding to the symbol): "*Rogo et admoneo vos, Fratres carissimi, ut* Quincunque vult salvus esse, Fidem *rectam et* Catholicam *discat*, firmiter teneat inviolatamque conservet.—Deus Pater, Deus Filius, Deus et Spiritus Sanctus: *sed tamen non tres Dii, sed unus Deus. Qualis Pater, talis Filius, talis et Spiritus Sanctus. Attamen credat unusquisque fidelis, quod Filius* aequalis est Patri secundum divinitatem, et minor est Patre secundum humanitatem *carnis, quam de nostro assumpsit.*" [Trans. "I ask and admonish you, dearest brethren, that *whoever wishes to be saved, must learn the right and catholic faith, and keep it faithfully and hold it inviolate. The Father is God, the Son is God, and the Holy Spirit is God*: but nevertheless there are not three Gods, but one God. *As the Father is, so is the Son, and so is the Holy Spirit*. Yet let every Christian believe that the *Son is equal to the Father according to divinity, and less than the Father according to the fleshly.*"]

43 Who is supposed by Muratori, Waterland, and Köllner to be the author of the *Expositio fidei catholicae*, which assumes already the general reception of the *Symbolum Quicunque*, and defends the *filioque*. For this reason Gieseler denies said *Expositio* to Fortunatus, but without being able to assign it to any other source.

44. Con. Tolet. [*Concilia Toletana* or Council of Toledo] IV (anno 633) chapter 1. Conc. Tolet. VI. (anno 638) chapter l. Conc. Tolet. XI. (anno 675) preface, and Conc. Tolet. XIV. (anno 684) chapter 8. The close relation between these councils and several passages of the Athanasianum is undeniable, and the question is merely, whether the councils quote from the Symbol without naming it, as most writers suppose, or whether the Symbol borrowed from the councils, as Gieseler, *Kirchengeschicte*, Ibid., 110 thinks. [Thirty Councils of Toledo were held between the fifth and sixteenth centuries. A summary of the actions of the first eighteen are found in P. DeLuis, "Toledo" *Encyclopedia of the Early Church*, II:844–45.]

45. It is called Codex Usseri I. Archbishop Usser or Ussher saw it in a *Psalterium Latino Gallicum* of the *Bibliotheca Cottoniana*, and assigned it "*tum ex antiquo picturae generae, tum ex literarum forma grandiuscula*" [Trans. "not only because of the antiquity of the types of pictures, but also because of the slightly older form of letters"] to the age of Gregory I (590–604). But it has since disappeared. [The Cotton library is now in the British Museum and Library, London.]

46. The manuscript of Treves on the borders of Gaul and Germany.

47. Ms. Ambros in the Ambrosian library at Milan.

48. Codex Usseri II. (Cottoniana I) in a copy of the Gallican Psalter of King Aethelstan. Ussher says of it, De symb., 8: "*Psalterium illud anno aerae nostrae Christianae 703 longe ante Aethalstani regnantis tempora, ex regulis Kalendario in libri initio subjunctis scriptum fuisse deprehendi.*" [Trans. "That Psalter is from the year 703 of our Christian era, long before the reign of Athelstan, as indicated by the

If this view be correct, the *Symbolum Quicunque* is less individual and more catholic in its very origin, than any other confession of Christendom, with the only exception of the Apostles' and the Nicene Creed. This fact does not weaken, but rather strengthens its authority as a confession of faith. If Athanasius were an inspired apostle, then the case would be very different. But as all the teachers of the Church, since the apostles, are fallible men, their writings carry no more weight and authority with them than their merits justify, and the Church has given them by its own consent. The validity and value of the Athanasian Creed can in no case be made to rest on the authority of any individual, however great and good, and the more it is separated from individual authorship, the better for its catholic and churchly character.

[III.] Reception and Authority

As soon as the Athanasian Symbol clearly appears in history, we find it in high esteem and quietly assuming its position among the authoritative doctrinal and liturgical standards of the *Latin* Church, first in France about 550, then in Spain 630, in Germany 800, in England 880, in Italy 880, in Rome 930.[49] The Roman Church in this point did not lead but followed public opinion. The Creed was frequently commented upon,[50] embodied in copies of the Psalter and Breviary, ordered to be committed to memory by the priests, and introduced into the weekly or even daily worship.[51]

In the *Greek* Church the Athanasian Creed, when it first became known, after the tenth century, met with opposition, especially on account of the Latin doctrine of the procession of the Spirit *from the Son,* as well as from the Father.[52] Subsequently it was likewise introduced, but less extensively than in the Latin Church, and with some

---

calendar that was written in at the beginning of the book.] Waterland, *A Critical History*, 51, as quoted by Köllner, *Symbolik*, 62) remarks: "The Psalter, wherein this Creed is, is the Gallican Psalter, not the Roman; the title is *Fides Sancti Athanasii Alexandrini*: the oldest monument we have extant—*Codex Usseri I* being lost—ascribing this creed to Athanasius."

49. See Waterland, *A Critical History*, 51 and Köllner, *Symbolik*, 85.

50. By Venantius Fortunatus, Hincmar, Bruno of Würzburg, Peter Abälard, St. Hildegard, Alexander ab Hales, John Wycliffe, and others.

51. Hatto [or Haito, a Roman Catholic monk, Abbot of the Abbey of Reichenau,] Bishop of Basel, A.D. 820: "*Ut Fides S. Athanasii a sacerdotibus discatur et ex corde, die Dominico, ad Primam recitetur.*" [Trans. "So that the faith of St. Athanasius may be known by heart by priests, let it be recited on Sunday by heart."] A more explicit testimony for the liturgical use of this creed in the French and English churches is furnished by Abbo of Fleury [c. 945–1004] about 997 (quoted by Köllner, 65). Of later usage Bona (*Tract. de divina Psalmodia*, 863) says: "*Illud symbolum olim, teste Honorio, quotidie est decantatum, jam vero diebus Dominicis in totius coetus frequentia recitatur, ut sanctae fidei confessio ea die apertius celebretur.*" [Trans. "Formerly, according to the witness of Honorius, that creed was chanted daily, and indeed now is recited on all Sundays in the full assembly, so that the confession of the holy faith may be proclaimed publicly on that day."]

52. Some Greek divines denied that Athanasius ever wrote it; others maintained that he was drunk when he composed it; still others that the Latins corrupted his Creed by the insertion of the *et filio* ["*and son*"]. The last is also asserted in the *Confessio Metrophanis Critopuli*, compare E. J. Kimmel's *Monumenta Fidei Ecclesiae Orientalis*, Part II:23. [Schaff, *The Creeds of Christendom*, I:43.]

alterations, and with the omission of the και εχ του υιου, *et filio*[53] (corresponding to the *filioque* in the Latin versions of the Nicaeno-Constantinopolitan Symbol).[54]

From the Latin Church the Athanasian Creed, together with the other two ecumenical creeds, passed over into the orthodox *Protestant* Churches, and was either separately and expressly acknowledged, or substantially incorporated into their doctrinal or devotional standards.

The *Lutheran* Church received it among its symbolical books. Luther appreciated it highly and was disposed to regard it as the most important and glorious production since the days of the Apostles,[55] The "Augsburg Confession " substantially repeats its doctrine of the Trinity, and of Christ's person, without naming it.[56] The "Form of Concord" distinctly recognizes it as scriptural, true and authoritative.[57] Hence it is found in all the editions of the "Book of Concord" as the third symbol of the Lutheran Confession.

The *Reformed* Church of *England gave* it a place in the *Common Prayer Book* and ordered it to be sung or said alternately by the minister and people standing, in the morning service on several festival days, viz: Christmas, the Epiphany, St. Matthias, Easter, Ascension, Whitsunday, John the Baptist, St. James, St. Bartholomew, St. Matthew, St. Simon and St. Jude, St. Andrew, and on Trinity Sunday. In all these days it takes the place of the Apostles' Creed.

The *Reformed* Churches of the *Continent* have not given the Athanasian Symbol that direct formal sanction and prominence, as the Lutheran and the Anglican.[58] But

53. [Trans., "and from the Son, and Son."]

54. [Joseph] Bingham, 548–49. *Presenter Graeci eo utuntur nonnullis additamentis aucto et aliquantum mutato.* [Trans. "In public the Greeks use it with a few additions and some changes."]

55. "*Es ist also gefasset,*" he says, "*dass ich nicht weiss, ob seit der Apostel Zeit in der Kirche des Neuen Testaments etwas Wichtigeres und Herrlicheres geschrieben sei.*" Compare Martin Luther, *Werke*, ed. Johann Georg Walch (Halle, 1740–53), VI: 2313 sqq. [Trans. "It is thus understood," he says, "that I do not know whether something more important and glorious has been written since the apostolic times of the New Testament." See also *Luther's Works*, Helmut T. Lehman, ed., "Three Symbols or Creeds of the Christian Faith," 34:201–29.]

56. Article I and Article III, *Libri symbolici ecclesiae evangelicae, sive Concordia*, Karl A. von Hase, ed., 910. [Schaff, *The Creeds of Christendom*, III:710. Karl August von Hase (1800–90) was a popular German church historian and theologian who taught at Tübingen, Leipzig, and Jena.]

57. Epitome, 571, and more fully in the *Solida Declaration*, 682 (ed. Hase): "*Amplectimur etiam tria illa Catholica et generalia summae auctoritatis Symbola, Apostolicum, videlicet, Nicenum, et Athanasii. Haec enim agnoscimus esse breves quidem, sed easdem maxime pias, atque in verbo Dei solide fundatas, praeclaras Confessiones fidei, quibus omnes haereses, quae iis temporibus Ecclesias Christi perturbarunt, perspicue et solide refutantur*" [Trans. "And let us embrace those three catholic and widely used creeds of the highest authority, namely the Apostolic, Nicene and Athanasian. Indeed we acknowledge these to be outstanding confessions of faith—short, but especially faithful, and founded solidly on the word of God—which clearly and solidly refute all the heresies which trouble the churches of Christ in these times." The Epitome and Solid Declaration describe the two parts of the Formula of Concord, with the former very briefly stating the Formula's contents. Schaff, *The Creeds of Christendom*, I:312–13. For reference to the Athanasian Creed in the Formula of Concord, see Schaff, *The Creeds of Christendom*, III:95.]

58. Dr. Ebrard, on the contrary, thinks that the Reformed Church makes in some respect even more account of the ecumenical Creeds than the Lutheran (*Christliche Dogmatik*, II:89, 90). This

they unanimously profess, in their symbolical books, the same doctrine of the Trinity and the Incarnation; reject the errors of the Arians, Semiarians [Semi-Arians], Nestorians, Eutychians and Monothelites, and thus acknowledge in fact, if not always in form, the authority of the ancient ecumenical creeds, in due subjection, of course, to the supreme authority of the Holy Scriptures. The Second Helvetic Confession, drawn up by Bullinger in the name of the Swiss Churches in 1566, and approved by them, endorses, in very strong and unmistakable terms, the doctrine of the first four general councils and of the Athanasian Symbol.[59] Dr. David Pareus, the pupil and friend of Ursinus, and editor of his *Commentary on the Heidelberg Catechism*, wrote a special exposition of the Athanasian Creed, which, however, we have never seen.[60]

So far the faith in the doctrines of our Symbol was unshaken in the Church and was shared in common by the Greeks (if we leave out of view their dissent from the *filioque*), Romans and Protestants. The Socinians[61] alone differed from it and prepared the way for a still greater dissent. During the seventeenth century the origin of the Athanasian Creed was first made the subject of critical investigation by Continental

---

may be true as to the doctrine itself, but not as to the formal recognition of these creeds. Dr. Ebrard has overlooked the distinct recognition in the passage just quoted, in the preceding note, from the Lutheran Form of Concord, and the somewhat disrespectful manner in which Calvin at least (*De vera ecclesiae Reformatione*) [Trans. "On the true reform of the church"] speaks of the *Symbolum Nicaenum* as a "*carmen cantillando magis aptum, quam confessionis formula.*" [Trans. "Nicene Creed ... as a song more fitting to be sung than the formula of confession." For reference to the Anglican Thirty-nine Articles, see Schaff, *The Creeds of Christendom*, III:492. Johannes Heinrich August Ebrard (1818–88) was a German pastor, Reformed theologian, and professor.]

59. Chapter XI:487 in Niemeyer's *Collectio Confessionum in Ecclesiis. Reformatis publicatarum.*): "*Quaecunque de Incarnationis Domini nostri Jesu Christi mysterio definita sunt ex Scripturis sanctis, et comprehensa symbolis ac sententiis quatuor primarum et praestantissimarum Synodorum celebratarum Niceae, Constantinopoli, Ephesi et Chalcedone, una cum beati Athantasii Symbolo, et omnibus his similibus symbolis, credimus corde sincero et ore libero ingenue profitemur, condemnantes omnia his contraria. Atque ad hunc modum retinemus inviolatam sive integrum fidem Christianam, orthodoxam atque catholicam: scientes, symbolis praedictis nihil contineri, quod non sit conforme verbo Dei, et prorsus faciat ad sinceram fidei explicationem.*" [Trans. "We believe with sincere heart and openly declare with willing mouth whatever things are defined concerning the mystery of the incarnation of our Lord Jesus Christ from the holy scriptures and included in the creeds and sentences of the four of the first and foremost of Synods: Nicene, Constantinople, Ephesus and Chalcedon, together with the Athanasian Creed, and all similar creeds, condemning everything contrary to these. And in this way let us retain the Christian faith pure and whole, orthodox and catholic, knowing that nothing is contained in the aforementioned that does not conform to the word of God but what, in short, makes for the sincere explication of the faith." August Hermann Niemeyer (1754–1828) was a German theologian, poet, and professor at Halle, who had been influenced somewhat by the mild rationalism of his colleague Johann Salomo Semler (1725–91).]

60. [David Pareus,] *Symbolum Athanasii, notis breviter declaratum*. 1681 (as Walch has it, *Introductio*, 156), or 1619 (according to Köllner, 87). Probably the one gives the date of the preface, the other the date of publication. [David Pareus (1548–1622), a German Reformed pastor, theologian, and professor, studied with the celebrated Zacharias Ursinus and published several other works including biblical commentaries.]

61. [Socinianism was a non-trinitarian theology that arose in the 1540's in Italy and later took root in Poland.]

THE ATHANASIAN CREED

and Anglican divines, and resulted in the almost unanimous rejection of the ancient tradition as to its authorship. This had the effect to weaken its authority as a primitive symbol, without undermining the faith in its contents. But when the skeptical and rationalistic flood of the eighteenth century swept away from a large portion of the Church the orthodox faith in the Holy Trinity and the Incarnation of the Son of God, this Creed was almost forgotten and figured only in Church histories among the many idle fabrications of a superstitious and intolerant age.

The reviving faith of the nineteenth century led to a gradual return to the ancient confessions, first of the period of the Reformation and then also to those of the primitive Church. And although the Athanasian Creed is still comparatively neglected and even passed by in silence by eminent writers[62] on the very doctrines it so ably and clearly sets forth, it begins again to attract attention more and more and to be appreciated in its true worth without being unduly overestimated as in times past. Dr. Kling, an Evangelical divine of Würtemberg, claims for it a permanent significance in the Christian Church which will never give up its dogmatic substance.[63] Dr. Ebrard, one of the leading representatives of the modern German Reformed school of theology, makes still greater account of it in his "Christian Dogmatics,"[64] represents it as the completion of the ancient Catholic theology and christology, and asserts that it has been most fully taken up and best understood by the symbols and early divines of the Reformed communion.

As to our own country, I am not aware that the Athanasian Creed has ever been made the subject of serious discussion. The Episcopal Church, at its separate organization after the Revolutionary War, has thrown it out of its Liturgy, together with the Nicene Creed (which, however, was subsequently restored at the insistence of the English bishops). But this omission must be traced to the prevalence of the latitudinarian spirit of the eighteenth century, which proposed, in the General Convention held at Philadelphia in 1785, a number of other omissions and changes in the Liturgy, the Thirty Nine Articles and even in the Apostles' Creed.[65] If the Episcopal Church were

---

62. Dr. Baur in his learned and eminently scholarly, though unsound, work on the history of the Holy Trinity and the Incarnation of God, alludes to this Creed only *en passant* [in passing] in a footnote, Vol. II:33, 168. But what is more surprising still, is that Dr. Dorner, in his invaluable Christological work, should not even mention it, so far as we can see from a cursory glance over both volumes and the index. [Ferdinand Christian Baur (1792–1860) was a German theologian and professor at Tübingen who analyzed the New Testament from an Hegelian perspective. Isaak August Dorner (1809–84) was a German Lutheran theologian of the "mediating" school.]

63. Article in *Herzog's Encyclopaedia*, I:577 [Christian Friedrich Kling (1800–62), "Athanasius"].

64. Ebrard, *Christliche Dogmatik*, I: §188, p. 185f, and II: paragraph 377, p. 89.

65. Compare on this subject Bishop White's [William White (1748–1836)] *Memoirs of the Protestant Episcopal Church in the United States of America*, 102ff. and 448ff, and the "Proposed Book," i.e., the provisional Liturgy of that Church as revised by the Convention of 1785. Many of the alterations, especially also the omission of the Nicene Creed and the article on the descent into hades in the Apostles' Creed, were subsequently given up on the remonstrance of the English bishops, who refused ordination, except on condition of the restoration of that article and of the Nicene Creed.

to be reorganized now, as it was in 1784, the Athanasian Creed, as well as the Nicene, would probably keep its place in the Liturgy, and many of its ministers would gladly see it restored.—The Lutherans of the United States are still bound to this Creed as far as they respect at all the Book of Concord.—The Presbyterians and Congregationalists never, as far as I know, acknowledged it in form, but they teach substantially the same doctrine in their standards.—The Dutch Reformed Church has it as an appendix to its Liturgy, although it is probably never used there in public service.—The new Liturgy of the German Reformed Church, which is at yet, however, merely of a provisional character, has received it, together with the two older ecumenical creeds, among the Primitive Forms (p. 17–19), recommends its use on the last communion in the ecclesiastical year (p. 192), and requires the consent to it on the part of the candidates for the ministry in the ordination office (p. 245). This is a step in advance of every other Protestant communion of the country and just the reverse of the negative action of the Episcopal Church in 1785; but, as compared with the original position and doctrinal standards of the Churches of the Reformation, Lutheran, Anglican and Reformed, it is certainly no innovation, but a return rather to old usage under a modified, and we may say simplified and restricted form as to its actual use in public service. Whether the Athanasianum will retain its place at the final revision of this work, remains to be seen. The more closely it is examined, the less objectionable will it appear to those who cherish a strong and hearty belief in the ancient Christian doctrine of the holy Trinity and the Incarnation of the Son of God.

[IV.] Character and Contents

Let us now examine the theology of the Athanasian symbol, the nature of which must determine its value and use in the Christian Church.[66]

The third ecumenical Creed is an epitome of ancient Catholic theology and sets forth, in clear logical statement, the orthodox faith concerning the fundamental articles of the triune God and the divine-human Saviour, without attempting to explain these unfathomable mysteries. It embodies the permanent results of the trinitarian and christological controversies which agitated, with uncommon violence, the Nicene and post-Nicene age, and were decided successively by the four general synods held at Nice [Nicea] in 325, at Constantinople in 381, at Ephesus in 431, and at Chalcedon in 451.

For all practical purposes we may say the Apostles' Creed was sufficient, and it is so to this day, as a guide for catechetical instruction of the young and as a confession at baptism and confirmation. In this respect it can never be superseded or improved. Its very simplicity gives it a decided preference for popular catechetical and liturgical use over the Nicene and Athanasian creeds and every subsequent confession of faith. But theologically and scientifically considered, it is defective, inasmuch as it does not

---

66. On the theology of the Creed, which we regard as the most important part of the subject, Walch and Köllner are altogether superficial and unsatisfactory.

clearly and unmistakably teach the Godhead of Christ and of the Holy Ghost in the full sense in which the Church intended it from the beginning.

Hence it was found necessary to define it more fully at the councils of Nice [Nicea] and Constantinople, in opposition to the Arian and semi-Arian hypothesis which acknowledged Christ to have existed before the world and to be divine in some sense, but denied his equality with the Father, and which made the Holy Ghost the first creature of the Son, or a mere power and influence of the Godhead. The Nicene Creed calls Jesus Christ not simply the "only begotten Son our Lord," as the Apostles' Creed, but the "only begotten Son of God; begotten of the Father before all worlds, God of God, Light of Light, very God of very God; begotten, not made; of one substance (*homoousious*) with the Father, by whom all things were made." This is certainly an advance, not in faith, we may say, for this was the same in the beginning, but in knowledge and in expression.

But the theology of the Church could not stop here. The Nicene Creed even in the more explicit form which it received at the Synod of Constantinople in 381, teaches, indeed, the true Godhead of Christ beyond the possibility of mistake, but it gives by no means yet a complete view of the holy Trinity. For in the first place, like the Apostles' Creed, it speaks of the Father, Son, and Holy Ghost separately only, without bringing out their oneness of substance, their mutual relations and distinctive personal properties, so as to exclude every possible form of tritheism on the one hand, and subordinationism on the other. Secondly, it is especially defective in the doctrine of the Holy Ghost, which did not come into full view at all during the Arian controversy. In the third place, it is entirely silent on the exact relation which holds between the divine and human nature of Christ, which was brought out only during the succeeding Nestorian and Eutychian controversies.

In all these respects, and especially in the last, the Athanasian Symbol is a decided advance upon its two predecessors. It naturally divides itself into two parts. Each part is introduced by a prologue on the necessity and importance of holding the true faith as afterwards taught, and the whole concludes with an epilogue to the same effect. The first, and larger part, from v. 3–27,[67] teaches the true doctrine of the Trinity; the second, from v. 26–44, the doctrine of the Incarnation, or the proper constitution of Christ's Person.

1. The doctrine of the Holy Trinity, or the Theology, in the strict sense of the term. The Holy Trinity is the sacred symbol and type of the Christian religion, as distinct from the abstract monotheism of Judaism, Mahometanism, and deism on the one hand, and from the dualism and polytheism of the various forms of Paganism on the other. It comprehends all the truths and all the blessings of the revelation

---

67. The division in verses differs somewhat, although the succession is the same in all manuscripts and editions. The *Book of Concord* makes 42 verses, Weber, 43. The best critical edition of the text is said to be that of Waterland. But the Latin codices, of which Montfaucon compared 12, Waterland 24, present a very small number of *lectiones variantes* [variant readings], while the Greek copies, though less numerous (8), differ more materially.

or self-communication of God for the salvation of men. Hence it is expressed in the baptismal formula, and confessed in the Apostles' Creed at the very entrance into the Christian Church in the sacrament of baptism (Matth. 28: 19), and made the all-comprehending and concluding benediction by the Apostle (2 Cor. 18: 14).

It stands thus at the beginning and at the end of Christian worship and controls it throughout. But it is not simply in the two express passages alluded to, that the Bible teaches the Holy Trinity, nor in all the far more numerous passages which prove the Godhead of Christ, or of the Holy Ghost, and which can only be reconciled with the fundamental idea of the Divine unity on the assumption of a trinity of persons in this unity of substance. We may say the doctrine runs through the entire Scriptures from beginning to end in the form of living facts, or in the exhibition of the revelation of the one only true and living God as Father, Son and Holy Ghost in the work of the creation, redemption and sanctification of the world. We need not be surprised, therefore, that this article stands out so prominently in the faith, worship and theology of the early Church, and gave rise to a long succession of doctrinal controversies. In this article again the divinity of Christ, as the incarnate God and Saviour of the race, formed naturally the central interest and fills the greater portion of the ancient Creeds, since it is the starting point of the Christian consciousness, determines the true idea of God, and was the main object of attack on the part of the ancient heresies, both of Jewish and heathen origin.

The Holy Trinity is a mystery which transcends our present power of comprehension and will furnish food for sacred meditation and praise throughout the countless ages of eternity. Nevertheless, as faith is never irrational and unnatural but merely superrational and supernatural, the subject matter of this article of faith can and ought to be clearly known and stated.

This is done with admirable clearness, precision, brevity and completeness in the Athanasian Creed. It betrays a mind which had evidently mastered the entire subject and fully appropriated it to the intellect as well as to the heart. It not only rejects *Unitarianism* or *Monarchianism*[68], which either as Patripassianism,[69] or as Ebionism,[70] denies the Trinity altogether, but it avoids, also, with singular care and discrimination, the three erroneous forms in which the Trinity may be held and has been held at different times before and since. It excludes, in the first place, *Sabellianism* or *Modalism*, which teaches merely a Trinity of revelation, not of essence, and thus falls back at last upon Unitarianism or abstract monotheism; secondly, *Tritheism*, which teaches three

---

68. [Monarchianism was a theology that arose in the second century and persisted into the third. It emphasized the unity of God by positing a single locus of authority in the Godhead.]

69. [Patripassianism was another early theological movement that stressed the unity of God so much that it proposed that the Father became incarnate and suffered during the earthly life and death of Jesus.]

70 [Ebionism was the ideology of several Jewish Christian sects in the second century that denied the divinity of Jesus but affirmed that he was a human being who had been adopted by God for his messianic role.]

divine beings, and thus runs into polytheism; and thirdly, *Subordinationism,* which subordinates the Son to the Father, and the Holy Ghost to both, as partaking in part only, as it were, or to a limited extent, of the Divine essence, or dignity. These errors are not expressly mentioned, but necessarily denied by the positive statement of the opposite view.

The Symbol teaches the Unity in Trinity and the Trinity in Unity, neither dividing the substance, nor confounding the persons.[71] 1) The *Unity* of the Godhead as to being, substance or essence: "The Godhead of the Father, of the Son, and of the Holy Ghost, is all one, the glory equal, the majesty coequal. . . . There are not three eternal, but one eternal . . . not three uncreated, nor three unlimited; but one uncreated, and one unlimited . . . not three almighty, but one almighty . . . not three Gods, but one God . . . not three Lords, but one Lord. . . . We are forbidden by the Catholic religion to say: There be three Gods, or three Lords." 2) The *Trinity* of persons or hypostases. These terms, it is true, must be taken in a peculiar sense, if applied to God. For in human relations three persons constitute three different beings. Yet there is no other term equally expressive. The Trinity is in the first place immanent and essential, a distinction in God himself, independent of, and prior to, his manifestation in the world. It is a living relationship and process in God, the vitality, so to say, of infinite intelligence and infinite love. God was from everlasting Father, Son, and Holy Ghost, and will remain forever Father, Son and Holy Ghost as certainly as he is supreme wisdom and supreme love. This trinity of essence reflects and manifests itself in the economical trinity or trinity of revelation,[72] that is the threefold divine work of creation, salvation and sanctification. "There is one person of the Father, another of the Son, and another of the Holy Ghost. . . . The Father is God, the Son is God, and the Holy Ghost is God. . . . Each person by himself is God and Lord." 3) The internal *relation* of the three persons or their distinctive properties which, however, do not in the least interfere with the strict unity of substance. The Father is himself not made, nor created, but eternally *begetting* the Son; the Son is not made, nor created, but eternally *begotten* of the substance of the Father; the Holy Ghost is not made nor created, but eternally *proceeding* from the Father and the Son.[73] It is true, in this last point there is

---

71. Vss. 8 and 4. In vs. 27, there is an unimportant difference of reading as to the order. The *textus receptus*, as found in the *Book of Concord*, reads, *trinitas in unitate et unitas in trinitate* [trinity in unity and unity in trinity], while Waterland reverses the order, *unitas in trinitate et trinitas in unitate* [Trans. "unity in trinity and trinity in unity"]. The latter is the order in the old English version and in the revision.

72. We employ here a terminology which is much later, but the distinction itself between an essential or immanent trinity, and an economical or transient trinity enters unquestionably into the ancient Creeds and is implied already in the doctrine of the *eternal* generation of the Son, or the eternal Sonship of Christ.

73. Or to express it in nouns according to a later terminology, to the Father belongs negatively *the innascribilitas* or αγγεννησια, positively the *generatio activa* and *spiratio* (πνον) *activa Spiritus Sancti*; to the Son belongs the *filialatio generatio* (γενησιαια) *passiva,* and *spiratio activa* Spiritus s.; to the Holy Ghost the *precessio* (εκπορευσις) and *spiratio passiva*.

a difference of opinion between the Greek and the Latin Church, the former denying the procession from the Son as a later innovation and corruption. But the equality of the Son and the Father in its full sense necessarily requires the *filioque*. Here the Athanasianum follows the Latin view as brought out especially by St. Augustine,[74] and embodied also in the later clause to the Nicene Creed.

This same doctrine of the Trinity, including the *filioque*, was unanimously professed by the Reformers, reasserted in opposition to the Socinians and incorporated into the doctrinal standards of the evangelical Churches. Hase says that the view of the Athanasian Symbol "was received *without change* into the symbolical books of the Lutheran Church and defended as the most sacred mystery of orthodox Christendom against every kind of opposition."[75] The Reformed Church, in some of its standards, is even more full and clear on the subject than the Lutheran.[76] Let us hear the four Reformed symbols which are most extensively used and enjoy the greatest authority, the second Helvetic Confession, the Heidelberg Catechism, the Thirty Nine Articles, and the Westminster Confession.

The larger Helvetic Confession not only expressly endorses the ancient symbols, including the Athanasianum, as we have observed already, but also, in its exposition of the Trinity, is so clear and explicit as to leave no room for doubt whatever.[77] "We believe and teach that God is one as to essence and nature (*unum esse essentia vel natura*), self-subsisting and self-sufficient for all things, invisible, incorporeal, immense, eternal, the creator of all things visible as well as invisible, the highest good. . . . Nevertheless we believe and teach that this same infinite God one and undivided (*unum et indivisum*) is inseparably and without confusion distinct in persons (*personis inseparabiliter et inconfuse esse distinctum*) as Father, Son and Holy Spirit, so that the Father from eternity begat the Son (*ab aeterno Filium generaverit*), that the Son was

---

74. Compare Augustine, *De Trinitate*. IV:20: *Nec possumus dicere, quod Spiritus S. et a Filio non procedat; neque enim frustra idem Spiritus et Patris et Filii Spiritus dicitur. Nec video, quid aliud significare voluerit, quum sufflans in faciem discipulorum ait: Accipite Spiritum S. Neque enim flatus ille corporeus substantia Spiritus S. fuit, sed demonstratio per congruam significationem, non tantum a Patre, sed et a Filio procedere Spiritum*. [Trans. "Neither can we say that the Holy Spirit does not proceed 'and from the Son,' nor indeed is it called 'the Spirit of the Father and of the Son' in vain. Nor do I see that it means other than what he said, blowing into the face of his disciples, 'Receive the Holy Spirit.' Indeed the corporeal substance of the Holy Spirit was not blown, but this was a demonstration through a suitable sign that the Spirit proceeds not just from the Father but 'from the Son.'"]

75. Hase, *Hutterus Redivivus, oder Dogmatik der Evangelisch Lutherischen Kirche*. 171 of the 8th edition. Compare his quotations from the "Augsburg Confession," the "Apology," and the old Lutheran divines, on the subsequent pages. Also Hase's *Evangelisch Protestantische Dogmatik*, 515, 4th ed.: "*Die hergebrachte Lehre ging ohne alle Durchbildung in die evang. Kirche über, theils durch Reception des Athanasianum, theils durch Wiederholung seines Grundgedankens, wie seiner praktischen Anwendung.*" [Trans. "The traditional teaching was passed on in the Protestant Church without any academic effort, partly through the acceptance of the Athanasian Creed and partly though the repetition of its basic thought as well as its practical application."]

76. Compare Ebrard, *Christliche Dogmatik*, I:180 sqq.

77. Chapter 3 (not Chapter. 2, as Ebrard quotes), 470, ed. Niemeyer.

begotten by an ineffable generation (*filius generatione ineffabili genitus sit*), and that the Holy Ghost eternally proceeds from both and is to be adored with both (*Spiritus S. vero procedat ab utroque, idque ab aeterno, cum utroque adorandus*); so that there are not three Gods, but three persons consubstantial, coëternal and coëqual, distinct as to hypostases, and in order (not dignity) one preceding the other, yet without any inequality (*nulla tamen inaequalitate*)." Then the Confession quotes several Scripture passages in support of this doctrine, and condemns not only the Jews and Mahomedans and all who blaspheme "*sacrosanctam et adorandam hanc Trinitatem*," but also those heretics who deny or pervert it, as the Monarchians, Patripassians, Sabellians, Arians, Macedonians and the like.

The Heidelberg Catechism, necessarily more brief, but sufficient for its purpose, says, in the 25th question: "Since there is but one divine essence, why speakest thou of Father, Son, and Holy Ghost? Because God hath so revealed himself in his word, that these three distinct persons are the only true and eternal God."

The Thirty Nine Articles of the Church of England recognize the Athanasian Creed,[78] and teach in the very first article, which is retained unchanged in the Episcopal Church of the United States: "There is but one living and true God. . . . And in unity of this Godhead there be three persons, of one substance, power, and eternity; the Father, the Son, and the Holy Ghost."

The Westminster Confession which is held by the Congregational and Presbyterian bodies of England and the United States, approaches more closely to the phraseology and letter of the Athanasian Creed:[79] "In the unity of the Godhead there be three persons of one substance, power, and eternity, God the Father, God the Son, and God the Holy Ghost. The Father is of none, neither begotten, nor proceeding; the Son is eternally begotten of the Father; the Holy Ghost eternally proceeding from the Father and the Son."

Similar quotations might easily be multiplied, but it is not necessary, since the orthodoxy of the Protestant evangelical Churches on this article has never been seriously questioned, not even by Roman Catholic controversialists.

---

78. Article VIII "of the Three Creeds," in the original articles as they still obtain in England. The Episcopal Church of the United States has not only removed the Athanasian symbol from the liturgical service, but also stricken out its name from said article, in the revision of 1801, retaining, however, the Nicene and Apostles' Creeds, and also Articles I and II unaltered, which teach the same doctrine on the Trinity and the Incarnation.

79. Chapter II, Paragraph 8. Compare the *Larger Catechism* Questions. VIIIXI. The Westminster standards are hardly ever noticed by German writers, not even by Ebrard and Schweizer, in their works on Reformed Dogmatics, while they refer to every other symbol, the Scotch Confession among the rest, which was superseded by the far more full and accurate *Westminster Confession* and *Catechisms*. It is characteristic that Niemeyer in his *Collection of all the Reformed Symbols*, originally omitted the Westminster standards entirely, but furnished them afterwards in an Appendix, with the excuse that he was unable before to find a single copy of them anywhere (*quod ne unum quidem confessionis Westmonasteriensis sive Puritanae exemplar usquam reperire potueram*) [Trans. "not able previously to find a copy of the Westminster Confession or of the Puritans."].

Chapter 4: "The Athanasian Creed"

2. The doctrine of the Incarnation, or the Christology.

The doctrine of Christ is substantially contained in the confession of Peter, that Jesus of Nazareth is the Christ, i.e. the promised Messiah, the Son of the living God, or in the declaration of John: The word became flesh [John 1:14], or in the word of Paul: God manifest in the flesh [Col 1:19]. The Church has ever believed in the mystery of the incarnation or the abiding union of the divine and the human in the person of Christ, as the central truth of our holy religion and the foundation of all our hopes. Christ must be the Son of God and the Son of man in the fullest sense of the term, if he really is what he claims to be, the Mediator between God and man, and the Saviour of the world. To deny either his divinity, or his humanity, to reduce him either to a mere man, however great and good, or to resolve him into a gnostic phantom and spectral idea, is a radical heresy and overthrows the Christian salvation. Hence the uncompromising hostility of the ancient Church against Ebionism on the one hand, and Gnosticism on the other. But the exclusion of these two extreme errors is not sufficient. It may be admitted that Christ is both God and man, and yet the *relation* of the divine and human in him be so conceived as seriously to affect either their difference or their unity. The difference may be made so great, as virtually to result in two persons, or the unity may be so pressed, as to teach but one nature. The former is the Nestorian, the latter the Eutychian or Monophysite error. The one allows merely a mechanical and external relation between the divine and human nature in Christ, and substitutes the idea of an indwelling of the former in the latter or of a moral fellowship for the idea of an incarnation. The other assumes a total absorption of the human nature into the divine in the act of the incarnation, so that Christ ceases to be man and cannot be our model for imitation. In both cases the truth of the incarnation and its result, the redemption and reconciliation of man with God, are seriously endangered and virtually annihilated. Nestorianism falls back at last upon an Ebionite christology, while Eutychianism ends logically in Gnosticism and Pantheism.

Here now the Athanasian Creed, in the second part, steers with equally sound instinct and discrimination between the Nestorian and Eutychian heresies, as it steered in the doctrine of the Trinity between Tritheism and Unitarianism. It teaches that Christ is perfect God and perfect man, equal to the Father as to his divine nature, equal to man as to his human nature, sin only excepted, and yet one and the same Christ, not by confusion of substance, but by unity of person,[80] not by conversion of the Godhead into flesh, but by assumption of the manhood into God.

It is interesting to compare with it the confession of the Council of Chalcedon in 451, which rejected the Eutychian heresy and gave at the same time an exposition of the orthodox doctrine in these words:

---

80. *Unus omnino, non confusione substantiae, sed unitate personae*, v. 36. [Trans. "One altogether, not by confusion of substance, but by unity of person."] This sounds like a direct denial of the Eutychian theory and seems to point to a period after the fourth general Council [Chalcedon] in 451. But the same view was substantially advanced before Eutyches, and opposed in similar forms as in this passage. Compare Waterland and Köllner, 89 sq.

Following the holy fathers, we all teach unanimously that we confess one and the same Son our Lord Jesus Christ, perfect in Godhead and perfect in manhood, truly God and at the same time truly man, of a reasonable soul and body; of the same substance with the Father as to his Godhead, and of the same substance at the same time with us as to his manhood; in all things like unto us, except sin; eternally begotten of the Father according to his Godhead, but in the last days for our sake and for our salvation (born) of the Virgin Mary, the mother of God (της θεοτοκον), according to his manhood; one and the same Christ (ενα και τον αυτον Χριστον), Son, Lord, Only-begotten, who is known in two natures[81] without mixture and change,[82] without division and separation,[83] so that the difference of the natures is by no means abolished by the union, but rather the peculiarity of each nature is saved, and they are united in one person and one hypostasis,[84] not divided or torn into two persons, but one and the same Christ: as the prophets from on high and the Lord Jesus Christ himself have taught us, and the faith of the fathers has handed down to us.

The statement of the Athanasian Creed is more simple and condensed and omits the term "mother of God," which is not to be regretted,[85] but it is equally, if not more clear and explicit. It also illustrates the relation of the two natures in Christ by the union of soul and body in man. It then enumerates, like the Apostles' Creed, the leading facts in the life of the Saviour to his return in glory, and concludes with the doctrine of the last judgment, where the good shall receive everlasting life and the wicked everlasting damnation.

The christology of the Athanasian Creed has likewise passed over, without any material change, into the symbolical books of the Lutheran and Reformed Churches. Leaving out of view the Lutheran doctrine, we will confine ourselves again to the four leading confessions of the Reformed communion.

The Heidelberg Catechism teaches,[86] that Christ as a Mediator and Deliverer must be *very man,* and perfectly righteous, because the justice of God requires that

---

81. εν δυο φυστοι, *in duabus naturis,* as all Latin copies read, instead of the other reading, εκ δυο φυσετων [Trans. "from two natures"], which might be understood in a Eutychian or Monophysite sense.

82. ασυγχυτως, ετρεπτως—against Eutychianism.

83. αδιαιρετως, εχωριετως—against Nestorianism.

84. εις εν προσωπον και μιαν προστασιν.

85. It must be admitted that the term, θεοτοκος [Trans. "Godbearer"], so obnoxious to the Nestorians, has a good sense, and follows with logical necessity from the orthodox view of the Incarnation. But it is equally certain that it is onesided (χριστοτοκος [Trans. "Christbearer"] and θεανθρωποτοκος [Trans. "God/manbearer"] would be more complete), that it was not used by the apostles and ante-Nicene fathers, that it is liable to be grossly misunderstood by the illiterate, that it has been greatly abused and made the basis of an excessive, yea idolatrous worship of the Blessed Virgin in the Greek and Roman Churches. We prefer the Scriptural term, "Mother of our Lord" (Luke 1. 43).

86. Questions XVXVIII. Compare Questions XXIXXL. [Schaff, *The Creeds of Christendom,* III:312–13, 317–20.]

CHAPTER 4: "THE ATHANASIAN CREED"

the same human nature which has sinned, should likewise make satisfaction for sin, and one who is himself a sinner, cannot satisfy for others; and that he must be at the same time in *one person very God,* that he might by the power of his Godhead sustain, in his human nature, the burden of God's wrath and might obtain for and restore to us righteousness and life.

The second Helvetic Confession,[87] after teaching distinctly the eternal generation of the Son and his strict equality with the Father, goes on as follows: "The same eternal Son of the eternal God, we believe and teach, has become the Son of man of the seed of Abraham and David, without the cohabitation of man, as Ebion said, being conceived in the purest manner, by the Holy Ghost and born of the Virgin Mary, according to the evangelical history." Then after rejecting the Gnostic and Appollinarian[88] view of the humanity of Christ, it continues: "We acknowledge in one and the same Christ our Lord two natures, the divine and the human, and these we hold to be so connected that they are not absorbed, or confused, or mixed, but united or conjoined in one person, without destroying the permanent properties of the natures; so that we worship one Lord Christ, not two, who is very God, of one substance with the Father according to his divine nature, and very man, of one substance with us men according to his human nature, sin only excepted. Therefore we abominate the Nestorian dogma which makes two out of one Christ, and dissolves the unity of person; so also we utterly execrate the folly of Eutyches, the Monophysites and Monothelites who expunge the property of the human nature."

The Thirty Nine Articles of the Anglican Communion:[89] "The Son, which is the Word of the Father, begotten from everlasting of the Father, the very and eternal God, and of one substance with the Father, took man's nature in the womb of the blessed Virgin, of her substance: so that two whole and perfect natures, that is to say, the Godhead and manhood, were joined together in one person, never to be divided, whereof is one Christ, very God, and very man," etc.

The Westminster Confession is equally clear and distinct on this subject.[90] "The Son of God, the second person in the Trinity, being very and eternal God, of one substance equal with the Father, did, when the fulness of time was come, take upon him man's nature with all the essential properties and common infirmities thereof, yet without sin, being conceived by the Holy Ghost, in the womb of the Virgin Mary, of her substance: so that two whole, perfect, and distinct natures, the Godhead and the manhood, were inseparably joined together in one person, without conversion,

---

87. Chapter XI: *De Jesu Christo vero Deo et homino, unico mundi Salvatore,* p. 488f., ed. Niemeyer. [Trans. "Of Jesus Christ true God and man, only Savior of the world."]

88. [Appollinaris of Laodicea (d. 382) emphasized the unity of the person of Christ and the power of the divine nature so extremely that he denied that Christ possessed a rational human soul; its role had been taken over by the Logos.]

89. Article II. [Schaff, *The Creeds of Christendom,* III:488.]

90. Chapter VIII, paragraph 2. [Schaff, *The Creeds of Christendom,* III: 619–20.]

composition, or confusion. Which person is very God and very man, yet one Christ, the only Mediator between God and man."

It is perfectly plain, then, that the theology and christology of the Athanasian Symbol is to this day the public doctrine of the Evangelical as well as the Roman Catholic Churches. To recognize and acknowledge it in form is perfectly consistent with orthodox Protestantism. To reject it altogether, is at the same time to reject the corresponding articles of all our leading confessions of faith.

The only real difficulty in the way, is the *damnatory* clause in the prologue and epilogue of the Athanasian Creed, which makes the eternal salvation dependent upon the reception of this faith in the Holy Trinity and the Incarnation. This is the great objection to this symbol even in the eyes of many who otherwise altogether agree with its contents. No doubt the objection would be serious and valid, if the damnatory clause referred to the *form* as well as to the *substance* of faith, and required us to condemn any particular *persons*, especially all those who held loose and unsatisfactory philosophical views on the Holy Trinity, as was the case even with most of the ante-Nicene fathers, not to speak of such men as Milton, Watts, Schleiermacher, Neander, Bushnell and many other distinguished divines in the later ages of the Christian Church. But this is a false interpretation of the clause. The more it is examined and understood in its proper sense, the less objectionable will it appear.

For in the first place, if faith is at all saving, the rejection of faith must be condemning. The assertion of truth is necessarily also the negation of error. There is no avoiding the conclusion. "He that believeth," says the highest authority, "and is baptized, shall be saved; but he that believeth not, shall be damned."[91] "He that believeth on him, is not condemned: but he that believeth not, is condemned already, because he hath not believed in the name of the only begotten Son of God."[92]

Secondly, the energy and earnestness of faith in its negative as well as positive expression, must not be confounded with intolerance and uncharitableness. The question is here not of persons at all, but simply of truth and error. We are bound as Christians to love the sinner and heretic, and to labor for his conversion, while we abhor and condemn his sin and error.

Thirdly, the Protestant symbols, both Lutheran and Reformed, do substantially the same thing which is found so objectionable in the Athanasian Creed. The Augsburg Confession, the Articles of Smalkald, the Form of Concord, the Helvetic, Gallic, Belgic, Scotch, and other Confessions, expressly condemn, in the strongest terms, such as *damnamus, abominamur, detestamur, execramur,* the trinitarian and christological heresies of the Gnostics, Docetists, Ebionites, Apollinarians, Nestorians, Eutychians, Monothelites, Servetians, Socinians and others.

Finally, in all these cases salvation and condemnation is not made to depend upon the acceptance or rejection of the logical form of statement or any particular

---

91. Mark 16:16.
92. John 3:18. Compare 8: 2; 6: 40, 47.

Chapter 4: "The Athanasian Creed"

degree of knowledge of these mysteries, but only upon the presence or absence of *faith* in the doctrinal *substance* or the great truth contained in the statement. The form of expression is simply the outer hull to guard the kernel of truth against misapprehension and perversion. The strength and nourishment lies in the kernel, not in the hull. So it is the truth alone, as apprehended by faith, which can save, and can save a child and a barbarian as well as the ripest and profoundest scholar. But what is the central truth, the main object of saving Christian faith? It is undoubtedly the *one only true and living God, Father, Son, and Holy Ghost, who made us, who redeemed us, and who sanctifies us,* and the *one Lord Jesus Christ, very God and very man, the only Saviour.* This is the faith taught in the Protestant confessions, as well as in the three ancient Creeds; this faith is necessary for salvation, while its wilful rejection must exclude from it; this faith will remain the same to the end of time, however much its philosophical apprehension and logical expression may change and improve with the progressive march of theological science.[93]

It is in this sense, and in this only, that the ordination service in the new German Reformed Liturgy requires the assent of the candidate of the ministry to the Athanasian as well as the Apostles' and Nicene Creed. The question first gives the contents of these Creeds by way of comment: "Do you believe in one God the Father; and in one Lord Jesus Christ, the only begotten Son of the Father; and in one Holy Ghost, proceeding from the Father and the Son, and with the Father and the Son one God Almighty? And do you believe in one holy Catholic Church, in which is given one true Baptism for the remission of sins? *And do you* consent unto the *system of faith* set forth in the three Creeds, commonly called the Apostles' Creed, the Nicene Creed and the Athanasian Creed?[94] Here the "system of faith" to which the candidate is expected solemnly to declare his adherence, is just the belief in the triune God as stated before. But for the purpose of making it still more clear it might be better perhaps to substitute for the last *And do you,* the words, *Do you thus,* i.e., in the sense previously indicated.

---

93. Dr. Kling in his short article on the Athanasian Creed, in Herzog's *Encyclopedia*, takes the same view of the offensive clause: "*Das Vorurtheil,*" he says, "*wird schwinden in dem Maasse, als man sich darüber verständigen wird, dass es (die Athan. S.) uns nur angeht hinsichtlich seines wesenlischen dogmatischen Gehaltes, das heisst, insofern als es die Einheit der Gottheit in der dreifachen persönlichen Unterschiedenheit und umgekehrt, und die vollkommene Gottheit und vollkommene Menschheit des Einen untheilbaren Christus als unvermengt, unverwandelt und ungeschieden feststellt.*" . . . "*Darin liegt seine bleibende Bedeutung, und nie wird sich die christliche Kirche diesen Gehalt und unser Symbolum, insofern es denselben in sich trätgt, nehmen lassen, wie auch immer die positive theologische Vermittlung desselben sich ändern und vervollkommnen mag.*" [Trans. "This prejudice will disappear when one is in agreement that it (the Athanasian Creed) applies to us in terms of its essential dogmatic content, that it, to the extent that it determines the unity of the divine in its threefold personal diversity and its opposite, the total divinity and humanity of the one, undivided Christ as unmixed, unchanged, and unseparated. Therein lies its continuing significance, and the Christian Church will never allow this content and our Creed to be taken from it, to the extent that it bears this in it, however the positive theological transmission of the same changes and becomes more complete.]

94. Above on 238.

[V.] Value and Use

With this explanation of the damnatory clause we should think that no strong believer in the holy Trinity and the Incarnation of the Son of God as the fundamental doctrines of the Holy Scriptures, can justly deny the Athanasian Creed a great and permanent value, and object to its reception into the new Liturgy among the Primitive Forms, together with the Apostles' and the Nicene Creeds. This was not done without due consideration and precedent. Besides the formal recognition of it in several symbolical books of the Reformed Church, it has long had a place in the Anglican, and the Dutch Liturgies. It has also quite recently been embodied in the new hymn book and liturgy of the Reformed Church of Elberfeld, which is perhaps more strictly Reformed than any other congregation in Germany and Switzerland. This work, published in 1853, in addition to the Psalms and two hundred and forty-three well selected choice hymns, accompanied with the tunes, contains the Heidelberg Catechism, a number of prayers and short liturgical services, the three ancient Creeds, and also the doctrinal decisions of the Councils of Ephesus A. D. 431, and of Chalcedon A. D. 451.

It is not intended, of course, to place these Creeds on a par with the holy Scriptures in a Romanizing sense, or to weaken in the least the fundamental Protestant principle concerning the rule of faith. The authority of the Word of God is absolute, that of the Confessions of the Church is relative only and conditioned by their agreement with it; the former is, strictly speaking, the only rule of faith the norma normans fidei, the latter are only exponents of the true sense of the Bible and safeguards of sound doctrine, the norma normata doctrinae.[95]

Among these Confessions of faith the three Symbols of the ancient Church have always held, and should continue to hold, the highest place, because they are nearest the apostolic fountain; they really contain the fundamental articles of the Christian faith in the shortest and simplest form; they are ecumenical or universal, being received by all the branches of orthodox Christendom, and they form a link of union between the Church of the present with the Church of the past, up to the age of the confessors, martyrs and immediate disciples of the apostles. The most sacred associations of many centuries cluster around them; they are fraught with the piety, faith, hope, joy and spiritual experience of God's people of all generations and tongues. Why should the Athanasian Creed be banished from its former time-honored position, since it is only the legitimate completion of the Apostles' and Nicene Creeds, embodies, as we have seen, the purest results of the theology of the first five centuries, and gives the clearest and fullest expression to the Church's faith in the triune God and the divine-human Saviour of the world,—a faith so earnestly and emphatically re-confessed, as with one voice, by all the symbols of evangelical Christendom.

---

95. [Trans. "Norming norm of faith" and "normed norm of doctrine;" i.e., the first (the Word of God) is itself the norm, while the second (confessions) is a norm that is normed by the Word of God.]

Chapter 4: "The Athanasian Creed"

In addition to their doctrinal value the ancient Creeds have also from time immemorial been used for liturgical purposes. Here a proper distinction must be made.

The Apostles' Creed stands decidedly first on account of its simplicity for all practical and popular use. It alone, as already intimated, is properly adapted for catechetical instruction, for baptism and confirmation, and should also be more frequently confessed than any other in the regular service of the Lord's day, as the solemn utterance of the common congregation and a united act of worship, like singing and prayer.

The Nicene Creed, being already more artificially constructed and rising somewhat in its terminology above the ordinary popular comprehension, should be confined to communion or festival seasons, where it may take the place of the Apostles' Creed.

The Athanasian Symbol, finally, being still more theological and scientific in tone and expression, might be said and sung once a year, either as the new German Reformed Liturgy directs, on the last communion season, or what perhaps would be more appropriate, as the canticle for Trinity Sunday. The frequent use of it in the mediaeval Latin, and the Anglican Protestant Churches, is to be attributed in part to the former scarcity of hymns, now so happily supplied by our rich treasures of sacred poetry, and can, therefore, not to be taken as a precedent. The most solemn and impressive form of professing these Creeds in public worship is the chanting by the choir, either alone or in connection with the whole congregation properly trained for responsive liturgical worship.

Chapter 5

"Origin and Structure of the Creed" and "The Unity of the Apostles' Creed"

By John W. Nevin

Editors' Introduction

Nevin resigned from the faculty of the Mercersburg Seminary in 1851 and from the presidency of its sister school Marshall College in 1853 when it united with Franklin College in Lancaster, Pennsylvania, to become Franklin and Marshall College. Nevin moved to Lancaster in 1855. After serving on the college's faculty he was elected President of the recently united school in 1866. Meanwhile his former seminary colleague Philip Schaff had requested a leave of absence from the Mercersburg seminary in 1863 and moved to New York City where he spent the last thirty years of his life. His twenty-three year tenure on the faculty of Union Theological Seminary gave him much more visibility and celebrity, and during this period his scholarly output was both enormous and significant, although not in a uniquely "Mercersburg" way. With these changes James Hastings Nichols claims, "The creative period of the Mercersburg movement thus came to an end."[1] But, apparently, its influence did not abruptly cease.

Although his address changed, Nevin was not finished with his interest in the Apostles' Creed. Both Nevin and Schaff participated with other church leaders in developing liturgies which embodied the Mercersburg Theology, one of the lasting bequests to which the movement gave life. Another volume in this series will explore that phase of their labors.[2] Their liturgical efforts came to fruition in 1866 with the birth of the "Order of Worship" for the German Reformed Church. In the "Regular Service on the Lord's Day" the liturgy specified the use of the Apostle's Creed. Nevin's article "Theology of the New Liturgy" celebrated the place of the Creed in the newly formed liturgy and reemphasized its high value. He wrote:

> The Apostles' Creed thus is the deepest, and for that reason, most comprehensive of all Christian symbols. It lies at the foundation of all evangelical unity; it is the last basis and bond of comprehension in the conception of the Church. No sect refusing to stand on this basis can have any right to claim footing in the Gospel, or fellowship with the Apostles. All right theological thinking then, as

---

1. Nichols, *Romanticism in American Theology*, 308.
2. See also Maxwell, *Worship and Reformed Theology*, 185–322.

Chapter 5: "Origin and Structure of the Creed" and "The Unity of the Apostles' Creed"

well as all true evangelical believing, must start where this fundamental form of faith starts, and keep step with it at every point as far as it goes.[3]

It may have been the publication, circulation, and use of the "Order of Worship" and the prominent place of the Creed in it that prompted Nevin to publish two articles on the creed in *The Mercersburg Review* in 1869, neither of them breaking new ground, and both of which follow. They were written after Nevin became President of Franklin and Marshall College in Lancaster, a tenure that began in 1866. Given that rather late composition, they demonstrate strong continuities in his reflections about the Apostles' Creed.

The first article, which follows, reiterated basic positions he had staked out in his first series of three articles on the Creed in 1849. It deals with its title, origin, development, and form. Nevin again quoted Irenaeus, Tertullian, Origin, and Cyprian, early Christian thinkers whose writings reflect the content of the Creed. He stated that the Creed's use in eastern and western Christianity is well attested. Among Protestants including Lutherans, Reformed, Anglicans, it is accepted as a genuine statement of faith. So, he concludes, this Creed "lies at the foundation of Christianity in all centuries and through all times" and he repeated the words of the quote above from his article on the "Theology of the New Liturgy."

The second article complemented the first. Nevin affirmed again that "... no scheme of Christian truth or doctrine can be regarded as valid for faith at all, which has not started originally from this [Creed's] form of sound words, and which does not continue rooted and grounded in it to the last." There are two major points he wished to maintain. (1) He contended that the Creed is "organic."[4] It grows from a "single principle" so that its various parts compose one authentic statement of faith. The articles of the Creed are inseparably interrelated. (2) Those are seriously mistaken who believe that the Creed is antiquated and that a better formula of Christian belief is necessary. This is yet another attack he issued on the Puritan (Congregationalist) attempt to devise new "covenants," statements of faith, which may include some of the theological concepts found in the Creed, but also incorporate ideas which are not found in it, such as the inspiration and authority of Scripture.[5] Nevin's endeavors to defend the Creed from such views were articulated in his articles "Puritanism and the Creed" and the "Anti-Creed Heresy" the texts of which are found earlier in this volume.

---

3. Nevin, "Theology of the New Liturgy," in *MR* 14 (Jan., 1867) 34.

4. [As we have seen, "organic" concepts and metaphors were an essential component of the conceptuality of Romanticism.]

5. K. L. Spruner, "Covenant Theology." In Daniel G. Reid, et al., *Dictionary of Christianity in America*, 322–24.

Origin and Structure of the Apostles' Creed[1]

The title it bears does not mean that the symbol, as we now have it, was the work originally of the Apostles themselves. It has been indeed a very widely prevalent opinion in the Church, resting in long tradition, that it originated in this way.[2] Rufinus, a church father of the fourth century, speaks of it as a common belief in that age, handed down from earlier times, that the Apostles, before separating to their different fields of labor, met together in Jerusalem, and under the guidance of the Holy Ghost framed and adopted this compend, to be received by the infant churches everywhere as a common bond of faith.[3] The term symbol[4] was supposed to favor, as it probably at first suggested, this imagination, by indicating in its Greek etymology a joint composition made up of different parts contributed from different quarters; in conformity with which view then it was sometimes held also, that each Apostle had contributed separately a distinct article or clause to the work which was thus brought to pass. But this whole opinion is easily shown to be false.[5] No such Apostolic rule is spoken of in the New Testament. None of the church fathers before Rufinus,[6] Greek or Latin, make any mention of the tradition to which he refers; and in all their controversies and discussions, we meet with no appeal whatever to any such single fixed form of words, as of established authority from the time of the Apostles. On the contrary, the way in which they express themselves in regard to the subject, shows clearly that no fixed form of this sort was in existence. They refer frequently to a Christian rule or

---

1. [J. W. Nevin, *The Mercersburg Review* 16 (January 1869) 148–56.]

2. [See Bingham, III:500–511.]

3. [See Bingham, III:500–502.]

4. [Nevin uses the traditional term "symbol" as interchangeable with "creed." For more on the evolution of this usage see J. N. D. Kelly, *Early Christian Creeds*, 52–61.]

5. [See Bingham, III:502–4.]

6. [Tyrannius Rufinus of Aquileia (c.345–411), monk, translator, and early historian of the church, composed a commentary on the Apostles' Creed and provided a fourth-century text and commentary on the Creed employed at Aquileia and Rome. He is credited with the theory that the Creed was the collaborative creation of Jesus' twelve apostles. Rufinus, *A Commentary on the Apostles' Creed*. Later scholarship discredited Rufinus' view.]

canon of faith,[7] and occasionally give us the sum of its contents; but this always with such free variation, as plainly implies that the rule was regarded as standing in the substance of what it taught, rather than in any particular form of expression. Nay, the testimony of Rufinus himself is conclusive in regard to this point. He affirms expressly, that the form was not the same precisely in all the churches; additions were made to it in some cases, in opposition to particular new phases of heresy. What the title of the symbol means then is, not that it was composed by the Apostles, but that it contains, in a form universally approved by the Church, the sum and substance of what the Apostles taught, the fundamental rule and normative scheme of the Christian faith, as this had been established by them and handed down from the beginning.

The conception of such a normative scheme does not require continued sameness of words for its representation, but only sameness of substance and fact. Even the tradition mentioned by Rufinus, which in the fourth century referred the authorship of the creed to the Apostles, must be taken to have understood this more of its substantive matter than of the precise form of words in which it was uttered. For Rufinus does not pretend to restrict this honor to any one form of the general creed then in use; but takes it for granted rather, that all the churches enjoyed in this respect the same advantage, as being alike in possession of the faith received from the Apostles. No difficulty was felt among the churches in recognizing the identity of their faith, through all the variations that were allowed in the form of its expression.[8] It was known, that the general symbol admitted an utterance more or less free, as circumstances might require; that particular clauses had been brought into it with the progress of time, which did not belong to it in the beginning; and that it was not the same precisely at all points, in any two leading provinces of the Church. And yet it was felt none the less surely for all this, that the Church had but one creed, and that this was of truly Apostolical origin and force. Its unity stood in its substance. Its stability was not in the outward letter, so much as in the inward spirit.[9] It was written and preserved, as Jerome tells us, not on parchment, but on the fleshy tables of the heart.[10]

We may easily see in this way, how the symbol, as we now have it, may be said to refer itself back, through all its early changes and variations, to the very age of the Apostles, and to carry in itself as derived immediately from them what was the one

---

7. [A rule of faith (*regula fidei*) was a brief statement of the essence of Christian faith which was employed in the early church to set forth what were perceived to be orthodox teachings as opposed to heretical beliefs. Although there were varieties of these rules of faith, they represented common basic content and were the predecessors of creeds, which were more commonplace public statements of belief often used in conjunction with baptisms.]

8. [See Bingham, III:504–50.]

9. [The contrast of outward letter and inward spirit was typical of Herder and Neander, both of whom influenced Nevin.]

10. [Jerome is quoted in Bingham, III:510. Nevin's earlier attribution of Jerome's letter 61 to Pammachius on p. 39 is incorrect. Letter 61 is addressed to Vigilantius. The correct letter is to Pammachius "Against John of Jerusalem," Section 28.]

ORIGIN AND STRUCTURE OF THE APOSTLES' CREED

unvarying faith of the Church in following ages. It lies in the nature of the case, that the Christian profession must have involved some common rule of faith from the beginning; and we know from the New Testament, that this stood in the acknowledgment of the mystery of the Incarnation, the coming of Christ in the flesh. Christianity roots itself, both as doctrine and life, in that fact. Peter's memorable confession (Matt. xvi. 16. John vi. 68, 69) becomes thus the germ or principle of all right confessional belief: carrying in itself, we may say, the universal truth and power of the Gospel. The form of baptism, as prescribed by our Saviour Himself, is only an enlarged utterance of the same faith. The Holy Trinity is revealed only in and through Christ; to confess Him, is to confess at the same time the Father and the Holy Ghost; and this threefold confession gives us at once the outline and scheme of the entire creed. How far it may have become usual, before the death of the Apostles, to take into the scheme formally, the secondary clauses of the confession as it now stands, cannot be clearly determined. But no one familiar with the early history of Christianity can well fail to see, that this must have been done at least to some considerable extent; and there is good reason to believe, that early in the second century, if not before, nearly all the particulars now embraced in it were found more or less in current use.

Still, as already said, this current use remained irregular and free. There was one creed, but various forms of giving it utterance. These variations were not felt to trench at all upon the unity of the general tradition or rule; and this is frequently appealed to accordingly, by the early writers, as being of acknowledged and easily intelligible authority. Irenaeus speaks of such an "immovable rule of faith,"[11] and describes it as proclaiming the same particulars that are found in the later creeds; and he makes it to be, at the same time, of Apostolical and universal authority; a tradition handed down from the Apostles and their disciples, which was kept sacredly by the Church diffused throughout the whole world. "The dialects in which it is uttered," he says, "are different; but the tradition is in force the same. The churches founded in Germany have no other faith and doctrine; nor those in Spain; nor those among the Celts; nor those in the East; nor those in Egypt; nor those in Libya; nor those of more central situation; but as the sun, God's workmanship, is over the whole globe one and the same, so also the evangelical truth shines everywhere and illuminates all who are willing to come to its light."[12] Tertullian appeals frequently in the same free way, to the Christian rule of faith, and recapitulates several times its general contents, always in harmony with the sum of it as given by Irenaeus, for the purpose of confuting and confounding the heretics of his own time. His recapitulations are indeed always different, sometimes more and sometimes less full, showing that the Creed was life more than mere word; but they assume throughout, nevertheless, the clear identity belonging to it as a single apostolical tradition. "Regula fidei," he tells us, "uno omnino est, sola immobilis et

---

11. [Irenaeus, as quoted in Bingham, III:512. See also Tertullian, *de virginibus velandis*, Chapter 1.]
12. Irenaeus, *Adversus Haereses*, S. L. Greenslade, ed., *Early Latin Theology*, V:66.

Chapter 5: "Origin and Structure of the Creed" and "The Unity of the Apostles' Creed"

irreformabilis."[13] The amount of it is always: One God, the Almighty Maker of the world; His Son, Jesus Christ, born of the Virgin Mary, constituted Messiah, crucified under Pontius Pilate, raised the third day, exalted to heaven, and set at the right hand of God, from whence He shall come to judge the quick and the dead; the Holy Ghost sent forth vicariously, according to His promise, to sanctify those that believe in his name; the resurrection of the flesh, the damnation of the wicked, and the reception of the righteous into eternal life and the blessedness of heaven. This rule, he says, instituted by Christ, allows no questions, other than such as spring from heresy and go to make heretics; it is older than all heresies; their novelty, as exposed by it, serves to establish its antiquity; to know nothing beyond it, is to know all that is necessary.[14] Origen, in like manner gives a summary statement of the heads of Christian doctrine, "as plainly received by apostolical tradition," which corresponds in substance with the same rule.[15] From Cyprian again we learn, that the whole Creed, nearly as we have it now was made use of in Africa, in his time, as a rule of faith derived from the Apostles, in connection with the service of baptism.[16] These private testimonies show the presence everywhere in the early Church of an evangelical tradition, agreeing in its general contents with the Creed as it now stands, and accepted as of strictly apostolic origin and weight. They show also, that this tradition, though always of the same general type, was not regarded as a slavish form of words, but as a free doctrine rather which might be uttered in various ways. Cyprian gives us a glimpse into the general African formula, as it was everywhere of force in the first part of the third century. Other sections of the Church had similar standing forms; some more full perhaps than others; those of the East different from those of the West; but all handed down from the earliest time, and palpably expressing one and the same faith, as they belonged also to one and the same baptism. In the fourth century, these public formularies come more distinctly into view; and now it was that a sort of central dignity and preeminence, among the symbols of the Western Church, began to be claimed and allowed in favor of the form which had long been in use at Rome. Gradually this authority became more and more widely established; other local and provincial forms fell quietly into neglect; until finally the Roman symbol, in the fifth and sixth centuries, worked its way into universal use; and has thus come down to us, with the veneration of the whole Christian world, as the standard version or edition of the ancient rule of faith, the best and truest representation of the fundamental realities of the Christian religion, the proper "Apostles' Creed."

Thus it is that this form of sound words lies at the foundation of Christianity in all centuries and through all times. No confessionalism can be truly Christian, which

---

13. Tertullian. [Trans."The rule of faith is entirely one, uniquely fixed and unalterable." This was quoted in Bingham, III:516].

14. [For Tertullian, see Bingham, III:517.]

15. [For Origen, see Bingham, III:514.]

16. [For Cyprian, see Bungham, III:518.]

does not start from this confession as its original root and source. Here, as on a common basis, all Churches rest, whether Oriental [Eastern] or Western, Roman Catholic or Protestant. The object of the Reformation was to remove the rubbish which threatened to smother the life of the ancient faith, not by any means to set aside this faith itself. Both divisions of the Protestant Church, accordingly, the Lutheran and the Reformed, joined in acknowledging the ancient oecumenical symbols, and especially the root of all symbols as found in the Apostles' Creed. In the Lutheran Church, the three primary Creeds (Apostolical, Nicene and Athanasian) are made to precede the Augsburg Confession, in the Form of Concord;[17] to show, says Walch, "that Lutherans embrace not a new doctrine, but such as is old and apostolical, and profess thus the truly catholic faith."[18] The Reformed Church here was of one mind with the Lutheran. Thus in Calvin's Catechism the first section treats of *Faith;* which is said to have the sum of its contents in the "formula of confession held in common by all Christians, commonly called the Apostles' Creed, and always received from the beginning among the pious, as being either derived from the mouth of the Apostles or faithfully collected from their writings."[19] So in the Heidelberg Catechism the "articles of our catholic, undoubted Christian faith," as comprised in the same symbol, are made to underlie the whole doctrine of salvation. The Gallican,[20] Belgic,[21] and Helvetic[22] Confessions, as well as the Thirty-Nine Articles of the Church of England,[23] distinctly acknowledge the three Creeds, Apostolic, Nicene and Athanasian, as of universal obligation for the faith of Christians.

With the outward history of the Apostles' Creed corresponds in full its inward constitution. It agrees throughout with the actual objective movement of the Christian salvation, and represents the form it must necessarily have, as apprehended by faith, for the Christian consciousness. It is not the product of reflection, employed with the doctrinal statements of the Bible; it is drawn rather from the direct contemplation of Christ, the living principle of the Gospel, and is the first utterance of what the faith of the Church saw in Him from the beginning, as being the brightness of the Father's glory and the revelation of all grace and truth for the world. Apprehended in this manner, Christ and Christianity were no doctrine simply, no theory for the understanding, but a grand act or drama of the most real kind, by which God was seen entering the world through the mystery of the Incarnation, and carrying out the

---

17. [Schaff, *The Creeds of Christendom*, III:94–95.]

18. Johann Georg Walch, *Introduction to the Lutheran Confessions.* [*Historische und theologische Einleitung in die Religions-Streitigkeiten der Evangelische-Lutherische Kirche*, 5 volumes (Jena: Johann Meyers Wittwe, 1733–39), 1031.]

19. [John Calvin, "Catechism of the Church of Geneva," 22: 92.]

20. [Schaff, *The Creeds of Christendom*, III:362]

21. [Schaff, *The Creeds of Christendom*, III:393.]

22. [Schaff, *The Creeds of Christendom*, III:277.]

23. [Schaff, *The Creeds of Christendom*, III:492.]

work of man's redemption in an objective, historical way, reaching through all time. Thus objective and real, the Christian salvation necessarily determined its own form; and this then determined necessarily also the form of its believing apprehension in the mind of the Church. The fundamental consciousness of the Church here must be in harmony with its object, the fundamental movement of Christianity itself; otherwise it would be no faith at all, but fancy only or opinion. The early creeds then which were in truth as we have seen but one creed (authentically fixed for general use at last in what we now call the Apostles' Creed), as the expression of this consciousness, could have only one general order and shape, answerable to what was thus apprehended as real in the Christian mystery itself. The organization of the Creed, in this view, is not a matter of indifference; as though it were the result of accident or mere subjective schematization; it is ruled by the actual movement of its object, the historical manifestation of the Holy Trinity in Christ, and the historical consequences of his Incarnation in his own Person and in the Church, on to the resurrection of the dead and the life everlasting. The form of the symbol thus is just as necessary as its matter.[24] Christianity fundamentally is this array of facts, and this order of facts, and no other. In the Creed we have not only the primordial constituents of the Christian faith, but the only construction of them also which can be regarded as true. Those who dream of other possible better summaries of the "first principles" of Christianity, either in the way of different matter or in the way of different form, only show that they have not entered properly into the sense of the Creed, and that faith for them is not the same thing it was held to be in the early Church. As there is but one Christianity (one historical movement of the Mystery of Godliness) objectively, so there can be but one true way of apprehending it by faith; and that way we have presented to us in the Apostles' Creed.

It lies in the very conception of the symbol as now given, that it moves throughout in the sphere of faith. So much is signified at once by its name. It has to do from beginning to end with things, which are real and true only in the supernatural order of life that has been introduced into the world by Jesus Christ. All its articles are mysteries; not to be certified or measured by the natural understanding of men; not to be settled in the first place by empirical observation or logical proof; but authenticating themselves rather to the Christian consciousness in an *a priori* way, as necessary deductions from the primary fact of Christianity, the actual coming of Christ in the flesh. The assumption is, in this view, that they may be believed, nay *must* be believed if Christ is true, even where there is no power to understand or explain fully what they mean. To believe in Christ necessarily involves the belief of all that His advent is represented as drawing after it in the Creed; the consciousness of the Church, exercised with the problem of what it felt itself to possess in His Person, found itself shut up from the beginning, we may say, to each successive point, as the necessary expression

---

24. [The congruence of form and content in a text, both flowing from a common spirit, was a pervasive theme in Romantic aesthetic theory.]

of what was comprehended in its faith, over against all surrounding infidelity and heresy. And so still; we cannot break off the onward flow of this confession at any one point, so as to hold a portion of it only without regard to what comes after. All its parts are organically bound together. They represent the movement of one and the same fact. We must believe all or nothing.

We have a right to say thus, that the Apostles' Creed is the deepest, and for that reason the most comprehensive also of all Christian symbols or confessions of faith. It lies at the foundation of all evangelical unity, and forms in this way the last basis and bond of common comprehension in the general conception of the Church. No religious community refusing to stand on this basis, no religious teacher pretending to construct Christianity on any other foundation, can have any right to claim footing in the Gospel, or fellowship with the Apostles.

Works on the subject: Lord Peter King, *History of the Apostles' Creed, with Critical Observations,* 5th edition, Latin trans. by Adam Olearius, (London, 1738); Jan Gerhard Voss, *De Tribus Symbolis Dissertatione.* (Amsterdam, 1701); Hermann Witsius, *Dissertation on what is commonly called the Apostles' Creed*, trans. Donald Frazer, (Edinburgh, 1823); Bishop John Pearson, *An Exposition of the Creed* (London, 1715); Johann Adam Möhler, *Einheit der Kirche, oder Princip des Katholicismus im Geiste der Kirchenväter der ersten 3 Jahrhunderte*, (Tübingen, 1825); Andreas Gottlob Rudelbach, *die Bedeutung des Apostolischen Symbolums*, (Leipzig, 1844); J. Stockmeier, *über Entstehung des Apostolischen Symbolums*, (1846); Peter Meyers, *De Symboli Apostolici*, (Trier, 1849); W. Wigan Harvey, *The History and Theology of the Three Creeds*, 2 vols., (London, 1855). [Editorial changes have been made to this bibliography to provide additional information and clarity.]

The Unity of the Apostles' Creed[1]

What has been said of the origin and structure of the Apostles' Creed, in our article in the January number, has already brought to view, in some measure, its organic unity and its fundamental authority for the Christian world. It is not by chance, or through the arbitrary outward ordering of men in any way, as we have seen, that either the matter or form of the symbol established themselves, they have found acknowledgment as the one only sure basis of Christian belief in the universal Church of all ages. The Creed could not have carried with it historically this universal force, for the Oriental [Eastern], Roman Catholic, and Protestant worlds, if it were not in its own nature, and in its own essential constitution, of true ecumenical and fundamental character for Christianity itself; in such sort, and to such extent, that no scheme of Christian truth or doctrine can be regarded as valid for faith at all, which has not started originally from this form of sound words, and which does not continue rooted and grounded in it to the last.

The unity of the Creed, we say, is organic. It is so, both as to its matter and as to its form. The different articles of which it consists grow forth from a single principle; and the force of this principle reaches into all its articles, determining their existence, and imparting to them severally all their significance and truth. Each article is what it is as an object of faith, only through its relation to the general root out of which all grow; while the root also is what it is as an object of faith, only through its relation in like manner to what thus proceeds from it in the way of necessary derivation and growth; its articles make up a single whole. This oneness of matter, however, involves at the same time necessarily oneness of form also. Viewed as an organic whole, in other words, the articles, or parts of which the symbol is composed, are not only derived from a common principle or root, but they are so derived from this that their relation to it serves to fix and determine, at the same time, their relation also to one another; so that as objects of faith, they can be apprehended truly only in the order in which they are here made to challenge faith, and in no other order. This does not mean, of course, that each article must always be distinctly expressed, to give us a valid Christian confession. We have seen already that there was what may be called a

---

1. [J. W. Nevin, *The Mercersburg Review* 16 (April 1869) 313–17.]

historical development of the articles of the Creed in part, in the beginning; and it is quite possible still to make a good confession, that shall not go beyond the acknowledgment of the Holy Trinity, as we are bound to it in our baptism, or that shall be no more even than St. Peter's memorable act of faith, *Thou art the Christ, the Son of the living God* [Matt 16:16]. But the Creed in any abbreviated form is always potentially the Creed in its full form—the presence from the first implicitly of all that this is found to comprise at the last explicitly; and what we mean to say now is, that, when it comes to such explication and full utterance, all the articles of the Creed have not only their existence, but their position and place also, necessarily determined by the constitution of the symbol itself.[2] They necessitate and condition one another in the order in which they are actually put together, and allow no other.

This necessary organization of the Creed, we have already seen, proceeds from its correspondence with the actual movement of the Christian salvation, as it takes its rise in the mystery of the Incarnation, and runs its course onward to the life everlasting. It is the simple response of faith to what is thus comprehended objectively in the coming of Christ in the flesh—the true historical gospel ("good tidings of great joy") [Nah 1:15; Luke 2:10] carried out to its consequences and results. Only as answering in this way to the actual order of the gospel, may we conceive of faith here as being faith at all, and not simply fancy or speculation. The Creed is, by its very conception, the primitive and deepest (and therefore most necessary and universal) conciousness of the Christian Church, moving in full harmony with the fundamental movement of Christianity itself. As such it is the force for all ages. It can never be superseded by any other form of supposed sound words. There can be not getting back of it, or aside to it, to the apprehension of what Christianity is, in any different way. No scheme of Christian belief, not construction of Christian doctrine, can deserve to be considered sound or safe, which does not grow forth organically from the radical organization of Christianity as we have it in the Apostles' Creed.

They labor under a grand mistake, then, who imagine that it can ever be possible to form a better basis or platform of faith for the Christian world, than that which is comprised in this ancient symbol. There is, we know, a large amount of religious thinking at the present time, in this country particularly, which is of a different mind. Much of what claims to be the best form of Protestantism among us—Protestantism in its most enlightened and most evangelical character—considers itself to have outgrown entirely the leading-strings of the Creed, and to be more than equal to the task of providing in short order, at any time, a decidedly better scheme of fundamental Christian doctrine. In the view of this Puritanic school, the Apostles' Creed is entitled to a certain sort of traditional respect, or account of the honor with which it has been regarded in past ages; but it belongs properly to those past ages, we are told, and not to our age; it is now ecclesiastically dead, if not absolutely buried, and any attempt to set

---

2. [As we have seen, the theme that the subsequent development of a plant is implicit in its roots or seed is a pervasive trope in Romanticism.]

it up again as a living rule of faith can deserve only to be looked upon with pity and contempt. Such modern religionists can see nothing particularly worthy of admiration in the Creed, but much rather to be dissatisfied with. What of fundamental truth there is in it, they are ready to tell us, might be expressed in better terms; some of its articles are unscriptural, and involve actual error; material points of faith are not found in it at all; so that altogether, taken in its own original sense and without any sort of mental qualification, it seems to them to be anything but such a summary of the first truths of religion as the best interests of religion demand. They feel it to be at once crude in its matter and poor in its form, and look upon it as being a witness and proof of the spiritual weakness of the period to which it owes its birth, for more than an argument of its spiritual strength.

The fundamental articles of Christianity, for those who think in this way, group themselves always into a form very different from the Creed, which is felt by them at the same time to be far more logically methodical and complete. Where the scheme tends to be evangelical, in the technical sense of the term, it will be found to run, for example, in some such order as the following. Beginning with the existence and the leading attributes of God, we shall have in the next place the mystery of the Holy Trinity; then the inspiration and divine authority of the Bible (or it may be the Bible first, as the principle of all religion, and then the Trinity[3]); next the fact of the fall, and the state of sin and misery to which it has reduced our ruined race; then possibly, the decree of election, underlying the whole plan of redemption as in the Westminster Confession (or with a more liberal construction this can be left out); next the incarnation and the union of the two natures in Christ's Person; then the atonement, wrought by His death upon the cross, and followed by His resurrection from the dead; then the necessity of repentance and faith; then the doctrines of regeneration, justification and sanctification; all ending, finally, with the resurrection of the dead, the general judgment at the end of the world, the eternal blessedness of the righteous, and the going away of the wicked into everlasting damnation. Of the sacraments, baptism and the Lord's Supper, mention may be made possibly somewhere in the system; but not in a way to make them essential account in the constitution of the Christian salvation; while the article of the Church, in all probability, will be allowed to pass without any notice whatever.

Conventional platforms of faith, more or less in this form, have become common in modern times. Congregational Churches in particular, of the Puritanic way of thinking, are accustomed to form in some such style for themselves doctrinal "covenants" as they are called, to which all are required to assent and agree, who join themselves to their communion; this being especially what is to be considered their profession of the Christian faith. And there is not a single one of these societies probably, which is not fully persuaded that it has in its own particular platform, thus constructed, a far more exhaustive and efficient summary of the first truths of Christianity, and a

---

3. [This was, in fact, the order of topics in the Westminster Confession.]

far more sure and firm basis of theological orthodoxy, than any that has ever been supposed to be comprised in the Apostles' Creed. No one of them would be willing at all to substitute the Creed for its church covenant. To do so, would be felt to involve some want of sympathy with the full and proper sense of the Gospel, and could only be regarded in this view as a falling away from a higher to a lower faith. It must seem at once both lax and unevangelical.

But let no one be deceived by any pretensions of this sort. We have platforms of Christian doctrine different from the Creed, which for certain purposes are important and worthy of respect; but we never can have any, we repeat, that may deserve to come in the room of the Creed, or that may be entitled to confidence as original compends of Gospel truth on the outside of the Creed. The best of these modern platforms is but a synopsis of what are taken to be the chief articles of the Christian religion, considered in the way of outward reflection; it is the work of the understanding, rather than the direct product of faith; and as such can never be made to stand for the Creed, without derangement and damage to the whole of Christianity.

Bibliography

Appel, Theodore. *The Life and Work of John Williamson Nevin.* Philadelphia: Reformed Church Publication House, 1889.

Athanasius, *Opera sancti patris nostri Athanasii.* Vols. 1-2. Heidelberg, 1600-1.

———. "Epistle to All Bishops Everywhere." In *Historical Tracts of S. Athanasius,* translated by Miles Atkinson, 1-12. Oxford: John Henry Parker, 1843.

Aubert, Annette. *The German Roots of Nineteenth-Century American Theology.* Oxford: Oxford University Press, 2013.

Augustine. *Against the Epistle of Manichaeus, Called Fundamental.* Translated by Richard Stothert. Savage MN: Lighthouse, 2018.

———. *Confessions.* Edited by Albert C. Outler. *The Library of Christian Classics.* London: SCM Press, 1955.

———. *De Fide et Symbolo.* Edited by Joseph Zyka. Prague: F. Tempsky, 1900.

———. *Iohannis Evangelium tractatus.* In *Patrologia Latina,* edited by J. P. Migne, vol. 35. Paris: Imprimerie Catholique, 1845.

———. *Sancti Aurelii Augustini De Trinitate.* Edited by William John Mountain and Françoise Glorie. Turnhout, Belgium: Brepols, 1968.

———. *St. Augustine: Homilies on the Gospel of John. Homilies on the First Epistle of John. Soliloques.* Translated by John Gibb and James Innes. In *Nicene and Post-Nicene Fathers,* vol. 7, edited by Philip Schaff. Edinburgh: T. & T. Clark, 1888.

———. "Tractate 29:6 (John 7:14-18)." In *Tractates on the Gospel of John, 28-54,* edited by John Rettig, 14-21. Washington, D.C.: Catholic University of America Press, 1993.

Baronius. *Institutes of Ecclesiastical History.* New York, 1839.

Barrett, Lee. "The Distinctive World of Mercersburg Theology: Yearning for God or Relief from Sin?" *Theology Today* 71, no. 4 (2015) 381-92.

Basil of Caesarea. *Sancti patris nostri Basilii Caesareae Cappadociae, Opera Omnia quae Exstant.* Edited by J. Garnier. Paris: Gaume, 1839.

———. *A Treatise on Baptism.* Edited by Francis Patrick Kenrick. Philadelphia: M. Fithian, 1843.

Bellarmine, Robert. *Explication du Symbole des Apôtres. Catechismes Philosophiques, Polémiques, &c.* 2 vols. Paris: M. L. Migne, 1842.

Berger, Peter and Thomas Luckmann. *The Social Construction of Reality.* Garden City: Anchor Books, 1966.

Bingham, Joseph. *The Antiquities of the Christian Church.* In *The Works of Rev. Joseph Bingham, M.A.* Vol. III. Edited by Rev. R. Bingham. 2nd ed. Oxford: Oxford University Press, 1855.

Calvin, John. "Catechism of the Church of Geneva." *Calvin: Theological Treatises*. Edited by J. K. S. Reid. Philadelphia: Westminster, 1954.

———. *Institutes of the Christian Religion*. Edited by John T. McNeill. Translated by Ford Lewis Battles. 2 vols. Philadelphia: Westminster, 1960.

Catharinus, Ambrosius. *Apologia pro veritate catholicæ et apostolicæ fidei ac doctrinæ, adversus impia ac pestifera Martini Lutheri dogmata*. Wittenberg, 1546

Cave, William. *Scriptorum Ecclesiasticorum Historia Literaria*. London, 1688.

Chrysostom, John. *Sancti Patris nostri Joannis Chrysostomi, Opera Omnia quae Exstant*. Edited by Bernard de Montfaucon. Paris, 1718–38.

———. *The Homilies of St. John Chrysostom*. Edited by John Henry Parker. Oxford: J.G.F. and J. Rivington, 1842.

Coleridge, Samuel Taylor. *Aids to Reflection in the Formation of a Manly Character*. London: Taylor and Hessey, 1825.

Comber, Thomas. *Companion to the Temple*. Oxford: Oxford University Press, 1841.

Conser, Walter H. *Church and Confession: Conservative Theologians in Germany, England, and America, 1815–1866*. Macon, GA: Mercer University Press, 1984.

F. L. Cross and E A.. Livingstone, eds. *The Oxford Dictionary of the Christian Church*. Third ed. Oxford: Oxford University Press, 2005.

Cyprian. *Sancti Caecilii Cypriani Opera*. Edited by Bishop John Fell. Oxford, 1682.

DeBie, Linden J., ed. *Coena Mystica: Debating Reformed Eucharistic Theology*. By John Williamson Nevin and Charles Hodge. Edited by Linden J. DeBie. Mercersburg Theology Study Series, vol. 2. Eugene, OR: Wipf & Stock, 2013.

———. *Speculative Theology and Common—Sense Religion: Mercersburg and the Conservative Roots of American Religion*. Eugene, OR: Pickwick, 2008.

DeLuis, P. "Toledo." In *Encyclopedia of the Early Church*, edited by Angelo Di Bernardino, II:844–45. 2 vols. Oxford: Oxford, 1992.

Dennis, John. *The Athanasian Creed Examined*. 2nd ed. Exeter: E. Woolmer, 1815.

de Wette, Wilhelm Martin Leberecht. *Commentar über die Psalmen*. 3rd ed. Heidelberg: J.C.B. Mohr, 1829.

DiPuccio, William. *The Interior Sense of Scripture: The Sacred Hermeneutics of John W. Nevin*. Macon, GA: Mercer University Press, 1998.

———. "Nevin and Coleridge." *New Mercersburg Review* , no. 17 (1995) 59–63.

Ebrard, Johannes Heinrich August. *Christliche Dogmatik*. Königsberg: August Wilhelm Unzer, 1851.

Erb, William H. *Dr. Nevin's Theology, Based on Manuscript Class-Room Lectures*. Reading, PA: I. M. Beaver, 1913.

Erlington, Charles Richard. "The Life of Ussher." In *The Whole Works of the Most Rev. James Ussher, D.D.*, edited by Charles Richard Elrington, I:1–12. Hodges and Smith: Dublin, 1847.

Evans, William B. *A Companion to the Mercersburg Theology*. Eugene, OR: Cascade Books, 2019.

———. "General Introduction." In *The Incarnate Word: Selected Writings on Christology*. By John Williamson Nevin, Philip Schaff, and Daniel Gans. Edited by William B. Evans. Mercersburg Theology Study Series, vol. 4. Eugene, OR: Wipf & Stock, 2014.

———. *Imputation and Impartation: Union with Christ in American Reformed Theology*. Eugene: OR: Wipf & Stock, 2008.

Ferguson, Everett, ed. *Encyclopedia of Early Christianity*. 2nd. ed. New York: Routledge, 2013.

Gibbon, Edward. *The Decline and Fall of the Roman Empire*. London: Thomas McLean, 1825.
Good, James. *History of the Reformed Church in the US in the Nineteenth Century*. New York: Board of Publication of the Reformed Church in America, 1911.
Gieseler, Johann Karl Ludwig. *Lehrbuch der Kirchengeschichte*. 6 vols. Bonn: Adolph Marcus, 1824–57. English translation by Samuel Davidson as *A Compendium of Ecclesiastical History*, 2 vols. New York: Harper & Brothers, 1849.
Greenslade, Stanley Lawrence, ed. *Early Latin Theology*. Louisville: Westminster, 1956.
Gregory Nyssa. *Contra Eunomium*. Coloniae, 1617.
Hart, D. G. *John Williamson Nevin: High Church Calvinist*. Phillipsburg, NJ: P&R, 2005.
Harvey, William Wigan. *History and Theology of the Three Creeds*. 2 vols. London, 1854.
Hase, Karl August (von). *Evangelische Protestantische Dogmatik*. 4th ed. Leipzig: Breitkopf and Härtel, 1850.
———. *Hutterus Redivivus, oder Dogmatik der Evangelisch Lutherischen Kirche*. Leipzig: Johann Friedrich Leich, 1833.
———, ed. *Libri symbolici Ecclesiae evangelicae, sive, Concordia*. 2nd ed. Leipzig. 1837.
Hatch, Nathan O. *The Democratization of American Christianity*. New Haven, CT: Yale University Press, 1989.
Heidegger (Heideggeri), Johann Heinrich. *Dissertation de Symbolo Apostolico*. 2 vols. Zurich, 1680.
Herder, Johann Gottfried (von). *Ideen zur Philosophie der Geschichte der Menschheit*. 3rd ed. Leipzig: Johann Friedrich Hartknoch, 1828.
———. *The Spirit of Hebrew Poetry*. Translated by James Marsh. 2 vols. Burlington: Edward Smith, 1833.
———. *Treatise on the Origin of Language (1772)*. Translated by Michael N. Forster. Cambridge: Cambridge University Press, 2002.
Hilary of Poitiers. *De Trinitate*. Edited by P. Coustant. Paris, 1693.
Hincmar, *Hincmarii rehemensis archiepiscopi,Opera omnia*. Edited by J. P. Migne. Paris, 1852.
Hodge, Archibald Alexander. *The Life of Charles Hodge*. New York: Scribner's Sons, 1880.
Hodge, Charles. "The Idea of the Church." *Biblical Repertory and Princeton Review*, vol. 25, no. 2 (1853) 249–90.
———. Review of *The Inspiration of Holy Scripture, Its Nature and Proof*," by Henry Lee. In *The Biblical Repertory and Princeton Review*, vol. 29, no. 4, (Oct., 1857) 660–698.
———. *Systematic Theology*. 3 vols. New York: Scribner, Armstrong, 1873.
Holifield, E. Brooks. *Theology in America: Thought from the Age of the Puritans to the Civil War*. New Haven, CT: Yale University Press, 2003.
Hopkins, Samuel. *The System of Doctrines*. 2 vols. Boston: I. Thomas and E. Andrews, 1793.
———. *Two Discourses*. Bennington, VT: Anthony Haswell, 1793.
Irenaeus. *Adversus Haereses*. In *Patrologia Graeca*, edited by J. P. Migne, vol. 7. Paris: Imprimerie Catholique, 1857.
Jerome. *Operum Omnium divi Eusebii Heironymi*. Edited by Desiderius Erasmus. Basel: Johann Froben, 1516.
Justin Martyr. "First Apology." In *Early Christian Fathers,* translated by Edward Rochie Hardy and edited by Cyril C. Richardson, 225–88. Philadelphia: Westminster, 1953.
———. *Justinii Philosophi et Martyris Opera*. Edited by J. C. T. Otto. Jena, 1842–43.
Kelly, J. N. D. *Early Christian Creeds*. New York: Continuum, 2006.
Kimmel, Ernst Julius. *Monumenta Fidei Ecclesiae Orientalis*. Jena: Mauke, 1850.

King, Sir Peter. *The History of the Apostles Creed: With Critical Observations on its Several Articles*. London, 1703.

———. *History of the Apostles' Creed, with Critical Observations*. 5th edition. Latin translation by Adam Olearius. London, 1738.

———. *An Inquiry into the Constitution, Discipline, Unity and Worship of the Primitive Church*. London, 1691.

Klaasens, Harry. "The Reformed Tradition in the Netherlands." In *The Oxford History of Christian Worship*, edited by Geoffrey Wainwright and Karen Westerfield Tucker, 463-68. Oxford: Oxford University Press, 2006.

Kling, Christian Friedrich. "Athanasius." In *Real-Encyclopaedia für protestanische Theologie und Kirche*, edited by Johann Jacob Herzog, I:577. Gotha: 1858.

Köllner, Heinrich Dorotheus Eduard. *Symbolik aller christlichen Confessionen*. Hamburg: Friedrich Perthes, 1844.

Layman, David W. "Was Nevin Influenced by S. T. Coleridge?" *New Mercersburg Review*, no. 17 (1995) 54-58.

Littlejohn, W. Bradford. *The Mercersburg Theology and the Quest for Reformed Catholicity*. Eugene, OR: Wipf & Stock, 2009.

Locke, John. *The Reasonableness of Christianity, as Delivered in the Scriptures*. Edited by John C. Higgins-Biddle. Oxford: Clarendon Press, 1999.

Luther, Martin. "The Three Symbols or Creeds of the Christian Faith." In *Luther's Works*, edited by Lewis Spitz and Helmut T. Lehman, 34:201-29. Philadelphia: Fortress, 1960.

———. *Luther's Works, Letters II*. Edited by Gottfried Krodel and Helmut Lehman. 49:59-68. Philadelphia: Fortress, 1972.

The Lutheran Observer 17, no. 38 (September 21, 1849).

Maxwell, Jack Martin. *Worship and Reformed Theology: The Liturgical Lessons of Mercersburg*. Pittsburgh: Pickwick, 1976.

McKim, Donald, ed. *Historical Handbook of Major Biblical Interpreters*. Downers Grove, IL: InterVarsity, 1998.

Melanchthon, Philip. *Apologia pro Luthero, adv. furoisum Parisiensium Theologastrorum Decretum*. Wittenberg: Melchior Lotter, 1531.

Meyers, Peter. *De Symboli Apostolici*. Trier: F. A. Galli, 1849.

Möhler (or Moeller or Moehler), Johann Adam. *Die Einheit in der Kirche; oder, Das Princip des Katholicismus, dargestellt im Geiste der Kirchenväter der drei ersten Jahrhunderte*. Tübingen: Heinrich Laupp, 1825.

———. *Symbolik, oder Darstellung der dogmatischen Gegensätze der Katholiken und Protestanten nach ihren öffentlichen Bekenntnisschriften*. 5th ed. Mainz: F. Kupferberg, 1838. English translation by James Burton Robertson as *Symbolism: Exposition of the Doctrinal Differences between Catholics and Protestants as Evidenced by Their Symbolical Writings*. New York: Edward Dunigan, 1844.

Montfaucon, Bernard de. *Diatribe de symbolo Quicunque*. In *S. Athanasii Opera Omnia*, edited by Bernard de Montfaucon, II:719-35. 3 vols. Paris, 1698,

Morgan, Robert C. "David Friedrich Strauss." In *Historical Handbook of Major Biblical Interpreters*, edited by Donald McKim, 364-68. Downers Grove, IL: InterVarsity, 1998.

Morrell. John Daniel. *The Philosophy of Religion*. London: Longmans, 1849.

Mosheim, Johann Lorenz. *Institutionum historiae ecclesiastica antiquae at recentiors libri quator ex ipsis fontibua insigniter emendati*. Helmstedt: Christian Frederick Weygand, 1755. English translation by Archibald MacLaine as *An Ecclesiastical History: Ancient and Modern, from the Birth of Christ to the Beginnings of the Present Century.* 4 vols. New York: Collins, 1821.

Nautin, P. "Letter of the Church of Lyons and Vienne." In *Encyclopedia of the Early Church*, edited by Angelo Di Bernardino, II:844–45. 2 vols. Oxford: Oxford, 1992.

Neander, August. *Allgemeine Geschichte der christlichen Religion und Kirche*. 6 vols. Hamburg, 1825–52. Translated by Joseph Torrey as *General History of the Christian Religion and Church*. 9 vols. Edinburgh: T & T Clark, 1847–55.

———. *Lectures on the History of Christian Dogmas*. Translated by Jonathan Edwards Ryland. London: Henry G. Bohn, 1858.

Nevin, John. "Antichrist; or the Spirit of Sect and Schism," in *One, Holy, Catholic, and Apostolic: John Nevin's Writings on Ecclesiology (1844–1849)*, Tome One, 163–232. By John Williamson Nevin. Edited by Sam Hamstra Jr. Mercersburg Theology Study Series, vol. 5. Eugene, OR: Wipf & Stock, 2017.

———. *The Anxious Bench*. In *One, Holy, Catholic, and Apostolic, John Nevin's Writings on Ecclesiology (1844–1849), John Nevin's Writings on Ecclesiology (1844–1849)*, Tome One, 26–103. By John Williamson Nevin. Edited by Sam Hamstra Jr. Mercersburg Theology Study Series, vol. 5. Eugene, OR: Wipf & Stock, 2017.

———. "The Apostles' Creed." *The Mercersburg Review* vol. 1, number 2 (1849). The three parts of the series were: I. "Outward History of the Creed," (March 1849) 105–27; II. "Its Inward Constitution and Form," (May 1849) 201–21; III. "Its Material Structure or Organization," (July,1849) 314–47.

———. *The Apostles' Creed: Its Origin, Constitution, and Plan*. Mercersburg, PA: H. A. Mish, 1849.

———. "Athanasian Creed." *Mercersburg Review* (Oct., 1867) 624–27.

———. "Athanasius." *Mercersburg Review* (July, 1867) 445–57.

———. "Brownson's Quarterly Review." *Mercersburg Review* 2 (1850) 33–80.

———. "Catholic Unity." In *One, Holy, Catholic, and Apostolic, John Nevin's Writings on Ecclesiology (1844–1849)*, Tome One, 118–19. By John Williamson Nevin. Edited by Sam Hamstra Jr. Mercersburg Theology Study Series, vol. 5. Eugene, OR: Wipf & Stock, 2017.

———. "Christianity and Humanity," *The Mercersburg Review* 20 (1873) 469–86.

———. *College Chapel Sermons*. Philadelphia: Reformed Church Publishing House, 1891.

———. "The Dutch Crusade." *Mercersburg Review* 6 (1854) 67–117.

———. "Evangelical Radicalism." *Mercersburg Review* 4 (1852) 508–12.

———. "Faith." *The Weekly Messenger*, (February 12, 19, 23; March 4, 11, 18; 1840).

———. "The Heidelberg Catechism." *Mercersburg Review*, III, Number 2 (March 1852) 172.

———. *History and Genius of the Heidelberg Catechism*. Chambersburg, PA: Publication Office of the German Reformed Church, 1847.

———. *The Mystical Presence*. In *The Mystical Presence and the Doctrine of the Reformed Church on the Lord's Supper*. By John Williamson Nevin. Edited by Linden J. DeBie. Mercersburg Theology Study Series, vol. 1. Eugene, OR: Wipf & Stock, 2012.

———. "Religion a Life." *Pittsburgh Friend* 2, no 25 (December 25, 1834) 198; no. 28 (January 15, 1835) 222–23; no. 29 (January 22, 1835) 230; no. 30 (January 29, 1835) 238–39. Reprinted in *New Mercersburg Review*, no. 17 (1995) 37–45.

———. "The Sect System. In *One, Holy, Catholic, and Apostolic*, Tome 1, 233–71. By John Williamson Nevin. Edited by Sam Hamstra Jr. Mercersburg Theology Study Series, vol. 5. Eugene, OR: Wipf & Stock, 2017.

———. "Unity of the Apostles' Creed." *Mercersburg Review* 16 (April 1869) 313–17.

Newman, John Henry "The Episcopal Church Apostolical, Tract 7." *Tracts for the Times.* London: Rivington, 1840 (original 1833–34).

Nichols, James Hastings. *Romanticism in American Theology: Nevin and Schaff at Mercersburg.* Chicago: University of Chicago Press, 1961.

Niemeyer, H. A., ed. *Collectio Confessionum in Ecclesiis Reformatis publicatarum.* Leipzig: Klinkhardt, 1840.

Nyssa, Gregory of. *Encomium in Sanctum patriarch Ephraem Syrus.* Oxford, 1609.

Origen. *Opera Omnia.* Edited by C. Delarue. Paris, 1740.

Pareus, David. *Symbolum Athanasii, notis breviter declaratum.* Hanover, 1651.

Payne, John. "John Williamson Nevin: The Early Years." *The New Mercersburg Review* 36 (Spring 2005) 4–35.

Pearson, Bishop John. *An Exposition of the Creed.* London, 1715.

Penzel, Klaus. *The German Education of Christian Scholar Philip Schaff: The Formative Years, 1819–1844.* Lewiston, NY: Edwin Mellon, 2004.

———, ed. *Philip Schaff: Historian and Ambassador of the Universal Church: Selected Writings.* Macon, GA: Mercer University Press, 1991.

Porter, T. C. "Review of *Private Judgment—Address to the Suffolk North Association of Congregational Ministers, with Sermons on the Rule of Faith, the Inspiration of the Scriptures, and the Church*, by J. P. Lesley. *Mercersburg Review*, vol. 1(September 1849) 515–19.

Proudfit, John Williams. "The Apostles' Creed." *The Biblical Repertory and Princeton Review* vol. 24, no. 4 (October 1852) 602–77.

"The Mercersburg Theology." *The Puritan Recorder.* July, 1849.

Quasten, Johannes. *Patrology.* Utrecht: Spectrum, 1950.

Quesnel, Pasquier, ed. *Sancti Leonis Magni, romani, pontifices, Opera Omnia.* Paris: J. P. Migne, 1855.

Rauch, Frederick. "Faith and Reason." *Mercersburg Review* 8 (1856) 80–94.

———. *Psychology; or, A View of the Human Soul.* Fourth Edition. New York: M. W. Dodd, 1846.

Richards, George Warren. *History of the Theological Seminary of the Reformed Church in the United States, 1825–1934.* Lancaster, PA: Rudisell, 1952.

Richardson, Cyril, ed. *Early Christian Fathers.* Philadelphia: Westminster, 1953.

Rothe, Richard. *Die Anfänge der christlichen Kirche und ihrer Verfassung.* Wittemberg: Zimmermann, 1837.

Routh, Martin Joseph. *Reliquiae Sacrae.* Oxford: Magdalen College, 1846.

Rudelbach, Andreas Gottlob. *Die Bedeutung des Apostolischen Symbolums.* Leipzig, 1844.

Rufinus, Tyrannius. *Commentarius in symbolum Apostolorum.* In *Ruffini Aquileiensis, Opera Omnia*, edited by L. de la Barre. Paris, 1580. Translated by W. H. Freemantle as "A Commentary on the Apostles' Creed," in *Nicene and Post-Nicene Fathers, Second Series,* vol. 3:541–62. Edited by Philip Schaff and Henry Ware. Buffalo, NY: Christian Literature Publications, 1892.

———. *Tyrannii Rufini Aquileiensis Presbyteri Opera Omnia.* Edited by Dominic Vallarsi. Verona, 1745.

Schaff, Philip. *Christ and Christianity.* New York: Charles Scribners' Sons, 1885.

———. *The Creeds of Christendom.* 3 vols. 4th ed. New York: Harper Brothers, 1919.

———. *The Principle of Protestantism.* In *The Development of the Church: "The Principle of Protestantism" and Other Historical Writings of Philip Schaff*, 25–205. By John Williamson

Nevin. Edited by David R. Bains and Theodore Louis Trost. Mercersburg Theology Study Series, vol. 3. Eugene, OR: Wipf & Stock, 2017.

Schlegel, Friedrich. *Philosophische Vorlesungen.* Vienna: Carl Schaumburg and Co., 1830.

Schleiermacher, Friedrich Ernst Daniel. *Der christlich Glaube nach den Grundsätzen der evangelischen Kirche im Zusammenhang dargestellt.* 2nd ed. Berlin: Reimer, 1830. Translated and edited by H. R. Mackintosh and J. S. Stewart as *The Christian Faith.* London: T & T Clark, 1999.

———. Über *die Religion: Reden an die Gebildeten unter ihren Verächtern.* Hamburg: F. Meiner, 1958. English translation by John Oman as *On Religion: Speeches to its Cultured Despisers.* New York: Harper, 1958.

Scultetus, Abraham. *Medulla theologiae Patrum, Pars Secunda.* Neapoli Nemetum: Nicolaus Schrammins, 1605.

Simonetti, M. "Eunomius." In *Encyclopedia of the Early Church*, edited by Angelo Di Bernardino, I:297. 2 vols. Oxford: Oxford, 1992.

———. "Vigilius Thapsus." In *Encyclopedia of the Early Church*, edited by Angelo Di Bernardino, II:870. 2 vols. Oxford: Oxford, 1992.

Speroni, Dominicus Maria. *De symbolo vulgo S. Anthanasii.* Patavii, 1751.

Spruner, K. L. "Covenant Theology." In *Dictionary of Christianity in America*, edited by Daniel G. Reid, Robert Linder, Bruce Shelly, and Harry Stout. Downers Grove, IN: InterVarsity, 1990.

Stockmeier, Immanuel. Über *Entstehung des Apostolischen Symbolums.* Publisher unknown, 1846.

Strauss, David Friedrich. *Leben Jesu kritische bearbeitet .* Tübingen: C. F. Osiander, 1835–36. Trans. by George Eliot as *The Life of Jesus, Critically Examined.* Philadelphia: Fortress, 1973.

Synesius, *Opera.* Edited by D. Petavius. Paris, 1612.

Taylor, Nathaniel. *Lectures on the Moral Government of God.* 2 vols. New York: Clark, Austin, Smith, 1859.

Taylor, Isaac. *Ancient Christianity and the Doctrines of the Oxford Tracts.* Philadelphia: Herman Hooker, 1840.

Tertullian. *Opera.* Edited by Ernst Friedrich Leopold. 4 vols. Leipzig: Bernard Tauchnitz, 1839–41.

———. *Qu. Sept. Flor. Tertulliani Opera.* Edited by Johann Salomo Semler. 6 vols. Magdeburg: Christian Hendel, 1821.

Tillemont, Louis S. *Memoirs pour servir à l'histoire eccles.* Brussels, 1693–1712.

Ullmann, Carl. Über *die Sündlosigkeit Jesu.* Hamburg: Friedrich Perthes, 1833.

———. Über *den unterscheiden charakter oder das Wesen Christenthum.* Hamburg: Friedrich Perthes, 1845.

Ursinus, Zacharias. *Admonitio Neostadiensium.* Neustadt: Harnish, 1581.

———. *The Commentary by Dr. Zacharias Ursinus on the Heidleberg Catechism.* 2nd ed. Translated by George Washington Williard. Columbus, OH, 1852.

Ussher, James, Archbishop of Armagh. *De Symbolis Diatriba.* In *The Whole Works of the Most Rev. James Ussher, D.D.* Edited by Charles Richard Elrington. Vol. VII, 308 ff. Hodges and Smith: Dublin, 1847.

Vöetius, Gisbert. *De Symbolo Apostolico. Disputationes Theologicae Selectae.* Utrecht, 1648.

Voss, Gerhard Jan. *Dissertationes Tres de Tribus Symbolis. Theses Theologicae et Historicae.* Hague, 1658.

BIBLIOGRAPHY

———. *De Tribus Symbolis Dissertatione.* Amsterdam, 1701.

Walch, Johann Georg. *Historische und theologische Einleitung in die Religionsstreitigkeiten der evangelishe-lutherischen Kirche.* 5 vols. Jena: Johann Meyers Wittwe, 1733–39.

———. *Introductio in libros Symbolicos ecclesiae Lutheranae.* Jena: Meyer, 1732.

Waterland, Daniel. *History of the Athanasian Creed.* Cambridge: Cambridge University Press, 1728.

Weber, Georg Gottlieb. *Kritische Geschichte der Augspurgischen Confession.* Frankurt, 1782.

White, Bishop William. *Memoirs of the Protestant Episcopal Church in the United States of America.* New York: Swords, Stanford, and Co., 1836.

Whitehead, Alfred North. *Religion in the Making.* New York: Macmillan, 1926.

Witsius, Hermann. *Exercitationes sacrae in symbolum quod Apostolorum dictur.* Amsterdam, 1697. Volume IV. English translation by Donald Frazer as *A Dissertation on What Is Commonly Called the Apostles' Creed.* 2 vols. Edinburgh: A Fullarton & Co., 1823.

Index

Abälard, Peter, 234
Abbo of Fleury, 234
Albrecht of Brandenburg, 50
Albright, Jacob, 93
Alexander, Archibald, 192, 269
Alexander, Natalis, 227, 230
allegorical exegesis, 26
Ambrose, 17, 49, 203
American Board of Commissioners for Foreign Missions, 53
Ames, William, 53
Anglicanism, 215
Anselm of Canterbury, 58
Anthelmi, Joseph, 230
Apollinaris of Hierapolis, 139
Apollinaris of Laodicea, 246
Apostles' Creed, v–vi, ix–x, 7–11, 13, 17–18, 21, 23–29, 32, 34–38, 41–42, 45–57, 68–71, 76, 84, 91, 95–96, 101–6, 109–11, 114–16, 120, 125–28, 140–53, 156–63, 171, 182, 185, 194, 196, 199–208, 215–17, 230–32, 235–48, 250–65, 270–72, 274
Appel, Theodore, 24, 109, 126, 267
Aristides of Athens, 138
Arius, Arianism, 48, 49, 136, 145, 176, 177, 225, 230
Arminianism, 161, 206
Arnold, Gottfried, 203
Athanasian Creed, v, ix, 7, 9–11, 17–18, 199, 211, 213–17, 224, 227–28, 230, 232, 234–38, 240, 242–45, 247–49, 268, 271, 274
Athanasius, 9, 51, 137, 160, 175–77, 187, 193, 200, 202, 204, 207, 214–17, 224, 225–30, 232–34, 237, 267, 270–71
Athenagoras of Athens, 139
Aubert, Annette, 4, 12, 267
Augsburg Confession, 9, 12, 50, 111, 165, 235, 242, 247, 259
Augustine, 26, 44, 59, 121, 133, 137–38, 143, 153, 178, 201, 203, 207, 232–33, 242, 267

Avitus, Alcitus Ecdicius, 233
Ayre, John, 138

Baconian tradition, 82
Bains, David R., 19, 85, 90, 111, 152, 273
Baptism, 5, 12, 27, 36, 40, 43–44, 48–49, 51, 69, 74, 80, 87, 95, 134–38, 140–41, 158, 163, 178, 182, 187, 203–5, 208, 231, 238, 240, 248, 250, 256–58, 263–64, 267
Baronius, Caesar, 25, 153, 227, 229, 267
Barrett, Lee C., vii, x, 1, 7, 267
Basil of Caesarea, 137, 182, 187, 188, 267
Basnage, Jacques, 27, 45, 135
Bauer, Bruno, 152
Baur, Ferdinand Christian, 237
Baxter, Richard, 30, 192
Beleth, Jean, 227
Belgic Confession, 51, 161, 205
Bellamy, Joseph, 227
Bellarmine, Robert, 128, 144, 149, 151–53, 227, 267
Benedict XIV, 227
Berardino, Angelo di, 135
Berger, Peter, 20, 267
Bingham, James, 217
Bingham, Joseph, 8, 25–26, 41, 227, 235, 267
Blackstone, Sir William, 68
Blanchini, 231
Boehm, Martin, 16, 93
Bonaventura, 153
Bonhoeffer, Dietrich, 157
Bruno of Würzburg, 234
Bucer, Martin, 51
Buddeus, Johann Franz, 227, 230
Bull, George, 46
Bullinger, Heinrich, 51, 53, 236
Bushnell, Horace, 38, 104–5, 247

Caesarius of Aries, 233
Calvin, John, 11, 25, 51, 53, 87, 160, 259

INDEX

Calvinism, 3, 6, 121, 206, 228
Cambridge Platonists, 30, 60, 192
Campbell, Alexander, 206
Campbell, Thomas, 13, 206
Campbellites, 13, 206
Catechism of the Council of Trent, 10
Catharinus, Ambrosius, 157, 268
Cave, William, 156, 227, 268
Cerdo, 45–47
Cerinthus, 45
Channing, William Ellery, 74, 76
Charles II, 156
Charles the Bald, 224
Chillingworth, William, 90
Christ, 2–7, 19, 27, 29–36, 39–42, 48, 49, 63–80, 86, 88–91, 105, 129, 135–37, 142–43, 167, 170, 173, 180, 184–88, 221–24, 229–32, 239–40, 244–48, 258, 263–64. *See also* Incarnation
    as Atonement, 6, 58, 80, 94, 264
    as Second Adam, 6, 8, 26, 32, 80
    as Victor, 6, 80
    eternal generation of the Son, 241, 246
Christian perfectionism, 16
Chrysostom, John, 133, 136, 193–94, 200, 202–3, 207, 268,
church, ix, 1, 2, 7–10, 17, 18, 32–33, 39–53, 67–70, 73–76, 84, 91–93, 107–9, 131–33, 148–58, 165–72, 185–97, 201
    as Body of Christ, 2, 7, 52, 86, 106, 184
Church of England, 9, 11, 26, 51, 96, 115, 146, 160, 162, 218, 235, 243, 259
Church of God, 206, 13, 16, 93
Clement of Alexandria, 134–35
Clement of Rome, 135, 138, 228
Cocceius, Johannes, 53
Coleridge, Samuel Taylor, 30, 59–63, 69, 109, 268, 270
Colloquy of Thorn, 51
Comber, Thomas, 26, 268
come-outerism, 119
Common Sense religion, 4, 60, 268
Congregationalism, 15, 28, 52, 101
Conser, Walter H., 12, 268
Constantine, 134
Council of Chalcedon, 9, 229, 232, 244
Council of Constance, 156
Council of Ephesus, 48
Councils of Toledo, 233
Council of Trent, 9–10, 35, 143, 149, 150, 188
Coustant, P., 177, 269
covenant theology, 146
Cromwell, Oliver, 192
Cross, F. L., 46, 268

Cudworth, Ralph, 230
Cumberland Presbyterianism, 206
Cyprian, 27, 43–44, 138, 201, 203–4, 207, 231, 254, 258, 268
Cyril, 48, 140–41, 171, 178, 202–3, 269, 272

Davies, Samuel, 192
DeBie, Linden, 30, 60, 80, 112, 125, 268, 271
Decius, 46
Declaration of Thorn, 51
DeLuis, P., 268
Democratization, 14, 269
Demosthenes, 182, 192
Dennis, John, 216, 268
Descartes, René, 137
Dionysius, 134, 227, 230
Disciples of Christ, 13, 206
disinterested benevolence, 14
Docetic Christology, 46
Donatists, 47, 137
Dorner, Isaak August, 5, 30, 71–72, 213, 237
dualism, 46, 239
Duke Albert of Prussia, 50
Dupin, Louis Ellies, 227, 230

Ebion, Ebionism, 45–47, 240, 246
Ebrard, Johannes Heinrich August, 235–37, 242–43, 268
Edwards, Jonathan, 14, 30, 121, 271
Elizabethan Settlement, 167
Emerson, Ralph Waldo, 16, 61
English Deists, 16, 76, 77, 88
Enlightenment, 16–17, 32, 62, 69, 82, 88, 104, 110
Ephraim the Syrian, 181, 202
Epiphanius, 46, 141
Episcopius, Simon, 27
Erasmus, Desideria, 143, 163, 167, 182, 231, 269
Erb, William H., 4, 6, 113, 268
Ethelstane, 145
Etherius, 145
Eunomius, 136, 182, 273
Eusebius, 48, 134, 138–39, 145, 182, 230–31
Eutychus, Eutychianism, 229, 244–45
Evangelical Alliance, 12, 53, 55–56, 148, 155
Evangelical Association, 93
Evans, William, 6–7 80, 268

Fabricius, Johann A., 230
Fell, John, 138, 268
Ferguson, Everett, 46, 268
Fichte, J. G., 198
Finney, Charles, 16
First Council of Constantinople, 49
First Council of Nicea, 26–27

INDEX

Fortunatus, Venantius, 230, 233–34
Frazer, Donald, 261, 274
French Reformed, 27, 135

Gallican Confession, 11, 51, 160
Garnier, J., 137, 182, 186, 187, 188, 267
Gaume, J. J., 137, 182, 186, 187, 188, 267
German Reformed Church, 15, 18, 23, 33, 93, 152, 206, 215, 218, 238, 253, 271
Gibbon, Edward, 269
Gieseler, Johann Karl Ludwig, 227, 229, 230, 232–33, 269
Gnosticism, 47, 244
God, x, 3–7, 11, 13–16, 18–19, 27, 31–33, 36, 39–43, 46–48, 58, 61–65, 71–87, 90, 109, 112–14, 117, 129–33, 135, 136, 143–45, 152–62, 169–89, 191–94, 197, 198, 206, 215, 219, 220, 222–25, 235–49, 258, 259, 263, 264, 267. *See also* Trinity
Goethe, 109
Good, James, 16, 269
Grabe, Johannes Ernst, 27, 46
Great Awakening, 13–15, 121
Greenslade, S. L., 257, 269
Gregory I, 233
Gregory VII, 186
Gregory XV, 151
Grundtvig, Nikolai S. F., 25

Hales, Alexander, 234
Hall, Robert, 192
Hamstra, Sam, 17, 19, 28, 30, 52, 66, 89, 93, 119, 154–56, 180, 183, 185, 194, 271
Hardy, Edward Rochie, 171, 269
Hart, D. G., 6, 30, 32, 269
Harvey, William Wigan, 216–17, 261, 269
Hase, Karl August von, 157, 235, 242, 269
Hatch, Nathan, 14, 269
Hatto (Haito), 234
Hegel, Georg Wilhelm Friedrich, 5, 30, 66–69, 71, 92, 113, 117, 150, 152, 197, 213
Hegelianism, 5, 65, 67–68, 72–73, 90, 157, 213, 237
Hegessipus, 139
Heideggari (Heidegger), Johann Heinrich, 140, 145, 146, 153, 199, 216, 217, 227, 231, 269
Heidelberg Catechism, 19, 29, 33, 51, 55, 58, 71, 126, 140–41, 152, 159, 187, 205, 236, 242–43, 245, 249, 259, 271
Helvetic Confessions, 51, 160
Hengstenberg, Ernst Wilhelm, 213
Herder, Johann Gottfriend von, 32, 60, 62, 65, 85, 92, 256, 269
Higgins-Biddle, John C., 131, 270

Hilary of Poitiers, 145, 177, 269
Hildegard, 234
Hincmar of Rheims, 224
Hippolytus of Rome, 228
Hodge, Charles, 3–4, 6, 17, 19, 30, 38, 55–56, 80, 83, 89, 125, 129–30, 268–69
Holifield, Brooks, 30, 82, 269
Hopkins, Samuel, 14–15, 269
Howe, John, 192
Hughes, John, 187

Idealism, 4–5, 69, 149–50, 198
Impartation, 6, 268
Imputation, 6, 95, 268
Incarnation, ix, 2, 3, 6–7, 19, 31, 33, 52, 58, 64, 67, 71–72, 74–76, 78–79, 82–85, 90, 94, 105, 108–9, 136, 154, 204, 221, 229, 236–39, 243–49, 257, 259–60, 263–64
Individualism, 16, 119
Irenaeus of Lyon, 8, 26

Jansenism, 203
Jerome, 17, 39, 139, 143, 167, 178, 186, 203, 256, 269
Jesuits, 203, 151
Jovinian, 143
Judaism, 135, 152, 239
Julius I, 229
Justin Martyr, 46, 138, 171, 173, 200, 231, 269

Kant, Immanuel, 16, 63, 161
Kelly, J. N. D., 9, 35, 198, 255, 269
Kenrick, Francis Patrick, 187, 267
Kimmel, E. J., 269
King, Peter Sir, 45, 109, 128, 153, 261
Klaasens, Harry, 218, 270
Kling, Christian Friedrich, 237, 248, 270
Köllner, Wilhelm Heinrich Dorotheus Eduard, 216–17, 226–28, 230, 231, 233, 234, 236, 238, 244, 270
Kurtz, Benjamin, 101

Latitudinarianism, 46, 77, 216
Lehman, Helmut T., 235, 270
Lesley, J. P., 102, 118–19, 272
Lewis, Tayler, 94
life (as an ontological category), ix, 2, 6, 29, 30–32, 42, 60–64, 66–88, 152
Livingstone, E. A., 46, 268
Locke, John, 13, 131–32, 270
Lockean empiricism, 113
Lombard, Peter, 153
Luckmann, Thomas, 20
Ludlow, John, 202, 203

INDEX

Luther, Martin, 9–11, 50, 93, 111, 157, 165, 235, 270
Lutheranism, 9, 12, 46, 50, 101, 111, 157, 215, 228

Manicheaism, 177, 201, 267
Maran, P., 137, 182, 186, 187, 188
Marheineke, Philip, 5, 72
Martensen, Hans Lassen, 5, 71
Mayer, Lewis, 66
Maxwell, Jack, 253, 270
McKim, Donald, 67, 197, 270
mediating school, 5, 6, 30, 45, 71, 72, 82, 312, 237
Melanchthon, Philipp, 9, 111, 165, 175, 206, 270
Melito, 139
Menander, 45, 46
Mennonites, 16, 93
Mercersburg theology, ix–x, 1–20, 23–34, 101–2, 104, 213–16, 253–54
Meyers, Peter, 261, 270
Migne, Abbé M., 128, 151, 267, 269, 272
Miltiades, 139
Modalism, 48, 240
Moehler (Moeller, Möhler), Johann Adam, 146, 192, 193, 261, 270
Monachism, 203
Monarchianism, 240, 243
Monophysitism, 229, 244, 245, 246
Monothelitism, 232, 236, 246, 247,
Montanus, Montanism, 46, 166, 167, 168, 169
Montfaucon, Bernard de, 193, 216, 217, 227, 228, 229, 239, 268
Morgan, Robert C., 197, 270
Mormonism, 108
Morrell, John Daniel, 198, 270
Mosheim, Johann Lorenz von, 24, 168, 278
Muratori, Lodovico Antonio, 227, 230, 233
Muratorian Canon, 230
Mysticism, mystical philosophy, 126, 129, 149, 152, 155, 156, 159

Natalis, Alexander, 227, 230
Natural religion, 77
Nautin, P., 135, 271
Nazianzus, Gregorius, 228
Neander, Johann August Wilhelm, 5, 24, 29, 30, 32, 33, 44, 63, 73, 92, 111, 113, 193, 197, 203, 213, 227, 230, 247, 256, 271
Nebrissensis, Antonius, 153
necessary development, 73
neologians, 16, 77
neo-Pietist, 5, 213
Neoplatonism, 133, 178
Nestorius, Nestorianism, 48, 229, 232, 236, 239, 244–47

Nevin, John Williamson, 1–8, 17–20
  and Apostles' Creed, 23–97, 251–60
  and John Williams Proudfit, 125–209
  and Mercersburg Theology, 1–8, 17–20
  and Puritanism, 101–21
New Divinity, 14, 15
Newman, John Henry, 96, 146, 272
New Measures, 13, 16, 93, 206
Newtonian physics, 62
Nicene Creed, 10, 11, 18, 26, 48, 49, 141, 162, 204, 205, 213–15, 224, 227, 230–39, 242, 248–50
Nichols, James H., 13, 14, 29, 30, 32, 34, 60, 253, 272
Niemeyer, H. A., 160, 161, 236, 242, 243, 246, 272
Novatian, 43, 46, 47
Nyssa, Gregory, 136, 179, 180, 181, 185, 269, 272

"Old Lutheran" party, 242
Old Roman Creed, 35
Olearius, Adam, 261, 270
organic development, 2, 5, 7, 18, 24, 29 31, 62, 66, 67, 68, 79, 82, 88, 95, 104, 106, 107, 109, 110, 111, 148, 150, 151, 155, 169, 182, 183, 193, 194, 204
Origen, 17, 26, 27, 43, 173, 177, 200, 230, 258, 272
original sin, 9, 15, 26
Otho, 227
Otterbein, William, 16, 95
Otto, J. C. T., 138, 269
Outler, Albert C., 135, 267
Oxford Movement, 38, 146, 203

paganism, 178, 239
Pagi, Antoine, 227, 230
Pamelius, Jacobus, 143
Pammachius, 39, 143, 256
pantheism, 149, 244
Pareus, David, 236, 272
Pascal, Blaise, 203
Patavius, Albertus, 153
Patripassianism, 48, 240, 243
Payson, Edward, 192
Pearson, John, 45, 227, 230, 231, 161, 272
Penzel, Klaus, 213, 272
Petavius, Dionysius, 186, 227, 230, 273
Pietism, 32, 101
Pithoeus (Pithou), Pierre, 230
Pius V, 142, 144, 150
Platonic thought, 26, 121, 131, 133, 139, 169, 178
Porter, T. C., 102, 118, 272
Presbyterianism, 5, 28, 52, 115, 187, 206, 209
Protestant Armenian Church, 53, 56, 148

INDEX

Proudfit, John Williams, 8, 19, 34, 37, 125–209, 272
Prussian Union Church, 29, 89
Puritanism, 14, 28, 52, 54, 94, 95, 99–121, 191, 196, 198, 201, 205, 208, 254
Pusey, Edward Bouverie, 38, 85

Quadratus of Athens, 138
Quasten, Johannes, 227, 272
Quesnel, Pasquier, 227, 230, 272

Radbertus, Pachasius, 153
Rauch, Friedrich Augustus, 5, 65–69, 73, 92, 113, 117, 272
Reformed scholasticism, 146
Regius, Benet, 227
repentance, 41, 48, 86, 132, 264
Republicanism, 131, 155
Restorationist movement, 13
Revivalism, 13, 15–16, 19, 30, 101, 206
Richards, George, 23, 272
Richardson, Cyril C., 41, 171, 269, 272
Roman Catholicism 9, 10, 12, 26, 28, 34, 35, 50, 51, 90, 101, 102, 139, 140, 146, 150, 153, 154, 157, 163, 167, 187, 193, 216, 217, 227, 230, 234, 247, 259, 262
Romanticism, 4, 32, 59, 62, 65, 68, 69, 109, 110, 149, 254, 263
Rothe, Richard, 203, 272
Routh, Martin Joseph, 134–35, 272
Rudelbach, Andreas Gottlob, 261, 272
Rufinus, Tyrannius, 17, 35–38, 47–49, 128, 138–45, 153, 173, 182, 231, 255–56, 272
rule of faith (rule of truth), 8, 9, 17, 34, 36, 39, 41–44, 50, 70, 112, 113, 118, 138, 152, 162, 166, 167, 174, 175, 178, 197–202, 249, 256–56, 256–58, 264

Sabellianism, 48, 240
Sabellius, Gregory, 137
Sanctification, 7, 71, 132, 232, 240, 241, 264
Sarpi, Paolo, 188
Saturninus, 45, 46, 47
Schaff, Philip, 1–11, 17–20, 23, 24–28, 48, 50, 51, 55, 58, 68, 71, 85, 87, 90, 102, 111, 116, 117, 125, 134, 152, 160–62, 168, 88, 259
  and Athanasian Creed, 213–50
  and Mercersberg Theology, 1–11, 17–20
Schelling, Friedrich Wilhelm Joseph, 5, 30, 68, 71, 150
Schlegel, Friedrich, 109, 273
Schleiermacher, Friedrich, 5, 26, 29–32, 57, 58, 64–67, 71, 78–80, 90, 113, 149, 151, 197, 198, 203, 213, 247, 273

Schröckh, Johann Matthias, 227
Schweizer, Alexander, 243
Scotch Confession, 243, 247
Scottish Common Sense philosophy, 60, 113, 192
Scultetus, Abraham, 227, 228, 273
Second Great Awakening, 13, 15
semipelegianism, 233
Semler, Johann Salomo, 236, 273
Shorter Catechism, 115, 116
Simonetti, M., 136, 230, 275
sin, 3, 4, 6, 7, 9, 14, 15, 26, 41, 60, 80
Socinianism, 236, 242, 247
sola scriptura, 8, 34, 90
Sparks, Jared, 75
Speroni, Dominicus Maria, 217, 227, 228, 273
Spruner, K. L., 254, 273
Stapleton, Thomas, 167
Stockmeier, J., 261, 173
Stoicism, 138, 152
Strauss, David Friedrich, 67, 90, 156, 157, 168, 172, 194, 197, 270, 273
subjective turn, 29
Synesius, 182, 186, 273
Synod of Dort, 9, 27, 144, 162

tabula rasa, 113, 131
Tapsensis (Thapsus), Vigilius, 230, 232, 233
Tatian, 139
Taylor, Isaac, 202, 203, 273
Taylor, Jeremy, 227, 230
Taylor, Nathaniel, 15, 273
Tertullian, 8, 17, 26, 27, 42, 70, 71, 138, 139, 147, 149, 163, 166–72, 183, 200, 201, 231, 254, 257, 258, 273
Theodosius, 49
Theophilus, 139, 167
Theosebeia, 186
Theotimus, 186
Thirty-Nine Articles, 9, 11, 162, 236, 259
Tholuck, Friedrich August Gottreau, 5, 213
Tillemont, Louis Sébastien Le Nain de, 146, 217, 227, 230
Tractarian Movement, 96, 203
Transcendentalist movement, 16
Trinity, ix, 2, 19, 31, 33, 38, 40, 42, 46, 49, 71–76, 83, 114, 161, 219, 221, 224–26, 239–47, 257, 264
Trost, Theodore, ii, 19, 85, 90, 111, 152
Tübingen School, 146 150, 154
Turretin [Turretini], Francis, 35

Ullmann, Karl, 5, 30, 273
Unitarianism, 102, 196, 240, 244
United Brethren, 16, 93

279

Ursinus, Zacharias, 140, 141, 152, 159, 199, 236, 273
Ussher, James, 128, 141, 145, 146, 224, 227, 231, 233, 268, 273

Valentinus, 47, 164
Valla, Lorenzo (Laurentius), 25, 231, 272
Victorinus, Gaius Marius, 133, 178, 202
Vigilantius, 39, 256
Vöetius, Gisbert
Voss (Vossius), Gerhard Jan (Johann), 45, 128, 140, 143, 145, 146, 153, 199, 216, 217, 227, 230, 231, 261, 273
Vulgate, 139

Walch, Johann Georg, 46, 48, 50, 216, 217, 227, 230, 231, 235, 236, 238, 259, 274
Waterland, Daniel, 216, 217, 227, 228, 230, 233, 234, 236, 241, 244, 274
Watts, Isaac, 86, 247
Weber, Georg Gottlieb, 239, 274
Westminster Confession, 55, 89, 242, 243, 246, 264
Westminster Shorter Catechism, 116
Wette, Wilhelm Martin Leberecht de, 29, 60
White, William, 237, 274
Whitehead, Alfred North, 19, 20
Winebrenner, John, 13, 16, 17, 18, 93, 206
Wiseman, Nicholas, 187
Witsius, Hermann, 128, 146, 261, 274
Wittwe, Johann Meyers, 259
World Convention of London, 53, 55, 147
Wycliffe, John, 234

"Young Rome," 157

www.ingramcontent.com/pod-product-compliance
Lightning Source LLC
Chambersburg PA
CBHW081145230426
43664CB00018B/2807